PHYSIC...
GEOGRAP...

FLOWS, CYCLES, SYSTEMS AND CHANGE

David Wilcock

Maps and diagrams by John Shaw

Blackie

ISBN 0 216 91378 0

First published 1983

Copyright © David Wilcock 1983

Published by Blackie and Son Limited
Bishopbriggs, Glasgow G64 2NZ
7 Leicester Place,
London WC2H 7BP

Cover photo supplied by:
Atmospheric Physics Group,
Imperial College, London

Filmset by Advanced Filmsetters (Glasgow) Ltd
Printed in Great Britain by Scotprint Ltd, Musselburgh

Preface

This book is written for sixth-form geography students, but it should also prove useful to first-year students at university, polytechnic or college of education. Its principal objective is to introduce students to the basic flows of energy and materials that take place in natural systems and which lie at the heart of environmental change. This is done in a non-quantitative manner. A second theme of the book is the interrelatedness of different parts of the natural environment. Processes in the lithosphere, atmosphere, hydrosphere and biosphere interact, and it is this interaction that makes physical geography such a stimulating subject to study.

Many ideas in physical geography are currently in a state of flux. This is largely due to the explosion of information from such varied sources as satellites, deep-sea ocean cores, and inter-nationally-sponsored scientific programmes devoted to the continuous monitoring of processes in the atmosphere, biosphere and hydrosphere. The book stresses the important role that careful measurement plays in improving our understanding of modern processes and past events. This understanding, however, has to be kept under constant review as more and more information becomes available.

The format of the book is conventional: An introductory section on basic concepts is followed by sections on geomorphology, climate, and bio-geography. Although hydrology is an important theme of modern physical geography it is not given a section of its own. Instead, different aspects of hydrology are introduced at appropriate points in the other sections, and this stresses the integrating role of the hydrological cycle in the natural environment as a whole. The book concludes with a section on biogeography and the biosphere. More than any other, this aspect of physical geography links the subject to human geography, since it is on the natural ecosystems of the world that man ultimately depends for his existence, and it is on ecosystems that man's economic and social activities have had the most profound effects.

A textbook of this kind represents a synthesis of ideas and examples originally developed or described by other people. My principal sources of information are referred to in the text and detailed in the list of references at the end of the book. Also included in this list are articles in more accessible sources which students are encouraged to follow up for further ideas. Writing a text of this breadth necessarily involves generalization and simplification. All generalization is dangerous and I hope I have done no serious injustice to the ideas of those many people on whose work I have drawn. I should like to thank present and former colleagues at the New University of Ulster who read various chapters at the first draft stage and made many helpful suggestions for improvement. Palmer Newbould, Bill Carter, Geoff Fisher, John Roberts, Mike Tullett and John Wilson all helped in this way, as did Chris Park (University of Lancaster) and I am very grateful to them.

John Shaw drew all the diagrams and Isobel McClelland typed the manuscript. Shirley Tinkler helped with general advice and last-minute modifications to the illustrations. To these three people I should like to say a special thank you.

Finally, I should like to thank my wife, Fran, for her suggestions on content, format and presentation, but most of all for her unfailing understanding and encouragement throughout my work on this book.

David Wilcock

To my mother and father

Contents

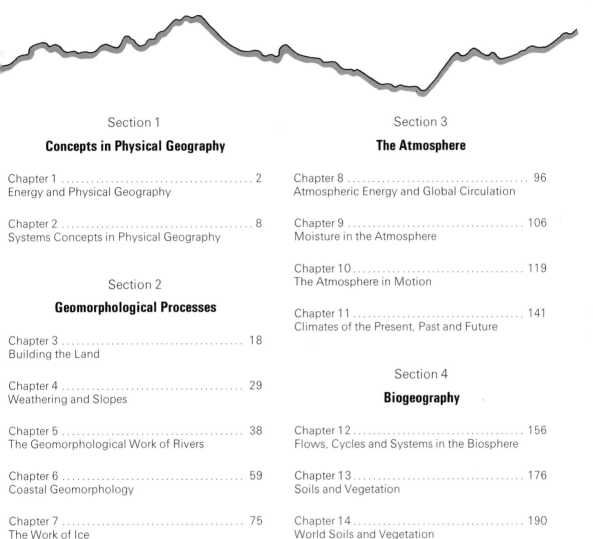

Section 1

Concepts in Physical Geography

Chapter 1 2
Energy and Physical Geography

Chapter 2 8
Systems Concepts in Physical Geography

Section 2

Geomorphological Processes

Chapter 3 18
Building the Land

Chapter 4 29
Weathering and Slopes

Chapter 5 38
The Geomorphological Work of Rivers

Chapter 6 59
Coastal Geomorphology

Chapter 7 75
The Work of Ice

Section 3

The Atmosphere

Chapter 8 96
Atmospheric Energy and Global Circulation

Chapter 9 106
Moisture in the Atmosphere

Chapter 10 119
The Atmosphere in Motion

Chapter 11 141
Climates of the Present, Past and Future

Section 4

Biogeography

Chapter 12 156
Flows, Cycles and Systems in the Biosphere

Chapter 13 176
Soils and Vegetation

Chapter 14 190
World Soils and Vegetation

References,
Other Sources of Information
and Suggested Reading   210

Index   215

Units and Symbols

1 Positive and negative exponents:

$$1000 = 10 \times 10 \times 10 = 10^3$$
$$100 = 10 \times 10 = 10^2$$
$$10 = 10 \times 1 = 10^1$$
$$0.1 = 1/10 = 10^{-1}$$
$$0.01 = 1/100 = 1/10^2 = 10^{-2}$$

2 Système International (SI) units have been used throughout this book—except where other work (in different units) has been referred to.

Length
μm	micrometre ($\times 10^{-6}$ m)
mm	millimetre ($\times 10^{-3}$ m)
cm	centimetre ($\times 10^{-2}$ m)
m	metre
km	kilometre ($\times 10^3$ m)

Area and Volume
ha	hectare
cm³	cubic centimetre
l	litre ($\times 10^3$ cm³)
m³	cubic metre ($\times 10^3$ l)

Time
s	second
min	minute
h	hour

Mass
mg	milligram
g	gram
kg	kilogram ($\times 10^3$ g)
t	tonne ($\times 10^3$ kg)

Energy and Power
J	joule
W	watt (Js^{-1})

3 The exponential method of expressing large and small fractions can be extended as follows:

e.g. 'metres per second' can be expressed as '$m s^{-1}$' and 'tonnes per km²' is equivalent to 'tonnes km^{-2}'.

4 The SI system has one unit—the joule (J) —for measuring mechanical and heat energy. The older c.g.s. system measures mechanical energy in ergs and heat energy in calories.

1 joule $= 0.2388$ calories
1 joule $= 10^7$ ergs

Other equivalent units in use are:

1 hectare $= 2.47$ acres
1 tonne $= 0.982$ tons

Section 1

CONCEPTS IN
PHYSICAL GEOGRAPHY

1

Energy and Physical Geography

SIX IMPORTANT TYPES OF ENERGY DEFINED

Physical geography studies the natural environment, particularly those aspects of it that affect, or are affected by, the development of human societies, past, present and future. The natural environment is subject to processes of change through time, most of which are natural but some of which are increasingly affected by mankind's own technology. Environmental change, whether natural or induced by man, involves the transformation of energy from one form into another, and an understanding of the different forms of energy in the environment is therefore fundamental to a modern understanding of physical geography.

Energy is not a substance but a concept developed by scientists over many centuries to explain why certain physical and chemical changes take place while others do not. Several forms of energy are recognized, but to the physical geographer six are particularly important. These are solar energy, chemical energy, gravitational energy, potential energy, kinetic energy and heat energy.

Solar energy

Like the earth, the sun is surrounded by electric and magnetic fields. The regular expansion and contraction of these fields generate waves, and these are sent out across the solar system as *electromagnetic radiation*. Solar energy is thus akin to the type of energy possessed by ocean waves. The earth intercepts only about $1/1\,000\,000\,000$ (10^{-9}) of the sun's total radiation, but this small amount is sufficient to provide all our light.

Radiation is classified by its wavelength, and the range of environmentally important wavelengths in solar radiation is shown in Figure 1.1. The total amount of solar radiation received by the earth at the edge of its atmosphere is defined by the *solar constant*[1] of 1360 watt metre^{-2} (Wm^{-2}). (A list of the principal units and symbols to be used is given on page (vi).) Only a fraction of this radiation reaches the earth's surface because much of it is reflected back into space (see Chapter 8). The earth also sends out electromagnetic radiation into space. However, because it is a colder and smaller body than the sun it radiates in longer wavelengths which contain less energy than the shorter wavelengths emitted by the sun.

Chemical energy

Chemical energy is the result of powerful forces that exist between atoms in the chemical bonds of molecules. These bonds bind the atoms together and when they are broken energy is released. At the subatomic level, nuclear forces within atoms hold together protons and neutrons in the atomic nucleus. Release of these forces, millions of times more powerful than the chemical bonds between atoms, produces *nuclear energy*.

Gravitational energy and potential energy

Any two separate bodies attract each other by the force we call gravity. The strength of this attrac-

---

1 Using the older c.g.s. system of measurement, the solar constant is 1.94 calories cm^{-2} min^{-1}. A calorie is the amount of heat required to raise the temperature of 1 gram of water 1 °C at 15 °C. 1 watt equals 0.2388 cal s^{-1}.

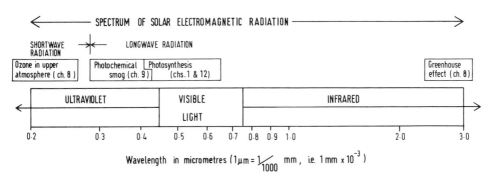

Figure 1.1 The wavelengths of solar radiation and some associated processes of interest to physical geographers. (Modified from J. C. Giddings, p. 55.)

tion depends on the masses of the two bodies and is inversely proportional to the square of their distance apart. At the earth's surface, and within the earth's atmosphere, the mass of the earth is so much greater than that of any other object that its attraction causes all other objects to fall towards it unless some other force prevents them from doing so. It is gravity, therefore, which causes water to flow downhill. It is also gravity which prevents molecules of water vapour in the atmosphere from flying off into space.

Gravitational energy is most frequently expressed as *potential energy* (E_p). Any body above ground level, such as the soil resting on a hillside, has energy of elevation proportional to its mass (m), the force of gravity (g) and its height above sea level (h):

$$E_p = mgh.$$

Kinetic energy

This form of energy is the product of motion. Any moving body (a flowing river, a mudslide, the wind, an ocean current) possesses energy, and is capable of doing work or of exerting a force on any other body with which it comes into contact. Kinetic energy (E_k) is defined mathematically in the equation

$$E_k = \tfrac{1}{2}mv^2$$

where m is mass and v is velocity.

Thermal energy or heat energy

This is the lowest (least useful) form of energy. Thermal energy is the motion of molecules in any

substance. More accurately, it is the kinetic energy of molecular motion.

ENERGY TRANSFORMATIONS IN PHYSICAL GEOGRAPHY—FOUR EXAMPLES

Other forms of energy are important in physical geography. The electrical energy in thunderstorms, for example, is believed to have played a very important role in the early chemical evolution of the earth. However, we need not consider all forms of energy. More important is the idea that energy is easily transformed from one form into another. Such transformations lie at the heart of all processes on earth and are absolutely fundamental to an appreciation of physical geography. To illustrate the variety of energy transformations that occur four important processes will now be described. All four processes will be referred to frequently throughout the book.

Photosynthesis—the transformation of solar energy into chemical energy

The chemical reaction involved is as follows:

$$6CO_2 + 6H_2O \xrightarrow{\text{sunlight}} C_6H_{12}O_6 + 6O_2$$

$$\left[\text{carbon dioxide} + \text{water} \longrightarrow \begin{array}{l} \text{glucose} + \text{oxygen} \\ \text{(carbohydrate)} \end{array}\right]$$

Photosynthesis produces glucose, a vital molecule in living things, and oxygen, the second most abundant element in the earth's atmosphere and another fundamentally important element for all higher forms of life on earth. Photosynthesis thus produces food for us to eat and oxygen for us to breathe. Only green plants can photosynthesize and these vary in complexity from phytoplankton (see Chapter 12) with a simple cell structure to large trees with complex cell structures. The molecules of glucose and carbohydrates contain chemical energy fixed by photosynthesis from incoming solar radiation.

Photosynthesis is such an important process that attempts have been made to measure how efficient different types of vegetation are in transforming solar radiation into chemical energy. In California[1] the solar radiation received by crops in the growing season is 20.94×10^6 joule metre^{-2} day^{-1} ($J\,m^{-2}\,day^{-1}$) according to Gates.[2] Each gram of carbon compounds in plant tissue contains $15\,662$ J and the amount of new plant matter produced every day equals 71 $g\,m^{-2}$. In energy units this is equivalent to 1.11×10^6 $J\,m^{-2}\,day^{-1}$ or 5.4% of incoming solar radiation. Some crops are more efficient than this in converting solar into chemical energy, but most are much worse.

Respiration—the transformation of chemical energy into kinetic energy, muscular energy, and heat

Respiration involves the combination of oxygen atoms with atoms in the glucose molecule, and occurs in all living organisms including plants. In its most familiar form respiration is the process by which animals, including man, convert glucose molecules taken in as food into kinetic energy of motion and other forms of physical activity. In this process oxygen from the atmosphere is consumed and the glucose molecule is destroyed, thus releasing its chemical energy. The chemical products of respiration are molecules of carbon dioxide and water. In the case of human respiration, oxygen from the atmosphere is consumed as we breathe in, carbon dioxide and water vapour are exhaled as we breathe out, and water also appears as perspiration. The more energy we expend in physical activity the hotter we become and the more heat energy we export into the

atmosphere around us. Photosynthesis and respiration thus form part of a cycle (Figure 1.2).

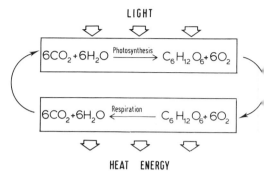

Figure 1.2 The photosynthesis-respiration cycle. (Modified from D. M. Gates, p. 48.)

Evaporation—the transformation of solar energy into heat energy

In evaporation, water molecules are agitated by incoming shortwave, high frequency, solar radiation. Agitation of the molecules raises their kinetic energy levels (increasing water temperature is the physical manifestation of increased kinetic energy) and great strain is placed on the chemical bonds binding the molecules together. These bonds, however, are very powerful (Figure 1.3) and considerable energy is required to break them. If radiation is intensive or continuous enough, the bonds are eventually broken and the water molecules gain sufficient velocity to fly off into the atmosphere as water vapour (Figure 1.3 B). Some water vapour molecules collide with others already present in the air above the water body, and these return to the water body with sufficiently less kinetic energy (Figure 1.3 C) to be caught up again by the strong hydrogen bond network. When more water molecules leave the water body than return to it in this way, evaporation is said to take place (Figure 1.3 D).

An important feature of evaporation is that escaping molecules take with them some of the heat energy they absorbed from the atmosphere before the hydrogen bonds were broken. Because this heat is a property of the escaping molecules and not of the water body, it remains hidden and is called *latent heat*. When the vapour molecules reach high levels in the atmosphere they are cooled and condense back into water droplets.

---

1 Compare ground level receipts of solar radiation in California with the solar constant of $1360\,W\,m^{-2}$. Only a fraction of solar energy received at the earth's outer atmosphere thus penetrates to the ground even in a relatively sunny part of the world like California.
2 See bibliography.

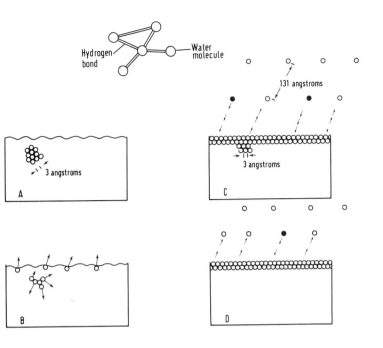

Figure 1.3 The evaporation process. The hydrogen bond is the strongest of all forces binding molecules together. The fact that water molecules are bound in this way means that a great deal of energy has to be applied in order to break the bonds and convert the liquid into vapour. When this is done, the space occupied by water molecules expands about 44 times. Thus the spacing of molecules in liquid water is 3 angstroms (an angstrom is 0.000 000 0001 m or 10^{-10} m) while in water vapour it is 131 angstroms. The amount of energy required to convert 1 g of liquid water into vapour at normal earth temperatures is about 2470 J. Since 1 cm³ of water weighs 1 g, 2470 J cm^{-2} day^{-1} would evaporate the top centimetre of all water bodies in 24 hours. 2470 J cm^{-2} day^{-1} is slightly more than the average amount of solar energy reaching ground level in an area with a Mediterranean type of climate.

The latent heat energy contained within them is then released to the atmosphere which is therefore warmed in the process. This atmospheric warming is sometimes visible as huge convection currents within cumulus clouds (see Chapter 9).

Evaporation is therefore a process in which solar energy is transformed into latent heat energy. Some solar energy used in evaporation is also transformed into potential energy, for water droplets in clouds possess potential energy proportional to their mass and height. When they fall, their potential energy is transformed into kinetic energy and the kinetic energy of rainfall impact can be a powerful agent of soil transport on slopes (Chapter 4).

Evaporation is also the process which maintains the hydrological cycle and as such is one of the most important processes in physical geography (see Chapter 2 and Chapter 12). It is also a cooling process in that fast-moving molecules containing large amounts of heat energy escape the liquid, leaving slower-moving molecules behind. These contain less kinetic energy and therefore less heat energy. It is important to realize that the process can take place at any temperature between freezing and boiling point, although pro-gressively less latent heat energy is required the higher the existing temperature of the water body involved. At 0 °C, for example, 2501 J are required to evaporate 1 g of water, while at 30 °C only 2430 J are required.

Mechanical work—the loss of potential energy

The three energy transformations so far examined are ultimately dependent on solar energy. The other principal source of energy in the earth's environment is gravity. This form of energy is independent of the sun and depends simply on the attraction of the earth's mass for all other objects on its surface and in its atmosphere. The concepts of potential energy and work are both derived from the concept of gravity. Physical geographers speak of 'the work of a river'. What do we mean by such an expression? Strictly speaking, we mean the loss of potential energy by the river as it moves downhill, transporting sediment and overcoming frictional forces on its bed and banks. Some of the potential energy lost is converted into kinetic energy of motion in both water and sediment, and that fraction lost in overcoming friction is converted into heat. The total amount of work done in these various ways is equal to the loss of potential energy. Potential energy in a large river can be stored and converted into electrical energy at a hydroelectric power station (Figure 1.4).

To illustrate how work is synonymous with the loss of potential energy, imagine a book on the edge of a table. The book possesses potential energy and falls 'naturally' to the floor if knocked off the table. In doing this it loses potential energy and cannot naturally rise back on to the table. To replace it, another source of energy has to be used. If we lift it on to the table, we do muscular work and burn off some of the glucose or protein taken in as food, i.e. we use chemical energy stored in our body. In the process of lifting the book on to the table, chemical energy is expended, work is done, and the book's potential energy of elevation is restored. This example illustrates two important principles:

1 Loss of potential energy is equivalent to the amount of work done. Potential energy is therefore a capacity to do work.
2 Loss of potential energy is a natural tendency because of gravity, and to restore it work has to be done. The energy for this work has to come from another source which in our example was chemical energy.

THERMODYNAMICS

Thermodynamics is a subject which deals with energy transformations and problems of natural change. As such, its concepts have much to tell us about how the natural environment functions. The processes of photosynthesis, respiration, evaporation and mechanical work are all illustrations of the *first law of thermodynamics*, which states that energy can neither be created nor destroyed but only changed from one form into another. Solar energy can thus be transformed into chemical energy, chemical energy into potential energy, potential energy into kinetic energy, etc., but after each transformation the total amount of global energy remains the same. The first law thus tells us that energy is *conserved*.

In the understanding of natural processes, however, the first law is less significant than the

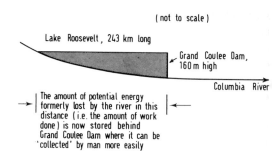

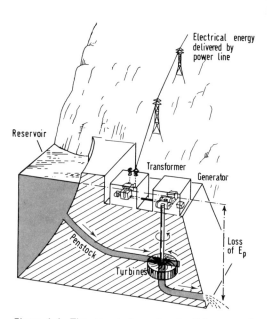

Figure 1.4 The conversion of potential energy into electrical energy at a hydroelectric power station. A typical river with few, if any, waterfalls loses potential energy gradually, and it is difficult for man to effectively harness the river's capacity to do work because it is dissipated over too great a distance. The construction of a dam (such as the Grand Coulee Dam on the Columbia river in Washington, USA) eliminates the loss of potential energy in a river for a distance upstream equal to the length of the impounded reservoir. In the drowned valley the river does no work. Instead its potential energy is stored behind the dam. The stored energy can be suddenly released as kinetic energy in the penstocks of the dam. This kinetic energy turns turbines which in turn drive generators. Generators spin electromagnets and these generate electricity which is then transmitted to the consumer. A hydroelectric power station, therefore, involves three energy transformations: stored potential energy becomes kinetic energy of motion in the penstocks; this in turn becomes electrical energy and this is eventually dissipated as heat in industrial and domestic consumption.

second law of thermodynamics. From the second law emerges the following very important principle: *Every transformation of energy produces a certain amount of low temperature heat energy which cannot naturally be transformed into any other form of energy*.

As an illustration, consider a single pulley system with two equal weights balanced on either side of the pulley (Figure 1.5). If an extra weight, W_3, is added to W_2 the rope moves clockwise over the pulley. This movement generates frictional heat and this heat disappears into the environment. If W_3 is removed, W_1 possesses more potential energy than W_2 and therefore falls, W_2 being forced to rise. When this happens, the rope moves in an anticlockwise direction over the pulley, heat is again generated by friction and again moves into the cooler atmosphere. Thus when work is done (by the addition of W_3) or when natural change is allowed to proceed towards a balanced state (by the removal of W_3), heat is produced at every transformation of energy and always moves in the same direction, i.e. into the neighbouring environment. What is true of the pulley is true generally. Every spontaneous transformation of energy in the physical environment generates heat, and this heat cannot be converted into useful energy by any natural means. Thus, all energy is ultimately transformed into useless heat.[1] When one contemplates the millions of energy transformations taking place every second it is not surprising that some scientists talk about the ultimate 'heat death' of the universe.

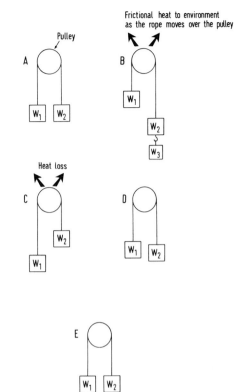

Figure 1.5   Generation of heat energy in a pulley system. Arrangement of the weights in (C) and (D) illustrate intermediate stages between the removal of W_3 and the restoration of final equilibrium (E).

1 Because all natural energy transformations produce heat energy, all forms of energy in the environment are most commonly expressed in heat energy units. The international unit of heat energy is the joule. The watt measures energy flows or fluxes.

2
Systems Concepts in Physical Geography

WHAT IS A SYSTEM?

The term 'system' is very general and can be defined in many ways. Because physical geography is largely concerned with energy and materials in the natural environment, a very useful definition is as follows: *a system is a group of objects within a boundary between which energy or material flows or has flowed*. Using this definition, three types of system can be recognized: *isolated, closed* and *open*. An isolated system can be defined as one with no exchange of energy or material across the system boundaries (Figure 2.1). Such systems are difficult to find in the natural world and physical geography is not usually concerned with them. More common are closed systems which can exchange energy across the system boundaries but not material, while open systems exchange both energy and material quite freely. This threefold classification of systems comes from thermodynamics.

FLOWS OF ENERGY AND MATERIALS IN SYSTEMS

One example of a closed system is the global hydrological cycle (Figure 2.2). In this cycle there is a fixed amount of material (i.e. water) within the boundaries of the system, and the circulation of this water is maintained by imported energy from the sun, which is of course outside the system. Throughout the earth's history the distribution of water in the global hydrological system has varied considerably, principally because changes of climate have greatly altered the amount of water stored in the oceans and ice caps at various times. Despite these changes, the total amount of water on the globe has remained fixed, and the system therefore appears always to have been closed.

A familiar example of an open system is the domestic water supply. In this system the material input is cold water, and the material output is waste cold water and/or waste hot water. Energy

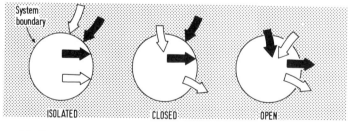

Figure 2.1 Isolated, closed, and open systems.

8

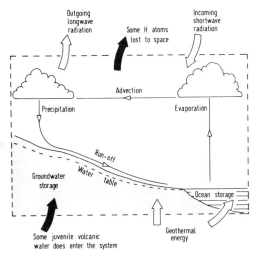

Figure 2.2 Flows of energy and water in the hydrological cycle. The principal inputs and outputs from this system are solar radiation, geothermal heat and longwave terrestrial radiation. Losses and gains of water molecules are infinitely small in comparison with water volumes already in the system which is therefore effectively closed.

imported into the system is kinetic energy from flowing water in the mains supply system and heat energy from domestic fires or boilers to provide hot water. Heat energy is also exported from the system through the pipe walls. Figure 2.3 illustrates the flow of water in the system and some of the significant energy flows and energy transformations that take place within it.

Open systems are the type of thermodynamic system most frequently studied in physical geography. Good examples are forests, lakes and drainage basins. All of these import and export matter and energy across their boundaries (Figure 2.4) and all will be referred to again in later chapters.

Four principles of open systems behaviour are helpful to an understanding of processes in physical geography:

1 Imported energy and matter are not always exported in the same precise form.

For example, shortwave solar energy imported into all natural systems is transformed into outgoing longwave energy. Some of the water falling as snow or rainfall on a drainage basin leaves it as water vapour. Coarse rock material in a headwater stream is transformed into finer material before it

finally leaves the river system and is deposited at sea.

2 The rates of input and output of energy and material need not balance in the short term (i.e. over hours, days or even months) because both can be stored within the system. In the long term however, (which might be measured in years, decades or even centuries), balance between inputs and outputs can often be demonstrated.

One example of this principle is the storage of rainfall as groundwater. Water flowing into a river from groundwater (see Chapter 4) may have been precipitated weeks or months earlier. Another example, this time of energy storage, is provided by deep-seated rocks in the earth's crust which store energy from the gradual movement of tectonic plates in much the same way as a spring can store potential energy when compressed. *Storage* is thus a very important mechanism in all open systems and is normally used to regulate short-term flows of energy and matter and thus to minimize rates of change. If released suddenly, however, materials and/or energy stored in a system can produce cataclysmic change. An earthquake, for example, represents the rapid release of stored tectonic energy, and a landslide the rapid release of stored potential energy in the soil mantle on the side of a valley.

3 In open (and closed) systems, the heat energy produced at each transformation of energy from one type into another is exported from the system, usually into the atmosphere, from where it is finally exported into space. To replace energy lost in this way other forms of energy are imported.

In the case of ecosystems, for example (Chapter 12), this imported energy is solar radiation. In the case of coastal geomorphological systems (Chapter 6) it takes several forms: wind, waves, tides and currents. Any open system in fact only maintains its organized flow of energy and its capacity to do work by the constant import of energy supplies from outside.

4 Despite the constant input of potential energy into open systems, the infinite number of energy transformations in nature produce so much useless heat energy that the ratio of useful work done to potential energy supplied is actually very small.

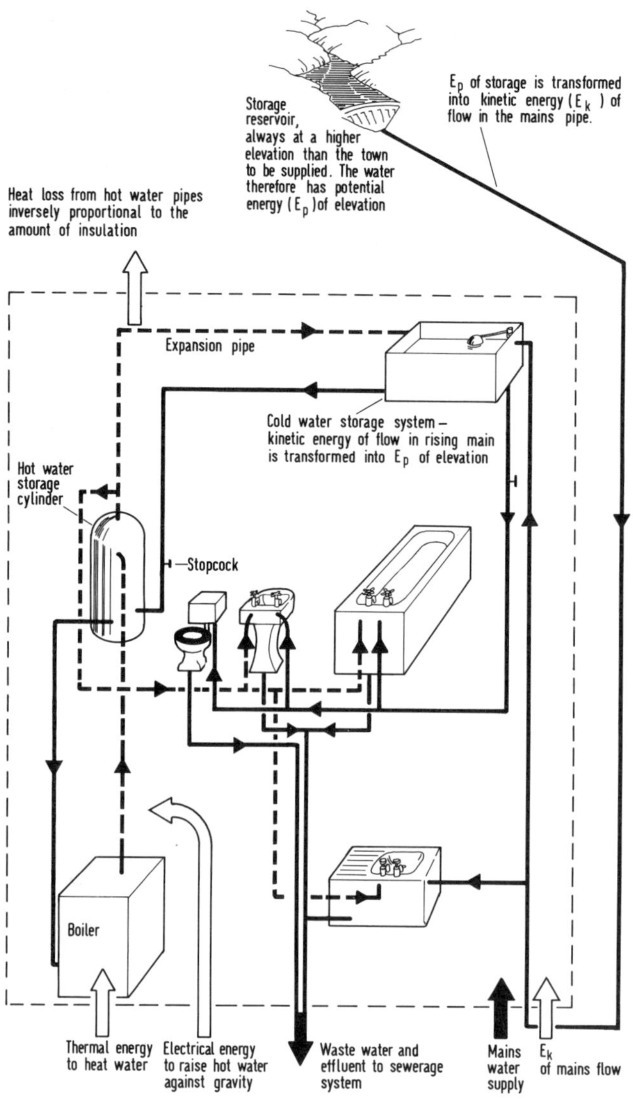

Figure 2.3 The domestic water supply as an open system.

E_p of storage is transformed into kinetic energy (E_k) of flow in the mains pipe.

Storage reservoir, always at a higher elevation than the town to be supplied. The water therefore has potential energy (E_p) of elevation

Heat loss from hot water pipes inversely proportional to the amount of insulation

Expansion pipe

Cold water storage system – kinetic energy of flow in rising main is transformed into E_p of elevation

Hot water storage cylinder

Stopcock

Boiler

Thermal energy to heat water

Electrical energy to raise hot water against gravity

Waste water and effluent to sewerage system

Mains water supply

E_k of mains flow

Natural systems, in other words, are inefficient. We shall see this idea explored further in Chapters 5 and 12.

RESPONSES TO CHANGE

System boundaries

A basic step in the analysis of any natural system is to measure, where possible, the major exchanges of energy and material between a system and its environment, and the flows of energy and material which take place within the system itself. Such measurements not only lead to an understanding of how the system works naturally, but also enable scientists to measure and interpret impacts upon the system brought about by changes in the system's external controls. Often such external changes are induced by man.

The easiest systems to examine in this way are those with well-defined boundaries, like a lake, a small forest or a drainage basin (Figure 2.4). In a drainage basin, for example, flows of energy and material take place principally in a downstream direction, the system boundary corresponds to the

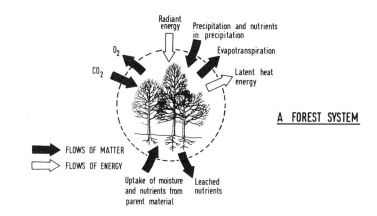

A FOREST SYSTEM

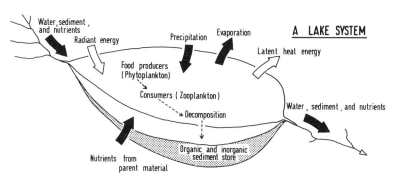

A LAKE SYSTEM

Figure 2.4 A forest, a lake and a drainage basin seen as open systems with some of their various throughputs of matter and energy. A drainage basin, for example, can be examined as a hydrological system, in which case the inputs are precipitation and solar energy, and the outputs are streamflow and evapotranspiration. Storage of water within the basin occurs in lakes, as soil moisture, and as groundwater. Examined as a geomorphological system, the inputs into a drainage basin are precipitation and weathered material. The outputs are streamflow and sediment (bedload, suspended load and dissolved load). Storage of water in the drainage basin takes the same forms as for a hydrological study, but sediment is also stored as weathered material on the drainage basin slopes and as bedload.

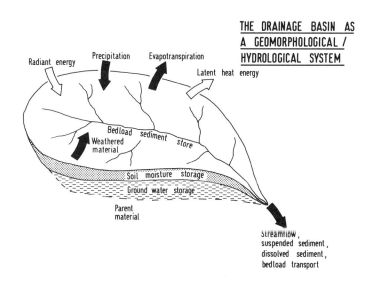

THE DRAINAGE BASIN AS A GEOMORPHOLOGICAL / HYDROLOGICAL SYSTEM

watershed (which is easily identified) and the principal routes along which energy and materials flow are clearly visible in the river network. A beach is a more difficult system to study. Here the boundaries, at least temporarily, may be under deep water, sediment transfers take place in many directions and energy inputs into the system take several forms.

Feedback loops

All systems are said to consist of *elements* or components. These might define routes along which energy and materials flow, like the river channels in a drainage basin. Alternatively, they might represent stores of energy and material like the trees or litter of a forest ecosystem. Relationships between elements in a natural system are often obtained by regression analysis. In this statistical technique, changes in the magnitude of one element are related to changes in the magnitude of another (Figure 2.5).

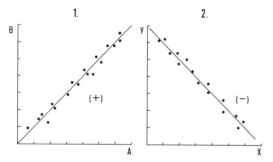

Figure 2.5 Positive and negative regression relationships. In (1) an increase in the value of A is accompanied by an increase in the value of B. Conversely, a reduction in A is accompanied by a reduction in B. These are features of the positive link/relationship between A and B. In (2) an increase of X is accompanied by a reduction of Y and a reduction of X by an increase in Y. This behaviour is a feature of an inverse relationship between two elements.

Analyses of relationships between several pairs of elements connected with a particular system are often able to demonstrate feedback mechanisms. *Feedback* occurs when a change in one particular element produces a sequence of changes in other elements which ultimately leads back to the element whose initial change set off the sequence in the first place. Two types of feedback loop exist: positive and negative. *Positive feedback* occurs when the direction of change for each element of a feedback loop is the same in second and subsequent cycles as it was in the first (Figure 2.6). Positive feedback therefore *reinforces* any initial change within the system brought about by external causes and tends to destroy any previous stability the system might have possessed. It implies exactly the same idea as the phrase, 'vicious circle'.

Positive feedback would have occurred as ice sheets expanded during the Pleistocene period.

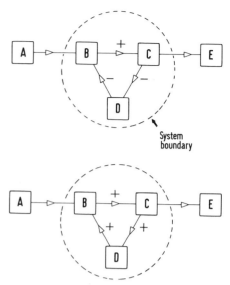

Figure 2.6 Possible links between elements in systems exhibiting positive feedback. In both diagrams, B, C, and D are elements of the system. A and E are elements of the system's environment. In the top diagram, any changes in B will be accompanied by similar changes of direction in C because of the + sign between them. Changes in D will be in an opposite direction to changes in C, and changes in B will be of opposite direction to changes in D. Imagine, therefore, that B increases in magnitude in response to a change in A, the external system element; C will correspondingly rise in response, D will fall and B will rise. In response to changes in D, B therefore responds in a direction similar to that of its original change. So too does E. This is positive feedback. In the lower diagram all signs are positive within the system and all changes between successive pairs of elements are therefore in the same direction. Again this is positive feedback.

Whatever initial mechanism caused ice to start accumulating at the poles, it must have involved a reduction in mean global temperature. As the ice caps grew, more and more solar energy would have been reflected back into space, because light-coloured objects reflect solar energy better than dark-coloured objects. Mean global temperatures would therefore have declined further, and more ice would have formed. The initial change would thus have been reinforced.

Negative feedback occurs when the direction of change on the second cycle of a feedback loop is in the opposite direction to the changes of the first cycle for all elements of the feedback loop (Figure 2.7). Negative feedback makes a change of state within a system difficult since no one element within the system is free for very long to move in one direction only. Negative feedback mechanisms are the ones which therefore maintain and

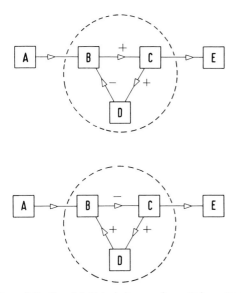

Figure 2.7 Possible links between elements in systems exhibiting negative feedback. In the top diagram, assume an initial increase in the magnitude of B following a change in A. C will then increase in magnitude as will D, and B will fall in response to the rise in D. Thus the feedback effect on B through elements C and D produces a change opposite in direction to that produced initially by changes in the external environment element A. This is negative feedback. Note also how the subsequent changes in C and D on the second cycle of responses will also be opposite in direction to those initially brought about. Thus after B falls in response to initial increases in D, C will also fall. This is a directional change opposite to the initial change in C. The bottom diagram illustrates a slightly different negative feedback mechanism.

regulate system stability, and they are of fundamental importance both to our understanding of how physical geography systems maintain equilibrium and of how they may best be managed. Systems in which negative feedback loops are dominant have a large capacity for *self-regulation*.

One often-quoted example of negative feedback in geomorphology involves the slumping of valley-side debris on to the bed of a river. Let us assume that this initially results in the formation of a local bed deposit which the river's erosive

capacity cannot cope with. The deposit reduces channel gradient and sediment transport rates on its upstream side, while at the same time increasing channel gradients and sediment transport rates on its downstream side. Reduced deposition upstream of the bar and increased erosion of its downstream end combine in time to remove the deposit altogether, and the effects of the initial change are ultimately eliminated from the system (Figure 2.8). Other examples of positive and negative feedback in geographical systems are described throughout the book.

EQUILIBRIUM

Equilibrium is a central concept in physical geography and implies the existence of some type of balance between a system and its environment. There are many types of equilibria (see Chorley and Kennedy, p. 201; Spanner, Chapter 8) but two are of special importance in understanding how natural systems function. These two types of equilibria are *steady-state equilibrium* and *dynamic equilibrium*. Both are most easily described with reference to open systems.

Steady-state equilibrium

There are two important characteristics of a system in steady state. These are:
1 There is no net change of storage inside the system with time. This applies to the storage of both energy and materials.
2 The inputs of material and energy equal the outputs.
Strictly speaking, the concept of steady state applies only to a system whose material and energy inputs enter along a different route from the ones by which they leave. As an example of a

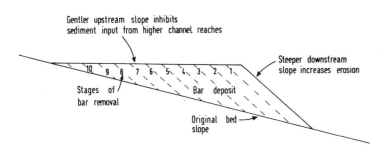

Gentler upstream slope inhibits
sediment input from higher channel reaches

Steeper downstream
slope increases erosion

Stages of
bar removal

Bar deposit

Original bed
slope

Figure 2.8 A simplified diagram showing the effects of deposition on the throughput of sediment in a river channel.

system in steady state, consider a tank (Figure 2.9) with a hole of fixed diameter in its base. It is a well-established physical law that the velocity of water *v* flowing through the hole is related to the depth of water *h* in the tank by the formula:

$$v = \sqrt{2gh}$$

where *g* is the acceleration due to gravity. Since discharge equals area multiplied by velocity, and the area of the hole is fixed, discharge from the tank is related solely to the depth of water. On being filled by water from a tap, such a system will eventually, and *quite spontaneously*, reach a stage at which the discharge of water through the hole equals input from the tap. Once this balance has been achieved it will be indefinitely maintained (and *h* will remain unchanged) just so long as inputs and/or outputs stay constant. In other words, there will be a constant throughput of water and a constant storage of matter and energy inside the system. The system is internally adjusted to the transfer, through it and out of it, of exactly the amount of material it receives from its environment. This is a condition of steady state.

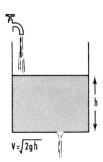

$$v = \sqrt{2gh}$$

Figure 2.9 To illustrate relationships between the inputs, outputs and storage of a system in steady state.

If input is changed, for example by increasing flow from the tap, there follows a short-lived period of adjustment in the system because the depth of water is initially insufficient to create a high enough outlet velocity for outflow to keep pace with inflow. The tank therefore fills up. Eventually, however, the increasing depth of water raises the outlet velocity to a value at which discharge equals the increased input. These adjustments are quite spontaneous. What happens is that negative feedback mechanisms automatically create new internal distributions of energy within

the system which eventually allow a new condition of balance to be achieved. In this case, the new distribution of energy involves storage of potential energy within the system.

The concept of steady state as just described has been applied to the flow and storage of energy and materials in many natural systems, including the earth's crust (Chapter 3), slopes (Chapter 4), river channels (Chapter 5), glacier flow (Chapter 7) and plant succession in ecosystems (Chapter 13).

Dynamic equilibrium

The phrase 'dynamic equilibrium' also refers to open systems and is used in two contexts. Physicists and chemists use it to refer to the exchange of matter and energy across the same surface between two stores. Water molecules, for example, are always leaving a lake surface and entering the atmosphere. Likewise some are always leaving the atmosphere and being caught up again in the liquid water of the lake. When the two processes are exactly equal there is no net loss of water molecules in either the lake or the atmosphere and both remain in equilibrium. The equilibrium in each system, however, is maintained by inputs and outputs across the same boundary. This is dynamic equilibrium. Recall that steady state, which is also characterized by no net storage change, is maintained by inputs and outputs along different routes.

The term 'dynamic equilibrium' has also been introduced extensively into geomorphology, where it is sometimes used synonymously with 'steady state'. It is useful, however, to use it in the context of longer spans of time than would normally be applied to steady state. Some landforms, and some statistical relationships, appear in some respects (though not all) to remain unchanged over long periods of time. For example, slopes are thought by some geomorphologists to retreat parallel to themselves (Chapter 5). This implies that the profile of the slope (its form) remains in equilibrium with the forces operating on it even though its actual position in the landscape changes. Such a combination of stability and change through time is appropriately called dynamic equilibrium.

A good example of statistical stability comes from the study of fluvial geomorphology where it has been found, from the examination of many rivers in different parts of the world, that channel width increases downstream in proportion to the square root of stream discharge (Chapter 5). This relationship appears to hold for river systems of very different ages and in very different climatic and geological environments. Clearly the result of water and sediment flow through drainage basins, the relationship appears, therefore, to be evidence of steady state. But if the relationship does not change through time, and there is no evidence that it does, the steady-state relationship must be maintained even as the landscape is lowered by the transfer of sediment along the river. Once again, therefore, the form of a system (i.e. the statistical relationship) remains stable as the system's physical position (i.e. its elevation) changes. This again is a type of dynamic equilibrium.

CONCLUSIONS

Several important scientific ideas are inherent in looking at objects from a systems point of view. One of these ideas is *interdependence*. All processes in physical geography are to some extent interdependent on one another, although for the sake of convenience they are usually examined separately. Vegetation cover in a drainage basin, for example, might be considered by most people as a subject of interest to biogeographers but hardly of interest to meteorologists or geomorphologists. Vegetation, however, affects evaporation rates. For example, it is now believed that in upland Britain coniferous trees evaporate more water than grass-covered areas (Chapter 14). Since evaporation is the first process to remove rainfall from the ground and from vegetation surfaces in a drainage basin, it necessarily determines how much water will eventually find its way into the river channel where it can do geomorphological work. Because of its direct effect on evaporation and its indirect effect on streamflow, changes in vegetation cover are therefore of very great significance to the meteorologist and geomorphologist as well as to the biogeographer. There are many examples in the chapters which follow of how we separate for convenience our study of different geographical features. But the idea of interdependence in the physical environment as a whole is vital to a proper understanding of how it works, and of how it should be studied and managed.

A second basic idea of open systems thinking is *equifinality*, a forbidding term which simply means that any particular system condition can be brought about in several different ways. In Chapter 5 we shall see that stream velocity is dependent on channel slope, channel depth and the roughness of channel boundaries. An increase of stream velocity can be brought about by an increase in depth, an increase in slope, a decrease in roughness or by any combination of these changes. This illustrates the principle of equifinality, and it is a principle of very great importance in the study of complex open and closed systems, for it stresses that in such systems *a given effect can have several possible causes, and that any particular environmental change can have several different effects*. This principle, of course, makes environmental explanation and prediction very difficult.

A third concept basic to the study of open and closed systems in the natural environment is *diversity*. This measures the number of components or links in a system. The importance of knowing how many components and links exist within a system is illustrated by Figure 2.10, which shows how the

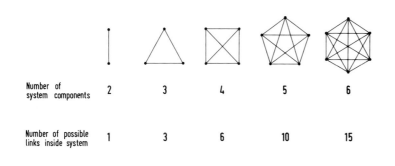

Number of system components	2	3	4	5	6
Number of possible links inside system	1	3	6	10	15

Figure 2.10 To illustrate how links multiply faster than elements as systems increase in complexity.

number of possible links increases more rapidly than the number of components. The more links there are between individual components inside a system the smaller tends to be the impact of any external change on each component. This is because the effects of the change are divided between a large number of components each of which is changed by only a small amount. If, in contrast, there is a small number of components inside the system to absorb all the change from outside, then each component changes by a relatively large amount and the overall state of the system may be transformed considerably. This, in essence, is the principle which lies behind the ecological maxim: diversity is the key to stability.

Section 2

GEOMORPHOLOGICAL PROCESSES

3

Building the Land

Geomorphology studies the origin and evolution of landforms on the earth's surface. The earth's largest landforms—continents, ocean basins, fold mountains, rift valleys, etc.—are created principally by forces operating in the earth's crust. Such forces are called *tectonic* or *endogenic*, and it is appropriate to begin this section on geomorphological processes with an examination of tectonic forces and their effect on the earth's morphology.

STRUCTURE OF THE EARTH

The earth has a diameter of 6370 km (Figure 3.1) and consists of a solid *lithosphere* (about 100 km thick), a solid *mantle* (about 3000 km thick) and a liquid *core*. The lithosphere is the solid crust of the earth together with the upper solid zone of the mantle. Material in the earth's crust is of two types. The continents, which cover about 30% of

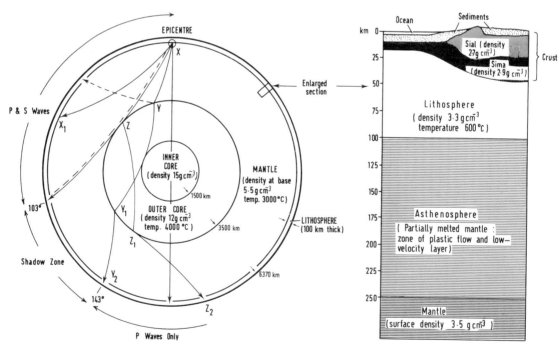

Figure 3.1 Structure of the earth's interior and the behaviour of earthquake waves. Solid lines represent P waves. Broken lines represent S waves. Note the reflection of S waves, and the refraction of P waves, at the junction between mantle and outer core. Paths of P waves emanating from X and affected by refraction are shown as X, Z, Z_1, Z_2, and X, Y, Y_1, Y_2. P waves travelling entirely in the mantle are not refracted (e.g. X, X_1).
(Modified from R. A. Muller, p. 9; and The Open University, 1971 (a), p. 44.)

the earth's surface, are made of light sialic material. *Sial* is somewhat like granite in chemical composition and has a density of 2.7 g cm^{-3}. Under the oceans, which occupy the remaining 70% of the earth's surface, the crust is made of *sima*, a denser material (about 3 g cm^{-3}) and somewhat like basalt in composition. Sima also underlies the sial of the continents.

Geophysicists have come to understand the earth's structure from a study of primary and secondary earthquake waves. When an earth tremor occurs, primary and secondary shock waves are transmitted through the earth from the *epicentre*, i.e. the point at which the earthquake occurs. These waves travel at different speeds and are therefore detected by seismographs around the world at different times. Primary (P) waves travel through solids and liquids. Secondary (S) waves travel only through solids. Both may be deflected at any boundary between materials of markedly different density and their velocities change as well. In general, earthquake velocities increase with depth. Two features of earthquake wave transmission are:

1 the absence of S waves in the antipodean region between 140° and 180° of the epicentre;
2 the absence of both P and S waves in the so-called *shadow zone*, between 103° and 143° of the epicentre (Figure 3.1).

The shadow zone is evidence of a significant change in the density of material about 3500 km below the earth's surface and this depth is taken as the base of the mantle. The fact that S waves are not transmitted beyond 103° suggests that the core is liquid.

Diamonds and the material in which they occur reveal something about the nature of the mantle. Diamonds are a type of carbon produced only at very high pressures such as occur about 250 km below the earth's surface. In South Africa they are found in pipes of material known as *kimberlites* which extend down to these very great depths. Study of kimberlites suggests that *peridotite*, an even denser rock than basalt in composition, is the crustal rock closest in character to the material of the earth's mantle. Although the mantle is described as a solid, it is not a rigid solid like the crust. The mantle is much hotter than the lithosphere and as a consequence behaves differently in the transmission of earthquake waves. A part of the

upper mantle is now in fact believed to be partially melted. This is the *asthenosphere*, about 100 km beneath the earth's surface. Geophysicists believe it to be melted because it only transmits earthquake waves slowly. It is sometimes called the low-velocity layer.

PLATE TECTONICS

Our modern understanding of the earth's crust and mantle and of continental structure, ocean trenches, mountain chains, and tectonic activity of all types is based on the theory of *plate tectonics*. In this theory the earth's lithosphere is believed to consist of eleven major plates (Figure 3.2) moving across the partially-melted asthenosphere. Some of the boundaries between the plates are diverging and others are converging. What happens at such boundaries is best illustrated by reference to the South American plate for this has been studied in considerable detail (Figure 3.3 A). The eastern edge of this plate is the mid-Atlantic ridge, a zone of divergence or *sea-floor spreading*. Here, parallel mountain ranges, 3000 m high and running in an approximate north–south direction along the middle of the Atlantic, are moving slowly apart, the space in between being filled with basaltic lava upwelling from the asthenosphere. The mid-Atlantic ridge, like all divergent plate margins, is therefore one of the youngest parts of the earth's surface. Here new crust is being constantly created.

Because of plate divergence, basaltic lava emerging from the spreading rift between the two plates is transported both east and west of the plate boundary. This produces topographical symmetry on the floor of the Atlantic Ocean, either side of the ridge (Figure 3.3 B). The amount of new crustal material added to each side of the ridge appears small, maybe in the order of 2 or 3 cm year^{-1}, but over a period of 1 million years this rate of activity would produce 50 km of new crust. Sea-floor spreading in both the Atlantic and Pacific oceans proceeds so rapidly that both oceans are now believed to be less than 200 million years old. The upwelling of magma at divergent plate margins makes them major zones of volcanic activity. Iceland, Surtsey, and the Azores, all of

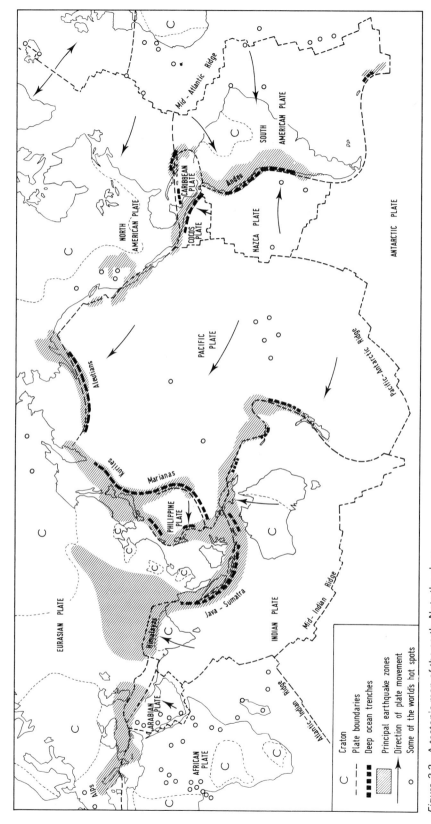

Figure 3.2 A tectonic map of the earth. Note the close association between earthquake zones and subduction zones, the location of cratons away from present-day plate margins and the heavy concentration of hot spots in Africa. Cratons contain the oldest rocks in each continent. Although much deformed in the ancient geological past, they are stable today. (Sources: M. N. Toksoz pp. 4–5; and K. C. Burke and J. T. Wilson, 1976, p. 52.)

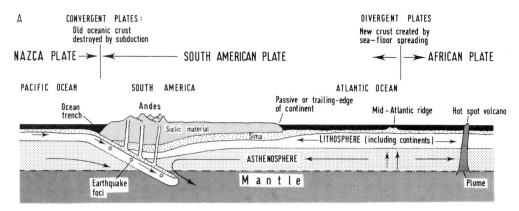

Figure 3.3 A Basic structure of the South American plate (not to scale).

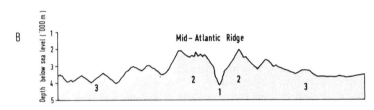

Figure 3.3 B Topography of the Mid-Atlantic Ridge.
1 The axial rift valley.
2 Central mountains.
3 Outer foothills.
(Source: The Open University, 1971 (b), p. 44.)

them areas of recent volcanic activity, are all on the mid-Atlantic ridge.

The western margin of the South American plate coincides with the western seaboard of South America. The Nazca plate, to the west, is moving from west to east while the South American plate moves west. When plates collide in this way, material from the lithosphere on one of the plates is *subducted* back into the mantle where it melts. Over the globe as a whole the processes of sea-floor spreading and subduction are in steady-state equilibrium and the total amount of lithospheric material at any one time is therefore constant (Figure 3.4). The process of subduction, like that of sea-floor spreading, might appear slow when measured on a human time-scale. When measured in volumetric terms over recent geological time it is seen to involve colossal amounts of lithosphere. One calculation states that 20 billion km³ of lithosphere would be sub-ducted in 160 million years at present rates of global subduction.

On the western margin of the South American plate the oceanic crust of the Nazca plate is heavier than the continental crust of the South American plate and is subducted below it. This always happens when continental crust con-verges on oceanic crust because continental crust is lighter and therefore more buoyant. To some geophysicists this suggests that continents are more stable and permanent features of the earth's surface than oceans.

As the oceanic crust of the Nazca plate descends beneath the South American plate, friction be-tween the two plates triggers off earthquakes along the fault systems of the South American coast. Material of the subducted block is partially melted as it is dragged deeper, and this melted oceanic crust possibly acts as a source of *magma* for active volcanoes in the Andes. Lava in these volcanoes is more like sial than sima. It is lighter and contains more silica than the basalts of the oceanic plate. If sialic lava does derive, at least partly, from melted oceanic plate then here is an

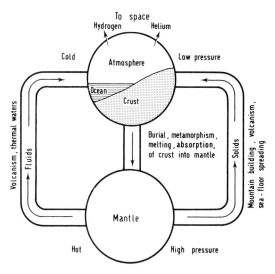

Figure 3.4 A steady-state model of the earth's mantle, crust, atmosphere, and oceans. Circulation is controlled by high pressures and hot temperatures in the mantle which cause partially-melted material to rise into the crust and liquids to rise into the atmosphere and oceans. At any one point in time over the globe as a whole, as much material is moving from the mantle into the crust, atmosphere, and oceans through mountain building, etc. as is being consumed at subduction zones. Models like this enable us to appreciate the inter-related nature of processes such as those identified in the diagram. This is a closed system; and very few materials are added to it or escape from it. Some helium and hydrogen atoms may be light enough to escape the earth's gravitational pull and move into space.
(Source: R. Siever, 'The Steady State of the Earth's Crust, Atmosphere and Oceans'. Copyright © 1974 by Scientific American, Inc. All rights reserved.)

important mechanism by which new continental material is created from oceanic crust. It could be the principal mechanism by which continents have expanded over geological time. However, many geophysicists believe that the lighter lava in these volcanoes results from simple melting of original continental crust.

Subduction therefore is a very important process involving the creation of new continental material at the margins of existing continents. It is also responsible for the creation of new land in the form of volcanic island arcs such as those in the Kurile, Aleutian and Marianas islands. Such islands are created when oceanic plates are melted by increased pressure, heat and friction, as they are subducted at convergent plate margins. Melted material of the subducted plate rises to the surface in a line of volcanoes. The neighbouring deep ocean trenches, the Kurile trench, the Aleutian

trench and the Marianas trench represent the subduction zones themselves.

STRUCTURE OF THE CONTINENTS

The highest parts of any continent are its young *fold mountains*, formed by *orogenic uplift*. This is the process by which large parts of the earth's surface are raised up as a result of horizontal earth movements and folding. There are two principal belts of young fold mountains: the Alpine–Himalayan belt and the almost continuous range of mountains on the western seaboard of North and South America consisting of the Cascades, the Sierra Nevada and the Andes. The principal tectonic difference between the two systems is that the Alpine–Himalayan belt originated on destructive plate margins between continents whereas the fold mountains of North and South America were formed between oceanic and continental plates.

How are fold mountains formed and what is the process of orogenic uplift? This is a complex question to which no definite answer can yet be given. It is known that fold mountains are formed at destructive plate margins from a combination of extreme pressure and intense volcanic activity of all kinds. One popular school of thought among geophysicists argues that continental crust cannot be subducted much below 40 km because of its buoyancy. At this depth, temperatures are not high enough to cause remelting and continental crust therefore responds to the very great pressures by folding and shearing. Sometimes 'wedges' of the leading continental edge appear to be 'broken off' and to be thrust upwards by compressional movement. This creates a very thick layer of extremely buoyant crust which therefore rises high above the rest of the neighbouring continent. Several layers of continental crust may accumulate on top of each other as a result of repeated shearing and upward thrusting, and this could account for the very great altitude of young fold mountains. An important part of orogenic uplift may be the release of pressure when two plates temporarily stop converging. Thick layers of crust previously held down by compression might rapidly rise thousands of metres, if the pressures are suddenly released.

Young fold mountains are about 40–60 million years old. Earlier phases of orogenic mountain building occurred in Hercynian times (250 million years ago) and in the Caledonian era (about 400 million years ago) and fold mountains formed during these periods may once have been as impressive as today's Alps. They have long since been eroded by water and ice, however, and remnants of the Caledonian chain in Britain and Ireland are now found in the relatively low mountains of northern Scotland and Donegal. Remnants of the Hercynian chain exist in Brittany, Cornwall and Wexford. Many geophysicists argue that the old fold mountains, like today's young fold mountains, were formed by *continental accretion* (i.e. by the transformation of dense oceanic crust into lighter continental crust at subduction zones). The fact that rocks tend to become progressively older towards the interior of continents is frequently quoted in support of this theory.

The oldest parts of the continents contain cratons (Figure 3.2). These areas represent the most stable parts of the continents, are at least 2.5 billion years old and are most typically situated well away from plate margins. An exception to this rule is the Indian craton which is currently being driven under the Eurasian plate at the rate of 5 cm year^{-1}.

Hot spots and continental drift

Nearly all the world's volcanoes (99%) occur at plate margins. The rest are far away from these margins, often in the middle of plates. These are the *hot-spot volcanoes* and they have a distinctive lava, somewhat like the basalt lavas of the divergent plate boundaries but containing more of the metallic elements sodium and potassium. These volcanoes are believed to sit on top of *plumes* (Figure 3.3) which ascend directly from the mantle. If this is true, they must derive their lava from deeper sources than any other type of volcano.

Hot spots help us to determine the direction and rate of plate movement. The majority of active plumes (35%) are in Africa, notably in the rift valley system of the north-east. The African volcanoes tend to be stationary and successive lava flows, each of which can be dated, build up one on top of the other. This suggests that the African

plate has remained stationary relative to the mantle. Elsewhere, hot-spot volcanoes can be highly mobile. For example, the Pacific plate near Hawaii has moved north-westwards over a single plume and this motion has produced a chain of volcanoes which becomes progressively younger towards the south-east. The age of each volcano has been dated by radioactive dating techniques (Figure 3.5), and the distances travelled by the volcanoes allow plate motion rates to be determined.

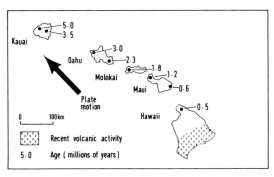

Figure 3.5 A line of hot-spot volcanoes in the Hawaiian Islands. Volcanic age is determined by potassium-argon dating. For a discussion of radioactive dating methods see Chapter 11. The half-life of potassium-40 (^{40}K) is 1.3 billion years. Radioactive decay produces argon-40 (^{40}A). Dates are determined by measuring the ratio of ^{40}K to ^{40}A in the rocks.
(Source: R. A. Muller, p. 22.)

Plate movement of course is the mechanism by which continents have drifted apart. All the continents once formed one supercontinent called *Pangaea* (Figure 3.6). We know this from the similarity of geological structures in continental regions of the world now far removed from each other. The founder of the continental drift theory, Alfred Wegener, used quite simple evidence on which to build his theory in the early twentieth century. He argued that the presence of coal deposits in Pennsylvania, for example, formed from tropical vegetation, meant that Pennsylvania must have drifted to its present position near latitude 41°N from somewhere south of the Tropic of Cancer. Wegener's theory was not finally accepted until plate tectonic theory provided a mechanism capable of explaining how the drift took place. We now believe that as plates drift apart the continents drift with them like rafts of sial embedded in the deeper sima. Why and how did the supercontinent break up? Some geologists

Figure 3.6 The supercontinent of Pangaea which probably began to break up about 2 million years ago. Shaded areas are cratons.
(Source: S. Moorbath, p. 95.)

believe that the gentle crustal warping and faulting which characterizes such stable hot-spot areas as the African Rift valley are signs that a single plate is beginning to break up into two or more plates along the rift system stretching from Kenya to the Red Sea. Stable hot-spot volcanoes, on this interpretation, represent an initial phase of plate subdivision. This may be how the supercontinent broke up.

IGNEOUS ACTIVITY

The word 'igneous' means formed by fire, and *igneous rocks* are those formed from molten magma upwelling from the asthenosphere, the mantle or from melted lithosphere in the subduction zone. Magmas are classified according to the amount of silica they contain. *Basic* or *mafic lavas* contain only 45% silica and are relatively rich in

ferromagnesian metals such as calcium (11%), iron (9%), and magnesium (8%). Magmas are described by their *viscosity*. The lower the viscosity of any substance the easier it flows. Motor oil for instance has a higher viscosity than water. Basic lavas have a viscosity 100 000 times greater than motor oil. Nevertheless, this is quite low for magma, and these lavas flow over long distances quite easily if *extruded* from a vent in the earth's crust on to the surface. Basalt and diorite are extrusive volcanic rocks. Basalt often forms extensive plateaux such as those on the ocean floors. Continental basalt flows are less extensive. Examples include the Deccan plateau in India and the Snake plateau in Idaho. In Britain and Ireland smaller basalt flows cover much of County Antrim and south-western Scotland (Figure 3.7).

Acidic or *silicic magmas* have more silica (70%), less calcium (5%), less iron (4%) and less magnesium (2%) than basic lavas. They flow slowly, sometimes hardly at all, and do not spread over large areas. The viscosity of acidic lava may be 100 million times that of basic lava and it is often erupted with great violence. Acidic lava moving up the central vent of a volcano cools from the top downward. As it cools, gas bubbles may form near the surface. Such bubbles cannot form at depth because of the great pressure. When the bubbles expand and eventually burst, large masses of molten material and gas are ejected

Figure 3.7 Basalt lava flow lying on top of chalk, County Londonderry, Northern Ireland.

from the volcano at great speed. Ejected material is called *tephra* and some tephra is ejected at speeds of 600 m s⁻¹.

Some forms of igneous activity

Extruded forms

The smallest volcanoes, under 300 m high, usually consist solely of unconsolidated tephra, ranging in size from dust and 10 cm long cinders to volcanic bombs 50 kg or more in weight. These are the *cinder cone volcanoes*, often violently explosive.

Composite volcanoes or *stratovolcanoes*, have alternating layers of lava and cinders. Most of the volcanoes in the Cascades and Sierra Nevada are of this type. So are Vesuvius, Stromboli, Etna and Fujiyama. Often 3000 m or more in height, these volcanoes can produce violent eruptions. The 1980 eruption of Mt St Helens in the Cascade mountain range of north-west USA was the most recent example of a long history of violent eruptions in this region. However, it was not as violent as the eruption of ancient Mount Mazama which produced the *caldera* at Crater Lake, Oregon (Figure 3.8).

Intrusive forms

Not all magma moving into the crust from the asthenosphere reaches the surface. Some is intruded only into deeper layers of the crust where it cools slowly, producing rocks like granite with large crystal structures. The largest intrusions are termed *batholiths* (Figure 3.9). Magma intruded along the bedding plane of a sedimentary rock is called a *sill*. When intruded across bedding planes it is termed a *dyke*. A *laccolith* is not unlike a batholith though it is usually smaller and has an identifiable base, often a former bedding plane. All these intrusions have one thing in common. They are only revealed as landscape features after long periods of erosion have removed overlying rocks into which they were intruded. Former batholiths in Britain and Ireland are Dartmoor and parts of the Mourne mountains. Dyke swarms are abundant along the north coast of Ulster and throughout western Scotland from Arran to Skye (Figure 3.10).

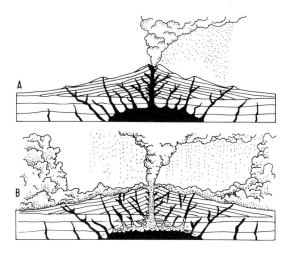

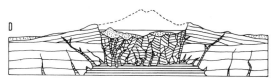

Figure 3.8 Origins of Crater Lake, Oregon. Eruptions of the volcano Mount Mazama (A) began 7000 years ago. Three years of intermittent but violent activity produced 30 km³ of tephra which rained down over large areas of what is now Oregon and Washington and greatly reduced the volume of the magma chamber feeding the volcano. The superstructure of the volcano began to sag (B and C), and eventually collapsed (D), leaving a huge amphitheatre-like depression known as a caldera. This eventually filled with melted snow and rainwater.
(Source: L. R. Kittleman, 'Tephra'. Copyright © 1979 by Scientific American, Inc. All rights reserved.)

SEDIMENTARY AND METAMORPHIC ROCKS

Continental parts of the crust are subject to weathering and erosion. Between them these processes produce sediment which is removed by rivers and deposited in ocean basins (Figure 3.9 C) where it may attain considerable thickness, especially in the deep subduction troughs at convergent plate margins. It also accumulates on the

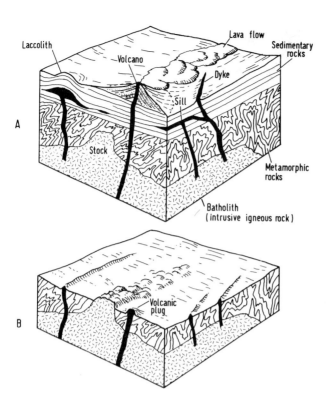

Figure 3.9A Various forms of igneous activity.

Figure 3.9B The same area as in (A) after erosion of sedimentary and some metamorphic rock.

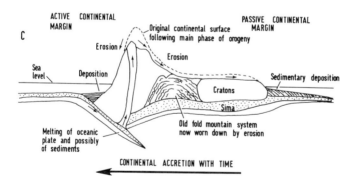

Figure 3.9C Idealized relationships between continental structure, continental growth, erosion and sedimentation.

continental shelves, which are particularly well developed where continental margins do not co-incide with plate margins as for example around Britain and Ireland. The accumulation, compression and cementation of sediments in these environments produces *sedimentary rock*.

Sedimentary rocks, like sandstone, shale and limestone, are transformed into metamorphic rocks by great heat and/or pressure. Sandstone becomes quartzite, shale becomes phyllite and schist,

limestone becomes marble. At convergent plate margins pressure and heat are most intense and here most of the world's metamorphic rocks are produced. *Metamorphism* literally means 'change of state', and igneous rocks as well as sedimentary rocks can be metamorphosed at convergent plate boundaries. On the passive margins of continents, like the eastern seaboard of the United States, metamorphism is not so intense and sedimentary rocks are more easily preserved.

Figure 3.10   Basaltic dyke through schist, north coast of Donegal.

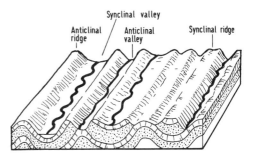

Figure 3.11   Idealized examples of four possible relationships between folding and topography. (Source: W. D. Thornbury, p. 226.)

FAULTS AND FOLDS

Sedimentary rocks originally laid down horizontally are folded and faulted by convergent movement between oceanic and continental plates. The most vivid expression of folds and faults is in the rocks themselves and is principally the concern of the geologist. There are topographic expressions of folds and faults, however, which are often locally very dramatic and/or regionally extensive. These features are often the indirect effects of the original folds and faults in that the surface we see today is not the original surface produced by the earth movements.

Folding produces some good examples of how structure indirectly affects landscape. Sometimes geological 'highs' (anticlines) coincide with topographic 'lows' (river valleys or simple depressions of the land surface). Sometimes geological 'lows' coincide with topographic 'highs' (hills, ridges, etc.). These are examples of *inverted relief* (Figure 3.11). Even when there is agreement between geological and topographic elements of the landscape it may not be the originally folded landscape we are looking at. Whole series of strata above the present landscape may have been stripped away by earlier erosion.

Faulting is spasmodic and usually results from the sudden release of energy stored in the rocks on either side of a fault as they are displaced relative to each other by plate movement. It takes many forms. A *normal fault* may produce a fault

scarp. This is a scarp *originally produced* by the uplift of land on one side of a fault relative to land on the other side. A *fault-line scarp* is *originally produced* by the differential erosion of rocks brought into contact with each other by faulting (Figure 3.12). Sub-parallel sets of faults are common especially at plate edges. Between these faults, huge blocks of land may be uplifted or downfaulted giving rise to *block-faulted mountain ranges* such as the basin and range topography of south-western USA. On a more local scale,

A

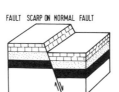
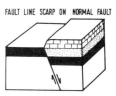

Figure 3.12 A   Two types of scarp along a normal fault. The fault scarp (left) was initiated by faulting, the scarp itself being located on the upthrown block. The fault-line scarp (right) is on the downthrown side, indicating that erosion of material from the upthrown side has taken place and that the scarp has been brought into existence by erosion.

B

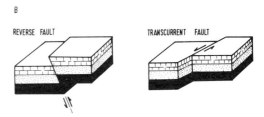

Figure 3.12 B   Reverse and transcurrent faults. Normal faults are usually associated with tension in the earth's crust. Reverse faults are associated with compression.

grabens are small blocks depressed between a pair of normal faults. A block elevated between such faults is a *horst*. As the names imply, these landforms were first described in Germany. The Rhine valley is considered to be a graben. *Rift valleys* are sometimes considered to result from the downfaulting of extensive blocks of land. However, as we have seen, more recent interpretation sees them as emerging plate boundaries rather than as relatively shallow products of faulting in the earth's crust.

ISOSTACY

Some minerals in the earth's mantle can exist in two phases, dependent upon pressure. High pressure compresses the atomic structure and the mineral becomes more dense. Release of pressure causes the atomic structure to expand and the mineral becomes less dense. These changes are called *phase changes* and involve no change in chemical composition. Removal of sediment from continents by erosion reduces the pressure on underlying minerals in the earth's upper mantle, some of which, especially olivine, are then believed to move into their less densely packed phase. The increased volume occupied by these minerals under conditions of reduced pressure causes the overlying continent to rise. The reverse chemical processes happen at continental margins where sediment accumulation compresses atomic structures in the upper mantle. The overlying parts of the crust therefore sink. Vertical movement of the earth's crust in this way is called *isostacy*. Any major redistribution of sediment on the earth's surface produces associated isostatic adjustment, and for every centimetre of continental rock removed by erosion there is approximately 0.42 cm of counteracting isostatic uplift. In this way the buoyancy of continents counteracts forces of erosion as well as of subduction.

4

Weathering and Slopes

INTRODUCTION

Fluvial geomorphology studies how land masses are lowered by rivers, and the basic unit of study in the subject is the drainage basin. The two principal inputs into a drainage basin (see Chapter 2) are precipitation and rock material broken down by weathering. These inputs combine to produce a mixture of water and sediment which moves downhill under the influence of gravity. On the slopes of the drainage basin, the mixture moves downhill slowly because it contains more sediment than water. In the river, the mixture moves quite rapidly because it contains more water than sediment. The slow downhill movement of soils on slopes and the relatively fast flow of water and sediment in rivers are, therefore, the two ends of a continuous process, and are studied as such in geomorphology. The present chapter deals with the first phase of this process, namely the production and gradual movement of weathered material on slopes. Chapter 5 examines how channel systems transport the products of weathering out of the drainage basins and into the oceans.

WEATHERING

The unconsolidated material between our feet and solid rock is called the *regolith* and is produced by *weathering*. As weathering proceeds with time, the size of material in the regolith becomes smaller. This is the process of *reduction*.[1] Reduction followed by regolith transport is called *denudation*.

[1] This process of reducing the physical size of material in the regolith is not to be confused with chemical reduction, the process whereby oxygen is removed from a compound.

There are two types of weathering: *physical* (or mechanical) *weathering* and *chemical weathering*. *Biological weathering* is sometimes recognized as a third type. This includes the widening of rock joints by plant roots and the burrowing activities of certain animals which create routeways for water movement in the regolith. These processes, however, do not themselves cause reduction, but serve rather to encourage other forms of physical or chemical weathering. They are best not regarded as a separate category.

Physical weathering

This involves the breakdown of rock without any change in chemical composition. One familiar example is *freeze–thaw*. On freezing, water trapped in a rock joint expands 9% by volume and exerts very high pressures on neighbouring materials. Sudden application of high pressures, followed by subsequent rapid release of pressure on melting, causes some rock materials to disintegrate very rapidly. Freeze–thaw is most effective when temperatures fluctuate frequently across 0 °C. This occurs in most temperate climates at high altitude, where freeze–thaw is therefore a powerful agent of weathering. It is a less effective weathering agent in climates like that of Antarctica which are constantly very cold.

Freeze–thaw involves the alternate formation and destruction of ice crystals. In dry areas a similar process of *crystal growth* in rock joints occurs when dissolved salts are precipitated from surface moisture following evaporation. Sulphate, gypsum, and calcium carbonate crystals can all be formed in this way, and their growth can exert sufficient force to break off small pieces of rock.

It used to be thought that a third type of physical weathering resulted from the different rates at which different minerals within rocks would expand on heating. Until quite recently, this process was believed to produce internal stresses which could fracture most rock materials, especially in hot, arid areas. Following laboratory experiments, however, in which rocks were heated and cooled very frequently and rapidly without showing any signs of disintegration, it was concluded that the importance of the process has probably been over-estimated.

A more important process of physical weathering is *pressure-release*. This produces a type of jointing typical of many intrusive igneous rocks like granite. Such rocks, formed under very great pressure deep in the earth's crust, are believed to expand slightly as surface rocks are gradually stripped off by denudation. The release of pressure as surface rocks are removed produces a joint system which runs parallel to the surface of the intrusion. This process is called *exfoliation*.

A final example of physical weathering is *colloidal swelling and contraction*. This takes place in rocks containing clay minerals, which expand when wet and contract when dry.

In American literature the wearing down of rock particles by *abrasion* as they move along in streams is sometimes regarded as a weathering phenomenon. This is unwise for weathering is an *in situ* process which does not involve transport by water, wind, or ice.

Chemical weathering

Physical weathering only involves changes in the size and shape of rock particles. Chemical weathering, however, involves chemical alteration of rock materials. Because of this distinction, physical weathering can be described as a process of rock disintegration and chemical weathering as a process of rock decomposition.

Most chemical compounds within the earth's crust exist in what the chemist calls a *reduced state*, i.e. they contain no oxygen and their electrons (subatomic particles with a negative charge) are easily removed in the right conditions. The earth's crust also contains very little water. When chemical compounds formed in this environment are exposed at the earth's surface, where both water and oxygen are abundant, they prove to be very unstable and decompose quite rapidly. Chemical weathering can therefore be described as a set of processes, involving principally oxygen and water, which convert unstable chemical compounds into more stable forms. In the study of chemical weathering it is well to remember that rocks consist of different minerals and that rates of chemical change are different in each mineral. Rock decomposition is therefore controlled by the rate at which the least resistant mineral is broken down.

An important chemical weathering process is *oxidation*. This occurs when dissolved oxygen in the water or atmosphere combines with other elements, principally metallic elements such as calcium, magnesium, sodium and iron. A good example of the oxidation process involves iron, which naturally exists in two states, ferrous oxide and ferric oxide. Ferrous oxide is unstable at the earth's surface because it can take on additional oxygen. In this way it is transformed into ferric oxide. Ferric oxide cannot take on any more oxygen and is therefore a stable mineral at the earth's surface. As a chemical reaction this transformation is written:

$$4FeO + O_2 \longrightarrow 2Fe_2O_3$$

[ferrous oxide + oxygen $\longrightarrow$ ferric oxide]

This particular oxidation reaction is believed to represent an important milestone in the earth's history. Insoluble ferric oxide is red. Ferrous oxide is not. Sedimentary rocks more than 1.8 billion years old are devoid of red colours, which suggests that there was no free oxygen (O_2)[1] in the earth's atmosphere to combine with the abundant ferrous oxide in the earth's crust. If there were no free oxygen, there was no life. This equation is therefore of central importance not only to geologists and geomorphologists but to biologists interested in the earth's evolution.

---

1 For the non-chemist, free oxygen (O_2) is not to be confused with the oxygen atom in the water molecule. O_2 contains two oxygen atoms and is produced by photosynthesis (Chapter 1). Oxidation is very different from hydration and hydrolysis, processes by which substances are dissolved in water. Indeed O_2 and H_2O do not react well together. O_2 can dissolve in water but only to a limited extent. At saturation, i.e. when water holds as much dissolved oxygen (DO) as possible the concentration of DO in the water is only 10 p.p.m. (parts per million).

A second form of chemical weathering is *hydration*, the general process whereby certain materials dissolve in water. Water is a good solvent and can dissolve most materials in the regolith, to some extent at least. For this reason, perfectly pure water is very rare. In hydration, ionic compounds[1] dissolve by interaction with the water molecule, the structure of which is very important in accounting for its solvency properties. Because oxygen atoms have a tendency to attract electrons, there is a very slight negative charge on the oxygen atom in the water molecule. The hydrogen atoms, which tend to lose electrons, have a small positive charge. When ionic substances like common salt come into contact with water the forces of attraction between the ions in the salt are smaller than those between the individual ions and the water molecule itself. The positive ion is therefore attracted to the oxygen atom in the water molecule while the negative ion is attracted to the hydrogen atom. In this way, a substance like common salt is easily dissolved (Figure 4.1).

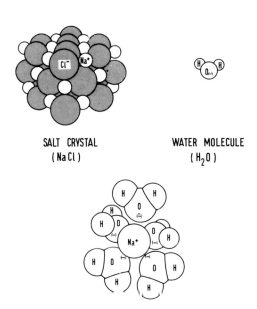

SALT CRYSTAL   WATER MOLECULE
(NaCl)   (H_2O)

Figure 4.1 Solution of common salt (NaCl) by the process of hydration. The attraction of positive sodium ions (Na^+) towards the partial negative charge on the water molecule is simultaneous with the attraction of the chloride ion (Cl^-) to the hydrogen atom (not shown). The salt crystal is thus broken up and dissolves in the water. The partial negative charge on the water molecule results from the oxygen atom's capacity to attract electrons. The oxygen atom develops a negative charge while the hydrogen atom, which tends to lose electrons, acquires a positive charge.

Hydrolysis is a different process from hydration. In natural waters the water molecule tends to dissociate very slightly into its constituent ions.

$$H_2O \underset{\longleftarrow}{\longrightarrow} H^+ + OH^-$$

[water $\underset{\longleftarrow}{\longrightarrow}$ hydrogen ion + hydroxyl ion]

The longer of the two arrows in the above formula indicates that the combination of H^+ and OH^- ions[2] is a stronger natural tendency than the dissociation of the water molecule. Once H^+ and OH^- ions have been formed, however, they may become electrically attracted to the crystal framework of various minerals. The incorporation of H^+ and OH^- ions in this way expands the crystal and weakens it. This is the process of weathering by hydrolysis. It is very important in the breakdown of the mineral mica and of siliceous rocks in general. It has also been identified as a possibly important process in the exfoliation of desert rocks.

The principal difference between hydration and hydrolysis is that in hydration the water molecule remains intact and the mineral crystal structures are ruptured, whereas in hydrolysis the water molecule itself dissociates, the H^+ and the OH^- ions being incorporated into the mineral crystal structure.

A fourth form of chemical weathering, *carbonation*, results from the slightly acidic nature of natural rainwater. Rainwater is acidic because carbon dioxide in the atmosphere reacts with some of the water droplets present to produce a weak solution of carbonic acid:

$$H_2O + CO_2 \longrightarrow H_2CO_3$$

[water + carbon dioxide $\longrightarrow$ carbonic acid]

---

1 A compound containing two different types of atom. One type of atom loses an electron and thereby becomes positively charged. The other type of atom gains the lost electron and thereby becomes negatively charged. Such charged atoms are called *ions*. The positively charged ion (cation) is attracted to the negatively charged ion and this attraction binds the compound together. In NaCl (common salt), for example, the Na (sodium) ion loses an electron and becomes positively charged while the Cl atom (chloride) gains the sodium's lost electron and becomes negatively charged.
2 H^+ is a chemical symbol which means that a hydrogen atom has lost 1 electron. This leaves it with a positive electric charge. The OH^- ion has gained 1 electron and has a single negative electric charge. Positively charged ions are called *cations*. Negatively charged ions are called *anions*.

An acid, by definition, is any solution which tends to lose hydrogen ions (H^+), and the hydrogen ions in H_2CO_3 are therefore less tightly held than they are in the water molecule. As a result, they are easily exchanged for any cations[1] such as magnesium (Mg^{2+}) and potassium (K^+) which may be present in the soil regolith. The exchange of hydrogen for magnesium produces magnesium carbonate ($MgCO_3$) and the exchange of hydrogen for potassium produces potassium carbonate (K_2CO_3). Carbonation, therefore, is another process by which hydrogen ions become available to separate cations from their original mineral assemblages. Like all other processes of chemical weathering, it is one which weakens and breaks down the original chemical composition of rock materials in the earth's mantle and in the regolith.

In a similar process to carbonation (Figure 4.2), sulphur oxides in the atmosphere can combine with water to produce weak solutions of sulphuric acid (H_2SO_4). Hydrogen ions might then break from the acidic solution to leave the polyatomic hydrogen sulphate ion (HSO_4^-). This has a negative electric charge and can combine with any other positive ion like potassium or calcium in the regolith. Material containing these cations might thus be broken down.

The role of this particular chemical reaction in weathering processes is not yet perfectly understood and it may prove to be insignificant. However, since acids lose H^+ ions so very easily, the increasing *acidification* of rainwater over certain parts of the industrial world is of great interest to soil scientists and geomorphologists alike.

Acidity is measured by the pH scale, which ranges from 1 to 14 and defines the number of H^+ ions per litre of solution. A solution in which the

1 Mg^{2+} is a chemical symbol to show that the magnesium has lost two electrons.

concentration of hydrogen ions is $1:10\,000\,000$, or 10^{-7}, is said to have a pH of 7, and represents neutrality, half-way along the scale from 1 to 14. A tenfold *increase* in the hydrogen concentration, from $1:10\,000\,000$ to $1:1\,000\,000$, *lowers* the pH from 7 to 6. Acid solutions therefore have low pH values, while alkaline, or basic, solutions have high pH values (i.e. low concentrations of H^+ ions).

Natural rainwater has a pH of between 5 and 6.5, a value controlled principally by the concentration of dissolved carbon dioxide in the atmosphere. Throughout western Europe and the north-eastern seaboard of North America, however, pH values in atmospheric precipitation have recently been falling, and in Scandinavia values as low as 2.8 have been recorded. It is now believed that emissions of sulphur into the atmosphere from industrial parts of Britain and West Germany are principally responsible for the low pH values in western Europe (Figure 4.3).

This brief description of chemical weathering has identified four separate processes. It is well to remember, however, that these processes do not act independently, but in quite close association. A second point to remember is that the chemical breakdown of rocks produces some end-products which are soluble in water and others which are not. The soluble products are removed in the water which percolates through the regolith, and the insoluble products accumulate in the soil. Carbonation, for example, breaks down orthoclase feldspar into insoluble kaolinite and soluble potassium. The kaolinite accumulates, and the potassium is removed in soil water.

Products of weathering

Perhaps the most obvious products of mechanical weathering are *screes*. These accumulate below exposures of solid rock in upland and arid areas.

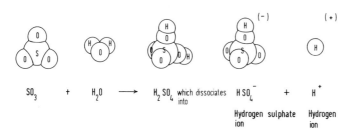

SO$_3$ +   H$_2$O   →   H$_2$SO$_4$ which dissociates   HSO$_4^-$ +   H$^+$
into
Hydrogen sulphate ion   Hydrogen ion

Figure 4.2 The breakdown of sulphuric acid into hydrogen sulphate and hydrogen ions.

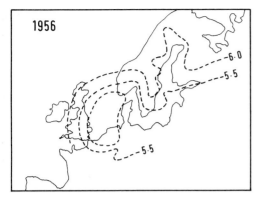

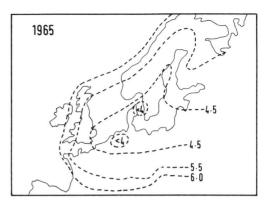

Figure 4.3 Acidification of rainwater over western Europe between 1956 and 1965. The figures refer to pH values. (Modified from S. Oden, 'The acidity problem— an outline of concepts' in *Water, Air and Soil Pollution,* Vol. 6, 1976, p. 144.)

They are produced by frost action and may, or may not, be mobile today. If they are mobile, vegetation does not easily grow on them and is therefore sparsely distributed or non-existent. If they are fossil features of the landscape, un-related to today's climate, vegetation cover may be extensive.

The principal product of mechanical and chemical weathering is of course the regolith itself. Where deep sections exist in a regolith they ideally have profiles like that shown in Figure 4.4. At the base is fresh rock with closed joints. Towards the surface, joints become widened for they are the principal routes along which water percolates downward from the surface. Chemical weathering therefore proceeds most rapidly in the joints. As the joints widen, so the *corestones* diminish in size, until at the surface no trace of the original rock structure remains. An interesting question is whether or not a steadily-increasing thickness of regolith hinders the weathering of fresh rock be-neath by impeding the downward movement of water. The answer to this question is not known, but most geomorphologists believe that weather-ing is most effective in the upper layers of the regolith and that breakdown of fresh rock is most rapid if the mantle of weathered material is steadily removed.

A conspicuous landform thought to be pro-duced largely by weathering is the *tor,* a loose group of boulders often standing on top of one another in the form of stacks. The principal theory as to the origin of tors envisages an initial phase of rock rotting in the zone above the water table (Figure 4.5). Where joints are closely spaced, this phase of weathering breaks down the bedrock into relatively small fragments. Where jointing is widely spaced, weathering is incomplete and large corestones are produced. These ultimately form the large boulders of the tor itself. The second phase of tor formation occurs when the finer products of weathering are mechanically removed. In Britain the most probable agents of removal were ice, meltwater, or simple downslope gravita-tional movement when the whole weathered mass was saturated with water. The most probable date for the production of British tors was towards the end of the last glaciation, about 30 000 years ago.

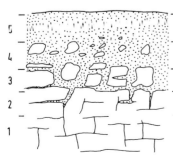

Surface soil with or without well-marked soil horizons. Colour due to soil processes and not parent rock

Most of the material is soil. Some rock fabric clearly present

Most material is rock. Well weathered corestones very evident. Weathering proceeds along much widened joints

Zone of slight discoloration along joints – the routes of initial weathering

Parent rock

Figure 4.4 An idealized profile through a regolith.

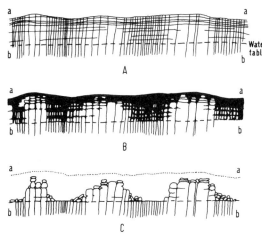

Figure 4.5 Linton's explanation of tor formation. Tors are usually located on watersheds.
(Source: D. L. Linton, 1955, 'The problem of Tors', *Geographical Journal*, Vol. 121, p. 475.)

SLOPES

Processes

Geomorphological processes operating on slopes are largely determined by how water moves in and across the regolith. All soil materials have a certain *infiltration capacity*. This defines the maximum rate, usually measured in millimetres per hour ($mm\,h^{-1}$), at which they can absorb rainfall. If the rainfall rate is less than the infiltration capacity, water will move downward through the soil pores driving out any air that is present. When all soil pores are full of water the soil is said to be saturated. The *zone of saturation*, which rises after prolonged rainfall and falls in dry weather, lies below the water table. Water in this zone is called *groundwater*, and moves towards the river at a rate determined by *soil permeability* and by the slope of the water table itself. Soil permeability is a measure of the soil's ability to transmit water. Because it moves slowly, groundwater has time to establish chemical equilibrium with many of the

chemical compounds in the soil, and water flowing into streams from this source typically contains large amounts of dissolved solids (see Figure 5.14).

Some water percolating downward through the soil from the surface may be forced by a relatively impermeable soil horizon to flow laterally. Water which thus flows downslope between the ground surface and the water table is termed *throughflow* or *interflow* (Figure 4.6), and like groundwater it may be an important source of dissolved solids in river water.

A third type of water movement takes place across the ground surface itself and is termed *saturated overland flow*. This occurs after long periods of heavy rainfall have totally saturated the soil and raised the water table to ground level. An alternative form of overland flow occurs when precipitation intensity exceeds infiltration capacity, and surplus water which cannot be absorbed into the soil is forced to flow across the ground surface. Such conditions may occur even when the water table is well below ground level. For example, if rainfall intensity is 75 $mm\,h^{-1}$ and infiltration capacity is 50 $mm\,h^{-1}$, the excess 25 $mm\,h^{-1}$ will flow across the ground surface whatever the sub-surface conditions. Robert Horton, an American geologist, was first to recognize this type of surface water flow, which is termed *Horton overland flow* to distinguish it from saturated overland flow.

In Britain, Horton overland flow is not now thought to occur very widely because infiltration capacities are rarely lower than rainfall intensity. Saturated overland flow is also thought to be restricted to a very narrow zone adjacent to river channels where the water table could quite conceivably rise to the ground surface. Elsewhere in a drainage basin it is unlikely to do so. For these reasons, throughflow and groundwater flow are now thought to be the principal ways in which

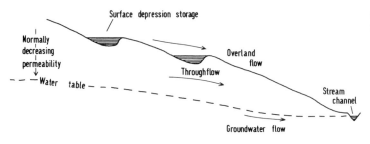

Figure 4.6 Water movement within and on a slope.

water reaches rivers in Britain, although in arid and semi-arid areas, where precipitation intensities can be very high indeed, Horton overland flow may well be an important geomorphological process.

When it does occur, overland flow is *laminar*, unlike water flow in rivers which is *turbulent* (Figure 4.7). This means that it lacks random vertical flow eddies necessary for suspended sediment transport. Instead, water flows in parallel layers which do not mix with each other. Although it cannot therefore transport by suspension, overland flow can theoretically roll very fine particles across the ground surface, and this is believed to take place in a process called *surface wash*. This process is difficult to measure because it takes place over large areas and is not confined in channels.

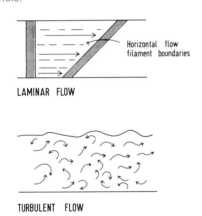

LAMINAR FLOW

Horizontal flow
filament boundaries

TURBULENT FLOW

Figure 4.7 Laminar flow showing the relative displacement of a water column, and turbulent flow showing the random motion of individual eddies. The direction of water flow is from left to right.

Another process contributing to the downhill movement of surface particles on slopes is *rainfall impact*. During heavy rainfall, soil particles have been observed bouncing up to heights of 50 cm above ground level. This is due to the very considerable kinetic energy contained in heavy rainfall. On level ground the net transport produced by rainfall impact is zero, but even on gentle slopes of 10° three times as much soil material moves downhill as uphill. This is because particles which move downslope after impact travel further in the air than particles displaced uphill (Figure 4.8). The process is most effective in arid and semi-arid areas where rainfall is often intensive

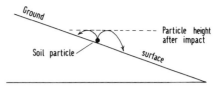

Figure 4.8 Relative displacement of soil material on a slope by rainfall impact.

and vegetation cover, which elsewhere protects soil from rainfall impact, is sparse.

Intermediate in nature between the *in situ* processes of weathering and the *erosive* processes of transport by water are the various processes of *mass movement* which are so important in determining the morphology of slopes. Three types of mass movement are particularly important. These are soil creep, mudflows and landslides. Each of these processes, and other slope-forming factors, are comprehensively described by Young (1972).

Soil creep is the slow continuous downhill movement of regolith, and is brought about as individual rock particles are first disturbed by the various processes of weathering and subsequently settle under the influence of gravity. The gravitational settling produces a net downslope movement of every part of the regolith initially disturbed. A sign of active soil creep is the accumulation of soil material on the uphill side of a wall built along a contour. Another is the downhill curvature of tree trunks sometimes to be seen on railway embankments or steep valley sides.

Mudflows and *landslides* are examples of rapid mass movement. Mudflows have a characteristic basin-shaped source area, a narrow mud track bounded by well-defined shear planes, and a large depositional lobe. Mudflows on glacial till at Minnis North in County Antrim have been monitored by Prior and others. Prior's field notes for the afternoon of November 4th, 1971, graphically describe the sequence of events involved in a mudflow surge.

'It was raining heavily at 4.15 p.m. and surface water could clearly be heard running down tributary mud tracks. At 4.25 p.m. the noise of moving surface water suddenly stopped, even though it was still raining, and a layer of mud 30 cm thick moved down one of the tributary slides. Its speed was about 5 m min⁻¹. The weight of this mud on the material in the main mudflow channel caused

this in turn to surge forward and cover the main road at the base of the slide with a lobe of mud 50 cm thick and 400 m² in area (Figure 4.9). The noise of running water was then heard again, the whole episode having lasted five minutes.' (Hutchinson *et al.*, p. 371.)

Landslides involve rapid movement of weathered rock or regolith across a well-defined failure surface or shear plane. Material above this surface remains relatively undeformed (Figure 4.9). They usually involve larger quantities of material than mudflows, which may in fact subsequently occur

within the slipped material of the landslide itself. This has in fact happened in NE Antrim. One of the world's largest landslides in modern times occurred at Hope in British Columbia and was triggered, many scientists believe, by two small earthquake shocks. The material involved was weathered metamorphic schists, dipping at 30° in the same direction as the steep valley sides. The landslide involved 130×10^6 tonnes of regolith, felled extensive areas of coniferous trees, and buried a road to a depth of 78 m, killing the occupants of a coach (Figure 4.10).

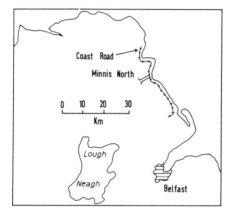

Figure 4.9 Plan and cross-section of a mudflow track in N.E. Antrim. (Modified from J. N. Hutchinson, D. B. Prior, and N. Stephens, pp. 364 and 365.)

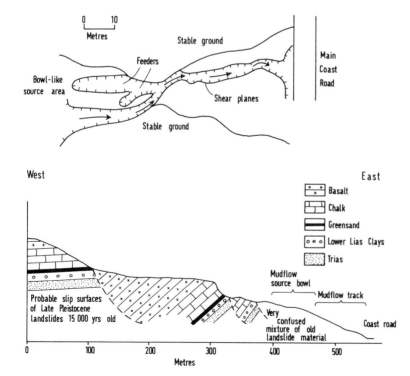

Figure 4.10   The Hope landslide occurred in 1965.

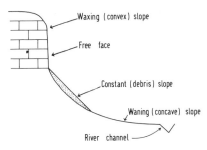

Figure 4.11   The four-facet model of an ideal slope. A constant (scree) slope beneath a free face of basalt and chalk is shown in Figure 3.7.
(Modified from L. C. King, 1962, *Morphology of the Earth*, p. 137, Oliver and Boyd.)

Factors causing rapid mass movements are complex. Areas in which they occur, however, probably possess some of the following characteristics: deep regoliths or steeply-dipping sedimentary rocks; clays which swell easily; very wet climates; temperatures which oscillate frequently around 0 °C; and a high earthquake frequency.

Wood's model of slope evolution

The processes and landforms described in this chapter so far are ones that can be observed and may be measured. When it comes to explaining how slopes evolve over long periods of geomorphological time, however, observation is not possible and deductions have to be made. Such deductions give rise to models and theories, and one model of slope evolution was devised by Wood in 1942. In this model the *free face* (Figure 4.11) is the surface of active mechanical weathering, and this retreats backwards as weathering proceeds. Rocks falling from the free face as a result of weathering accumulate as scree on the constant slope and are further broken down there by physical and chemical weathering. The constant slope abuts on to a concave slope across which various forms of wash possibly take place. Above the free face is the convex slope produced by weathering.

Not all four facets need be present in any one locality. For example, if physical weathering produces more scree than can be removed by erosion on the concave slope, the constant slope will build up to eventually obliterate the free face. This sequence of events represents a form of negative

feedback in that the transport of sediment through and out of the system is successively regulated by decreases in the height of the exposed weathering surface. Decreasing the input of sediment from the free face in this way gives the limited system output facilities a better chance of coming into balance with the input rates and of thus creating a steady state of sediment throughput.

The stability of the free face determines the presence, or absence, of the convex element above it. If the free face is retreating, any convex element present will be removed by rock fall and will not therefore be prominently developed. Conversely, if the free face is static because weathering on it is limited, the convex turnover may be very pronounced.

CONCLUSIONS

Like all environmental systems slopes are very complex and this chapter has concentrated on a simple description of processes which operate within and upon slopes at the present time. It is well to remember, however, that slopes may be more related to past than to present-day processes. Perhaps the easiest example to illustrate this point is the widespread existence today of U-shaped valleys in areas now devoid of ice. Slopes on the sides of such valleys are principally the product of glacial erosion and they have not yet been obliterated by those slope processes which have been operating in the 10 000 years since the glaciers retreated.

5

The Geomorphological Work of Rivers

RIVER CHANNELS AS OPEN SYSTEMS

Any particular stretch of river channel is an avenue of sediment transport through which is carried the products of weathering and erosion from higher up the drainage basin. Consider a channel segment (Figure 5.1) with an upstream input of water (Q_w) and sediment (Q_s). To maintain a continuous flow of water and sediment through a channel network, each such segment between the source of a river and its mouth should discharge at its downstream end all the water and sediment delivered to it from upstream.

In order to transport sediment delivered from upstream with whatever discharge is provided from the upstream drainage basin a channel segment is able to adjust its width (w), depth (d), slope (s) and velocity (v). It is also able to adjust its planform between three conditions: *braided*, *meandering* and *straight*. It is now known that some combinations of width and depth favour the transport of coarse bed material, while others favour the transport of fine sediment. If a channel

segment therefore receives a lot of coarse sediment without any increase in streamflow, as for example after a valley side landslip, it adopts that shape most suited to remove the increased sediment supply. In the final analysis, channel morphology is a response to the discharge-sediment ratio.

It is possible to recognize three basic conditions relating to the transport of sediment through an individual reach. In condition A (Figure 5.2), the total input of sediment from upstream ($Q_s(I)$) exceeds the output downstream ($Q_s(O)$). When this condition persists over many years sediment accumulates within the reach. This process is called *aggradation*. In condition B, total input of material is less than the channel's ability to transport sediment. The flowing water is able to pick up previously-deposited material and to erode its bed and banks. This process, if it persists at one site, is called *degradation*. Degradation occurs downstream from many of the high dams on the rivers of western USA. Behind these dams suspended sediment is trapped in the reservoirs and

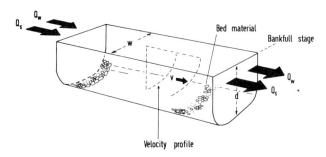

Figure 5.1 Independent and dependent variables in a river channel. The inputs Q_w and Q_s are determined by upstream drainage basin characteristics and channel processes. They are independent of the channel system. Any variations in their values are principally brought about by climate or by changed land use. The channel morphology variables (width, depth and slope) are dependent on, and adjust to, Q_w and Q_s. Such adjustments bring about changes in velocity, which is also a dependent variable.

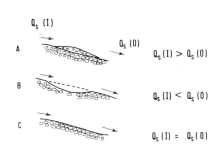

Figure 5.2 Three relationships between the input of sediment into a reach, $Q_s(I)$ and output, $Q_s(O)$.

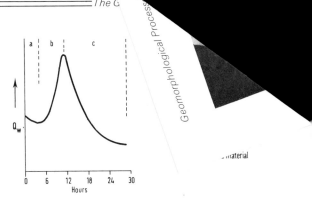

Figure 5.3 A flood hydrograph and associated changes in bed elevation. In this example the net effect of the flood is to raise bed levels.

the water which leaves the dams has a small load, and is thus able to pick up fine calibre sediment quite easily. As a result many of the alluvial channels downstream from the dams are actively degrading. In condition C, the total input of sediment into a reach is just balanced by the output of an equivalent amount from the downstream end. Material leaving the reach need not necessarily be (and seldom is), physically, the same material that enters from upstream for a balance to exist between input and output. The condition of balance is a net effect and exists when the transporting ability of a channel reach, as determined by slope, cross-sectional shape and velocity, is sufficient *just* to transport the size and quantity of material provided from all parts of the drainage basin upstream. This condition represents an example of *open system steady state*. Inputs into the system equal outputs because the internal distributions of energy in the system are delicately adjusted to the transfer of sediment and streamflow from upstream. If the steady state condition lasts over an extended period of time, say a few hundred years, during which the whole river system may be lowered by erosion, the river is usually said to be in a condition of dynamic equilibrium (see Chapter 2). Such a river is said to be *graded*.

Care must be taken not to confuse aggradation and degradation, which are long-term adjustments, with the short-term build-up and removal of sediment which can take place in any channel segment as a result of normal sediment transfer downstream. During the passage of a flood, for example (Figure 5.3, stage b), velocities in a channel are high, and may be sufficiently high to pick up sediment from the stream bed. This sediment is transported downstream and the bed level

is lowered. As the flood peak recedes (Figure 5.3, stage c), sediment already in transport from upstream is deposited in the channel, and the bed accordingly rises. Bed lowering on this timescale (such as the 6 hours or so in Figure 5.3) is called *scouring* and deposition is called *filling*. Either process may exceed the other during any one flood, so that the net effect may be a temporary lowering or elevation of the bed. But the effects of successive floods cancel each other out over a number of years in a graded channel, and no net change occurs in bed elevation over this extended time period. In a degrading reach scouring is the dominant process in successive floods over a period of years. In an aggrading reach the dominant process is filling.

MEASUREMENT OF STREAM DISCHARGE AND SEDIMENT

Stream discharge (or streamflow) (Q_w)

Because stream discharge and sediment movement are the principal agents of change in channel networks it is important that they are both measured as accurately as possible if we are to understand how channel morphology is adjusted to them. Stream discharge is usually measured by means of a current meter. A *current meter* (Figure 5.4) consists of a propeller which revolves in flowing water at a speed proportional to the flow velocity. In current metering, the channel cross-section is divided into equal segments (Figure 5.5) each of known width. Discharge through each segment equals the product of velocity and cross-sectional area. At the mid-point of each

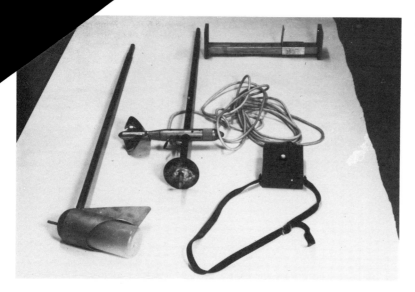

Figure 5.4 A current meter
(centre) together with
revolution counter. To the left
is a suspended sediment
sampler fitted with $\frac{1}{2}$ litre
sampling bottle, and to the
rear is a pebbleometer.

Figure 5.5 Principles of
calculating stream discharge
by current metering.

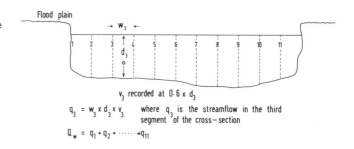

$q_3 = w_3 \times d_3 \times v_3$ where q_3 is the streamflow in the third
segment of the cross-section

$Q_w = q_1 + q_2 + \cdots\cdots + q_{11}$

segment, depth is measured and the current meter
is lowered into the water to a point at 0.6 of the
depth as measured down from the water surface.
This is the point at which the actual velocity in any
vertical column of water is closest to the average
velocity throughout the column as a whole. Total
discharge through the section equals the sum of
discharges in all the individual segments.

Measurement of stream discharge over long
periods of time (hours, days, years, etc.) is based
on the continuous measurement of water depth.
At the measuring cross-section, water is transferred into a *stilling well* to remove wind disturbances on the water surface. A float recorder
incorporating a clockwork or electric mechanism
is mounted on top of the stilling well (Figure
5.6 A) and produces a continuous trace of water
level usually for a period of one week or a month.
This continuous trace of depth can be converted
into a continuous trace of stream discharge by use
of a *rating curve*. Rating curves are unique for

each station and are simple graphical plots of
stage height (or depth) against measured streamflow for a number of different stages throughout
the flow range experienced (Figure 5.6 B). A
continuous plot of stream discharge is known
as a *hydrograph* (Figure 5.6 C) and from such a
graph total flow, peak flow and low flow values
can easily be determined for any period of time.
A typical streamflow gauging station at which
current-metering techniques are used is shown in
Figure 5.7 A. A more sophisticated gauging structure is shown in Figure 5.7 B.

Sediment

Sediment in a stream channel falls into four categories: *bedload, saltation load, suspended load*
and *dissolved load*. Bedload is the largest material
and travels by rolling along the bed. As it rolls,
it is worn down by constant collision between
individual particles in motion. This process is

A

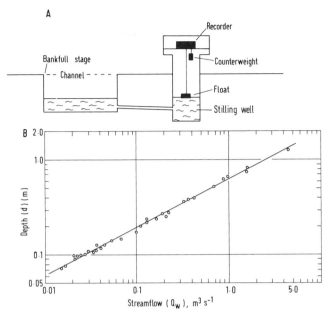

Figure 5.6 A   Principles of a water-level or stage recorder.

B

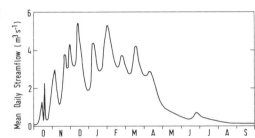

Figure 5.6 B   A stage-discharge rating curve.

C

Figure 5.6 C   An annual hydrograph.

Figure 5.7 A   A cableway installation for measuring streamflow on the Kellswater river in Northern Ireland. The cableway is stretched across the river and the current meter is suspended from it. Water level recorders are housed in the building on the right of the picture.

Figure 5.7 B   Artificial structures define cross-sectional area more precisely than natural channels and permit more accurate streamflow measurements than those made at natural sections. The weir is part of the Institute of Hydrology's experimental catchment study at Plynlimon (see Chapter 14).

called *attrition*. The saltation fraction, which consists of smaller particles than the bedload, moves in a 'hopping' manner; while the suspended sediment, the finest fraction of sand and silt, is carried in the body of the flowing water (Figure 5.8 A) by turbulent eddies. Dissolved matter is not transported mechanically like the other three categories of sediment. It is transported in solution in the streamflow.

It is difficult to measure the quantity of bedload that moves although this can be attempted by means of sediment traps (Figure 5.8 B). In these devices, sediment is allowed to accumulate in pits sunk into the stream bed, or behind weirs, and is periodically lifted out and weighed. Regular survey of bed profiles (Figure 5.9) is another method of monitoring the net movement of bedload. Bed-

load size is more easily determined than the amount moved. Pebble length for example can be measured on a wooden or metal *pebbleometer* (Figures 5.4 and 5.8 C) and samples of bedload taken at a number of sites along a river's length can be used to determine the manner in which particle size changes downstream or in what way it is related to slope.

Suspended sediment is difficult to measure. One type of sampler (Figure 5.4) mounted on a rod, is manually lowered from the water surface to the bed of the stream and back to the water surface again. The concentration of suspended sediment is usually expressed in milligrams per litre (mg l^{-1}) or parts per million (p.p.m.), and is determined by filtering a water sample through a filter paper and then drying the filter paper over-

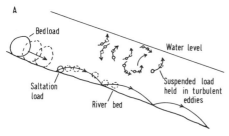

Figure 5.8 A The three principal means of sediment transport in streams.

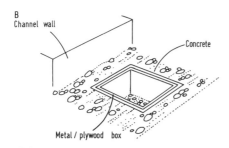

Figure 5.8 B A bedload trap.

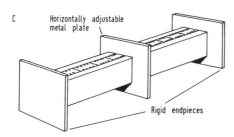

Figure 5.8 C A pebbleometer.

Figure 5.9 A Bedload trap on the Institute of Hydrology's experimental catchment at Plynlimon. The level of the bed in the reach between the concrete sidewalls is plumbed from the datum plane straddling the river, and volumes of sediment added to or removed from the reach are determined by contouring the bed surface.

Figure 5.9 B Periodically, material is mechanically removed from the trap and dumped on the bank for subsequent weighing and particle size analysis.

night at 105 °C. The weight of sediment retained on the filter paper can be found by subtracting the average weight of a number of dry filter papers from the combined weight of the dried filter paper plus retained sediment. Suspended sediment concentration is calculated as follows:

$$\text{concentration} = \frac{\text{grams of retained solids} \times 10^6}{\text{volume of water sample (cm}^3)}.$$

Total dissolved solids (TDS) in water may be determined by evaporating percolate from the suspended sediment determinations and weighing the residue. This weight, divided by the sample volume and multiplied by 10^6, also gives a TDS value in mg l^{-1}.

STREAM DISCHARGE (Q_w) AND SEDIMENT TRANSPORT

Competence

An important concept in the understanding of bedload transport is that of *stream competence*. A large range of sediment sizes is present on the bed of an upland river, and at low flow, when velocities are also low, only the finest sand grains can be moved, the vast bulk of coarser bedload remaining immobile. At somewhat higher flows and velocities, pebbles as well as sand may be moved. Only at very high flows when velocities approach

their maximum value do the larger boulders move. At any particular discharge the size of bedload that a stream is able to move defines its competence (Table 5.1). The term *capacity* refers to the *amount* of sediment transported. Of course, much material in upland streams is not moved by even the highest flows likely to be encountered under present-day conditions (Figure 5.10). These very large boulders are probably 'residual' under present conditions and before they can be moved they have to be worn down by the collision impact of smaller particles or by subaerial weathering *in situ*. The first of these processes is called *abrasion*. Residual bedload in the upland streams of northern Britain is principally derived from the deposits of glacial boulder clay which mantles the valley sides. Whereas ice sheets and glaciers were evidently

Figure 5.10   Coarse bedload in an upland stream.

Table 5.1. Probable relationships between bedload size, flow conditions and competence in stream channels

Bedload calibre Channel flow condition	Sand <2 mm	Pebbles 2–16 mm	Cobbles 16–256 mm	Boulders >256 mm
Low (from groundwater souces only)	probably competent	incompetent	incompetent	incompetent
Intermediate (groundwater and some throughflow)	competent	probably competent	incompetent	incompetent
Bankfull[1] (throughflow and/or overland flow)	competent	competent	probably competent	probably incompetent

1 This condition exists when flow in the channel is level with the adjacent flood plain.

43

competent to carry such boulders, modern upland rivers are not. In Dartmoor, large residual material is derived from tors on the valley sides.

More precise relationships between velocity, erosion, transportation and deposition (sedimentation) are illustrated in Figure 5.11. Two features of this diagram, derived in 1935 by Hjulstrom, a Swedish geologist, are worth noting.

1 The easiest material to erode has a diameter of about 0.1 mm. Coarser bedload, as might be expected, is more difficult to erode because of its greater size, while finer material, especially clay, is also more difficult to erode, partly because it is bound together by chemical bonds which are difficult to overcome.

2 Higher velocities are always required to initiate movement (i.e. to cause erosion) than are required to maintain transportation for all sizes of sediment. This is also true of erosion by wind (Chapter 6). Clay material 0.001 mm in diameter, for example, requires velocities of 100 $cm\,s^{-1}$ to initiate motion but can be maintained in transportation at velocities 1000 times lower. The lines separating erosion and sedimentation velocities for coarse material are very close together in comparison.

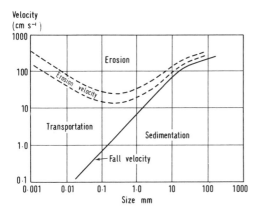

Figure 5.11 Phases of erosion, transportation and deposition defined in terms of velocity for material of different sizes.
(Source: M. P. Morisawa, p. 50, after Hjulstrom.)

As might be expected from Table 5.1, quantitative measurements of bedload transport show that most of it is accomplished by floods.[1] In a study of bedload movement at four sites in Devon, for example, Gregory and Park (1976) showed that movement was infrequent, or *episodic*, in char-

acter occurring as a result of individual storms. Most of the bedload transport in one of the gullies studied was accomplished in two short periods (marked 1 and 2 in Figure 5.12), which lasted 11 or 12 weeks out of the 52 for which observations were made.

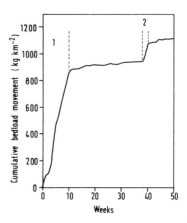

Figure 5.12 Bedload movement as measured by bedload traps in a Devon gully, 0.55 km² in area. Altogether, 46% of the total volume moved was transported in under 6% of the time.
(Source: K. Gregory and C. Park, p. 80.)

Suspended sediment transport

When suspended load is plotted against Q_w for a particular gauging station or site it is often found that the concentrations of suspended sediment are much larger at high flows than they are at low flows (Figure 5.13 A). Where this effect is most pronounced it probably occurs because the higher flood discharges reach the river channel across the ground surface of the drainage basin and are able to pick up unconsolidated soil particles. In addition, the expanded channel network (see later) taps new sources of sediment. Conversely, low flows reach the stream from groundwater and contain little or no suspended sediment. In the downstream direction a different effect occurs. Because the greatest suspended sediment yields from the drainage basin are provided from the steepest slopes, and because these normally occur

---

1 A flood can be defined hydrologically as any high flow produced by overland flow and/or throughflow. These are the most rapid routes by which precipitation on a drainage basin can be delivered to a channel (see Chapter 4) and always produce high flows, but not necessarily ones that overtop the banks.

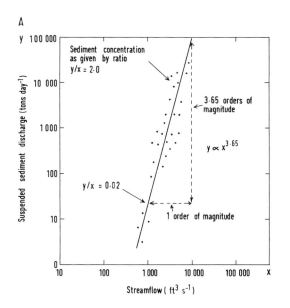

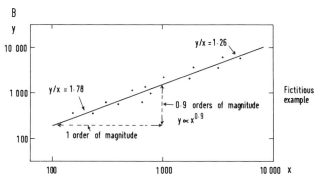

Figure 5.13 Typical logarithmic relationships between streamflow and suspended sediment discharge in rivers. (A) The relationship at a station. (B) The relationship in the down-stream direction.

in the headwater regions, it is often, though not always, found that suspended sediment concentrations at the mouth of a large river are lower than they are upstream (Figure 5.13 B) although total load ($Q_w \times$ concentration) increases downstream.

The solute load in rivers

The relationship between stream discharge and TDS concentration at any particular gauging station is exactly the opposite of that between stream discharge and suspended sediment. Because groundwater travels slowly through regolith and parent rock it has more time to absorb chemical elements released by weathering and by the breakdown of organic matter than does water travelling towards the stream via the relatively rapid routes of overland flow or throughflow. Low

flows tend, therefore, to be much richer in dissolved calcium, magnesium and other soluble elements than are the higher flows (Figure 5.14).

Magnitude and frequency

The amount of bed material and suspended sediment transported by a river can be used as a measure of effective mechanical work done by a river in its drainage basin. Dissolved load is not included because this load is derived from chemical solution and not by the transformation of potential energy into mechanical work. Since large flows carry most sediment it might be assumed that such flows do most work. Some caution is necessary, however, before this conclusion is reached. Consider the five fictitious floods ranked by order of magnitude in Table 5.2. As

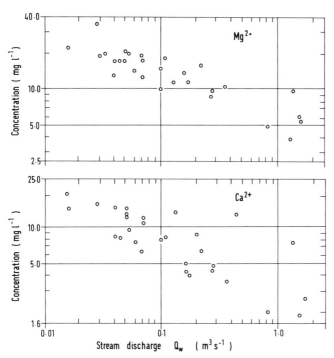

Figure 5.14 The concentration of magnesium and calcium ions in relation to stream discharge on the Agivey River, Northern Ireland. The gauging station at which these measurements were made has a drainage area of 15 km².

might be expected, the transporting capacity increases with flood magnitude. In considering the cumulative importance of each flood over a 50 year period, however, some account has to be taken of how frequently it recurs in this period. When the expected frequency of each flood in the 50 year period is multiplied by the quantity of sediment it moves, it is seen that the flood of smallest magnitude in this particular set of data is cumulatively the most important. This example illustrates the very important idea that the *frequency* of an event is important as well as its *magnitude* in considering its long-term significance.

Most studies on rivers suggest that floods which recur about once every 1.5 or 2 years are cumulatively the most important flows in terms of the mechanical work they do. Floods of such frequency on most rivers just about fill the channel without overtopping the banks and are therefore called *bankfull floods*. Floods which overtop the bankfull stage are individually more effective than the bankfull flood in carrying suspended sediment and bedload, though cumulatively less important in the long term. Small floods, which fall well short of the bankfull stage, carry less sediment than the bankfull flood and are cumulatively less important in the long term as well.

Table 5.2. Total suspended sediment load transported by five fictitious floods over a 50 year period

Flood rank (Largest = 1)	Frequency of occurrence in 50 years	Sediment load (i.e. concentration × Q_w) (tonnes)	Total load transported in 50 years (tonnes)
1	1	200	200
2	5	100	500
3	10	80	800
4	20	60	1200
5	25	50	1250

To calculate the amount of geomorphological work done by rivers at low flow, the quantity of dissolved solids transported at a particular discharge can be multiplied by the discharge frequency. From such calculations it has been shown that the discharge of dissolved solids may represent a large fraction of all sediment discharged from river basins. It may often account for more than half a river's total annual sediment load, even in rivers not flowing on soluble rocks such as limestone. Low flows are often, therefore, just as important geomorphologically as high flows, visually more dramatic and exciting though these may be.

Rates of erosion

Various studies of worldwide rates of erosion have been made using information on suspended sediment and stream discharge. One such study is that by Holeman who ranked the major rivers of the world according to their suspended sediment loads (Table 5.3). Also presented in Table 5.3 are figures for the four most important rivers of Europe ranked in the same way. Only rivers with drainage basins larger than 150×10^3 km² are included. Information on bedload and soluble load is not generally available and Table 5.3 has to be interpreted with this fact in mind.

From this study, Holeman concluded that some 20.2×10^9 tons of sediment per year are removed from continental to oceanic areas. Asia produces the highest yields with 591 tons km^{-2}. The other continents are ranked as follows: North America (94 tons km^{-2}), South America (62 tons km^{-2}), Australia (44 tons km^{-2}), Europe (35 tons km^{-2}), and Africa (27 tons km^{-2}).

Asia's high yields result from several factors. It is a continent of very great relief and steep slopes. Large areas have monsoonal or semi-arid climates and these two climatic types are associated with some of the highest sediment yields in the world.

Table 5.3. Selected rivers of the world ranked by sediment yield (After Holeman)

Name	Location	Drainage area (km² × 10³)	Average annual suspended load		Average streamflow at mouth
			(tons × 10³)	(tons km⁻²)	(m³ s⁻¹ × 10³)
Yellow	China	673	2 080 000	3091	1.50
Ganges	India	956	1 600 000	1674	11.75
Brahmaputra	Bangladesh	666	800 000	1201	12.18
Yangtze	China	1943	550 000	283	21.18
Indus	Pakistan	969	480 000	495	5.55
Amazon	Brazil	5775	400 000	69	181.30
Mississippi	USA	3222	344 000	107	17.84
Irrawaddy	Burma	430	330 000	767	13.57
Missouri	USA	1370	240 000	175	1.95
Mekong	Vietnam	795	187 000	235	11.05
Colorado	USA	637	149 000	234	0.16
Nile	Egypt	2070	122 000	41	2.83
Europe:					
Danube (mouth)	USSR	818	21 420	26	8.02
Volga	USSR	1350	20 770	15	6.17
Tisza (Danube tributary)	Hungary	156	11 040	71	?
Rhine	Holland	150	504	3	2.20

In the monsoon areas the principal reason for high erosion rates is the extremely intensive rainfall. In the semi-arid areas, where average annual rainfall is only 250–300 mm, high erosion rates are caused by periodically heavy storms which fall on un-vegetated surfaces. The soil has no protection from the impact of rainfall and no extensive root systems to prevent its removal.

Europe has low rates of erosion because rainfall intensity is generally light. Precipitation usually infiltrates into the soil and is transferred to the rivers via groundwater flow. Erosive run-off across the ground surface is therefore rare. Africa's low figure is more difficult to explain. It may partly be incorrect because data are scarce, especially from the large expanses of semi-arid desert where erosion rates are probably quite high. Studies by Douglas and by Dunne, however, confirm low yields in Africa from areas under tropical forests. Several reasons for these low yields are possible. Africa, for example, is tectonically stable and plateau-like over large areas. It lacks the extensive areas of steep slopes typical of the orogenic mountain belts in Asia, Europe, North and South America. Part of the explanation also lies in the stability of ecosystems in the undisturbed tropical rain forests. Many of these are thought to have matured over somewhat longer periods of time than other world ecosystems, and in an environment of intense chemical weathering. Soils are deep, and weathered minerals are cycled efficiently between the soils and the vegetation (see Chapter 14), few being allowed to escape into the river systems. The only method of escaping this closed system of mineral cycling in the tropical forest is by the slow process of soil creep. Sediment yields are therefore low (25 tons $km^{-2} year^{-1}$) although removal of protective vegetation for agriculture has been known to raise these yields to 1000 tons $km^{-2} year^{-1}$.

HOW ARE CHANNEL CHARACTERISTICS RELATED TO WATER AND SEDIMENT DISCHARGE?

Channel size and shape

In the late nineteenth and early twentieth centuries, British engineers in Egypt and India had the task of designing irrigation canal systems in the unconsolidated flood plain silts of such major alluvial valleys as those of the Nile and Indus. The purpose of these canals was to distribute irrigation water from the main river to the more remote parts of the flood plain, along a network of branching canals. It was essential that these canals did not erode their channels or systematically deposit sediment within them over a long period. Erosion would have destroyed large parts of the flood plain that the engineers were trying to irrigate, while deposition would have produced unwanted flooding and inadequate water transfer. After several years of experiment, formulae describing stable conditions in the canals were established from measurements taken on stable unlined canals. A stable system was one in which there was no erosion or deposition within the canals over a period of years. It was a perfect system of transportation: all water and sediment entering the canal naturally from the river was successfully distributed through the network. Such canals were called *regime canals*. We would define regime canals as being in steady state.

In regime canals, shape and velocity were found to be related to streamflow (Q_w) as follows:[1]

$$\text{width} \propto Q_w^{0.5}$$
$$\text{depth} \propto Q_w^{0.33}$$
$$\text{velocity} \propto Q_w^{0.17}$$

In 1953 two American geomorphologists, Leopold and Maddock, showed that natural rivers could be described by similar relationships. To describe graphs which show how width, depth and velocity change with discharge on natural rivers they suggested the term *hydraulic geometry*, and in the downstream direction hydraulic geometry graphs have the following relationships:

$$\text{width} \propto Q_w^{0.5}$$
$$\text{depth} \propto Q_w^{0.4}$$
$$\text{velocity} \propto Q_w^{0.1}.$$

A typical set of hydraulic geometry graphs is shown in Figure 5.15.

---

1 Power function relationships are explained in graphical terms in Figure 5.13. The hydraulic geometry relationship relating to width, for example, means that as Q_w rises by 1 order of magnitude (say from 1 to 10 $m^3 s^{-1}$ or from 100 to 1000 $m^3 s^{-1}$) width increases by only 0.5 order of magnitude.

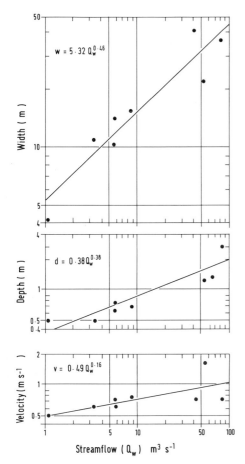

Figure 5.15 Graphs of downstream hydraulic geometry for the Palouse River, Washington State, USA, derived from analyses of data at eight stations along the river.

The close similarity between regime and hydraulic geometry equations suggests that rivers are 'naturally' trying to establish channel geometry characteristics which regime canals are provided with artificially but thereafter maintain naturally. From the evidence of the regime canals these shape characteristics appear to be the ones which distribute available energy within the system in such a way as to bring about a balance between input and output of water and sediment and a stability of form. The hydraulic geometry of rivers is now seen as a similar response.

The regime and hydraulic geometry equations are maintained by negative feedback. We saw in Chapter 2 how negative feedback might operate to restore initial slope conditions in a channel after the deposition of sediment on the bed. The same type of adjustment occurs with regard to width, depth and velocity. If any of these channel and flow characteristics change locally, for any reason whatsoever, a set of reactions occurs among the other variables to absorb the effect of the initial change and to restore the original condition. If negative feedback mechanisms did not occur, then neither the condition of steady state nor the precise form of the regime and hydraulic geometry equations could be maintained.

These ideas can be illustrated by the following example. Assume that two surveys of a river are made, separated by a period of 20 years, and that width is carefully measured on the two occasions at 10 identical points. It is most unlikely that the width of flow will be exactly the same at each point on the second survey as on the first. At some stations width will increase slightly while at others it will decrease (Figure 5.16). Despite these random local changes the overall relationship between width and streamflow throughout the system will remain essentially unchanged. Width, in other words, is free to vary, but not so far from a mean condition at any point that it upsets its relationship with other parts of the channel upstream and downstream, and thus destroys the channel system as an effective means of transporting sediment and water. If local changes of width, depth and velocity, at any point on a stream and in whatever direction, were to be progressive with time (i.e. if positive feedback were to reinforce initial changes) the regime and hydraulic geometry equations would not exist. This is what the early civil engineers meant when

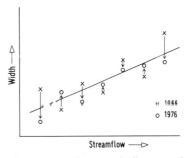

Figure 5.16 The general nature of adjustments between width and discharge along a fictitious river. Although values of width in relation to discharge at any particular station may vary slightly between surveys, the relationship between width and discharge throughout the channel system remains essentially unchanged, unless, of course, changes in climate and/or land use permanently alter the discharge–sediment mixture which the river has to transport.

they said that the dimensions of a channel to carry a given discharge and sediment load were fixed by nature.

Velocity

One of the interesting facts which emerged from the hydraulic geometry studies is that stream velocity tends to increase downstream for flows of a particular frequency (say once a year). Many people find it difficult to accept this idea and prefer to believe that velocity must decrease downstream because slope does. Stream velocity in a channel, however, is not controlled simply by slope but by depth and frictional effects related to the roughness of the channel. A very useful relationship in fluvial geomorphology, devised originally by Manning, a civil engineer, states that

$$\text{velocity} \propto \frac{\text{depth} \times \text{slope}}{\text{roughness}}$$

In the downstream direction channel depth increases while both slope and roughness (governed mainly by bed irregularities and channel curvature) tend to decrease. Of these three tendencies only that applying to slope acts in a manner that would cause velocity to decrease downstream, according to Manning's equation. The increase in depth and the decrease in roughness both operate to increase velocity downstream, and their combined effect overcompensates for any reduction of slope. In a recent survey of hydraulic geometry studies undertaken since 1953, it was shown that in only four natural channel systems out of seventy studied in different parts of the world did velocity decrease downstream.

Sediment characteristics and channel morphology

Several general relationships between channel morphology and sediment load are by now well established. For example, braiding (Figure 5.17) can be seen as a response to the deposition of relatively coarse sediment on the channel bed. When bedload entering a reach is beyond the channel's competence to carry it, the excess load is deposited. Flow is diverted round the deposit and erodes the bank, thus widening the channel. Excessive deposition may create several channels separated by islands. Each of the smaller channels

Figure 5.17 Braided channel on the Nooksack river in Washington State, USA. This river drains the western Cascade mountains, before entering the Pacific.

represents a return to upstream conditions in that it is narrower than the initial channel and steeper. Overall, however, the total width of the divided channels is greater than before deposition occurred. The sum total of all these effects is as follows: width increases relative to depth; slope increases; and turbulent energy is concentrated on the bed of the channel (where it is required to transport the excess load) rather than on the channel sides. Braiding is thus a good example of negative feedback. The channel system is seen to make a set of adjustments designed to reduce or remove the effects of an external change (the original supply of excessively large sediment) on the system.

Efficiency in rivers

One final point about the adjustment of river channels to sediment transport is worth emphasizing. It concerns the general efficiency of channel systems in transforming available potential energy into geomorphological work. Most of the potential energy available for mechanical work is dissipated as heat by friction between the flowing water, the channel sides and the channel walls. Potential energy is also lost at bends and at every place where flow is deflected from a straight path. The number of such flow diversions in river channels is so enormously large that very little of the river's potential to transport sediment is in fact used for this purpose. Only about 1% of available energy, for example, might be used for coarse bedload transport although this might rise to 25%

or fine sand. The channel system, in other words, is usually inefficient at transforming available energy into useful geomorphological work. In this respect it is like other natural systems such as eco-systems (see Chapter 12). The reason for these low efficiencies, of course, is the irreversible nature of heat energy described in the second law of thermodynamics (Chapter 1) and the very large number of energy transformations, all of them producing low-temperature heat, that occur spon-taneously in natural systems. To compensate for energy lost, the river system needs to import fresh supplies of potential energy in the form of pre-cipitation.

LONG PROFILES AND BASE LEVEL

Although long profiles are for the most part con-cave upward in appearance they are rarely smooth. Waterfalls or rapids, for example, occur where rivers flow over locally resistant rocks. They also occur in response to changes of base level. *Base level* is the lowest height to which a river can degrade its bed and the grand base level for all rivers is sea level. Local base levels, however, may exist. Some take the form of rock outcrops, others occur as lakes. Rivers upstream of a lake, for ex-ample, cannot degrade their beds lower than the lake's elevation without having to flow uphill before flowing into the lake itself. Since this is impossible, the lake acts as a downward limit of vertical erosion for all points of the river upstream; it is the *local base level* of erosion.

The concept of base level can be taken a stage further. Since streams cannot flow uphill it follows that the elevation of any particular stream seg-ment is the base-level control for the next stream segment above it, and this segment in turn is the base-level control for the segment flowing into it, and so on. No stream segment, in other words, can cut down or degrade its bed to a lower elevation than its downstream neighbour.

When sea level falls or land masses rise, potential energy is introduced into river systems and rivers proceed to cut new and lower profiles adjusted to the new base level. Rivers affected by falling base levels in this way are said to be *rejuvenated*. Renewed downcutting takes place initially at the coast, and lower bed levels must be transmitted

upstream. Where the new lower levels intersect the older long-profile a waterfall or zone of rapids may be produced. Such a feature is termed a *nickpoint*. In areas where sea level has fallen repeatedly several nickpoints may be evident. In ideal circumstances the most recent phase of downcutting is marked by an incised valley, above which are paired terraces on either side of the river, the relics of former flood plains (Figure 5.18).

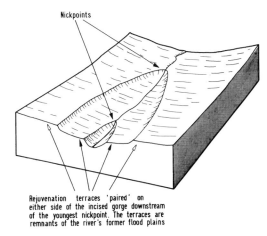

Nickpoints

Rejuvenation terraces 'paired' on either side of the incised gorge downstream of the youngest nickpoint. The terraces are remnants of the river's former flood plains

Figure 5.18 Idealized relationships between nickpoints and terraces resulting from successive falls of sea level.

MEANDERS AND FLOOD PLAINS

In its search to find a form which can most effi-ciently transport sediment with whatever stream discharge is available, a river can adjust its cross-sectional shape and its slope. These were the principal conclusions arising from Leopold and Maddock's work. Meandering is now believed to be another such adjustment a river can make, but how and why it makes this adjustment is still unclear. One theory notes that pools and shallow riffles alternate with each other in both straight reaches and meanders, each successive pool and riffle being spaced about 5–7 channel widths apart in both types of channel. It has been suggested that meanders may develop from straight reaches, as shown in Figure 5.19.

An interesting application of meander geometry relationships is in the interpretation of *underfit streams*. One form of underfit condition occurs when a meandering channel with relatively small

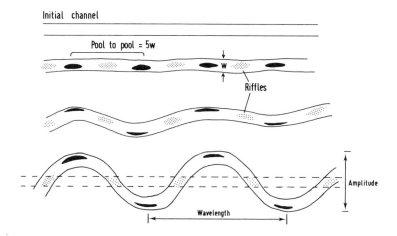

Initial channel

Pool to pool = 5w

Riffles

Amplitude

Wavelength

Figure 5.19 A possible sequence of stages in the evolution of a meandering stream from an initially straight one. Throughout the development from straight to meandering channels the riffles (shallow areas of deposited sediment) remain anchored in a more or less straight line. (Sources: G. H. Dury, 'Relation of Morphometry to Runoff Frequency' (in) R. J. Chorley, *Introduction to Fluvial Processes*, 1971, p. 180 and Dury, 1963, p. 28.)

width, wavelength and amplitude is seen to exist within a meandering valley characterized by very much larger wavelengths and amplitudes (Figure 5.20). This condition has been examined in some valleys of central England by Dury. If channel width is related to stream discharge as Leopold and Maddock suggested, it is clear that the discharge producing the valley meanders must have been much larger than today's discharges to which the smaller channel geometry features are adjusted. Some people have argued that these larger channels were produced by glacial meltwater discharges cutting through thawed-out unconsolidated surface soils lying on a frozen regolith at the end of the Ice Age. It is also possible that the valley meanders were produced in an early postglacial period which was colder and wetter than today, although average discharges some 5–10

times today's values would be required to account for the valley meanders. [See Dury (1977a) for a discussion of these features.]

One final aspect of meanders concerns their relationship to flood plains. Flood plains are extensive flat areas adjacent to river channels. Periodically these areas may be inundated by water, the normal frequency of such flooding being approximately once every 2 years (Figure 5.21). As we saw earlier, many rivers flow at their bankfull stage once every 1.5 years on average. A flood plain usually consists only of the gravel or finer material that a lowland river is competent to carry. If its profile is convex-upward in appearance it probably derives most of its sediment from overbank flooding (Figure 5.22 A). Flat flood plains in contrast probably owe their origin more to meandering. As the river migrates laterally it

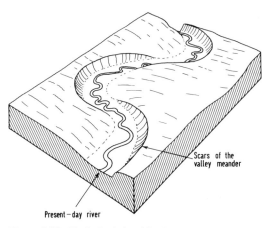

Scars of the valley meander

Present–day river

Figure 5.20 Typical relationships between channel and valley meanders in an underfit river.

Figure 5.21 Overbank flooding on the River Main flood plain, County Antrim, Northern Ireland. Flow in the channel when the photograph was taken is just about at bankfull.

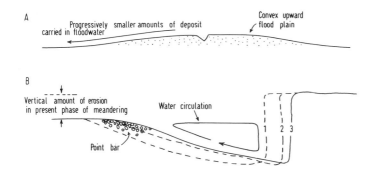

Figure 5.22 Flood-plain profiles built up principally by overbank flooding (A) and by lateral channel migration (B).

undercuts material deposited in an earlier flood plain. Some of this material is immediately re-deposited on the opposite point bar but some is also transported to point bars downstream and ultimately out to sea. As the outer bend is eroded, a new flood plain at a lower level is built up out of successive migrations of point bars on the inner convex side. Figure 5.22 B shows how meanders can thus lower flood plains. They do not only cut laterally.

DELTAS

Deltas (Figure 5.23) are produced where a river's velocity and hence its ability to transport sediment is rapidly diminished on entering a lake or the sea. Sea water in addition helps fine clay particles to flocculate so that they become heavier

Figure 5.23 A recently formed delta at the mouth of the Nooksack River, Washington State, USA. Notice how the delta is extended by deposition in the form of dunes on the sea bed.

and sink more easily. According to Holmes, the relative densities of the flowing and standing water bodies are critical in determining the type of delta formed. If the river water is more dense than that of the lake or the sea, perhaps because of its very high suspended sediment load, its waters may dive beneath the surface waters of the lake or sea, carrying the finest sediment some distance away from the coastal margin in the form of a *turbidity current*. Only the coarsest material is left to form a delta in this instance. If the reverse is the case, as for example in the Mississippi where suspended sediment concentrations are remarkably small, the low density river water flows over the surface of the denser sea water at quite high velocities and for considerable distances. On the margins of this flowing surface water, however, velocities are low and deposition occurs in the form of lateral accumulations of material which build up to confine the flowing water in well-defined channels. When these are periodically over-topped in large floods new channels are formed and a characteristic *bird's foot delta* builds out from these breaches. Studies on the Mississippi delta have shown the delta to be slowly sinking under its own weight. The delta is tending to grow in vertical thickness rather than lateral extent, and as the delta sinks so the areas inland are slowly rising (Figure 5.24).

The formation of both deltas and flood plains is much affected by the construction of dams and reservoirs in the tributary drainage basins. The impact of such basin management schemes on the rates of fluvial sediment supply to downstream reaches is best illustrated by the Colorado River on which the US Bureau of Reclamation has built many large dams since the 1930s. These dams, which trap large volumes of sediment, have led to

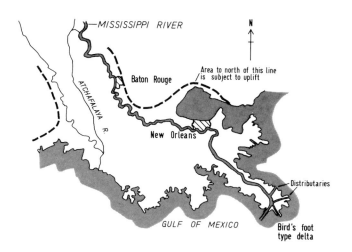

Figure 5.24 The Mississippi delta in plan and cross-section.
(Simplified from G. H. Matthes, p. 7.)

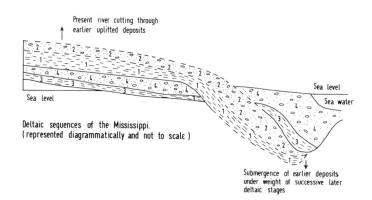

an annual reduction in the river's suspended sediment load at its mouth from 180×10^6 tons year^{-1} to 13×10^6 tons year^{-1}. Many downstream flood plains and deltas of the world's largest rivers, which have traditionally provided some of the most fertile land in the world, are similarly being deprived of the flood-deposited silt which built up their fertility in the first place. This trend is causing concern in many parts of south-west USA and in Egypt below the Aswan Dam.

STREAM NETWORKS

Stream networks can be classified by appearance. *Trellis* patterns are developed on belts of alternating 'hard' and 'soft' rocks as in the Weald of south-east England, *pinnate* patterns develop on unusually steep slopes, and *dendritic* patterns are usually representative of horizontal sedimentary strata or igneous complexes where structural and/or topographic controls are not very prominent (Figure 5.25).

More recently, quantitative classifications of stream networks have been devised using the concept of *stream order*. A first-order stream is one of the extremities of the network which receives no tributaries. Two order-1 streams unite to produce an order-2 stream segment, and two order-2 stream segments unite to produce an order-3 segment, and so on (Figure 5.25).

Two other useful measures of drainage network organization are *drainage density* and *stream frequency*.

$$\frac{\text{drainage}}{\text{density}} = \frac{\text{total stream length in a basin}}{\text{drainage area}}$$

$$\frac{\text{stream}}{\text{frequency}} = \frac{\text{total number of stream segments}}{\text{drainage area}}$$

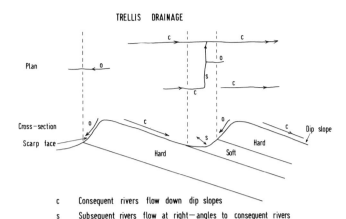

Figure 5.25 Three types of drainage network classified qualitatively according to their relationships to under-lying structure or topography. The bottom diagram shows how individual stream segments can be classified by stream order.

TRELLIS   DRAINAGE

Plan

Cross-section

Scarp face

Hard   Soft

Hard

Dip slope

c   Consequent rivers flow down dip slopes

s   Subsequent rivers flow at right—angles to consequent rivers
     at 90° to the dip of the rocks (i.e. along the strike)

o   Obsequent streams flow down scarp slopes

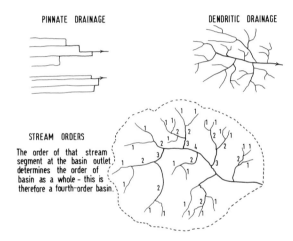

PINNATE DRAINAGE   DENDRITIC DRAINAGE

STREAM ORDERS

The order of that stream
segment at the basin outlet
determines the order of
basin as a whole – this is
therefore a fourth-order basin.

Both these properties affect the manner in which surface run-off at times of heavy rainfall is collected and transmitted down the channel network to the basin outlet.

Drainage networks, of course, are dynamic and not static. The length of channel contributing streamflow to a basin outlet is greater in wet weather (e.g. during winter floods) than it is in dry weather (e.g. during the 1975–6 British drought). So too, therefore, is drainage density. Stream frequency, however, need not necessarily increase with increasing rainfall: in times of flood, existing first-order channels may be extended but new ones do not necessarily come into existence. In south-west England drainage density during individual floods is sometimes 15 times the drainage density at low flow.

From an analysis of British Ordnance Survey maps (Ovenden and Gregory) it has recently been shown that drainage networks over the past 140 years have probably been expanding. The actual change taking place is the collapse of sub-surface *flushes* or *pipes*, which can be recognized in the field before collapse by well-defined lines of moss and/or reed vegetation which thrive in wet places. The conversion of flushes and pipes into open first-order channels are all caused by man's activities over the last century. The causes range from increased surface run-off following road drainage, to the trampling activities of cattle.

FLUVIAL PROCESSES IN DESERTS

Arid environments cover one-third of the world's land area, and although wind is an important agent of erosion here, it is probably less important than water action in creating landforms.

Run-off in the desert is infrequent and much of it occurs as overland flow (Chapter 4), although throughflow may be important. Even though heavy rainfall concentrated in short periods of time produces the most effective run-off, excessive amounts of rainfall are not necessarily essential for run-off to occur. Cooke and Warren quote studies undertaken in Arizona which claim that run-off is possible after only 6.6 mm of rainfall, and run-off has been observed in the Sahara and Mojave deserts after daily rainfall totals of 16 mm and 34 mm respectively. Such totals are not large by world standards (see Chapter 9), but in deserts they are infrequent. Whereas such daily rainfall amounts may occur several times per year in the wetter parts of Britain and Ireland they would recur in deserts only once a decade. These infrequent events of moderate magnitude in deserts are more effective in transporting sediment than they would be in temperate areas because weathered sediment is not cohesive in these dry environments and there are few roots to bind the soil together. In technical language, the *erosion threshold*[1] tends to be lower in deserts than in moist temperate areas. Dry areas of the world embrace a wide variety of conditions, however, and erosion rates vary between zero and 300 $m^3\,km^{-2}\,year^{-1}$, being highest in semi-arid areas.

Water and sediment is transported as slope wash on gentle slopes. This takes the form of laminar flow in thin sheets which is quite capable of transporting small particles in the 2–5 mm size category. Several geomorphologists argue that *sheetfloods* can occur across gently-sloping areas in deserts although few such events have been observed and doubt exists as to whether they occur. Water also flows in channels as turbulent flow. Most channels in deserts, however, are dry for most of the year (Figure 5.26) and when flash floods do occur in these *ephemeral streams*, much of the water infiltrates into the dry bed. Although large amounts of sediment may therefore be moved by floods, the largest particles do not move very far.

River systems in deserts have clearly experienced alternating periods of aggradation and degradation reaching back into the Pleistocene

Figure 5.26   Ephemeral channel in northern Arizona.

period (see Chapter 7). This story, however, is still being pieced together. Geomorphologists know more about the phase of degradation in historical times which produced deep, steep-sided *arroyos* in the semi-arid south-west of the USA (Figure 5.27). Much of this trenching was started in the nineteenth century by settlers whose cattle overgrazed the land and removed the thin vegetation which had previously provided some degree of protection against erosion. It is very easy to inadvertently increase the velocity of water in channels and to initiate scouring. The removal of channel vegetation, for example, reduces channel roughness and this likewise may lead to an increase in velocity. A recent study (see Graf) has shown that on average about 5 kg of vegetation per square metre of channel bed is sufficient to resist trenching, but if vegetation is removed to below this amount, trenching may commence. In other words, 5 $kg\,m^{-2}$ represents a *threshold value* of vegetation cover in desert stream beds. In areas with more than this amount of vegetation cover,

Figure 5.27   Vertical-walled arroyo in southern Utah.

1 This is often defined as the critical velocity at which erosion occurs for a particular size of sediment (see Figure 5.11).

hannels are relatively stable and well adjusted to present streamflow and sediment discharges. In reas with less than this amount of cover they re unstable and actively degrade their beds. The concept of threshold values separating two different levels of intensity at which a particular process might operate is important throughout geomorphology.

The topography of deserts is divided into mountains and plains. The piedmont plain (Figures 5.28 and 5.29) can be divided into a concave-upward pediment cut in rock and an alluvial plain, also concave-upward but less so than the pediment. On pediments, material has been collected in traps to confirm that unconcentrated surface wash across these gentle slopes is quite capable of transporting finer sediment.

The origin of pediments has been a subject of controversy for many years. One theory is that steep slopes are worn back by weathering and erosion on the free face which thus retreats. Material from the free face may accumulate at its base as alluvium or *talus* but this material is continuously or intermittently removed across the pediment which is created as the free face retreats. This is the theory of *parallel retreat*, and it owes much to Wood's model of hillslope evolution described in the last chapter.

Figure 5.29 Mountains and piedmont plain in the Mojave desert, south-west USA.

There are other theories to explain pediments and the student should consult more specialist texts for further details.

Two features of deposition in the desert are alluvial fans and playas. *Alluvial fans* are cones of sediment built outward by rapid deposition from streams flowing out of the mountains. The stream channels often braid across the accumulating debris which builds outward into a semi-circular shape as viewed from above.

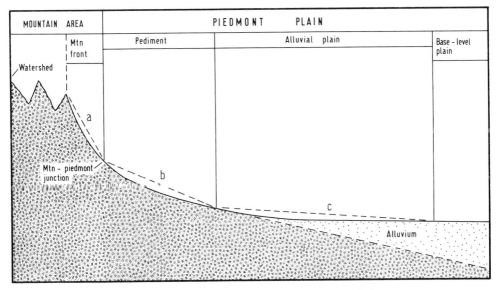

Figure 5.28 Morphological units of mountains and plains in desert areas. The broken lines a, b, c are the average slopes of the mountain front, pediment and alluvial plain respectively.
(Source: R. U. Cooke and A. Warren, p. 172.)

Playas are enclosed depressions into which sediment from adjacent piedmont plains is washed. They are low areas in the desert environment and may accumulate silts and clays to great thickness. They are very saline environments because water which accumulates in them is very easily evaporated, leaving behind thick deposits of salts. These are the environments in which solonetz and solonchak soils form (Chapter 14).

The depositional record contained in alluvial fans and playas helps geomorphologists to construct a picture of past climatic variability. In phases of degradation, channels were cut into the fans and the shape of these channels is often preserved, although filled in by subsequent aggradation. Some phases of degradation and aggradation can be related to long-lasting changes of climate. Other phases of degradation may simply represent a relatively short period in which floods

were infrequent but very large, intervening phases of aggradation occurring when floods were more frequent and smaller. During wetter periods of the past, playas were often quite extensive lakes, and their terraces (see Chapter 11 and the discussion on former Lake Bonneville) provide important evidence of past climatic change. In drier periods encrusted sediments in the playas were baked hard and often removed by wind action leaving *deflation hollows*. These can often be detected within the sometimes thick stratigraphic record. Playas (and alluvial fans less so) preserve a sedimentological record of recent geomorphological ecological and climatic history for desert areas just as lakes do for moist temperate and tropical areas of the world, and as oceans do for adjacent continents. Geomorphology is not simply a study of erosion. The study of depositional environments is important too if the sequence and timing of past geomorphological events is to be unravelled.

6

Coastal Geomorphology

INTRODUCTION

The coast is an open system although its geographical limits are often difficult to define. One possible set of boundaries on an indented coastline is shown in Figure 6.1. In such a system seaward limits might be set by the so-called *wave base* (i.e. the deepest point of transport by waves), and landward limits by the rear of a sand-dune belt if sand dunes are present. Other boundaries may be located at headlands which, like the watershed of a drainage basin, frequently determine the limits from which sediments normally enter coastal embayments on an indented coastline. Littoral drift, however, may bring a small amount of material round the headland from the coast beyond.

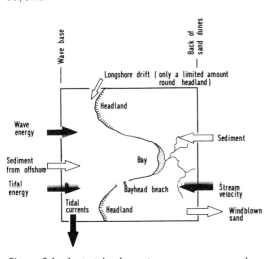

Figure 6.1 A stretch of coast seen as a geomorphological system. The offshore limit is here taken as the wave base, the landward limit as the back of a sand-dune system. On some coasts sand dunes may not be present, and other system boundaries would have to be chosen.

The principal inputs of energy into the system from outside are wind, waves and tides. Longshore currents result from interactions between the principal inputs of energy and local coastal topography. All these inputs principally contain kinetic energy although waves and tides also contain potential energy. To these three sources of energy in a coastal system can be added the kinetic energy of river flow when this is present. The principal input of sand into some systems is from rivers. The finer silt and clay which they bring down to the coast from their drainage basins, however, is usually deposited beyond the wave base. Sand also moves into the coastal zone from offshore areas on rare occasions although, as we shall see, this is less important now than in the past. A third mechanism transferring material along the coast is littoral drift.

Output of energy from the coastal zone, like the input, is most obviously in kinetic form. Tidal currents and various forms of wave action transfer material through and out of the system. The wind blows sand off the beach and out of the dunes, often depositing it far inland. Along some parts of the British coastline, recent research has shown that movement of sediment into and out of coastal systems is very limited. Such systems are better classified as closed rather than open, and we shall say more about these later.

AGENTS OF CHANGE—WAVES, TIDES AND WIND

Waves

Waves are formed by frictional drag between ocean and atmosphere as the wind blows over the

ocean surfaces. The process is not fully understood but clearly involves a transfer of energy
from the atmosphere to the ocean. Since the
earth's wind systems are themselves caused by
the unequal distribution of solar energy on the
earth's surface (Chapter 8), it is quite realistic to
regard ocean waves breaking on the coast as a
downgraded form of solar energy.

Waves are described by their height (h), wavelength (λ), and period (T) (Figure 6.2 A). Height
and wavelength are self-explanatory. Period is the
time taken for two successive crests to pass a
fixed point. Deep-water waves are 'rotational'.
This means that some of the water in the body of
the wave moves in a direction opposite to the
wave itself (Figure 6.2 B), so that over one wave
period each water particle makes a complete orbit.
Next time you see a ball in wave-affected water,
observe how it appears simply to go up and down
as successive wave crests pass. The ball has a
slight horizontal to and fro movement but no net
horizontal motion. This is because forward movement of water particles at the top of a wave
is cancelled out by backward movement at the
bottom. The wave moves forward. The water does
not. The wave transmits energy not matter.

Another interesting characteristic of waves is
that they are features of the water surface only
and extend to no great depth (Figure 6.2 A). At
the surface the orbits of individual water particles
have a diameter equal to the height of the wave.
At a depth equal to one wavelength there is no
orbital movement at all.

Two types of wind-generated wave are recognized. Those still within the area where they were
initially formed are called *sea*, and those that have
travelled beyond the generating area are termed
swell. Sea is characterized by waves of great
height, short wavelength and short period. They
are therefore very steep with high h/λ ratios and
do great damage. Swell has flatter waves of low
amplitude and long wavelength. The wave period
of swell is long and it therefore tends to be less
erosive than sea, though this is not always the
case.

Fetch is the distance over which wind generates
waves, and length of fetch determines how long
wind energy can be continuously applied to the
sea surface. The west coasts of Scotland and
Ireland have much greater fetches than the east

coasts. Southern Californian coasts have very
long fetch distances of 8000 km and the swell
arriving here may have amplitudes of 9 m.

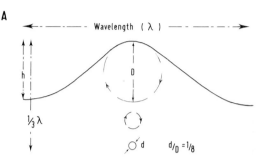

Figure 6.2 A The decreasing size of water particle orbits
under a wave.

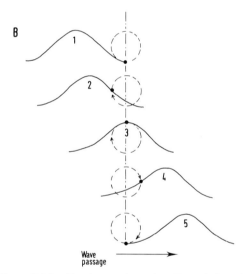

Figure 6.2 B Circular motion of a float during the
passage of a deep-water wave. There is no perceptible
net horizontal movement of the float.

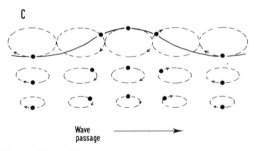

Figure 6.2 C Elliptical motion of water particles in a
shallow-water wave.
(Source: J. R. L. Allen, p. 156.)

When a deep-water[1] rotational wave enters shallow water important changes take place. Frictional drag on the bottom begins to slow down the wave motion. Wavelength shortens and the wave front steepens. As this happens water motion under the wave becomes increasingly elliptical (Figure 6.2 C). Most critically, the velocity of water at the top of the wave starts to exceed the velocity of the wave itself. When this happens the wave topples and breaks. Normally this occurs in water which is only as deep as the wave's height. After breaking, waves cease to be rotational and become *waves of translation*. That is to say, the water itself now moves in the same direction as the wave. *Swash* is a wave of translation.

Wave energy takes two forms. Potential energy (E_p) is measured by the height of a wave above the water surface. Its kinetic energy (E_k) is contained in the orbital motion of the water. Total wave energy E equals the sum of E_p and E_k. Potential energy lost in a breaking wave is principally converted into kinetic energy of motion, and heat. The kinetic energy is transferred:

1 to the water moving up the beach; and
2 to the sediment moving up the beach after being disturbed by the breaking wave.

Areas of high and low wave energy can be recognized along any stretch of coast. High-energy coasts occur where a specific width of wave crest in the deep water zone is concentrated into a shorter width of coastline at the moment of breaking. The opposite situation characterizes a low-energy coast. The principal cause of wave energy concentration on the coast is wave *refraction*. Incoming wave trains are slowed down as they meet shallow water. This means that when a wave train approaches at an oblique angle to submarine coastal contours it tends to swing round, until it is almost parallel to the coast when the waves finally break (Figure 6.3 A). When a wave train approaches an indented coast, wave energy is concentrated on the headlands. This may be because of wave refraction if submarine topography is favourable. Or it may be because deeper water at the headland allows more energetic waves to break. Whatever the reason, headlands do tend to be areas of relatively high wave energy. Bays in

1 Deep water is defined as having a depth d more than half the wavelength: i.e. $d/\lambda > 0.5$. In shallow water d/λ is less than 0.2.

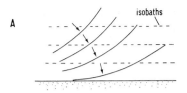

Figure 6.3 A Wave refraction on a shoaling beach. Notice how an originally oblique wave train is transformed into one almost parallel to the beach.

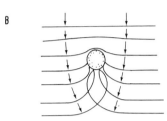

Figure 6.3 B Wave refraction round an island. Wave trains cross each other in the lee of the island. Wave trains which cross each other are common in other situations too, as when swell waves and sea waves arrive simultaneously from different directions.

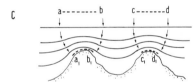

Figure 6.3 C Wave refraction round headlands. Notice how wave energy in the crests 'ab' and 'cd' is concentrated on the headlands, while the same amount of wave energy in the crest 'bc' is dispersed over a greater length of coastline in the bay.

contrast are relatively low-energy zones (Figure 6.3 C).

The movement of sediment on beaches is very complex, and is brought about principally by waves and currents and the interaction between the two. Three types of breaking wave are generally recognized. *Plunging breakers* have a near-vertical front, and water at the crest of the wave plunges down with great force on to the beach beneath. The wave front in a *spilling breaker* has a steep gradient towards the shore but it is less steep than in the plunging breaker. Water from the crest of such a breaking wave tumbles down the wave front and produces great amounts of foam. *Surging breakers* do not break in a conventional manner but collapse, causing water to rush up the beach.

Like spilling breakers these waves also produce large volumes of foam.

As they break, waves throw sediment into suspension, a fact that anyone can confirm by observation on a sandy beach. As in streams, sediment on beaches is moved as bedload, suspended load and saltation load. Suspended loads are highest in the inner surf zone and swash zone, especially where incoming waves meet backwash moving down the beach. According to Komar, suspended loads in the breaker zone tend to be low, probably because breakers here do not reach the bed to throw sediment into suspension but have much of their energy absorbed by the water into which the wave breaks. Turbulence in water within the breaker zone is less than in the inner surf zone and swash zone. Sediment here therefore moves principally as bedload, and keeps very close to the beach surface.

A large amount of sediment is moved in the nearshore zone by longshore currents. These result from the oblique approach of waves on to the shore which causes large volumes of water to move along the coast, away from the line of approaching waves. These longshore currents may move sediment if their bed velocities are high enough to initiate movement. They may also combine with wave action in the following manner. As the orbital motion of water particles in contact with the beach surface increases, a stage may eventually be reached when beach particles begin to move. Since water movement in waves is only a to-and-fro motion, no net transfer of sediment may occur by this process alone. However, if longshore currents also exist, their velocity may be sufficiently large to transport the sediment initially thrown into suspension by the waves. It is this type of interaction between processes which makes the study of beach processes very complicated, and this brief account, derived principally from Komar, has done no more than introduce a few very basic ideas.

Tides

Tides are caused by the gravitational effects of the moon and the sun on the earth and its oceans. Although the mass of the sun is much greater than that of the moon, it is nearly 400 times more distant. Its absolute effect on tides is therefore only half that of the moon. The effect of the moon is as follows. The moon's mass attracts oceanic water on that part of the earth nearest to it, and a bulge in oceanic water level is created (Figure 6.4 A). This produces high tides. Water in this bulge is provided by the rapid evacuation of water from adjacent oceans, and water levels here therefore fall. This produces two zones of low tides, one on either side of the primary tidal bulge. On the far side of the earth, where the moon's gravitational pull is lowest, movement of water towards the moon is minimal and water levels here therefore remain relatively high. A second zone of high tides is thus produced.

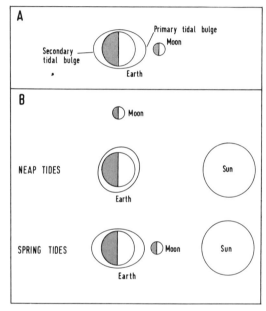

Figure 6.4 Tidal bulges of water in relation to the position of the moon (A) (the size of the bulges is greatly exaggerated); and (B) earth, moon and sun relationships at neap tide and spring tide. (Modified from R. A. Muller, p. 400.)

As the earth rotates on its axis once every 24 hours most parts of the earth experience two high tides and two low tides per day. Twice a month, however, at approximately 14 day intervals, the sun and moon are in approximate alignment so that the sum of their gravitational effects is exerted on the earth and its waters (Figure 6.4 B). This produces extreme elevations and depressions in oceanic water levels, and at such times the high tides are very high and the low tides are very low, i.e. tidal range is at its greatest. These are the so-called *spring tides*. They occur at full moon and new moon. Seven days after full moon, and seven days after new moon, the sun and moon are not aligned. The sun's gravitational effect now works against that of the moon and the tidal bulges are at their smallest. High tides at this time of the month are at their lowest and low tides are at their highest, i.e. tidal range is at its smallest. These are the so-called *neap tides*.

Coastal configuration can affect tidal range. Where rising and falling tides are channelled up and down narrow estuaries, tidal range can be very great. This is the case in the Bristol channel where tidal ranges exceed 6 m. When the flood tide in this estuary finally reaches the lower stretches of the River Severn it produces the famous Severn bore, a small wall of water up to 2 m in height, which moves upstream as a quite distinctive series of waves. In other areas tidal range can be very small. The Mediterranean, for example, is virtually cut off from the Atlantic ocean by the Straits of Gibraltar. The volume of water flowing into and out of the Mediterranean on the flood and ebbing tides is therefore quite small, and tidal range is small as well. Two extreme types of tidal environment can be recognized. A *macrotidal coast* can be defined as one with a spring tide range of more than 4 m. A *microtidal coast* has a spring range of under 2 m. In between these two extremes is the *mesotidal* environment where tidal range is 2–4 m (Figure 6.5).

The geomorphological significance of tides and tidal range is threefold.

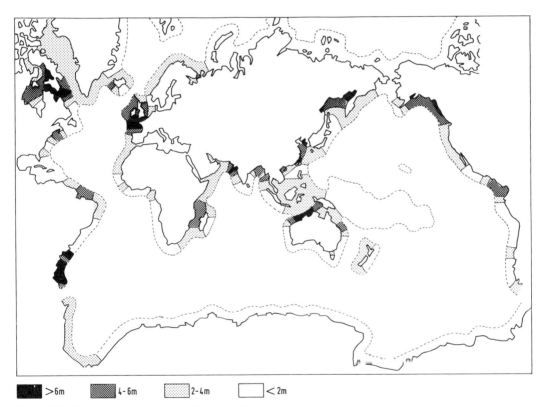

■■ >6m ▦ 4-6m ▒ 2-4m □ <2m

Figure 6.5 Spring tidal ranges around the world. Notice how ranges on the south-west coast of Britain are among the largest in the world. In contrast, many enclosed seas, like the Mediterranean, the Red Sea and the Baltic, have very small tidal ranges.
(Source: J. L. Davies, 1972(a), p. 51.)

1 Tides help to determine the vertical range over which waves can erode or deposit material.
2 Ebb and flood tidal currents, which are especially pronounced in and around estuaries on macrotidal coasts, can have a pronounced scouring effect in narrow estuaries. Tidal scouring in the Mersey, for example between Liverpool and New Brighton, is very important in removing sediment from the estuary.
3 Tides cause alternate wetting and drying of the intertidal zone. Many burrowing organisms such as clams, worms and barnacles are well adapted to this environment, according to Komar, and many help to break down rock material for subsequent removal by waves. Alternate wetting and drying also leads to mechanical weathering in the form of salt crystallization (see Chapter 4). This is a particularly important process in drier tropical areas, where evaporation rates and salt crystal growth at periods of low tide can be very rapid.

Wind

There are three environments in which wind becomes an important agent of erosion. These are:
1 arid and semi-arid deserts;
2 glacial outwash plains;
3 sandy coasts.
Although important in all these environments wind is not necessarily the most important geomorphological process in any of them.

In coastal geomorphology the most effective wind is called the *dominant wind*. On windward coasts, such as the west coasts of Britain and Ireland, the direction of this wind coincides with that of the prevalent wind, and therefore occurs more frequently than on leeward coasts where the dominant and prevalent winds blow from different directions. The distinction between windward and leeward coasts is important because on the latter, landforms tend to be adjusted to less frequent processes than they are on windward coasts.

Wind can be regarded as a fluid. As it moves across a sand surface, friction between the wind and the ground dislodges particles of sand. Friction also causes velocity to be lowest near the ground, much as in the vertical velocity profile of a river (Figure 5.1). As wind strength increases, it eventually reaches a velocity at which sand

particles start to move. This is the *fluid threshold velocity*. For material with the same density as quartz sand this velocity is lowest when grain diameter is 0.10 mm. Finer materials (silt for example) require higher fluid threshold velocities. So too do coarser sands (Figure 6.6). Once moving, sand particles move in discontinuous short jumps. This is called *saltation*. Particles moving in this manner splash into other particles and disturb them. These disturbed particles may then start to saltate. Alternatively, they may move by *surface creep* without leaving the ground, or by *suspension* in the air (if they are fine enough to be lifted). In this way the whole sand surface may become mobile. Once the wind contains a large amount of sand, it becomes progressively easier to initiate movement of particles at rest because the impact of saltating particles creates the initial disturbance. *Impact threshold velocities* are therefore lower than fluid threshold velocities for any size of material (Figure 6.6). The broad principles of sediment transport, outlined above for wind, are really typical of all fluids flowing across loose boundaries. Sediment transport by rivers and by waves is subject to similar processes.

Deposition of sand by wind is very complex. Bagnold, a pioneer in the study of wind action,

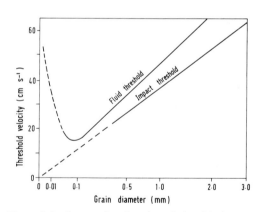

Figure 6.6 Curves showing the relationship between threshold velocities and particle size in air.
(Source: R. A. Bagnold, p. 88.)

recognized three types of deposition. *Precipitation* or *air fall* occurs when particles fall vertically in still air. Such particles have no ability to disturb other particles on impact and the deposit accumulates vertically. *Accretion*, which occurs over continuous sand surfaces, is a horizontal type of accumulation. It occurs as wind velocity falls and when more saltating particles come to rest than are disturbed by impact. A principal difference between precipitation and accretion is that in precipitation there is no particle movement after hitting the ground. In accretion, horizontal movement may continue until the particle settles in a convenient hollow. A final form of deposition is *encroachment*. This only affects particles moving by surface creep. On the steep lee side of a dune, for example, coarse particles too heavy to saltate roll over the face where they are then protected from the wind. Here they settle while finer material saltates over and beyond them. Encroachment deposits therefore consist of coarser materials.

Extreme events as agents of change: tsunamis and storm surges

Incorrectly called tidal waves, *tsunamis* have nothing to do with tides. They are formed by a sudden disturbance of the ocean surface, often after earthquakes or volcanic eruptions. A tsunami is a train of waves which travels very rapidly, often at speeds of more than 500 km h^{-1}. Wavelengths can reach 50 km. When they reach shallow water, tsunamis are progressively slowed down, and their kinetic energy is transformed into potential energy. In extreme form, this process can produce waves 5–10 m high above the still-water line. Such waves are capable of great damage when they break. Fortunately tsunamis are relatively rare events with a frequency of once every ten years in the Pacific. They are rarer still in the Atlantic.

Storm surges are caused when strong onshore winds pile water up against the coasts to heights much above normal. The most famous recent storm surge to affect Britain occurred during the spring tides of January 31st 1953 (Figure 6.7). At 0600 hours on January 31st a deep depression to the north-east of Scotland caused south-westerly winds to blow across the southern North Sea. These winds transferred large volumes of water from the Flemish Bight to the centre and eastern areas of the North Sea, and depressed tides around south-east England to abnormally low levels. As the depression moved to the south east, north-westerly winds built up to gale force, exceeding 180 km h^{-1} at some places on the east coast.

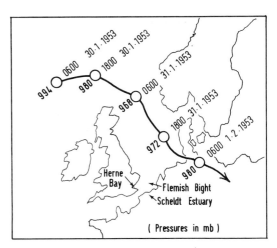

Figure 6.7 Path of the depression which caused the 1953 storm surge around the coasts of the southern North Sea.
(Source: A. H. W. Robinson, p. 136.)

The water previously evacuated from the Flemish Bight now surged back into the bottleneck of the Dover Straits and tide levels along the east coast of southern England rose to heights of 2 m above normal spring tide level. In the Scheldt estuary they reached 3 m above normal. The effects of the surge were dramatic. Cliff lines at Herne Bay for example were cut back 3 m. Sand-dune systems all along the east coast were breached. Altogether 64 000 hectares (ha) were inundated in Britain and 141 000 ha in the Netherlands.

The 1953 storm surge was but one in a series of similar events that have affected the east coast for several centuries. Similar surges are known to have occurred in 1825, 1894, 1906 and 1916. A minor surge occurred in 1977. These rare events are believed to have played a major role in determining the geomorphological evolution of Britain's east coast. They may be rare events on a human timescale but the changes they bring about in one or two days probably exceed the changes that occur on all intervening days put together.

To protect London against the effects of another storm surge, possibly larger than the one in 1953, a tidal barrage has been constructed across the Thames at Woolwich. The problem of protecting London against such a flood has progressively become more acute because south-east England is isostatically subsiding at a rate of about 1 mm year^{-1}, a fact which favours an increased frequency of flooding along this coastline.

Other agents of geomorphological change

There are other important agents of erosion on the coast. Subaerial processes of weathering and mass movement operate on some cliffs, various types of wave-induced and tide-induced currents transport sediment, and man himself is an important agent of change. These are best described in the context of individual coastal landforms which we shall now examine.

GEOMORPHOLOGICAL DIVISIONS OF THE COASTAL ZONE

A wide range of terms is used to classify landforms and processes on the coast. The backshore, foreshore and inshore zones are used in descriptions of beach morphology. The terms nearshore, swash zone, surf zone and breaker zone are used to classify processes. Relationships between these zones are shown in Figure 6.8 A, which should be studied carefully. Also shown are some of the important changes which affect the profiles of the inshore zone in winter and summer. These are referred to later. The seaward limit of the offshore zone, not shown in Figure 6.8 A, is the wave base. Some writers define this limit at the edge of the continental shelf. All the zones landward of the offshore zone constitute a very narrow belt when seen against the scale of the continental margin, principal elements of which are shown in Figure 6.8 B.

LANDFORMS OF THE COASTAL ZONE

The most dramatic features of the offshore zone are *submarine canyons*. These deep trenches often lie offshore from large river systems like the Hudson on the east coast of the USA, and were once thought to have been formed by these rivers when sea level was lower than today. Another theory is that they are formed by *turbidity currents*. These are concentrated flows of water, very heavily laden with sediment. These currents have a greater density than surrounding water and are powerfully erosive.

Beaches extend between high water mark and the lowest limit of effective wave action. Their form is very dependent on wave type. If wavelength is long, and the arrival of successive waves is separated by a long time interval, the backwash from the first may drain away before the second wave breaks. This sometimes enables swash to build up the beach levels. Such waves are therefore called *constructive waves*. *Destructive waves* have short wavelength and short periodicity. Backwash from one wave impedes the up-beach movement of the next swash wave and destructive effects dominate, i.e. material is combed from the beach.[1] It is because destructive 'sea' waves tend to be

1 This is a crude distinction between constructive and destructive wave action, for much depends on sediment size, infiltration rates into the beach and existing beach slopes.

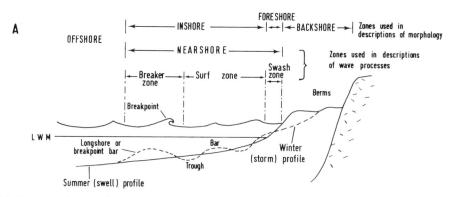

Figure 6.8 A Terms used to describe coastal morphology and the different zones of wave activity. Beach gradients are related to sediment size as well as to wave activity. Water percolates easily through gravel beaches and backwash is often ineffective. Such beaches may have gradients of 1:5. Beaches on fine sand may have gradients as low as 1:50.
(Source: J. L. Davies, 1972(a), p. 120 and E. Derbyshire, K. Gregory and J. R. Hails, p. 131.)

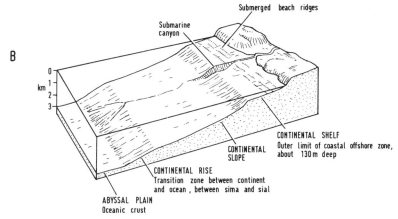

B

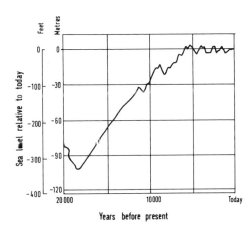

Figure 6.8 B Components of the continental margin. Actual widths and slopes of individual elements vary from coast to coast. On coasts which coincide with the edge of an advancing plate, for example, continental margins tend to be narrow and steep. If the coast is not on a leading edge, continental margins tend to be wide and gently sloping.
(Source: M. G. Gross, p. 42.)

more common in winter than summer around British coasts that beaches here tend to develop depositional bars in the nearshore zone at this time of year. These bars represent material combed down from the foreshore and deposited in the nearshore zone (Figure 6.8 A). In summer, material in these bars tends to be pushed up the surf zone towards the foreshore by the greater frequency of constructive waves at this time of year.

The tide also plays a part in beach construction. During rising tide when the beach is dry, water tends to percolate into the beach from breaking waves. This reduces backwash and constructive effects tend to predominate. On the falling tide, beach water content is often high, and percolation from breaking waves may be less. Backwash in these circumstances becomes stronger and sand is combed down from the upper to the lower swash zone.

A lot of our knowledge about beaches is the result of careful regular surveying. The winter and summer changes in beach levels, described earlier, can often be demonstrated by regular surveying over a twelve-month period. Regular surveys over a longer period, backed by map evidence and aerial photography, can help to establish if material is being systematically added to or removed from the beach. In many parts of Britain, such measurement techniques have demonstrated that the total volume of beach material is not changing at the moment, and has probably not changed much in the recent past. This has been demonstrated for many of the beaches on the north coast of Ireland, and for Chesil Beach which has been described as a virtual closed system. Where then does the material in such beaches come from? Much of it is now thought to have been deposited, far beyond our present coastline, by glaciers and fluvioglacial action during those parts of the Pleistocene period when sea level was lower than today. This material was gradually pushed onshore by the rising sea level which accompanied the melting of the ice in the post-glacial period. The main rise in sea level started about 20 000 years ago and stopped 6000 years ago, since when sea level has tended to oscillate gently about its present level (Figure 6.9).

Figure 6.9 The worldwide rise in sea level since the last glaciation of the Pleistocene period, some 20 000 years ago. Ice melt raised sea level some 100 m and drowned extensive areas of former coastline.
(After R. W. Fairbridge, 1960, p. 76.)

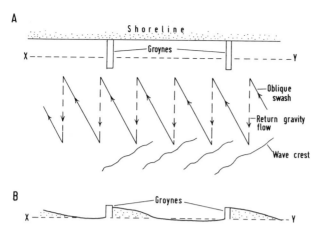

A

Shoreline

Groynes

X ---------- Y

Oblique swash

Return gravity flow

Wave crest

Figure 6.10A The zig-zag movement of beach material by littoral drift. On the British coastline littoral drift tends to be southward on the east coast, eastward on the south coast and northward on the west coast. There is thus a coastal drift of material towards the south-east coast and away from the south-west.

B

Groynes

X ---------- Y

Figure 6.10B Beach profiles along the transect XY. The side of the groyne on which beach material accumulates is the side from which littoral drift originates.

The progressive movement of sediment along coasts is called *littoral drift*. One form of littoral drift occurs when slightly oblique swash waves push material diagonally up the beach and gravity-controlled backwash returns it straight back down (Figure 6.10). This process occurs on many beaches, and sometimes in different directions at different times of the year. Komar, for example, points out that on the California coast, waves from the north-west in winter often transport material southward, while in summer swell waves from the southern Pacific return much of it northward. The net effect of these two movements in California may be quite small although the southwards movement is always the stronger of the two.

Much of the beach material on California's coast is derived from rivers. According to some writers, reservoir construction on major rivers like the San Joaquin and Sacramento may be depriving some beaches of their present-day sediment input. A traditional response to the loss of beach material, here and elsewhere in the world, has been the construction of groynes. The long-term build-up of sand on one side of a groyne is a useful indication of the net direction of littoral drift. The groynes help to slow down littoral drift and thus conserve beach sediments.

As sediment moves along a coast it may become trapped, temporarily or permanently. Various forms of sediment trap have been recognized by Davies and are shown in Figure 6.11. A typical *re-entrant trap* is the bayhead beach, characterized by the

seasonal movement of sediment across the beach but not along the coast. Where sediment does move freely along the coast *salient traps* occur. *Steady state* or *equilibrium traps* occur where erosion and deposition of sediment, often involving separate modes of transport, appear to be more or less balanced. A final category of coastal sediment trap is the *deep sink*. These are depressions in the continental shelf, sometimes submarine canyons, into which sediment may sink and be permanently lost to the coastal beaches. A good example is the La Jolla submarine canyon in southern California which traps a great deal of material drifting southward along the Californian coast.

A *spit* is a type of salient trap, especially well developed on a coastline where littoral drift is strong and where the coastline suddenly turns

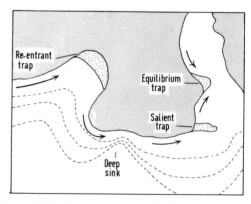

Re-entrant trap

Equilibrium trap

Salient trap

Deep sink

Figure 6.11 Four types of coastal sediment trap. (Source: J. L. Davies, 1972(a), p. 105.)

away from the sea towards the land. Hurst Castle spit in the Solent is a particularly good example of a *recurved spit* (Figure 6.12). Here littoral drift is principally from the north-west, and the spit is orientated in a north-west to south-east direction at 90° to the longest fetch which is from the south-west. At the end of the main spit subsidiary shingle spits have developed, and are in turn orientated at 90° to the direction of second-longest fetch which is from the north-east down the Solent (see Sawyer).

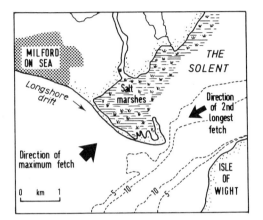

Figure 6.12 Hurst Castle spit, Hampshire. Notice the deep water off the end of the spit. Depth contours are in fathoms.

According to several authorities, recurved spits like that at Hurst Castle require at least two conditions:

1 the presence of subsidiary waves with a different fetch from those causing the principal littoral drift; and
2 the presence of deep water and a large tidal range at the end of the spit.

Shallow water would tend to refract waves parallel to the feature itself and the recurved ridges would not then be able to develop. A word of caution is appropriate here. Many interpretations of spits and of other coastal landforms are based on morphology alone. Sometimes processes have to be inferred from landforms, but it is always best to measure processes directly whenever possible.

Cuspate forelands represent the best examples of equilibrium traps, although the length of time over which the equilibrium can be demonstrated may appear very long. Perhaps the most famous cuspate foreland on the British coastline is

Dungeness. A similar example, at the mouth of the Foyle estuary on the north coast of Ireland, has recently been examined by Carter (Figure 6.13, Figure 6.14).

Magilligan Point is made of quartz sand, probably derived from material laid down as end moraine (Chapter 7) at the edge of a late-glacial ice sheet which moved into north-east Ireland from Scotland. It has evolved over a period of some 6000 years by steady growth towards the north-east. It seems initially to have been formed around the Giant's Grave, a gravel storm ridge in the south-west. The Point itself lies at the boundary of two different wave environments. Atlantic swell waves from the north-east break parallel to beaches on the east side of the Point, while sea waves of low periodicity generated in Lough Foyle affect the west side. The last 30 years has seen a marked extension of the Point by about 240 m. Material for this build-up of land has been derived from erosion of the Point at other places, principally on the Lough Foyle side but also on the Atlantic side. The long-term future of the Point is uncertain but two facts emerge from analysis of old Ordnance Survey maps and from modern field surveys:

1 little if any new material is now being added to the feature as a whole—the total sediment budget appears to be finite;
2 over the past 150 years periods of deposition at the tip of the Point have alternated with periods of erosion.

About 30 ha have been affected by each phase of erosion and deposition, and each phase lasts about 40 years. The lack of any net change over the last 150 years in the volume of stored sediment suggests that the feature is more or less in equilibrium over this time period. Whether or not it will remain for ever in equilibrium is a matter for speculation.

Important morphological features which may be present on any beach include longshore bars, crescentic bars, cusps and berms. All four are principally sand beach features and are largely unknown in gravel, with the exception of cusps. *Longshore bars* are formed of material eroded from the surf zone and swash zone. They are present on indented and straight coastlines and although they are probably best developed in winter, when they act as stores for sand combed

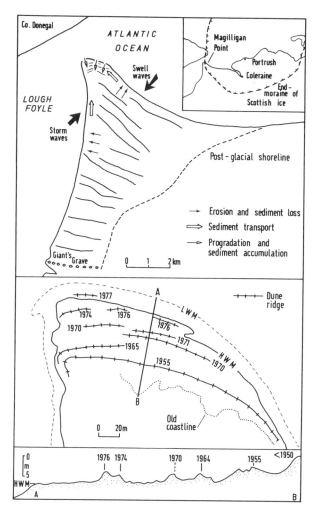

Figure 6.13 Patterns of erosion and deposition on Magilligan Point. Note the location of Magilligan Point along the line of a glacial end-moraine. The lower diagrams show how the tip of the Point has grown over the past thirty years. (Source: R. W. G. Carter, 1979, pp. 18 and 20.)

Figure 6.14 Magilligan Point, looking across the entrance of Lough Foyle (left) towards Inishowen in County Donegal. (Courtesy, G. Bond.)

down from the upper beach by storm waves, they are often present all year round. Most beaches have more than one longshore bar. In general, the number increases as beach slope decreases, the outer ones being formed at the position where the largest waves break while the inner ones are related to smaller, probably calm weather, waves.

Beach cusps (Figure 6.15) are scalloped-type ridges of material often seen on the middle and upper beach. They form in material of all sizes and may be associated with deltas as shown in Figure 6.16. The cusps act as boundaries of small circulation cells, each cell with its own swash and backwash. Backwash is concentrated into the middle of the depression between each pair of cusps and takes the form of a *rip-current*. Cusps may be associated with *crescentic* (or *lunate*) *bars* in the surf zone. These are large deposits, concave towards the shore (Figure 6.16 C), and are particularly well developed on bayhead beaches. Like cusps their precise origin is unknown.

The *berm* is a feature of the backshore. Constructive waves, on breaking, carry material up the beach and deposit it at the limit of swash action. The highest part of the berm is the product of constructive wave action at spring tide. Berms are therefore highest and of greatest extent in summer. Destructive waves, more frequent in winter, cut the berms back. At this time of year these features are therefore at their lowest and narrowest. Eroded material from the berms finds its way to the various bars of the inshore zone. These bars absorb wave energy and thus serve to protect the backshore from excessive erosion. This exchange of

Figure 6.15 Beach cusps at different levels on a gravel beach, Malin Head, County Donegal.
(Copyright, R. W. G. Carter.)

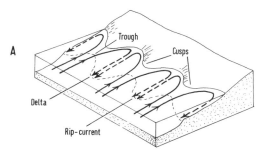

Figure 6.16 A Patterns of wave swash and concentrated backflow between cusps.
(After P. D. Komar, p. 270.)

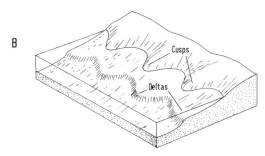

Figure 6.16 B Beach cusps and associated underwater deltas.
(After P. D. Komar, p. 266.)

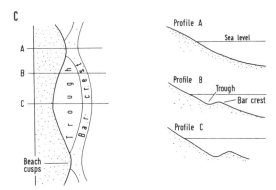

Figure 6.16 C Plan and profiles through a cusp and its associated crescentic bar.
(After P. D. Komar, p. 266.)

sediment between the berms and the inshore bars provides an example of negative feedback, in that berm erosion is followed by inshore deposition which then restricts further berm erosion.

Where there is no beach to absorb wave energy, waves may break directly against cliffs. When this happens air within rock joints is compressed by the impact of the wave, and equally rapidly it expands as the wave recedes. This pressure-release mechanism, particularly effective in a high-energy coastal environment, helps to loosen rock material from the base of the cliff face which is thereby undercut. The cliff may eventually become so unstable that large masses of rock fall into the sea and the cliff face recedes. Rock at the coast is also subject to chemical weathering which may be very rapid. Some rocks, basalt for example, weather more rapidly in sea water than in fresh-water.

Rock fragments accumulating at the base of cliffs may be thrown by wave action against the cliff face. This is *abrasion*, a term referring to the process by which waves wear away and break up rock material. Abrasion also occurs in rivers and glaciers. The end-product of cliff retreat by weathering and abrasion is a *wave-cut platform*. This is a gently-sloping shelf extending seaward from the base of a cliff.

The form a cliff takes on being undercut by wave action depends very much on geological structure. Landward-dipping rocks tend to produce steep cliffs because rockfalls are relatively infrequent and contribute only a limited amount of material when they occur. Weathering of cliff faces on seaward-dipping rocks disengages blocks of rock which more easily slide down bedding planes to produce gently-sloping cliffs. Much of this weathered material of course protects the cliff from further undercutting by wave action, and thus increases the relative impact of weathering on the slope form. A frequent form of cliff profile is the *slope-over-cliff*. The gently sloping upper portion of such cliffs are inherited features from an earlier period when sea level was lower. This slope facet was then undercut by the rising sea levels of post-glacial times to produce the compound cliff profile we see today (Figure 6.17 C).

Sand dunes

Davies has summarized ideal conditions for coastal sand dune development. A principal requirement is for frequent winds over the fluid threshold velocity. For this reason the largest dune complexes occur on coasts, like the Landes region in France, which are exposed to the regular passage of frontal depressions. A large tidal range also helps in that it exposes extensive areas of beach sand (preferably dry) from which the dunes can derive fresh supplies of sand. Wind helps to dry out the beach sand by encouraging evaporation.

There are two basic types of coastal sand dune. *Primary dunes* are derived from the beach and are parallel to it. The first line of primary dunes at the back of the beach are the *foredunes*. *Secondary dunes* are derived from these and are often at right-angles to them. Secondary dunes include blowouts and longitudinal dunes (see Davies).

Foredunes may initially grow around high spring-tide debris. Berms may provide the nucleus. Foredunes represent yet another reservoir of sand storage in the coastal sedimentary environment, and another means of absorbing wave energy at times of very high tide when they may be undercut by wave action. If the crest of the foredune is breached, wind action tends to be concentrated along the col produced by the breach, and sand is progressively eroded from the foredune and deposited behind. The huge amphitheatre-type depressions which develop from this process are called *blowouts* and the *longitudinal dunes*, which form in the lee of the foredunes from original foredune sand, are orientated parallel to the prevailing wind and quite frequently at right-angles to the beach.

It is clearly important to maintain foredune systems for three reasons:

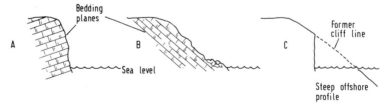

Figure 6.17 Landward dipping strata (A) tend to produce steep cliffs. A point worth emphasizing is that the very dramatic coastal features frequently described (e.g. stacks, blowholes, etc.) are in fact very rare and occur only when local geology is favourable. Seaward-dipping strata (B) tend to produce gently sloping cliffs. A slope-over-cliff profile is shown in (C). The upper, gentle, slope is all that now remains of a more extensive cliff face, the lower part of which was drowned by the rising sea levels of post-glacial times. Wave activity associated with present sea level has produced the steep cliff.

1 they absorb wave energy at high tide;
2 they are a source of sand for the beach should beach levels be lowered for any reason;
3 along with other landward dunes they protect inland areas from windblown sand.

Vegetation helps with this last aspect, marram grass and *Spinifex* providing two examples of how plants protect sand from wind removal (Figure 6.18). In many parts of the world, however, vegetation is being removed by rabbits, and destroyed by human trampling. In these circumstances erosion of the dune systems easily sets in (Figure 6.19). Quarrying of dune and beach sand for agriculture and industry can also be locally important. At Portrush in Northern Ireland, 100 000 m³ of sand were removed from one beach between 1950 and 1970. These practices are serious and reduce the level of protection the beach-dune system provides for the area inland. A significant conclusion to emerge from studies of the 1953 storm surge was that areas worst affected by inundation and erosion were those with low beach levels and small dune systems. Areas with high beach levels and large dunes fared better, because the sand stored in these systems absorbed a large proportion of the storm's wave energy. Many consultancy reports on coastal protection recommend the addition of sand to the beach as an anti-erosion device.

Figure 6.19 Eroded foredunes at Portstewart, County Londonderry, Northern Ireland. The large depression running away from the beach is a blowout. Incipient, smaller, blowouts in the dune crest are apparent. Evidence of intense human pressure on this fragile system is evident in the numerous footpaths.

COASTAL CLASSIFICATION

Problems of coastal classification have been reviewed by Shepard and Fairbridge in the *Encyclopedia of Geomorphology*. For many years coasts were classified as emergent, submergent or stable. *Emergent coastlines* were said to show signs of a recent fall in sea level and/or uplift of the land. They were said to be basically straight, with offshore bars a common feature. *Submerged coastlines* showed signs of a recent rise in sea level and were commonly indented in plan view, the indentations being drowned river valleys. *Stable coasts* showed no evidence of emergence or submergence. This classification is now considered too simple for two reasons:

1 over the last 20 000 years all coastlines have suffered more submergence than emergence (Figure 6.9); and
2 where emergent features occur they are often found on coastlines containing features of submergence as well.

The *fall zone* on the eastern seaboard of the USA is a line of rejuvenation waterfalls in the rivers draining to the Atlantic. These provide evidence of recent emergence and/or falling sea levels along this coast. Yet the same coastline is highly indented and contains many 'drowned' river valleys, such as those around Chesapeake Bay, which are more typical of submergence.

A more basic classification is into primary and secondary coasts. *Primary coasts* occur where the

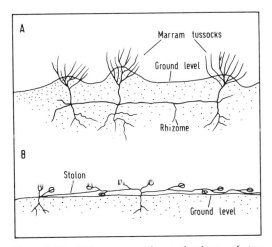

Figure 6.18 Different growth mechanisms of two common sand-binding plants. Marram grass (A) (*Ammophila arenaria*) widely planted to protect against dune erosion, binds sand through its underground network of rhizomes. *Spinifex* (B) protects against windblow by its surface vines called stolons. (Source: J. L. Davies, 1972(a), p. 67.)

sea's influence in determining the overall character of the coastline is minimal. Drowned river valleys (*rias*), drowned glaciated valleys (*fjords*), *deltaic coasts* and *diastrophic coasts* (Figure 6.20) provide examples. *Secondary coasts* owe their character principally to marine agencies. Wave-eroded coasts containing steep undercut cliffs, coasts of marine deposition containing such landforms as spits, and coasts built by marine organisms such as coral: all are examples of secondary coasts.

A classification based on the present balance of processes at the coast divides coasts into *receding* and *advancing coasts*. Receding coasts occur when marine erosion and/or submergence exceeds deposition and/or emergence. Advancing coasts occur when marine deposition and/or emergence is greater than erosion and/or submergence. This classification stresses the need to observe and measure processes and trends happening today.

Other classifications are possible. Tidal range has been adopted as one criterion (Figure 6.5). One might also use wave energy. Coasts however are difficult to classify. They depend on so many factors (lithology, geological structure, wave processes, subaerial processes, marine ecology, orientation, previous history) that the attempt to recognize a few basic types of coast is almost bound to be unsatisfactory.

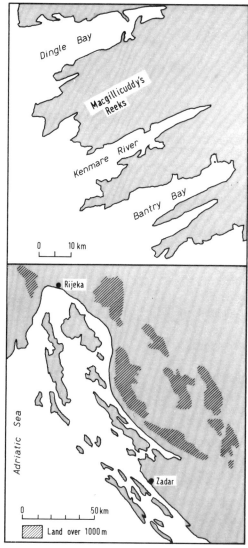

Figure 6.20 Two different types of diastrophic coast. The Kerry coastline (top) is an example of highly indented 'Atlantic' type coast in which geological structure and the consequent pattern of coastal inlets runs transverse to the direction of the coast itself. Here in south-west Ireland the SW/NE geological structure is Hercynian in age. On the west coast of Yugoslavia the geological structure runs parallel to the coast. When sea level rose, mountain ranges running parallel to the coast were drowned, producing the elongated, narrow, offshore islands. This type of coast is termed a 'Dalmatian' coast.

7
The Work of Ice

THE BUILD-UP AND DECAY OF ICE SHEETS

Snow is transformed into ice by the melting and settling of individual snow grains. Owing to the irregular shape of snowflakes, accumulating snow has a low density (0.05 g cm^{-3}) and air is able to circulate between the snowflakes melting their outer edges and making them more spherical. With greater sphericity the snowflakes are able to settle, the snowmass becomes more compact and dense, and air is driven out from between the snowflakes. When the density of the snowmass reaches 0.7 g cm^{-3} it is called *firn*. At this stage it has a very granular structure. Air can still circulate, though now with more difficulty, and melting and settling continue. When air can no longer penetrate the accumulating solid mass, the firn becomes ice. The density of ice is about 0.89 g cm^{-3}.

The growth of large ice masses takes many years and clearly cannot succeed by the relatively slow processes just described if spring and summer are warm enough to melt the preceding winter's snowfall. Many parts of the British Isles today have large winter snowfalls which disappear within weeks. Clearly a drop in summer temperatures is required in such areas if glaciers are to develop. The amount by which temperature might have dropped in the last ice age can be crudely approximated by the following simple calculation outlined by Andrews. If the base of an icefield was 800 m lower during the Pleistocene ice age than it is today, and if temperatures decreased with height then as they do now (i.e. at 0.6 °C per 100 m) the warming that has taken place since the ice retreated is the equivalent of a 4.8 °C temperature change. Calculations like this from

around the world show that today's mean annual temperatures in polar regions are probably about 2 °C warmer than in glacial times. In areas closer to the equator (e.g. East Africa) the temperature increases may have been as much as 6 °C. It is stressed, however, that temperature does not adequately represent all the energy inputs and losses that affect glacier expansion and contraction, and that estimates of temperature change based on altitudinal limits have to be interpreted with caution. It must also be remembered that temperature change is as much a result as a cause of glaciation.

The development of a complete ice cover over any region is technically known as *glacierization* and is believed to consist of three stages. The first (Figure 7.1) is called *the corrie stage* and occurs with a high snowline when permanent snow is

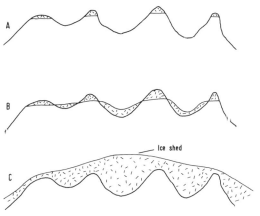

Figure 7.1 Stages in the glacierization of a region: (A) the corrie stage; (B) the valley glacier stage; (C) the ice sheet stage. The highest peaks which may protrude through an ice sheet at a stage intermediate between (B) and (C) are called *nunataks*.

Figure 7.2 The Aletsch glacier, Switzerland.

confined to the highest peaks. The *snowline*, incidentally, is the height at which winter snow continues to exist throughout the following summer. As temperatures become colder, the snowline falls and ice begins to flow from the mountains into the valleys. Valley sides are left clear of ice or only thinly covered. This is the *valley glacier stage* and ice flow follows lines of pre-glacial drainage (Figure 7.2). Continued lowering of temperature allows ice to build up and to bury large land masses under extensive *ice sheets*. At this stage ice flow follows the direction of the ice-surface slope and not that of the underlying topography. Flow now is multi-directional and radiates outwards from the highest parts of the ice sheet which do not necessarily coincide with the highest parts of the land surface. This is the case today in Greenland which consists of a large basin fringed by mountains. Ice was initially formed in these mountains but subsequently flowed into the central basin where it accumulated. When ice levels in the central basin eventually grew above the snowline, the basin for the first time started to receive its own supply of fresh snow. This accelerated the build-up of snow above the basin and here ice levels subsequently exceeded those in the surrounding mountains, which at maximum glaciation were finally engulfed. A similar situation existed in Ireland at the time of maximum glaciation when a major ice shed stretched from Sligo to Belfast, which then as now was a lowland rather than an upland axis.

Ice decay

Ice disappears from an area when ablation exceeds accumulation over a long period. The decay of an ice sheet is thought to pass through the three phases of Figure 7.1 in reverse order. This is important for it means that glaciated valleys and corries in today's landscape may well have experienced at least two periods of development, one at the beginning and one at the end of each major glacial phase.

Various attempts have been made to calculate how long deglaciation might take by comparing annual rates of meltwater production with the volume of water contained as ice in the bulk of individual glaciers. It has been calculated that small corrie glaciers in temperate areas such as Colorado or the Alps might disappear in about 30 years at present ablation rates and in the absence of any further accumulation, whereas polar ice caps would take 20 000 years or so to disappear.

There are three reasons why ice caps take longer than temperate glaciers to melt, other than their greater bulk:

1 Ice disappears from ice caps largely by sublimation (the process of converting ice directly into vapour), and this requires nearly ten times the energy input required for melting which is the primary process by which temperate glaciers disappear.

2 Ice caps tend to be clean and to reflect more incoming solar radiation than temperate glaciers, the surfaces of which tend to be dirty and to absorb more solar radiation because of their consequently darker colour.

3 Warm air currents carrying large amounts of sensible heat from oceanic areas fail to penetrate often into the interior of polar ice caps whereas in temperate areas such air streams are more common.

It is well to remember that when glaciers melt they shrink vertically as well as horizontally. This is important for as glaciers or ice sheets become thinner as well as less extensive, isolated pockets of ice come into existence cut off from the main ice mass and therefore without any internal horizontal movement. Such ice is called *dead ice*. This forms most easily near glacier margins and the distinctive landforms it produces are very useful in tracing former glacial limits.

GLACIERS AS OPEN SYSTEMS

Mass budgets

Many modern authors (e.g. Andrews) stress the importance of studying glaciers as open systems. Using this approach, it is possible to calculate mass budgets and energy budgets which help to determine the flow of materials and energy, into, through, and out of a glacier. The principal inputs of material are snowfall and sediment. The principal outputs are snowmelt and morainic material. Although it is not yet possible to measure sediment flows in a glacier, mass budgets for inputs and outputs of snow can be determined and tell us a great deal about how glaciers flow. The principal input of snowfall takes place above the snowline in the *zone of accumulation* (Figure 7.3). Here the glacier consists of ice covered by firn and snow. Most melting takes place below the snowline in the *ablation zone* where the glacier is 100% ice. When annual snowfall gains in the accumulation zone equal losses due to melting in the ablation zone the glacier is said to be in a steady state with its environment. To find out if this condition exists in a glacier, surface profiles are measured, ideally at the end of summer. Steady state equilibrium exists if these profiles remain unchanged from year to year.

The question arises as to how a constant profile drawn through a glacier can be the same at the beginning and end of any twelve-month period if, during that period, all the accumulation takes place in only one zone of the glacier and all the melting in another. The answer is revealing. The balance is maintained by *glacier flow*. Ice moves from the zone of accumulation to the zone of ablation, and the volume of ice transferred is equal to the net annual gain in the accumulation zone and the net annual loss in the ablation zone.

The mechanics of this transfer are very significant. To transfer excess ice from the zone of accumulation, ice flow is forward and downward from the surface of the glacier towards its base (Figure 7.3 C). In the ablation zone ice flow is forward and upward. The point at which there is little or no annual change in the height of the glacier, and at which flow is therefore parallel to the surface, is known as the *equilibrium line altitude* (ELA). This point divides the accumulation zone from the ablation zone. Of course, not

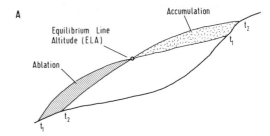

Figure 7.3 A Zones of accumulation and ablation in a small valley glacier and position of the equilibrium line altitude (ELA).
(Modified from J. T. Andrews, pp. 33 and 34.)

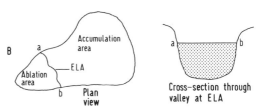

Figure 7.3 B Plan of the valley glacier and the shape of its cross-section through the ELA.
(Modified from J. T. Andrews, pp. 33 and 34.)

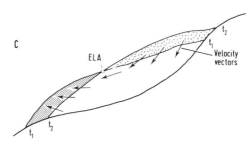

Figure 7.3 C Flow paths within a steady-state glacier. These flow patterns must exist if the glacier profile is to return to t_1 at the end of summer, after winter accumulation and summer ablation. At the ELA, flow is parallel to the glacier's surface and here the glacier's velocity is greatest. The profile t_1 would change into t_2 after one year's accumulation and ablation if glacier flow were zero.
(Modified from J. T. Andrews, pp. 33 and 34.)

all glaciers are in equilibrium. If accumulation exceeds ablation they are said to have a *positive economy* and they therefore advance. If ablation exceeds accumulation they have a *negative economy* and retreat.

The mass budget concept can also be used to identify active glaciers and passive glaciers. *Active glaciers* have high rates of snow accumulation and high rates of ablation. If accumulation and ablation are in balance, such glaciers must have a compensatingly large transfer of ice within the system from the input zone (accumulation zone) to the output zone (ablation zone). Velocities in such glaciers are high, and considerable volumes of sediment as well as of ice are transferred down the glacier. In *passive glaciers*, low rates of accumulation and ablation produce low velocities and therefore relatively little transfer of ice and sediment. Velocities in active glaciers such as those of the Alps may reach 15–20 m day^{-1}. The best examples of passive glaciers are the ice sheets of Greenland and Antarctica in which the movement of ice is much slower. Paterson quotes flow rates of under 30 cm year^{-1} in a small Canadian ice cap.

ICE MOTION

How does ice move in an active glacier and why is there so little movement, if any, in a passive glacier? The answer has to do with the presence or absence of meltwater. Two basic mechanisms of ice movement are commonly recognized: *internal flow* and *basal slip*. We know little about internal flow other than that ice crystals orientate themselves so that their basal planes point in the flow direction. This enables ice crystals to slide past each other more easily. Internal flow, however, is very slow. Much more rapid is basal slip. This occurs when meltwater penetrates to the base of the ice. Here it acts as a lubricant and helps the glacier to slide over the bedrock. The glacier can thus transfer sediment frozen within it. It can erode.

According to Davies and others, changes of pressure at the bottom of a glacier affect basal slip. Increased pressure on the upstream side of a knoll, for example, may cause ice at the base of a glacier to melt. On the downstream side of the knoll, pressure is lower and ice can reform. This is *regelation*. Temperature is important in this process, for if ice temperature at the base of a glacier is very much below *pressure melting point*,[1] as in parts of the polar ice caps, the ice may never melt and the glacier remains frozen to the bed-

rock. Little or no basal slip can occur in these conditions and ice movement is principally by internal flow. Glacier velocities are very low and erosion is probably minimal. This is one reason why some geomorphologists believe that ice sheets protect rather than destroy underlying land-scapes. In active glaciers of temperate latitudes, temperature is close to melting point throughout the profile, meltwater is more abundant (especially in summer when most movement occurs) and basal slip, with its associated erosion, can there-fore take place.

It should not be concluded from this brief account of ice motion that basal slip never occurs under ice sheets. In deep depressions ice may be so thick and pressure so high at the base that pressure melting occurs and basal slip is possible. Recent studies suggest that some large polar ice sheets may only be frozen to their beds at their margins and that near their centres their thickness is great enough to cause pressure melting and sliding at the base. Debris may thus be transported outward from the centre by basal sliding. Nearer the margins, where pressure is lower, meltwater refreezes and debris is refrozen into the base of the glacier. Here shear planes (see later) carry the debris upward, above that part of the ice sheet permanently frozen to bedrock. In this way, debris is brought to the surface and edges of the ice sheet where it accumulates. Ablation of the ice at the margin allows sediment to move down the outer slope of the glacier where it accumulates as end moraine.

In support of this theory is the observation that many ice sheets have a dirty peripheral zone some 150 m wide where shear planes bring debris to the surface. Being dirty, this ice melts easily and debris is deposited. Beyond this zone, towards the centre of the ice sheet, the surface of the glacier is very clean. It has to be stressed, however, that this explanation is only theoretical. No obser-vational proof yet exists that the interior part of an ice sheet can slide across its bed, although theoretical physics suggests that this is probable.

PROCESSES OF EROSION AND DEPOSITION

Glaciers acquire their load in several ways. Freeze–thaw on the bare rock slopes above valley glaciers

---

1 Very large pressures, such as occur under thick ice caps and ice sheets, may lower the melting point substantially below 0 °C.

produces rock debris which falls on to the glacier to become *supraglacial material*. This supraglacial material may become *englacial* as it is trapped by annual firn accumulation and as it moves downward and forward in the zone of accumulation. Englacial material is sediment which moves in the body of the ice itself, well away from the surface, sides, or base of the glacier.

Quarrying, or *plucking*, involves subglacial freeze–thaw weathering, and is particularly pronounced in well-jointed rocks. Locally high pressures at the base of a glacier produce supercooled meltwater which penetrates rock joints. Release of pressure further downvalley allows the water to refreeze and to incorporate loose fragments of weathered rock into the base of the glacier by regelation. Once incorporated into the base of a moving glacier, weathered rock material forms a very powerful abrasive tool. When basal load is very thick it scratches and polishes rock outcrops over which it passes. This is *abrasion*. Individual fragments in the load will themselves become polished and *faceted* in this process. The slow, grinding, process of abrasion tends to produce fine sediments such as sand, silt and clay. Plucking produces coarse boulders. Between them they produce *boulder clay*, an active glacier's most distinctive sedimentary deposit.

Deposited glacial material is variously called 'till', 'boulder clay', or 'drift'. We shall use *till*. Glacial till in the zone of ablation is sometimes let down vertically, or *superimposed*, on to underlying topography when an ice cap melts *in situ*. This process is also typical of dead ice. Sediments deposited in this way are loose and unconsolidated. In contrast, glacial till deposited by moving ice at the bottom of a glacier is often very compressed. This is *lodgement till*, and the stones it contains are often aligned with their long axes parallel to the flow direction. In *ablation till* there is no such preferred stone orientation and this is a principal way of distinguishing the two types.

Meltwater plays an important role in the deposition of material from ice. Meltwater flows in supraglacial, englacial, ice-marginal and subglacial channels. The environment immediately adjacent to the margin of a glacier is known as the *proglacial* environment. Here, meltwater is the most important agent of landscaping.

EROSIONAL LANDFORMS

The best-known glacial landform is the *corrie* or *cirque*. These are believed by some writers to develop initially from *nivation hollows*, which in turn develop from small depressions in the preglacial landscape. Snow masses which accumulate in these depressions expand and contract significantly in relation to their overall dimensions during the course of a year, and thus allow freeze–thaw to affect relatively large areas at their edges. Meltwater removes some of the weathered material produced and lubricates the base of the snowmass as it builds up. With continuing climatic deterioration, vegetation thins out, mechanical weathering becomes more intense, and the nivation hollow deepens. The transition from small nivation hollow to large-scale corrie however is never fully explained, and many would dispute that it actually occurs.

A corrie's most distinctive feature is its high semicircular headwall and the knob of rising ground at its outlet. This is sometimes termed the *threshold*. The recession of two corrie headwalls towards each other produces an *arête*. The recession of three or four towards each other produces a *horn*.

The development of corries is particularly difficult and dangerous to study but the headwall gap is believed to play an important role. Here, gravity pulls ice away from the headwall and the headwall gap may reach the surface via a *randkluft*. If ice adheres to the backwall, the headwall gap sometimes reaches the surface via a *bergschrund* (Figure 7.4). Meltwater from the glacier surface is able to flow down these avenues and freeze–thaw attacks the base of the headwall. So long as there is a continuous supply of meltwater down the headwall gap, freeze–thaw can continue at the base in a zone of relatively low ice pressure. Meltwater also helps basal slip beneath the corrie ice and this removes the frost-shattered rock. Abrasion at the base of the glacier produces the overdeepened depression between headwall and threshold which is thought to reflect the rotational pattern of flow lines often found in small glaciers and described earlier (Figure 7.3 C). The net effect of these flow lines is to produce a scouring action. It has to be stressed, however, that no complete

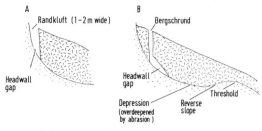

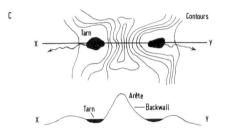

Figure 7.4 A and B Idealized sections through a corrie glacier showing how the position and form of the headwall gap may vary. Sometimes neither randkluft nor bergschrund exist and the headwall gap is not connected to the ice surface. Water in the headwall gap may then be derived principally from groundwater sources. (Modified from J. L. Davies, 1972(b), p. 136.)

Figure 7.4 C How corries and arêtes typically appear on contour maps.

and universal theory of corrie formation is yet available.

Another distinctive feature of glacial erosion is the U-shaped valley. These are produced by valley glaciers, and their cross-profile is often contrasted with the characteristic V-shape of a river valley. This is somewhat misleading for the post-glacial U-shaped trough is in fact the former channel of a glacier and not its valley, and many river channels are also U-shaped or rectangular in cross-section.

U-shaped troughs are characteristically straight because ice is a very viscous material which does not deform easily. Protruding spurs in the former river valley are therefore *truncated* by the combined action of pressure melting on the upstream side of the spur, associated freeze–thaw at the base of the glacier, and removal of weathered rock by basal slip. Intense freeze–thaw in the *peri-glacial period* immediately preceding the onset of glaciation may have played an important role in weathering valley-side bedrock so that it was more easily removed by subsequent valley glaciers. Freeze–thaw may have been quite intense at the base of valley sides where pre-glacial water tables would have been close to

the surface. Removal by glaciers of any material weathered in this way might quickly have transformed the cross-section of the former valley from a V-shape to a U-shape (Figure 7.5 A). The critical factor in this explanation is the depth to which initial freeze–thaw action would have penetrated before the onset of glacial conditions, and the volume of weathered material it would have produced.

A typical cross-section through a valley glacier is presented in Figure 7.5 B. All valley glaciers derive their load from weathering and erosion at their base and sides, but where tributary glaciers converge into main glaciers their basal and lateral moraines may become englacial and medial moraines respectively. In a composite valley glacier, debris is therefore transported as supra-glacial, englacial, medial, lateral and basal moraine.

Formerly glaciated valleys are distinctive in other respects. Ice erosion by valley glaciers is very much related to ice volume, and small glaciers do not therefore erode as much as large glaciers. As the ice melted, tributary valleys were therefore left *hanging* above the larger troughs. The former

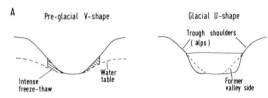

Figure 7.5 A Possible stages in the transformation of a V-shaped valley into a U-shaped glacial trough.

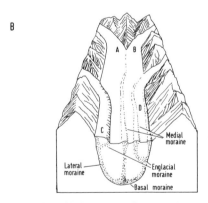

Figure 7.5 B Various types of moraine in a valley glacier. The basal moraine of glaciers C and D is superimposed on glaciers A and B respectively, and becomes englacial within them.
(Source: R. G. West, p. 45, after Sharp.)

junction of small and large glaciers are often today marked by a waterfall.

Valley steps are another characteristic of glaciated valleys and have a wide variety of possible origins. Over-deepening at the junction of two corrie glaciers often created a valley step. Some steps represent former nickpoints in the pre-glacial river valley while others are possibly related to glacier flow. On the upstream side of valley steps, ice pressure is considerable and compressing flow occurs. Shear planes in the ice slope upward towards the surface (Figure 7.6 A). Downstream of the step, pressure is released, freezing of meltwater therefore occurs and plucking can take place. This is the region of extending flow and shear planes slope downward towards the bed, encouraging scouring of the valley floor.

Another theory on the origin of valley steps relates them to joint patterns. If joints are close together glacial plucking scours the valley floor and over-deepens it. Widely spaced joints resist glacial plucking and remain as relatively elevated steps in the valley floor (Figure 7.6 B). Valley steps in all probability are seldom produced in any one single way, but from a combination of the above processes. Often the depressions between

valley steps are filled with lakes. Strings of such lakes, in plan view rather like a string of beads, are termed *paternoster lakes*.

Roches moutonées are rock mounds, gently sloping and smooth on the upstream side, steep and irregular on the downstream side (Figure 7.7). As with valley steps, a popular general theory relates them to abrasion on their smooth upstream side and to plucking on their downstream side. A refinement of this explanation involves another mechanism, that of *pressure-release jointing*. According to this idea the pressure of ice on the upstream side produces large volumes of meltwater and at the same time compresses the rock material on the valley floor (Figure 7.8 A). Downstream, the rigid ice is unable to mould itself to the subglacial topography, and a small subglacial cave is formed in which meltwater can refreeze by regelation due to the lower pressures at the base of the ice. This is also a zone of stress release, for the rocks as well as for the base of the glacier, and shallow stress-release joints may be formed running parallel to the surface. These are

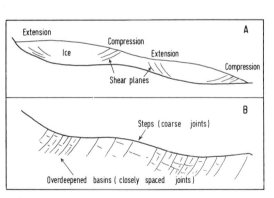

Figure 7.6 A   Types of flow zone in a glacier. Extending flow occurs in the zone of accumulation and where velocity increases on steep slopes. Compressing flow occurs in the ablation zone and on gentle slopes where velocity decreases and ice volume builds up. Plucking and scouring take place in the zone of extending flow. Much of the transported material is brought to the surface by the shear planes in the zone of compression. The combination of these two processes produces hollows in the underlying rock between each valley step.
(Source: J. L. Davies, 1972(b), p. 93, based on original ideas by J. F. Nye, 1952.)

Figure 7.6 B   Valley steps as they are sometimes related to jointing.

Figure 7.7   Roche moutonée, Connemara, Ireland. The direction of ice flow was away from the observer.

A

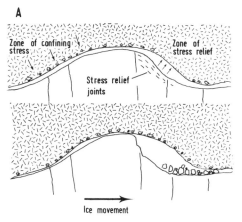

Figure 7.8 A The possible roles of ice pressure, melt-water, and rock joints in the production of roches moutonées.
(Source: E. Derbyshire, K. J. Gregory and J. R. Hails, p. 232.)

B

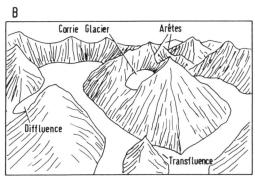

Figure 7.8 B Glacial diffluence and transfluence in a glaciated upland.
(Source: J. L. Davies, 1972(b), p. 146.)

attacked by freeze–thaw weathering, and regelation processes then incorporate the weathered products into the bed of the ice for subsequent transport. If the downstream side of a roche moutonée is subsequently plastered with boulder clay it is termed a *crag and tail*. The orientation of both roches moutonées and crag-and-tail features tells us a great deal about the direction of ice flow, and both can be classified as *ice-streamlined landforms*.

Distinctive features of glacial erosion in uplands are produced by *diffluence* and *transfluence*. These processes occur when the volume of ice in a valley glacier increases to such a depth that it overtops the valley divide and spills over into an adjacent valley. Diffluence occurs if a glacier

diverges into two ice streams. Transfluence occurs if a branching glacier flows into another (Figure 7.8 B). Both processes may leave U-shaped cols in the ridges between former valley glaciers and these may or may not be deep enough to affect post-glacial drainage. Good examples of diffluence and transfluence exist in the Muckish–Errigal range of Donegal, and in the Lowther Hills of the Clyde valley. They were most probably formed in the late valley glacier stage of glaciation or, conversely, in the phase of deglaciation when ice sheets contracted back into the valleys.

DEPOSITIONAL LANDFORMS

Morainic material is deposited in various ways. *Terminal moraines* are deposited at the snout of glaciers and several types can be recognized. *Dump moraines* (Figure 7.9), for example, are

Figure 7.9 Small dump moraine in the Alps. Note the asymmetrical shape of the moraine, the unconsolidated debris and the unmelted ice incorporated into the moraine fabric.

considered to represent periods of stillstand when glaciers are in steady-state equilibrium with their environment and the ice front is stationary. The larger the moraine the longer the stillstand. When ice sheets are not in equilibrium but constantly advancing or retreating, morainic material is laid down as *ground moraine* or as a *till plain*.

Another category of terminal or end moraine is the *push moraine*. These form at the snout of glaciers when supersaturated till at the base of a glacier is compressed by readvancing ice and carried upward by shear planes to form a wedge between the ice and the ground moraine (Figure 7.10 A and B). For comparison the profile through a dump moraine is also shown in Figure 7.10 C. It too is asymmetrical in long profile, but unlike

the push moraine its ice-contact (*proximal*) slope is steeper than its *distal slope*. All the material in a dump moraine is the product of ablation till from supra-, en- and subglacial sources. It is therefore ill-sorted and has no preferred orientation. The same is true of material forming the distal end of a push moraine. In this case, the lack of a preferred orientation results from the slumping of material down the distal slope. Near the ice-contact end of a push moraine coarser sediments may have a preferred orientation as the sediment here was compressed during formation. Material here may also be faulted and folded. This would indicate that the ground moraine was deeply frozen rather than saturated when it was forced up by advancing ice (Figure 7.11).

The retreat of glaciers from any region was frequently marked by periodic stillstand, at which time terminal moraines may have been laid down. A sequence of such moraines are called *recessional moraines*. Clearly, recessional moraines represent events which took place during the deglaciation of an area for they would have been destroyed by any subsequent ice advance. Lateral and medial moraines may be left as conspicuous features of glaciated valleys but are less useful than terminal moraines in indicating the speed and general nature of ice retreat.

Drumlins are distinctive features of ice deposition. They are streamlined landforms like roches moutonées, and occur in swarms, the most famous of which are in Ireland. Drumlins are composed of boulder clay, although they may sometimes be

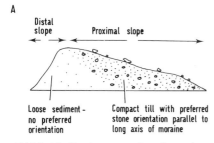

Figure 7.10A Idealized cross-section of a push moraine.

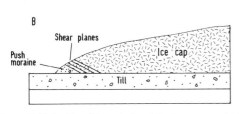

Figure 7.10 B Possible relationship between glacier shear planes, subglacial till, and push moraine. (Modified from J. T. Andrews, p. 151.)

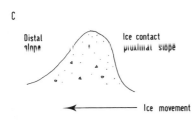

Figure 7.10 C Idealized cross-section of a dump moraine laid down by ablation. The distal slope of a moraine is the slope furthest away from the glacier. The proximal slope is, or once was, adjacent to the glacier. (Modified from J. T. Andrews, p. 148.)

Figure 7.11 Reverse faults in fluvioglacial sands and gravels, Gweedore, County Donegal. The vertical extent of faulting indicates the depth of freezing which must have occurred during one of the cold phases that followed initial deposition of the sediments.

rock-cored. Their steeper end points upstream in contrast to roches moutonées. Their long axes, like those of roches moutonées, point in the direction of ice flow and drumlin orientation is often used in tracing the direction of regional ice movements. There is considerable controversy as to whether they are truly depositional forms, or whether they are eroded by ice from previously-deposited ground moraine laid down in an earlier phase of glaciation.

Other features of glacial deposition are *knob and basin topography* and *erratics*. Knob and basin topography, as its name implies, is irregular hummocky landscape, the product of ice ablation. Moraine containing lenses of unmelted ice, is let down vertically. As the ice melts within the moraine, the overlying material collapses. The hollows in this type of landscape are termed *kettle holes*.

Erratics are not landforms but rock fragments. They are found in glacial deposits and are totally unlike local rock types from which they could not possibly have been eroded. One of the most famous erratics in the British Isles is a microgranite which outcrops only on Ailsa Craig, a small island in the Firth of Clyde. Pieces of Ailsa Craig granite, however, are found as far afield as Donegal, south-east Ireland and north Wales and show clearly the southward and westward movement of Scottish ice throughout the Irish Sea basin during the last glaciation.

FLUVIOGLACIAL ICE-CONTACT DEPOSITS

Fluvioglacial deposits are laid down by water draining from the ice in some way. *Eskers*, for example, are sinuous ridges of sediment laid down originally in supraglacial or englacial channels. When a glacier melts this material is superimposed on to the underlying topography. In today's landscape eskers often traverse hills and intervening hollows without any break in continuity. This is strong evidence that they were superimposed from passive glaciers or dead ice.

Kame terraces are deposited from meltwater flowing on the margins of valley glaciers. Although both are the products of meltwater, kame

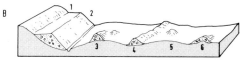

Figure 7.12 A and B Origins of ice-contact fluvioglacial deposits.
1 Kame terrace.
2 Ice-contact slope of kame terrace.
3 Crevasse filling.
4 Esker.
5 Kame.
6 Moulin kame with till nucleus pushed up by ice pressure.
(Source: R. G. West, p. 32.)

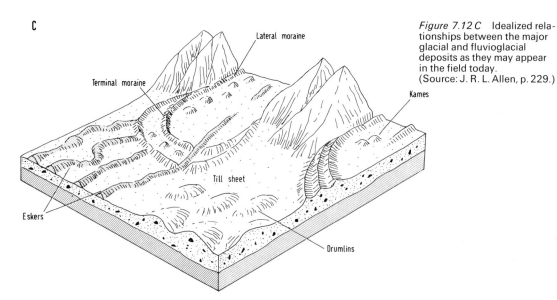

Figure 7.12 C Idealized relationships between the major glacial and fluvioglacial deposits as they may appear in the field today.
(Source: J. R. L. Allen, p. 229.)

erraces and eskers are partly moulded by the ice with which they are in contact during their initial formation. They can therefore be classified as fluvioglacial ice-contact features. The origin and appearance of other ice-contact features are shown in Figure 7.12.

PROGLACIAL LANDFORMS

The most extensive of all proglacial landforms is the *outwash plain*. It is formed, as its name implies, of material 'washed' from glaciers and glacial drift by meltwater streams issuing from a glacier. These streams are usually competent enough to transport fine clays and silts but not coarser sands and gravel. The 'fines' are therefore transported far away from the ice margin and the coarser material is left behind as a residual deposit. Outwash material is therefore well sorted, sediment size decreasing away from the ice front.

The ratio of sediment volume to meltwater at an ice margin is usually very high and streams do not therefore have the capacity to remove all the available sediment. Stream channels as a result are usually braided and quite steep. They also change position quite frequently, in response to the closure of individual meltwater outlets and the opening of new ones at the glacier snout. During the period in which each channel operates, a small *alluvial fan* may be built up. This may be cut into by a second meltwater channel and subsequently buried beneath the alluvial fan of a third. Sediments of outwash plains are therefore not only well sorted in a horizontal sense. They are also well stratified and often very thick. Outwash material in the Canterbury Plains of South Island, New Zealand, is 500 m thick. Other well known and recently deposited outwash plains are the sandur of Iceland.

Other features of the proglacial environment are proglacial lakes and overflow channels. These can originate in several ways but are often produced in association with cross-valley or *De Geer-type* moraines. As ice retreats from an upland area (Figure 7.13, Stage 1, long profile) a meltwater lake may be dammed up between the ice and the high land. At the margin of the glacier, moraine is laid down across the line of valleys draining from

the upland. These are the so-called cross-valley moraines and are laid down under water. They are a kind of push moraine, and are produced when great ice pressure squeezes out supersaturated till at the glacier's edges. As the lake level rises, water eventually overflows at high level across a col in the upland divide and into an adjacent valley on the other side (Figure 7.14). The large volumes of water involved sometimes cut deep, meandering, incisions into the watershed, and these remain today as relics of the former *overflow channels*. Retreat and thinning of the ice (Figure 7.13, Stage 2) lowers the lake level and leaves the initial overflow channel stranded. New, lower, levels for the ice-dammed lake come into operation and a second overflow channel may be formed. Ideally, overflow channels, cross-valley moraines and lake strandlines are preserved in association with each other (Figure 7.13, Stage 3). Unfortunately this is not often the case. Perhaps the best examples of former proglacial lakes are the parallel roads of Glen Roy in the Grampians where lake strandlines exist at 350 m, 305 m, and 260 m. Such strandlines are important in helping to trace the sequence of events in the deglaciation of an area.

Other features of proglacial lakes which help in the dating of glacial events are *varves*. These are alternate bands of sand and silt laid down as lake sedimentary deposits. Both are originally picked up by the high flows of the spring meltwater but whereas the coarser and heavier sands settle out almost immediately in early summer, the finer silts remain in suspension until autumn or winter when they finally settle out. Each pair of sand and silt bands therefore represents one year's sedimentary cycle, and the total number of pairs in a lake provides an estimate of the length of time the lake was fed by glacial meltwater (Figure 7.15).

Glaciers did not always impound lakes as they retreated from an area. Often the relief was too low for this to occur. On occasions rivers draining from ice-free areas flowed into ice sheets and were diverted by them. In north-west Germany, for example, northward-flowing rivers were blocked by Scandinavian ice retreating northward at the end of the last glaciation. A series of east-west ice-marginal channels were cut by the rivers as they were diverted westward into the North Sea. These are called *urstromtaler*.

PLAN VIEWS

VALLEY PROFILES

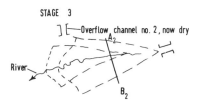

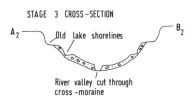

Figure 7.13 Idealized sequence of stages in the laying down of cross-valley moraines and the associated de-velopment of pro-glacial lakes and overflow channels. (Modified from J. T. Andrews, p. 159.)

Figure 7.14 Former overflow channel across a topo-graphic divide in the Bowland area of the Pennines. Note the meandering shape of the channel which indi-cates its fluvial origin.

Figure 7.15 Varved clays, Ballymoney, Northern Ire land.
(Courtesy, J. Shaw.)

INDIRECT EFFECTS OF GLACIATION

Since there is only a fixed volume of water on the Earth's surface, the growth of large ice caps necessarily reduces the remaining volume in the world's oceans. World sea levels therefore drop during periods of glaciation and rise again when the glaciers melt. This process is termed *eustacy*. During the most intense period of the Pleistocene glaciation eustatic effects operating alone would have lowered sea level about 160 m. Sea level, however, never actually fell by this amount because the build-up of ice on land isostatically depressed the continents and this process was in turn compensated by isostatic uplift of the ocean floor. The average thickness of Pleistocene ice sheets has been estimated at 1.5 km and they exerted a pressure of 1000 tonnes m^{-2}. The net effect of a eustatic fall in sea level and of compensating isostatic uplift was a fall in sea level variously estimated between 90 m and 110 m. The isostatic adjustments involved in the transformation of oceanic water into continental ice and back again are complex and lag behind eustatic processes by several thousand years. Post-glacial isostatic uplift in fact is not yet complete, and oceanic basins are still sinking as continental land masses under the greatest thickness of ice in the last glaciation continue to rise. Scandinavia has risen by 100 m since the end of the Pleistocene period and is still rising at about 1 mm $year^{-1}$ (Figure 7.16).

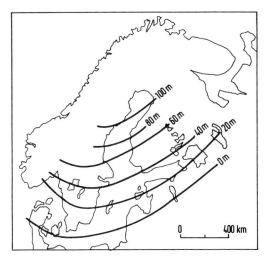

Figure 7.16 Isostatic uplift of Scandinavia since the melting of the Pleistocene ice-sheets 10 000 years ago. Some 200 m of isostatic recoil is still to take place before isostatic balance is achieved. Isopleth units are in metres. (Source: R. W. Fairbridge (ed.), 1968, p. 885.)

Isostatic and eustatic processes during the Pleistocene period are difficult to unravel, and are bound up with longer term changes in world sea level. World sea levels had been dropping throughout the Tertiary period. This fall is difficult to explain but is thought to be possibly connected with an increasing capacity of the ocean basins consequent upon renewed orogenic and plate activity in the early Tertiary (Table 7.1), and the early glacierization of Antarctica and Greenland which would have withdrawn water from the

Table 7.1. Geological succession over the last 70 million years

Era	Period		Epoch	Age (10^6 years)	Events
Cenozoic	Quaternary		Recent	0.01	
			Pleistocene	2	Growth and decay of ice sheets
	Tertiary	Neogene	Pliocene	11	210 m platform in SE England
			Miocene	22	Red Sea starts to open
		Palaeogene	Oligocene	40	
			Eocene	60	
			Palaeocene	70	Uplift of new fold mountains starts

oceans. This process is now thought to have started in mid-Tertiary times (see Sugden).

One morphological effect of a falling sea level is to leave former coastline features stranded above present sea level. Sometimes only wave-cut notches exist. Sometimes beach deposits can be found at very great heights above today's coastline. These are called *raised beaches*. Only those below 70 m can be explained by the eustatic effect of glaciers alone for if all ice on the earth's surface today were suddenly to melt, this is the height to which world sea level would rise (Figure 7.17). How then are we to explain the marine-cut platforms at a height of 210 m on the chalk dip slopes of the North and South Downs? These are interpreted as pre-Pleistocene shorelines, related to higher sea levels of the Tertiary period.

The Pleistocene period (strictly it should be termed epoch) is traditionally believed to have consisted of four major ice advances separated by warmer periods, the *interglacials*. At glacial maxima sea level was low, while during inter-glacials it was high. The ice did not expand and retreat to the same limits on each of these four occasions. The most intense glaciation was the penultimate glaciation. Minor advances and re-treats also took place within each major period of advance and retreat, and evidence for these can be seen in the minor oscillations of sea level depicted in Figure 7.17. The most interesting feature about Figure 7.17 is that during each interglacial period sea level rose to a lower level than that attained during the preceding inter-glacial. This evidence is critical in confirming the

belief that Pleistocene sea level changes were superimposed on longer term changes. If sea level changes in the Pleistocene were exclusively the result of ice sheet build-up and decay the highest sea levels would have occurred between the second and third glacial periods. This was the longest of the interglacial periods and if tempera tures during each interglacial rose to much the same level (which from oceanic fossil evidence we believe that they did) then most ice would have melted at this time.

During the last of the four principal glaciations sea level was about 100 m below today's mean sea level. During this period, rivers extended their courses across the continental shelves often cutting deep valleys into them. Glaciers were able to cut U-shaped valleys below present sea level and land bridges between islands existed where none exist today. The Dover Straits, for example, were dry and Britain was joined to Ireland. Land bridges provided very important overland routes for plant and animal migration, routes which are now closed. Much of the plant diversity in our western islands has its origin in these periods. Altogether the lowering of sea level during the Pleistocene increased world land area by 8%.

The post-glacial rise of sea level subsequently buried the river and glacial channels that had been cut into continental margins. At the present time sea level continues to rise as glaciers recede although it is probably unwise to regard this twentieth-century change as necessarily part of a long-term trend. Since 1900 world sea levels have risen about 12 cm on average.

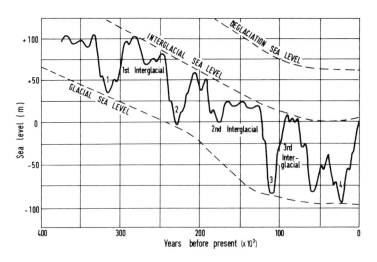

Figure 7.17 Changes in sea level during the four main glaciations of the Pleistocene period. Notice how sea level falls in glacial periods and rises in interglacials. The shorter duration warm periods within each glacial period are called interstadials. (Source: R. W. Fairbridge, 1960, p. 77.)

PERIGLACIATION

The development of large ice sheets over polar regions was associated with profound changes of world climate. At glacial maxima, 18 000 years ago, the Kalahari desert, for example, was cooler and moister than today and areas of African tropical rain forest less extensive. Sand deserts in the southern Sahara expanded southward while those in the southern hemisphere extended into the Zaire basin on the equator. Changes in tropical climate, however, were less dramatic than in mid-latitudes, and according to Butzer (1978, p. 201) the Tertiary and Pleistocene are essentially a continuum in tropical Africa. This was not so in mid-latitudes. Here, adjacent to the ice sheets *peri-glacial* conditions existed, as they do today in the high latitude tundra belts (Figure 7.18). Processes associated with periglaciation have been well described by Davies and French and are characterized by intense frost action and mass movement on very gentle slopes. These processes are most effective in the absence of trees which warm the lower atmosphere close to the ground and reduce the number of freeze–thaw cycles.

The periglacial zone is characterized by a layer of *permafrost* or permanently frozen ground. In modern Siberia the permafrost zone is 500 m thick in places. Seasonal thawing of the surface soil produces a ground layer of saturated regolith and it is this material which slips easily over the permafrost zone in a distinctive mass movement process called *solifluction*. Solifluction may occur in sheets or in well-defined channels. Rates of sheet movement may reach 7 cm year^{-1}.

The periglacial zone has certain distinctive sediments and landforms. Weathering products are very angular and there is little transport by fluvial processes. Soil profiles often show very contorted *involutions* in the seasonally thawed surface layers (Figure 7.19). Freezing in winter causes saturated materials to expand, and thawing in spring makes the soil very mobile. This variation of the freeze–thaw cycle often produces vertical sorting in soil profiles. Freezing raises the soil and thawing allows

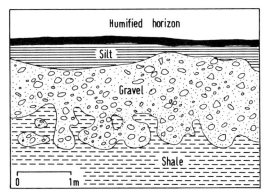

Figure 7.19 Involutions produced by frost action between gravel and shales in Montana.
(Source: J. L. Davies, 1972(b), p. 22.)

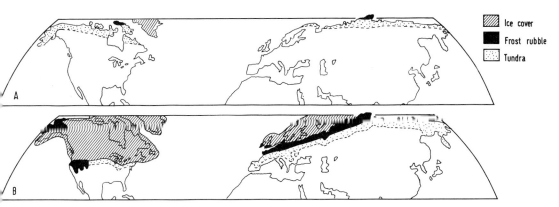

Figure 7.18 Cold climate regions of today (A) and cold climate regions of the late Pleistocene (B). The area of true periglaciation is divided here into a frost rubble zone where vegetation is very limited and broken-down rock material is abundant, and the more southerly tundra zone (see Chapters 13 and 14) where vegetation is scant but definitely more extensive than in the frost rubble zone.
(Source: J. L. Davies, 1972(b), p. 2.)

it to settle gravitationally. In the settling process, the finer material slips down between the coarser particles towards the base of the seasonally thawed soil layer, leaving coarser material close to the surface.

Frost action on saturated ground produces *stone polygons* the origin of which is not thoroughly understood. When viewed from above, polygons have between four and eight sides although sometimes they are circular in shape. Sometimes the material is well sorted, with the coarsest at the sides of the polygon and the finest in the middle. Sometimes no horizontal sorting exists. Polygons are found on flat ground. On slopes of between 2° and 7° there is considerable movement of surface material and polygons cannot exist. Instead elongated stone stripes develop parallel with the slope.

Two other distinctive features of the periglacial zone are *ice wedges* (see Figure 7.20) and *pingos*. Careful examination of sandpits in several parts of

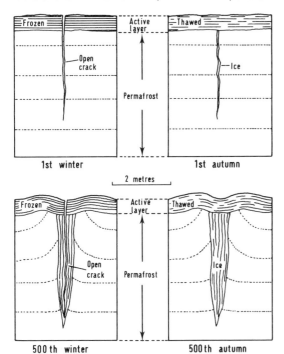

Figure 7.20 Evolution of an ice wedge by contraction. Winter freezing of the active layer (the surface soil layer which melts annually) causes soils to contract and thin cracks to appear. These fill with water which subsequently freezes the following autumn and winter, causing the crack to expand. The process is repeated in each successive year until the wedge-shaped depression is formed. When the ice in a wedge melts, overlying sediments may slump into it to preserve the cast of the ice wedge.
(Source: C. Embleton and C. A. M. King, p. 469.)

the British Isles may reveal fossil ice wedges Pingos are mounds, sometimes 100 m high, often lowest in the centre, and somewhat like a miniature volcano in overall appearance. One type of pingo is found where groundwater under artesian pressure is forced up underneath the permafrost zone where it freezes. The resulting ice core forces the ground surface into a dome which then stretches, and tension cracks appear. When the ice melts, the centre of the dome collapses because of its structural weakness and the resulting hollow may be filled with a lake (Figure 7.21).

Two other effects of periglaciation need to be remembered. During the Pleistocene glaciations streamflow in periglacial areas was much reduced while mechanical weathering became intense. The volume of sediment produced by weathering exceeded the rivers' ability to transport it, and the upper courses of rivers therefore experienced a period of aggradation. At the same time sea level was eustatically lowered and downstream river courses therefore degraded their beds to the new, low, base level. As interglacial periods were reestablished, run-off increased in the upland areas and the rivers here cut through their aggraded channels to new, low, levels leaving the aggraded material stranded on the valley sides as terraces In the lower reaches, aggradation characterized interglacial periods as sea level rose. This sequence of events was repeated several times in the Pleistocene period and gave rise to several 'cut and fill' cycles in the river valleys of the periglacial zone (Figure 7.22). Terraces produced by these events in the higher parts of drainage basins are often called *climatic terraces*. The lower ones are called *thalassostatic terraces*. The terraces of the Thames above London are thought by some to be climatic terraces produced by aggradation during cold climates while those below London are thalassostatic. This model of events has been much refined by recent work (see Bowen, for example) but it serves as an introduction to the cyclical types of geomorphological change that may have taken place.

A final erosive agent of the periglacial zone is wind. The lack of vegetation, the strong winds blowing off the polar ice caps, and the great abundance of finely ground sediment combine to produce an ideal environment for *wind deflation* Wind deposited material is called *loess* and many

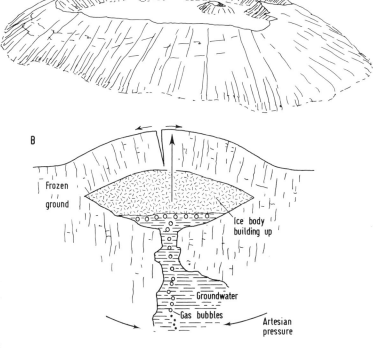

A

Figure 7.21 A Typical appearance of a pingo. From a photograph of a pingo in north-west Canada.

B

Frozen ground

Ice body building up

Groundwater

Gas bubbles

Artesian pressure

Figure 7.21 B Hypothetical evolution of a pingo by groundwater under artesian pressure. Other modes of pingo formation have been suggested. Pingos thought to be formed by artesian pressure tend to occur in groups. Isolated pingos probably have a different origin.
(Source: A. L. Washburn, p. 158.)

of the world's loess areas were formed during periods of periglacial climate. In Britain, loess deposited during periglacial conditions is exposed on top of the chalk at Ramsgate in Kent. It also occurs elsewhere in southern England although a much more extensive loess area is the Palouse region of Washington state, USA.

PLEISTOCENE CHRONOLOGY

The Pleistocene period is now thought to have begun about 2 million years ago though recent evidence suggests earlier dates of 3.4 million years BP (before present-day) for the onset of glaciation in Antarctica and Greenland (see Sugden). Ice sheets are even thought to have existed 14 million years ago in parts of Antarctica. During the Pleistocene period the ice sheets advanced and retreated at least four times. These oscillations were originally determined from analysis of fluvioglacial deposits, moraines, and associated terraces in southern Germany in the late nineteenth century. More recently, ocean floor sediments have thrown additional light on

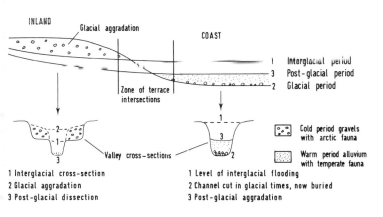

INLAND

Glacial aggradation

COAST

Zone of terrace intersections

Valley cross-sections

1 Interglacial period
3 Post-glacial period
2 Glacial period

1 Interglacial cross-section
2 Glacial aggradation
3 Post-glacial dissection

1 Level of interglacial flooding
2 Channel cut in glacial times, now buried
3 Post-glacial aggradation

Cold period gravels with arctic fauna

Warm period alluvium with temperate fauna

Figure 7.22 Inland and coastal river terraces resulting from changes of climate and from changes of sea level.
(Source: N. Stephens and F. M. Synge, p. 14.)

Sequence	Great Britain	Alps	Northern Europe	North America	Age (years before present × 10⁶)
Last glaciation	Newer Drift/ Devensian	Würm	Weichselian	Wisconsin	0.12
Last interglacial	Ipswichian		Eemian	Sangamonian	0.34
Fourth glaciation	Wolstonian	Riss	Saale	Illinoian	0.42
Third interglacial	Hoxnian		Holstein	Yarmouthian	1.06
Third glaciation	Anglian	Mindel	Elster	Kansan	1.20
Second interglacial	Cromerian			Aftonian	1.38
Second glaciation		Günz	Pre-Elster	Nebraskan	1.50
First glaciation		Donau		Pre-Nebraskan	

Table 7.2. Regional names of the major glacial and interglacial phases

the events of the Pleistocene (see Chapter 11). From this sedimentological record, at least eight warm and eight cold phases have been recognized and dated in the last 500 000 years of the Pleistocene period.

The four principal glaciations and the intervening interglacials are given different names in different parts of the world (Table 7.2). In all areas the last but one glacial period was the coldest and it was during this period that ice advanced furthest. In Britain the maximum advance occurred during the Wolstonian glaciation when ice reached as far south as London. Glacial deposits laid down by this ice sheet are termed older drift. During this phase Ireland was almost entirely covered by ice.

The last glacial phase laid down the newer drift in Britain, the southern limit of which is the Devensian moraine of about 20 000 years ago (Figure 7.23). The period of ice retreat from the British Isles after this last glaciation was not continuous. Minor cold phases saw various re-advances, three of which are shown in Figure 7.23. The most recent of these was the Loch Lomond re-advance of 10 500 years ago. At this time, most of Britain and Ireland was ice-free save for the few corrie and valley glaciers in the north-west of Scotland. Considerable controversy surrounds the location of the various retreat stages and Figure 7.23 should not be taken too literally.

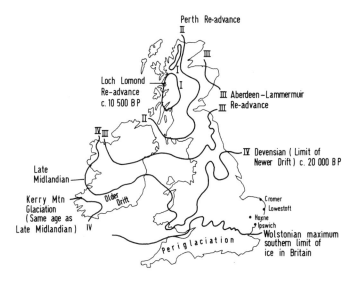

Figure 7.23 Possible correlations between ice limits in Britain and Ireland during the last two major glaciations of the Pleistocene period. Ice was most extensive in the Wolstonian glaciation. The southernmost limit of ice during the last glaciation is marked by the line labelled Devensian. The location of some important sites in British glacial stratigraphy is shown.

CONCLUSIONS

Several important facts have to be remembered when studying glacial and periglacial geomorphology.

1 We know very little about glacial processes directly because research on today's glaciers is expensive and dangerous. Much of our knowledge about glacial processes is therefore derived from observation of landforms and sediments, i.e. from the effects of processes rather than from observation of the processes themselves.

2 Most depositional glacial landforms have been highly degraded by weathering and erosion since they were first laid down. The determination of chronological events from such evidence is therefore difficult. Fluvial processes since glaciation, however, have not completely removed the legacy of the Pleistocene period, and much of our landscape was primarily formed in this period.

3 Fluvial processes, as well as ice action, were important in the Pleistocene period. Warm interglacials lasted far longer than the periods of glaciation themselves. It is therefore wrong to think of the ice age as one uninterrupted period of glaciation.

4 Finally, and perhaps most important, is the role of periglaciation which everywhere preceded the development of glacial conditions themselves. Periglaciation provided much of the weathered material which glaciers subsequently used to erode the landscape into the distinctive forms we see today. In the immediate postglacial period it probably also modified those forms a great deal. It certainly left an impact on the landscape of the British Isles. Landforms that probably originated wholly or in part as a result of periglaciation are:

(a) fossil pingos, found in the Cledlyn basin, Cardiganshire, and in County Wexford;
(b) fossil ice wedges formed throughout Scotland and Ireland;
(c) the tors of south-west England;
(d) underfit streams and dry valleys in central and southern England;
(e) stone polygons in South Devon;
(f) climatic terraces of the upper Thames basin;
(g) solifluction 'head' deposits (locally called Coombe Rock) in southern England; and
(h) the loess of southern England.

Section 3

THE ATMOSPHERE

8

Atmospheric Energy and Global Circulation

COMPOSITION OF THE ATMOSPHERE

Table 8.1 gives details of the principal gases contained in dry air. Nitrogen is most abundant but is chemically unreactive at normal atmospheric temperatures. Its role in natural atmospheric processes is therefore limited, and its principal importance in the physical environment is as a source of nitrogen for plant growth (see Chapter 12). At high temperatures, however, nitrogen is very reactive and it combines readily with oxygen in all fuel combustion processes. Nitric oxide (NO) and nitrogen dioxide (NO_2) are the oxidation products of combustion in motor cars and domestic heating, and both are important atmospheric pollutants. According to Giddings, the worldwide annual emission of NO_2 into the atmosphere from coal burning is 26.9×10^6 tons, from the burning of oil 22.3×10^6 tons and from the burning of natural gas 2.1×10^6 tons. NO_2 is very toxic and causes breathing problems and other forms of physical distress in humans.

Oxygen (O_2) is the next most abundant element in the atmosphere. The product of worldwide photosynthesis, it is a necessary part of all respiration and combustion processes, and combines readily with other elements under normal atmospheric conditions as we saw in Chapter 4. Argon is the most abundant of several chemically inert gases in the earth's atmosphere. Others are neon, helium and krypton. As far as we know they do not significantly affect weather and climate.

Three gases which together constitute a small fraction of the earth's atmosphere are water vapour (H_2O), carbon dioxide (CO_2) and ozone (O_3). All three have very important roles in atmospheric

Gas	By volume %
Nitrogen (N_2)	78.088
Oxygen (O_2)	20.949
Argon (A)	0.930
Carbon dioxide (CO_2)	0.030
Neon (Ne)	0.0018
Helium (He)	0.0005
Ozone (O_3)	0.00006
Total	99.9994

Table 8.1. Atmospheric composition

processes and all are vulnerable to disturbance by man. Nitrogen and oxygen, it should be emphasized, are not vulnerable to such disturbance. Water vapour may locally rise to 4% of atmospheric volume though an average worldwide figure is about 0.2%. Water exists in the atmosphere as solid, liquid and vapour and at each change of state latent heat is taken from or released into the atmosphere (see Chapter 1). These changes of state are very important atmospheric processes. Water vapour also scatters, absorbs and reflects incoming shortwave solar radiation (insolation) and absorbs outgoing longwave radiation from the earth. It thus plays a very significant role in the earth's radiation budget.

Carbon dioxide in the atmosphere is principally the product of respiration, although the burning of fuel also releases significant quantities. It is used by plants in the process of photosynthesis and is significant in the atmosphere as an absorber of radiant energy from the earth. The third of these three important gases, ozone, is important for its role as an absorber of solar radiation in the upper atmosphere. Ozone absorbs ultraviolet radiation less than 0.3 micrometre[1] (µm) in wavelength. These rays are very damaging to humans and plant life, and atmospheric ozone therefore protects all living systems from biological damage. It is therefore important that existing O_3 concentrations in the stratosphere are not depleted. If they are, the earth's lower atmosphere could become uncomfortably hot as more solar radiation would then penetrate to these levels than does now. Conversely, any increase of O_3 concentrations in the stratosphere would cause the lower atmosphere to become cooler.

A final constituent of the atmosphere is dust. It may be derived from natural processes like volcanic eruptions or from industry, and soil erosion is also thought to release significant quantities. Dust may reach heights of 10–50 km, although most is concentrated in the lower atmosphere. Dust scatters solar radiation and acts as *condensation nuclei* in cloud formation.

ATMOSPHERIC STRUCTURE

The atmosphere can be divided into four layers. The lowest layer, the *troposphere*, is about 8 km deep over the poles and 16 km deep over the equator. It is deepest over the equator because atmospheric convection here is strongest and vertical air currents reach great heights. All gases in the atmosphere are compressed by the weight of the overlying atmosphere, the effect of which is to concentrate 75% of the atmosphere's total mass into the troposphere.

The troposphere is turbulent and therefore well mixed. It is turbulent because it is primarily heated from the earth and not from the sun (we shall discuss this later). It therefore follows that the warmest air (which tends to rise) is near the ground and the coldest air (which tends to sink) is at higher levels. This is confirmed by observation from weather balloons which send back radio signals of temperature conditions at varying heights in the atmosphere. Evidence from such

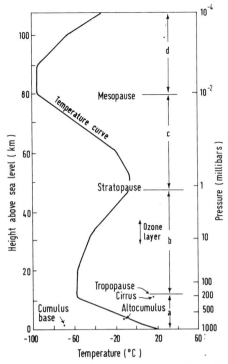

Figure 8.1 The four layers of the atmosphere: (a) the troposphere, (b) the stratosphere, (c) the mesosphere and (d) the thermosphere. Also shown is the variation of temperature with height and the typical location of certain cloud types.
(Source: R. A. Muller, p. 58.)

radiosonde balloons normally shows a decrease of temperature with height (Figure 8.1). The gradient of this curve, *the environmental lapse rate*, is 6 °C km^{-1}. With such a lapse rate turbulent mixing is automatic.

Occasionally the normal state of affairs is reversed and temperatures increase with height. Such a situation is termed a *temperature inversion* and occurs when warm air overlies cold air. This happens most often at night near the ground surface when the earth cools. Inversions form most rapidly in the absence of clouds and produce atmospheric stability with cold air near the ground, where gravitationally it is most stable, and warm air up aloft. An inversion usually breaks up when the ground is heated by the sun on the following day, although some inversions last for several days. Inversions trap pollutants near the ground where we have to breathe them.

Above the troposphere is the *stratosphere*. In the lower 15 km of the stratosphere temperatures

1 Formerly 'micron' ($\times 10^{-6}$ m).

remain more or less constant but towards the *stratopause*, where ozone concentrations are greatest, temperature increases with height. This is because ozone absorbs incoming solar energy. The stratosphere, unlike the troposphere, is therefore primarily heated from above. Here, warm air lies on top of cold air to produce great stability, turbulence is minimal and mixing is virtually non-existent. There is no vertical air movement and little cloud formation. Because of its stability the stratosphere is very vulnerable to pollution and one possible source of pollution was long thought to be supersonic transport (SST). According to figures quoted by Giddings, a supersonic airliner flying in the stratosphere emits in 1 hour 83 tons of water vapour, 207 tons of CO_2, 3 tons of carbon monoxide and 3 tons of NO. It was originally thought that water vapour emissions might increase cloudiness and the reflection of solar radiation. This is now thought unlikely and fear of pollution in the stratosphere is now receding as the number of operational SSTs like Concorde is much smaller than originally envisaged. In the early 1970s some climatologists envisaged a world supersonic jet fleet of 500 aircraft which could have depleted the ozone layer by 50% according to one calculation. This number now seems unlikely.

Above the stratosphere lies the *mesosphere*. Here temperatures once again decrease with height, principally because the concentration of ozone rapidly decreases above the stratosphere. The highest zone of the atmosphere is the *thermosphere*. As in the stratosphere, temperatures here increase with height, because like the stratosphere and mesosphere the thermosphere is primarily heated by the sun. Temperatures at the outer edge of the thermosphere probably reach 1500 °C, although such a temperature would not feel as hot here as it would at ground level. This might appear strange but remember that temperature is a measure of the mean kinetic energy of molecules in a substance, whereas heat measures their total kinetic energy. Small and large bodies can therefore have the same temperature, but the larger one has more heat. In the thermosphere it is the small number of molecules which explains the low heat energy level, not the kinetic energy of the molecules themselves, which in fact is very high.

THE GLOBAL ENERGY BALANCE

So far as scientists are able to determine, the earth as a planet is not getting any hotter or colder. In other words, the earth is not storing energy, even as heat, nor is it losing energy. This in turn means that the total output of energy from the earth–atmosphere system must equal the input of energy from the sun.

Solar energy is received at the edge of the earth's atmosphere in the form of electromagnetic radiation. Because the sun's temperature is very hot, 5730 °C, all solar radiation is shortwave radiation in the ultraviolet, visible and near infrared part of the electromagnetic spectrum (Chapter 1). The earth in contrast is much colder, 12 °C, and emits longwave radiation (Figure 8.2). Instruments for measuring radiation and sunshine are shown in Figure 8.3.

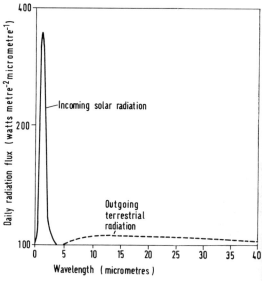

Figure 8.2 Solar radiation (insolation) is emitted in short wavelengths because of the sun's high temperature (5730 °C). The earth's radiation is spread over a broader spectrum of wavelengths because it is much cooler (12 °C). Maximum terrestrial radiation occurs at wavelengths of 12 μm. Since the earth receives from the sun as much radiation as it radiates to space the area under the two curves is equal.
(Source: A. H. Oort, p. 20.)

The way in which shortwave radiation behaves after entering the atmosphere (Figure 8.4) is critical to an understanding of atmospheric processes. Assuming 100 units of energy reach the outer edge of the atmosphere, 6 are scattered and

Figure 8.3 A Two solarimeters, the far one set up to measure total solar radiation (direct and diffuse) on a flat surface, the near one to measure the diffuse (scattered and reflected) sky radiation component only. Direct solar radiation is cut out by the shading ring. The difference between the two measures gives direct solar input. The measurement of radiation input into natural systems is important for the study of energy flows in the physical and biological environment.

Figure 8.3 B Foreground: a Campbell–Stokes sunshine recorder for measuring the duration of bright sunshine. Also shown are: a tilting syphon rain gauge for continuous measurements of rainfall (right), a group of anemometers mounted on a mast to determine wind velocity profiles close to the ground, and a conventional Stevenson screen for housing thermometers (left).

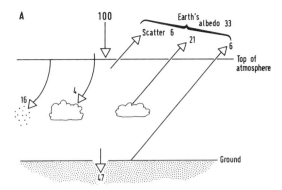

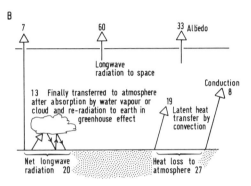

Figure 8.4 Energy budgets of the earth and its atmosphere: A—incoming radiation; B—outgoing terrestrial radiation and heat energy. At the top of the atmosphere the radiation balance is zero. Radiation inputs from the sun total 100 units. Output to space totals 100 radiation units, 33 in shortwave form, 67 in longwave form. Within the atmosphere the total energy balance is also zero. Radiation inputs total 33 units, 20 shortwave units from the sun, and 13 longwave units from the earth. Heat energy inputs from the earth (27 units) bring the total number of energy input units to 60. These 60 are all exported to space as longwave radiation. At the earth's surface the total energy balance is again zero. Short-wave inputs from the sun total 47 units. These 47 units are emitted as longwave terrestrial radiation (20 units) and as heat energy (27 units).

reflected back into space by dust, 21 are reflected back by clouds and 6 are reflected back by the earth's surface itself. The *albedo* of any surface is the ratio of reflected radiation to radiation received and the earth's albedo is therefore 33%. Light-coloured objects (snow, ice, clouds, etc.), reflect more than dark-coloured objects (soil, coniferous vegetation, etc.), and the 6% reflected from the earth's surface is principally from ice.

Incoming radiation greater than 1 μm in wavelength tends to be absorbed in the lower atmosphere. Altogether 20 units are thus absorbed, 16 by dust and other suspended solids, and 4 by water vapour. A small proportion of these 20 units is absorbed by ozone in the upper atmosphere, but we do not know precisely how much. Some of this absorbed energy is used to power atmospheric circulation in the upper atmosphere although the mechanisms are imprecisely understood at the moment.

The remaining 47 units of incoming solar radiation reach the earth's surface. This fraction is nearly all in the 0.4–0.7 µm wavelength range, the visible part of the spectrum. To maintain an energy balance of zero at the earth's surface, these 47 units have to be re-exported, and they are. But only 20 are exported as net longwave radiation. The other 27 are finally exported as degraded heat energy. The fact that less than 50% of incoming radiation units (20 out of 47) are re-exported as radiation creates a positive *radiation balance* or *radiation surplus* at the earth's surface. Such radiation balances, sometimes called *net radiation*, are positive at all latitudes except at the poles.

Let us look in more detail at the 20 units of terrestrial radiation, and in particular at how they are affected by water vapour and carbon dioxide in the lower atmosphere. Although transparent to shortwave radiation, H_2O and CO_2 can both absorb certain types of longwave radiation, though not all. Water vapour, for example, cannot absorb in the 8–14 µm range and CO_2 only absorbs in the 12–17 µm range (Figure 8.5). This leaves a 'hole' in the middle of the water vapour/carbon dioxide

'blanket' between 8 and 12 µm, and it is through this 'hole' that 7 of the 20 terrestrial radiation units escape into space. Since there is more water vapour than carbon dioxide in the atmosphere, water vapour is cumulatively more important in trapping longwave radiation. If these two gases were not present in the lower atmosphere, all longwave radiation would escape quickly and the earth's mean surface temperature would be about −45 °C instead of today's 12 °C. As it is, the earth's surface receives longwave *counter-radiation* from water vapour and CO_2. The earth in turn re-radiates this counter-radiation back into the atmosphere only to receive it back once more. The total number of longwave units radiated from the earth in this way is variously estimated between 98 and 113, a figure to be compared with the *net* figure of 20 mentioned earlier.

The process of trapping longwave radiation in the lower atmosphere is called the *greenhouse effect*. It is so called because H_2O and CO_2, like glass, are transparent to shortwave radiation but prevent the escape of longwave radiation. A greenhouse thus protects plants from the damaging effects of frosts on clear nights when, in the absence of clouds and water vapour in the lower atmosphere, longwave radiation easily escapes and leads to very low temperatures at ground level. The importance of the atmospheric greenhouse effect is given by the following figures. Although the atmosphere allows 47% of incoming solar radiation to pass through to earth, the greenhouse effect allows only 7 of 98 (or 113) longwave radiation units (7%) to escape directly back into space.

Twenty of the incoming units to the earth's surface have thus been accounted for. What of the other 27? These are transferred to the atmosphere not as radiation but as heat. The earth's continental and oceanic areas, in other words, absorb some of the incoming solar radiation and return it to the atmosphere as degraded heat energy. Conduction, the process of heat transfer between two bodies of unequal temperature in contact with each other (in this case the ground and atmosphere) accounts for 8 of the 27 units. Air, however, is a poor conductor and only the lowest centimetres of the atmosphere are warmed in this way. Of more importance is the process of latent heat transfer by evaporation. Each gram of

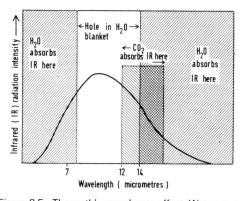

Figure 8.5 The earth's greenhouse effect. Water vapour absorbs most of the earth's outgoing infrared (IR) radiation, but the 'hole' in the vapour blanket (between 7 and 14 µm) is partially closed by carbon dioxide (CO_2). (Source: J. C. Giddings, p. 202.)

water evaporated at the earth's surface and carried into the atmosphere transfers with it some 2470 J of heat energy which is released into the atmosphere when the water vapour condenses (Chapter 1). This process accounts for the remaining 19 units. Together, therefore, longwave radiation and heat energy transfer dispose of exactly 47 units of incoming solar energy, and maintain an overall energy balance of zero at the earth's surface. In much the same way the atmosphere and the earth–atmosphere system can be seen to be in overall energy equilibrium (Figure 8.4).

Altogether some 40 units of energy are transferred to the atmosphere from the earth in the form of radiant energy and heat energy, but only 20 units of shortwave radiation are absorbed in the atmosphere from the sun. The atmosphere therefore receives most of its energy input from the earth. It is heated primarily from below.

HEAT TRANSFER FROM EQUATOR TO POLE

Although the annual global *radiation balance* at the edge of the atmosphere is zero, this is not the case for the earth's surface which annually receives 47 units of shortwave radiation but only exports 20 longwave radiation units. As we have seen, the difference between input and output is called the radiation surplus. The atmosphere conversely receives 33 units of radiation (20 from the sun and 13 from the earth) and exports 60. The atmosphere therefore has a negative radiation balance. We also saw that these radiation 'imbalances' are converted into overall energy balances by the *vertical transfer of heat energy from the earth to the atmosphere*.

As well as a vertical transfer of heat energy there is also a horizontal transfer of heat energy from low latitudes to high latitudes. This is heat described by Sellers and can be summarized as follows. North of 40°N, and south of 30°S, the radiation deficit in the atmosphere is greater than the radiation surplus at the earth's surface, and there is therefore an overall radiation deficit. In the tropical areas between 40°N and 30°S there is an overall radiation surplus because the radiation balance at the earth's surface is greater than the atmosphere's radiation shortfall.

The large radiation surpluses within intertropical areas is partly related to the angle of incidence of the sun's rays, which here strike the earth almost vertically. The angle of incidence becomes increasingly oblique towards higher latitudes, and the intensity of solar radiation therefore decreases (Figure 8.6 A). Moreover, the sun's rays pass through a greater thickness of atmosphere in

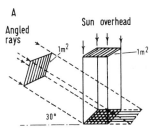

Figure 8.6 A Intensity of solar radiation is greatest when the sun is vertically overhead at noon. This occurs only in the intertropical zone, twice per year at the equator and in very low latitudes, but only once per year at the tropics themselves. Outside the tropics and even inside the tropics for most of the time, the sun's rays strike the earth's surface at an angle, and this angle decreases with increasing latitude. As the angle decreases, a specific amount of solar radiation is spread over increasingly large areas so that each area in high latitude receives less solar radiation than an equivalent area in low latitudes.
(Source: A. N. Strahler, p. 56.)

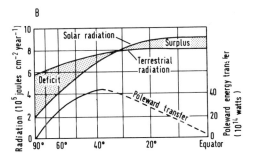

Figure 8.6 B Difference between absorbed solar radiation and emitted longwave radiation for each latitude in the northern hemisphere. Below about 38° latitude in each hemisphere there is a net input of radiation. Poleward of 38° there is a net annual loss of radiation. The flow of warm air from the tropics toward the poles compensates this radiation imbalance and releases latent heat energy in high latitudes, thus warming these areas and cooling the intertropical zone. Atmospheric circulation thus helps maintain an overall energy balance in the earth–atmosphere system. This circulation has been termed the atmospheric heat engine, the main source of heat being at the equator and the main heat 'sink' at the poles.
(Modified from R. G. Barry and R. J. Chorley, p. 64.)

higher latitudes and therefore suffer more atmospheric scattering and reflection.

To equalize the total energy budget for the earth's surface and atmosphere, there is a horizontal exchange of latent heat and sensible heat from low to high latitudes. The latitudinal imbalance of incoming and outgoing radiation, together with the poleward flow of heat energy, are shown in Figure 8.6 B. The transfer of heat energy towards the poles is initiated by equatorial heating. Warm air at the equator rises, carrying with it large amounts of latent heat in the form of water vapour evaporated from land and ocean surfaces. Expansion of rising air above the equator creates high pressure in the upper atmosphere and air flows northward and southward at high altitude. As this poleward-moving air invades areas of lower temperature in the middle latitudes, water vapour condenses and latent heat is released. In this way the atmosphere in middle and high latitudes is warmed.

It was originally believed that poleward-moving air in the upper atmosphere actually reached the poles where it subsided and then returned at low altitude all the way back to the equator. This *single-cell model* of atmospheric circulation in each hemisphere was proposed by Hadley, a British meteorologist, in 1735. Later observers found that Hadley's model could not account for the absence of surface winds blowing towards the equator between latitudes 30° and 60°, and a more sophisticated model was proposed by Ferrel. Consisting of three cells in each hemisphere (Figure 8.7 A). Ferrel's model has two zones of rising air, one at the equator and one at about latitude 60°, and two zones of subsiding air, one at the poles and the other in subtropical areas. This model of how vertical and horizontal air movements are inter-related on a global scale has long been one of the most basic models in physical geography. Two cells in each hemisphere are named after Hadley and Ferrel.

Ferrel's model describes average conditions in the atmosphere quite well, especially as they exist at the spring and autumnal equinoxes when the sun is overhead at the equator. But evidence described by Oort, from radiosonde balloons which can reach heights of 26 000 m, suggests that even Ferrel's model is inadequate to describe summer and winter conditions. At these periods only one

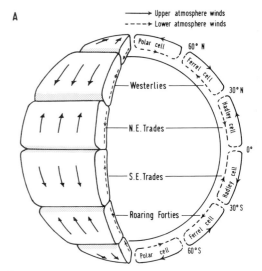

Figure 8.7 A   Atmospheric circulation cells as envisaged by Ferrel. Radiosonde evidence suggests that this pattern exists only at spring and autumn equinoxes when the sun appears to be vertically above the equator. (Modified from A. H. Oort, p. 21.)

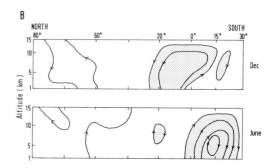

Figure 8.7 B   Radiosonde evidence defines this picture of atmospheric circulation at winter and summer solstices. The Hadley cell (shaded) is well developed in the winter hemisphere. Mid-latitude circulation is never well defined although the polar cell can sometimes be quite clear in winter. Arrows indicate the principal directions of air transport that can be detected by radiosonde.
(Modified from A. H. Oort, p. 23.)

well-defined intertropical cell seems to exist, and it is a feature principally of the winter hemisphere (Figure 8.7 B). In December, for example, during the southern hemisphere's summer, air rises at about latitude 15°S and travels northward across the equator to the Tropic of Cancer where it subsides giving a well-defined subtropical high pressure belt. A weak and smaller cell is sometimes evident in the southern hemisphere at about 17°S, but it is not so well defined as the cell of the winter hemisphere. In June the reverse situation exists. The sun appears to be over the Tropic of Cancer, but here only a weak cell of air circulation can be demonstrated. The principal cell involves rising air at the equator and sinking air in the vicinity of the Tropic of Capricorn. In both winter and summer the present radiosonde evidence is unable to define the two other cells of Ferrel's model with anything like the same clarity, although the north polar cell does appear reasonably defined in winter. Important observations of this type continue to be made, principally nowadays by satellites which measure infrared radiation. These enable temperature profiles to be constructed from the base of the atmosphere to the top and should soon improve our understanding of atmospheric circulation and heat energy transfers. Much remains to be discovered.

LOCAL ENERGY BALANCES

Figure 8.8 A shows a daily ground level radiation balance for Hertfordshire in summer. The radiation balance R_N is the difference between incoming shortwave solar radiation and incoming longwave counter-radiation on the one hand and outgoing shortwave and longwave radiation on the other. During the day incoming solar radiation ($R_S\downarrow$) reaches a marked peak around noon. Incoming longwave counter-radiation ($R_L\downarrow$) is more or less constant day and night. Both shortwave ($R_S\uparrow$) and longwave radiation ($R_L\uparrow$) from the earth are at a maximum in daytime, and losses are therefore considerable in these hours. During the night, of course, there is no shortwave radiation towards or from the earth although longwave terrestrial radiation continues to take place. The net effect of all these radiant energy transfers is to create a net surplus of incoming over outgoing radiation which is distributed throughout the day as shown (R_N), reaching a maximum about noon. As we have seen, radiation surpluses of this type (but not always this pronounced) are normal for all parts of the earth's surface except the poles.

Figure 8.8 B shows the daily net radiation curve for Wisconsin as described by Sellers and the way in which the surplus radiation received by the earth here is transformed into different forms of heat energy which, in turn, are subsequently

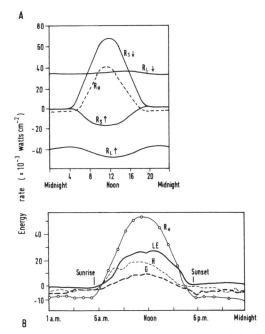

Figure 8.8 A Radiation balance over grass (albedo 26%) at Rothamsted Experimental Station on a cloudless August day. Symbols are explained in the text.
(Modified from K. Smith, p. 29, after J. L. Monteith and G. Szeicz, 1962, 'Radiative temperature in the heat balance of natural surfaces', *Quarterly Journal of the Royal Meteorological Society*, 88, pp. 496–507.)

Figure 8.8 B Daily variation of the surface energy balance at Hancock, Wisconsin, on September 7, 1957. Symbols are explained in the text.
(Modified from W. D. Sellers, p. 112.)

exchanged between earth and atmosphere to maintain the overall energy balance for this particular place. Over land areas $R_N = H + LE + G$, where R_N is the radiation balance, H is the transfer of sensible heat from the ground to the atmosphere, LE the transfer of latent heat between ground and atmosphere, and G the downward transfer of heat into the ground. Latent heat transfers most energy into the atmosphere during the day. The next greatest energy transfer during daytime is from the ground into the atmosphere, and the third is downward from the ground into the soil. At night, when the earth cools, the greatest heat losses involve the upward movement of heat energy in the soil towards the ground surface ($-G$). There is a downward transfer of heat from the atmosphere to the ground surface ($-H$) and a downward transfer of latent heat as well. This must take the form of condensation, most probably as dew and hoar frost.

LAND, WATER AND RADIANT ENERGY

Land and water surfaces respond very differently to radiation. Land surfaces heat up much more quickly than water because they have a lower specific heat capacity and because mixing of surface and deeper horizons is not possible as it is in water. Land surfaces also cool down quickly because all heat contained in the ground is stored near the surface. In contrast, water has a very high specific heat capacity and therefore heats up slowly. (Notice how a pan heats up more quickly than the water in it.) Waves and turbulence also mix surface water with deeper water and thus distribute incoming energy through a large volume. The greater the mixing, the greater the delay in warming up the water body relative to that of an adjacent land mass receiving the same amount of radiant energy. Another factor delaying the heating up of water is evaporation which as we have seen in Chapter 1 is a cooling process in its own right.

The net effect of these differences is that continental areas heat up and cool down quickly whereas land areas surrounded by water, in the same latitude, and therefore receiving the same amount of insolation, have a more even distribution of temperature (Figure 8.9).

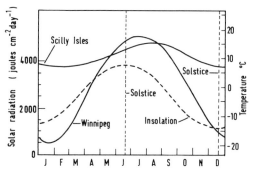

Figure 8.9 Annual temperature cycles for the Scilly Isles and Winnipeg (both in latitude 50 °N) in relation to radiation received (which is the same in both places). Note that maximum and minimum temperatures at Winnipeg occur about one month after the summer and winter solstices respectively. Maximum and minimum temperatures in the Scilly Isles are one month behind those at Winnipeg.
(Modified from A. N. Strahler, p. 67.)

MAN AND THE ENERGY BALANCE

One effect of man on the energy balance is seen in large cities, which are often warmer than the surrounding countryside. This is termed the *urban heat island* and results from the large surface area of buildings which can absorb more radiation than surrounding rural areas. Bricks also have a higher capacity to retain heat than soil. Another feature of city life is the burning of fossil fuels for heating and transport. This is another source of heat energy which can be absorbed in the building fabric of the city. The net effect of all these factors is to raise city temperatures. A temperature profile through London is shown in Figure 8.10.

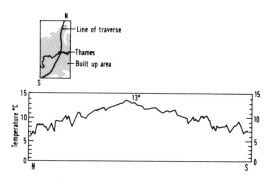

Figure 8.10 A night-time temperature profile through London from Enfield in the north to Epsom, October 1961. The heat island intensity at this time was about 7.8 °C.
(Source: T. J. Chandler, p. 170.)

Other modifications of the earth's surface by man include deforestation which usually raises the ground albedo, since grass which replaces forest has an albedo of 25%, and usually reflects more solar radiation. Coniferous forest, for example, has an albedo of 15% or less. Such changes have important local effects on the energy balance and on heat transfers in the lower atmosphere.

Man also affects CO_2 levels in the atmosphere. The principal source of CO_2 is respiration, but the burning of coal and oil also produces CO_2. Since 1850, the approximate beginning of the Industrial Revolution, global CO_2 levels appear to have risen (from 290 p.p.m. to 330 p.p.m.), and this has been associated by some climatologists with a rise in the mean temperature of the northern hemisphere during the same period. Increased

CO_2 levels enhance the greenhouse effect and tend to increase the retention of longwave radiation in the lower atmosphere. This is believed by some scientists to produce the warming effect. In 1945, mean temperatures in the northern hemisphere reached a peak. Since 1945 they have been falling. One possible mechanism for this fall is the release of fine dust into the stratosphere where rain cannot wash it out. Dust may increase the scattering of incoming insolation and reflect more of it back into space. One possible source of this dust is mechanized agriculture and the deforestation of large areas. A more likely source is increased volcanic activity which was spasmodic in the first half of the twentieth century although it has increased dramatically since 1960. We can leave an extended discussion of this important topic until Chapter 11.

9

Moisture in the Atmosphere

EVAPORATION AND TRANSPIRATION

The atmosphere gains its moisture through evaporation and transpiration and loses it through precipitation. We have already looked at the evaporation process in Chapter 1. Transpiration is basically similar though more complicated. In transpiration, plant roots absorb soil water which is then transferred upwards through microscopic passages in plant cells, finally escaping into the atmosphere through small pores in the leaves called *stomata*. The stomata, over 50 000 per square centimetre of leaf surface, open only during daylight to take in carbon dioxide for photosynthesis. Once they are open, water inside the plant is able to escape into the atmosphere, and soil water can move into the plant to replace any lost. The movement of water from soil, through plants, and into the atmosphere is called the *transpiration stream*. This vertical transfer of water takes dissolved nutrients from the soil and distributes them throughout the plant. Without these nutrients plants are unable to grow. At night, of course, there is no photosynthesis (remember that the process requires sunlight) and stomata close. Transpiration therefore occurs only during daytime whereas, in contrast, evaporation is a 24-hour process. The energy required for transpiration is the same as that for evaporation: 2470 J g^{-1} at normal temperatures.

Transpiration is an important plant function from a meteorological and ecological point of view, and it is worth examining in some detail. Plants take up water from the soil via root hairs and transmit it upward via plant cells. The membranes surrounding plant cells have such fine pores that molecules of water are only able to enter them very slowly. Molecules of mineral nutrients dissolved in the soil water are usually larger than water molecules and have even more difficulty in moving from cell to cell within the plant. Their dispersal through the plant is accordingly much slower.

Because nutrients move through the plant's sap solution more slowly than water the nutrient concentration of sap is higher than that of soil water. Expressed another way, the number of water molecules per cubic centimetre of soil solution is greater than it is in the transpiration stream. Since water flows from zones where the concentration of water molecules is highest to zones where the concentration is lowest, it quite naturally moves into and through the plant from the soil. This flow, the result of differences between the concentration of water solutions in the soil and in the plant, is called *osmosis*. Although other forces are involved in the upward transfer of water in plants against the force of gravity, this is thought by most plant physiologists to be the most important.

The upward transfer is set in motion when leaf surfaces are warmed by the sun. Solar energy transforms into vapour some of the water in the leaves and this leaves the plant as transpiration when vapour pressure in the plant exceeds that in the atmosphere. As water molecules escape from the leaves, other molecules from lower down the plant are forced upward to replace them. The quantities of water involved in transpiration are considerable. Penman shows that a crop can use 100 times its own harvest weight over a growing season, and at harvest may consist of 75% water and only 25% dry matter. Even the dry matter will contain hydrogen atoms split from the water molecule during photosynthesis and incorporated into the chemical structure of the plant.

One question that arises as a result of this discussion concerns the fate of the minerals in the soil water initially absorbed by the plant. The water absorbed leaks into the atmosphere. Where do the nutrients go? Most are absorbed in new plant tissue and thus stored as growth. They finally leave the plant as leaf-fall, windblow, or harvest (see Chapter 12).

We think of evaporation as primarily taking place from oceans and other water bodies. But it also takes place directly from surface soil, and over large vegetated surfaces the processes of evaporation and transpiration are impossible to measure separately. We therefore use the term *evapotranspiration* which refers to both processes.

Water vapour in a column of air above the ground exerts a pressure quite distinct from, and additional to, the pressure exerted by the dry atmosphere. This *atmospheric vapour pressure* increases as evapotranspiration proceeds. However, at any particular temperature there is a maximum amount of water vapour that the atmosphere can hold. It is then said to be saturated. The pressure of water vapour in saturated air is its *saturated vapour pressure*. At saturation, water molecules continue to enter the atmosphere, but a large number collide with water molecules already there. They therefore lose kinetic energy and fall back to the surface from which they were evaporated or transpired. When the number of water vapour molecules entering the atmosphere equals the number leaving it the air is saturated, and there is no net loss of water from the ground surface, i.e. there is no evapotranspiration. This is a condition of dynamic equilibrium (see Chapter 2).

Evapotranspiration can therefore only proceed when actual vapour pressure in the atmosphere is less than the saturated vapour pressure, i.e. when a vapour pressure deficit exists. As evapotranspiration proceeds, however, this deficit decreases and the bottom layers of the atmosphere may become saturated. Evapotranspiration is therefore helped by a gentle overturning of the lower atmosphere by light winds. This brings drier air into contact with the evapotranspiring surface and distributes the water vapour through a greater thickness of air.

There are two principal measures of atmospheric water vapour content besides vapour pressure. *Absolute humidity* measures the density (mass divided by volume) of water vapour in the air, usually expressed in grams per cubic metre ($g\,m^{-3}$). Relative humidity is a measure of the amount of water vapour in the air as a percentage of the amount it can hold at that temperature. Put another way,

$$\frac{\text{relative}}{\text{humidity}} = \frac{\text{actual vapour pressure}}{\text{saturated vapour pressure}} \times 100.$$

Figure 9.1 A shows the relationship between saturated vapour pressure and temperature in semi-logarithmic form. Careful examination of this diagram shows that at any temperature below 0 °C air is more easily saturated over a frozen surface (ice or snow) than it is over liquid water.

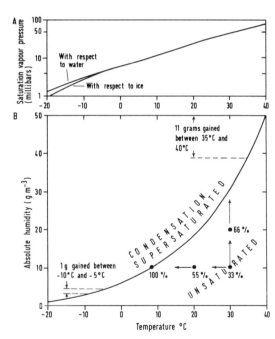

Figure 9.1 A Saturation vapour pressure (SVP) plotted against temperature. SVP is plotted on a logarithmic scale, temperature on an arithmetic scale. Such a graph is termed a semi-logarithmic or exponential graph. (Modified from R. G. Barry and R. J. Chorley, p. 33.)

Figure 9.1 B Absolute humidity plotted against temperature for saturated air. Notice how a relative humidity of 33% can be increased to saturation by a lowering of temperature without any change in absolute humidity. Notice also how relative humidity can be increased by raising the absolute humidity without any change of temperature. Saturation is thus brought about by increasing absolute humidity, lowering temperature, or by a combination of both.

As we shall see later, this is an important physical principle in one of the explanations of how raindrops are formed.

Figure 9.1 B shows the curve relating absolute humidity to temperature for saturated air (i.e. air with a relative humidity of 100%). The diagram illustrates three ways of bringing unsaturated air to saturation. The diagram also shows that saturated warm air holds more water vapour than saturated cold air. A rise of 5 °C, from 35 °C to 40 °C, increases water vapour content at saturation by 11 g. A rise of 5 °C, from −10 °C to −5 °C, increases water content at saturation by only 1 g. Since each gram of water vapour contains about 2470 J of latent heat energy it is obvious that warm air releases more heat into the atmosphere on cooling than cold air. This also is an important process in cloud formation.

Because evapotranspiration is the source of all atmospheric moisture, water vapour content decreases with altitude, and at 75 m height absolute humidity is only about 85% of its ground level value. However, very little precipitation is ever dropped on an area from which it was originally evaporated or transpired. This is because, as we saw in the last chapter, water vapour is transported horizontally over the earth's surface by the major wind systems. This is *advection*, a process which transfers heat as well as water vapour. Even in warm humid areas, where we might expect convection to contribute large amounts of rainfall, advection is usually the more important process. The Mississippi basin, for example, receives only 10% of its annual precipitation from local evapotranspiration and convection, according to Barry and Chorley. The rest is brought by advection.

The standard way of measuring evaporation is in an open evaporation pan (Figure 9.2). These may be circular or rectangular. The British Meteorological Office uses rectangular pans. The height of the water surface in the pan is read daily and the depth of water lost by evaporation or gained by precipitation in the preceding 24 hours is calculated.

The measurement of evapotranspiration is more difficult, but one way of measuring *potential evapotranspiration* (PE) is by use of an evapotranspirometer. PE is a measure of the atmosphere's ability to absorb water vapour when soil

Figure 9.2   A meteorological station in southern Spain. The circular pan is an evaporation pan of American design. Also shown are two rain gauges (mounted on staffs about 1.5 m above ground level) and, in the left foreground, a sunshine recorder.

moisture supplies are sufficient to meet the plant's water needs. One form of elementary evapotranspirometer consists of two or three grass-covered tanks (Figure 9.3) which are irrigated every day to ensure that there is always water in the soil profile to meet the evapotranspiration requirements of the grass. This being the case, there is always some percolation to measure every day at 0900 hours when meteorological recordings are usually taken. The difference between input and output, i.e. between precipitation and irrigation on the one hand and percolation on the other, is the amount of water lost to the atmosphere in evapotranspiration (see Ward, 1963). In this instrument the amount of water stored in the soil remains more or less constant and changes in storage are therefore ignored. *Actual evapotranspiration*, which may be less than PE, especially during a drought when the soil dries out considerably, is more difficult to measure experimentally and requires that changes in soil moisture storage are measured directly (Figure 9.4).

The volume of water annually involved in evapotranspiration around the world is 396 000 km³ (Leopold and Davis), of which 84% is derived from oceanic evaporation and 16% from terrestrial evapotranspiration. Evaporation is highest not at the equator, where cloud cover is often extensive, but over subtropical oceans, where clear skies allow solar radiation to reach the ocean surface

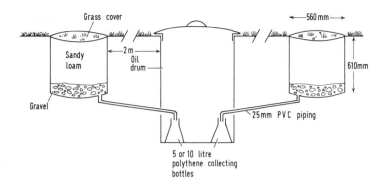

Figure 9.3 A An evapotranspirometer for measuring potential evapotranspiration from grass. Daily PE estimates from each tank usually differ slightly and the average of the two is therefore used. Grass levels inside and outside the tank are the same height so that the tanks are as representative as possible of the ground cover in which they are installed. The tanks should not cause any unnatural surface roughness which would alter ground-level windspeed and therefore evapotranspiration rates. Daily irrigation keeps the soil at field capacity or above (see Chapter 13) and there is therefore some percolate every day.

Figure 9.3 B An evapotranspirometer installation at Coleraine, Northern Ireland. There are three soil tanks at this site, shown here by dotted lines. Each drains to the central measuring tank on top of which is the $\frac{1}{2}$ litre cylinder used to measure daily percolate.

Figure 9.4 A lysimeter installation at the Institute of Hydrology's experimental catchment, Plynlimon, central Wales. The two grass plots are 10 m × 10 m in area and the walls are lined with impermeable material to a depth of several metres. Soil water draining from the plots (Q) is fed by pipes to the building in the background where it is continuously recorded. Rainfall (P) is also continuously recorded nearby and soil water content (S_m) in each plot is measured regularly. As with all mass budget studies, what goes in (in this case P) equals what comes out (Q) plus or minus any changes in storage (S_m). Actual evapotranspiration therefore equals P − Q +/− changes in S_m.

very freely. The Red Sea annually loses 3.5 m through evaporation. Such high evaporation rates, of course, are a principal cause of high salinity in these oceans. Over land surfaces evapotranspiration can be zero, as for example over hot deserts where there is simply no water to be evaporated. Within the British Isles, annual evapotranspiration ranges from under 400 mm in western uplands and parts of Ireland to over 600 mm in south-east England. Over surfaces where plant cover is continuous, transpiration can be three times the value of evaporation because plant roots tap a greater volume of soil water than does evaporation, which affects only the surface layers.

CONDENSATION

The temperature at which saturation occurs simply as a result of falling temperature, without addition of moisture and without any change of atmospheric pressure, is the *dew point*. This is theoretically the temperature at which condensation starts, but water vapour needs a cold surface on which to condense. Plants provide such surfaces after a clear night when they are cold after nocturnal radiation. Early morning condensation on the grass produces dew. If temperatures are below freezing, condensation on to grass and other plants produces *hoar frost*.

More usually, air cools because it is allowed to rise and to invade areas of lower atmospheric pressure. This type of cooling is called *adiabatic cooling* and we shall examine it further in the next section. On cooling adiabatically, relative humidities increase and eventually saturation occurs. For condensation to take place in these circumstances small *condensation nuclei* are necessary. These are small particles suspended in the atmosphere. Dust from volcanic explosions and agriculture, smoke from industry and forest fires, sulphur dioxide, common salt: all are good condensation nuclei. All have low densities and therefore fall very slowly. They remain suspended for long periods because the velocities of upward air currents exceed their own *fall velocities*. According to Barry and Chorley, ocean air may contain 1 million condensation nuclei in every litre of air whereas over the continents 5 million in every litre are not uncommon. Some of the condensation nuclei, notably salt spray, are *hygroscopic*. That is, they attract water. On such nuclei condensation can start at relative humidities as low as 80%.

Without condensation nuclei, air can cool beyond the temperature at which saturation should theoretically occur. It then becomes *supersaturated* and in supersaturated air actual vapour pressures can be three times the saturated vapour pressure. In reality, condensation does occur at or close to saturation level, even without condensation nuclei. But it seems that water droplets so formed lack cohesion without any nuclei, and disintegrate almost as soon as they are formed. If condensation nuclei are available, water droplets start to grow in only slightly supersaturated air and rapidly become cohesive enough not to disintegrate as they are swept around inside a cloud.

A water droplet is not a raindrop. Water droplets form round condensation nuclei and in turn combine to form raindrops. Some idea of relative sizes

is given in Figure 9.5. Condensation nuclei are less than 2 μm in diameter. Water droplets are usually less than 40 μm in diameter, while raindrops may reach 2000 μm in diameter and contain 10^{22} water molecules. Raindrops therefore contain millions of water droplets and the principal question in precipitation formation is: how do millions of water droplets combine to form raindrops? At the moment there are two *models* of raindrop formation: the coalescence model and the ice-crystal model.

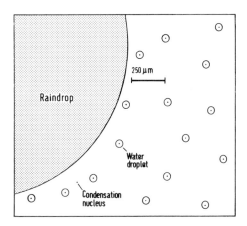

Figure 9.5 The relative sizes of condensation nuclei, water droplets and raindrops. Note that one condensation nucleus is required for each water droplet. A raindrop contains millions of droplets and therefore millions of condensation nuclei. Rainfall is consequently a most important way of cleaning the troposphere of dust. Condensation nuclei are also the cause of 'dirty rain'. (Source: R. A. Muller, p. 87.)

The coalescence model

Water droplets sometimes grow to more than 40 μm in diameter. This is very rare, however, and requires an initially large condensation nucleus more than 2 μm in diameter. Such *giant nuclei* are usually hygroscopic and this helps water droplet growth. Although very infrequent in any cloud (there may be only one or two giant nuclei in every thousand cubic centimetres) large droplets play a very important role in coalescence because of their relatively large mass. Droplets less than 40 μm in diameter have insufficient mass to overcome the airflow between them as they approach each other and, therefore, can never collide and coalesce. Droplets greater than 40 μm, however, do have the necessary mass to overcome such airflow and can grow by coalescence with smaller droplets.

As the droplets coalesce and grow they become heavier. Some droplets may fall from low cloud with weak vertical air currents when they are only 100 μm in diameter. Such small raindrops (large droplets really) usually evaporate in the dry air below the cloud before reaching the ground. Only initially large raindrops can eventually reach the ground because all raindrops evaporate to some extent on falling. In a cloud about 1.5 km thick it probably takes about half an hour for water droplets to grow by coalescence into raindrops large enough to reach the ground. The minimum initial size for such raindrops is probably about 250 μm.

The ice crystal model

The coalescence model is particularly appropriate for *warm clouds*, those that do not reach freezing level. In cold clouds (i.e. ones that reach freezing level) small water droplets may exist at temperatures as low as −40 °C. This is because water does not always freeze at 0 °C. Cloud water droplets are finely dispersed and often contain chemical impurities within them. Both these factors help to lower the freezing point. The smaller the water droplets the lower is their freezing point and all water droplets below 0 °C are said to be *supercooled*. At −40 °C, however, even the smallest droplets cannot remain unfrozen and ice particles form. For ice to form at temperatures well above −40 °C 'freezing nuclei' are required, in much the same way as condensation nuclei are required for water droplets. According to Sutton, clay and ash are good freezing nuclei. As we saw in Figure 9.1 A, saturated vapour pressures below 0 °C are lower above ice than above water, and as soon as ice crystals form, any water vapour in the air condenses on to the ice in preference to condensing on to existing water droplets. This process, in which vapour condenses directly on to ice without passing through a liquid phase, is called *sublimation*. (The same term applies to direct evaporation from ice.) During sublimation both the latent heat of vaporization (2470 J g⁻¹) and the latent heat of fusion[1] (335 J g⁻¹) are released into the atmosphere which is thus warmed. At temperatures below 0 °C the great attraction of ice

for water also strips water vapour molecules from supercooled water droplets, and the ice crystals grow as the water droplets shrink. Eventually, the ice crystals are big enough to fall through the cloud. On falling they become warmer and groups of them coagulate into snowflakes. These snowflakes in turn may melt into large water droplets which then coalesce with warmer, smaller, droplets near the cloud base. If the melting level is low, ice crystals have no time to melt and precipitation falls as snow. The ice-crystal theory of raindrop formation was developed by Bergeron, a Norwegian meteorologist.

ADIABATIC COOLING: STABILITY AND INSTABILITY

The rate at which atmospheric temperature decreases with height is called the environmental lapse rate (ELR). The ELR is normally 6 °C per 1000 m though it can vary. Atmospheric pressure also decreases with height, and if a part of the atmosphere is separated from the rest of the atmosphere and forced to rise as an individual, insulated,[2] parcel of air it will expand as it invades areas of lower pressure (Figure 9.6 C). The parcel expands because air molecules within it push against the surrounding atmosphere (i.e. they do work). As a result of expansion, air molecules within the parcel are forced to travel over greater distances and their kinetic energy levels decrease. The temperature of the parcel therefore falls. This is the process of *adiabatic cooling*.

Rising parcels of air with relative humidities less than 100% cool at the *dry adiabatic lapse rate* (DALR), 10 °C per 1000 m. As cooling proceeds, relative humidity reaches 100% and condensation starts, assuming condensation nuclei are present. Condensation, as we have seen, releases latent heat and the parcel of air is thus warmed from within as it were. Two contrasting types of temperature change thus take place simultaneously:

1 The latent heat of fusion is released on the transformation of liquids into solids.

2 There are no insulated 'parcels' of air in the atmosphere as such. Changes of temperature due to compression or expansion are so rapid, however, that they only affect quite well-defined volumes of the atmosphere. In adiabatic cooling or warming these well-defined volumes of air are not affected by conduction with the rest of the atmosphere. That is their essential characteristic.

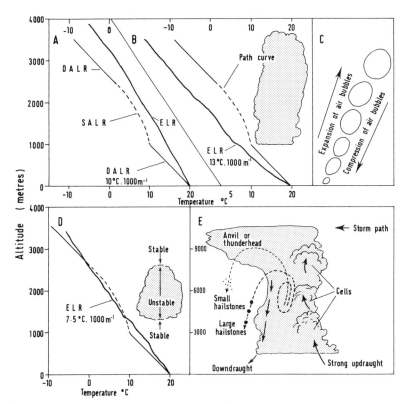

Figure 9.6 A A parcel of air separated from the rest of the atmosphere and forced to rise experiences a sequence of temperature changes defined by a path curve. The path curve shown here is at all altitudes colder, and air in the parcel is therefore denser, than the surrounding atmosphere. A parcel of air will not rise naturally in these conditions, which define atmospheric stability.

Figure 9.6 B Here a parcel of air is warmer than the surrounding atmosphere at all altitudes and is therefore lighter. Such a parcel of air will rise spontaneously. The situation depicted here is extreme instability.

Figure 9.6 C Expansion of an air bubble as it rises and invades areas of lower atmospheric pressure. Notice the converse principle of compression on descent. Compression, of course, induces warming of the parcel.

Figure 9.6 D Conditional instability. Here the ELR is intermediate in value between the DALR and the SALR. The path curve is therefore only to the right of the ELR between 1300 m and 2500 m. This is the only altitudinal range in which the parcel of air is warmer than the rest of the atmosphere and therefore unstable. Instability is here therefore conditional upon the parcel being forced through the stable layer at low altitude, maybe by forced ascent over a mountain range.

Figure 9.6 E Simplified cross-section of a cumulonimbus thundercloud. The initial uplift of air may result from intense local heating of the ground, from uplift over mountains (orographic uplift) or from the passage of moist air over a warm water surface. These are all major trigger actions of adiabatic movement. Cooling at the DALR takes place beneath the cloud but within the cloud individual cells form and latent heat is released. A typical thundercloud releases more heat in this way than an atomic bomb. The cloud builds up vertically until all moisture is condensed out or until it reaches a stable layer, maybe even the tropopause, where it spreads out into the familiar anvil shape. Hail is formed in the updraughts and grows rapidly from a small nucleus such as a snow pellet. Supercooled water droplets which collide with snow pellets freeze on collision; sometimes immediately, producing opaque ice with air trapped inside; sometimes more slowly, producing clear ice. Clear ice results if the supercooled water droplets have time to spread round the nucleus before freezing. Some hailstones circulate within the cloud several times and sometimes grow to the size of onions. The longer the period of circulation the larger is the hailstone. The fact that solid particles of such dimensions can exist within a cloud illustrates just how strong the updraughts of air are. The falling precipitation brings with it cold air in the form of downdraughts.

1 because of adiabatic cooling temperatures tend to fall; and
2 because of condensation temperatures tend to rise.

The first of these changes is always dominant, and even in saturated air temperatures decrease with height, but not at a constant rate.

At high humidities condensation releases large quantities of latent heat (Figure 9.1 B). The net fall in temperature within the air parcel is therefore quite low (about 4 °C per 1000 m). As condensation continues, absolute humidity falls and the latent heat liberated by condensation decreases. The net fall in temperature inside the parcel now rises towards 9 °C per 1000 m which is the maximum it attains. When all vapour has condensed out, cloud formation ceases and the parcel once again cools at the DALR. The *saturated adiabatic lapse rate* (SALR) is therefore not constant but takes a curved form. The DALR and the SALR together are known as the path curve, and when drawn in relation to the ELR the path curve helps to determine *stability* and *instability layers* within the atmosphere (Figure 9.6).

CLOUD FORMS

Clouds consist of millions of suspended water droplets. Physically, therefore, they are aerosols. There are two basic types of cloud: *convective* and *layer*. Air in convective clouds has high rates of vertical ascent, sometimes as high as 30 m s⁻¹. Layer clouds result from widespread gentle uplift such as occurs, for example, at warm fronts where typical upward speeds are much lower. Layer clouds are often formed when air is forced upwards through stable parts of the atmosphere. Before convective clouds can form, a parcel of air has to be separated from the rest of the atmosphere by some *trigger action*. Localized heating of the ground surface is one such trigger action and topography is another. Cloud initiated by either of these mechanisms can reach great heights in unstable air (Figure 9.6 B). Topography often causes air to rise in such a way as to produce condensation on the windward side of mountains and a *rain shadow* in the lee (Figure 9.7 A). A startling example of the rain shadow effect occurs on Mt Waialeale in the Hawaiian Islands. On the windward side of this mountain barrier annual rainfall is 1170 cm year⁻¹. In the lee, annual rainfall totals 81 cm. A spectacular *orographic cloud* produced by the forced ascent of warm, moisture-laden air, is the 'Table cloth' cloud of Cape Town's Table mountain in South Africa.

A rather special type of orographic cloud is the *lee-wave cloud*, formed best where stable air lies sandwiched between less stable layers. Mountains lying at 90° to the path of moist winds cause air to rise into the stable layer overlying them, and the stable layer in turn pushes the air down into the

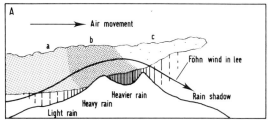

Figure 9.7 A A topographic barrier acts as a trigger action forcing air to rise and cool (a). Once the condensation level is reached precipitation falls. This is usually heaviest on the windward side of the summit (b). Note how the cloud base rises in the lee of the mountain (c) as absolute humidity decreases. Rainfall here is lower than on the windward side. This is the rain shadow effect, often associated with a dry descending föhn wind.
(Source: D. E. Pedgley, 1967, 'Weather in the mountains', *Weather*, 22, p. 270.)

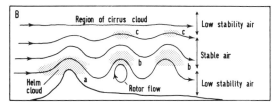

Figure 9.7 B Lee waves form best if the area behind the mountains is flat, in which case standing waves may develop with clouds perched on top of each wave crest where it reaches condensation level.
(a) Föhn wind effect.
(b) Roll clouds.
(c) Altocumulus lenticularis cloud.
(Source: C. E. Wallington, 1970, 'An introduction to lee waves in the atmosphere', *Weather*, 15, p. 270.)

unstable layer from where it once more tends to rise. A wave-type motion is thus set up in the lee of the mountain (Figure 9.7 B). From below, lee-wave clouds may appear as long parallel bands of altocumulus cloud separated by clear sky.

Classification of clouds is usually done on a basis of height. Three groups are recognized:
1 high clouds above 6000 m;
2 medium cloud between 3000 and 6000 m;
3 low cloud below 3000 m.
The principal types of cloud are illustrated in Figure 9.8.

Fog can be called a form of low level cloud, and two basic types can be recognized:
1 those resulting from cooling; and
2 those resulting from evaporation.
The first category includes radiation fog, advection fog, upslope fog, mixing fog and barometric fog

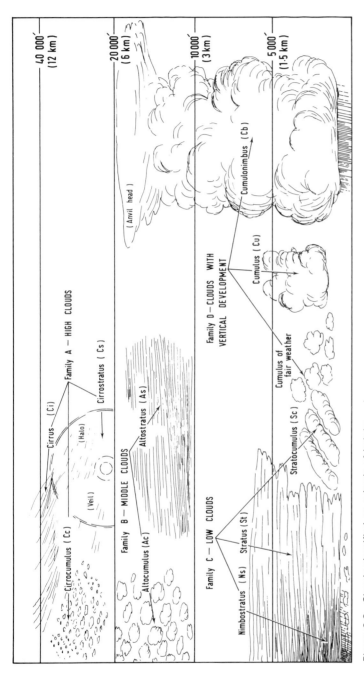

Figure 9.8 Clouds classified on a basis of height and
form.
(Source: A. N. Strahler, p. 99.)

see Critchfield). *Radiation fog* results from the nocturnal cooling of moisture by terrestrial radiation. A low level temperature inversion encourages its development and it is therefore a feature of land but not sea areas. *Advection fogs* occur when warm moist air crosses a colder surface. They are best developed along arid tropical coastlines such as the Chile coast where warm air crosses a cold offshore current, in this case the Humboldt current. They also form off the east coast of Britain in early summer when warm moist air from Scandinavia crosses the cold North Sea. This fog is called the *haar. Upslope fog* is produced by gradual uplift of air up mountain sides. Too much turbulence converts this fog into low stratus cloud. *Mixing fog* occurs when warm moist air and cool moist air, neither of them saturated, combine to produce a mixture of humidity and temperature appropriate for condensation. Mixing fog is common at fronts. *Barometric fog* is produced when pressure drops without uplift and moist air cools adiabatically to produce condensation. Like radiation fog it develops best in valleys. Fogs in the second of Critchfield's two categories are of two types. *Steam fog* or *sea smoke* occurs when warm water evaporates into very cold air and *frontal fog* forms when rain, formed along a front, descends through warm dry air underneath the cloud and evaporates only to condense again in cold air below the front.

A special type of fog forms in cities when fog and smoke are mixed together. The result is smog. A particularly unpleasant form of smog is called *photochemical smog*. This type of urban pollution affects cities with very large numbers of cars and long periods of sunlight. It will be recalled that at high temperatures, such as in the exhaust gases of automobiles, nitrogen is very active chemically and combines with oxygen to produce nitrogen dioxide (NO_2). This compound is responsible for the yellowish-brown appearance of air in cities like Los Angeles. Once NO_2 is produced high energy ultraviolet radiation comes into effect (see Chapter 1). It removes oxygen atoms from the NO_2 molecule and these oxygen atoms (O) combine with oxygen in the atmosphere (O_2) to produce ozone (O_3) which is thought to be a possible cause of bronchitis and reduced breathing capacity. Eye-burning compounds and other irritants are also produced in associated chemical processes which follow the splitting of the NO_2

molecule. Altogether photochemical smog is an environmental nuisance. It damages vegetation, reduces visibility and causes ill health.

PRECIPITATION

Precipitation takes many forms: rainfall, snow, hail, dew, frost. Daily rainfall in the UK is measured in a standard Meteorological Office copper rain-gauge 12.7 cm (5 in) in diameter and 30.5 cm (12 in) high. There are some 6000 such gauges in Britain at a density of about 1 gauge per 40 km². Many tests are currently being undertaken to determine what effect different types of rain-gauge installation have on the rainfall recorded (Figure 9.9).

Figure 9.9 Four rain gauges installed at one site to compare catches. In the foreground is a gauge made of PVC tubing to standard Meteorological Office dimensions. Behind is a ground-level gauge. Here a copper rain gauge is located in a shallow pit with its orifice at ground level. A metal grid covers the pit to prevent any rainfall splashing into the gauge. The grid also simulates the roughness of natural grass. This gauge represents an attempt to measure rainfall actually reaching the ground as opposed to some imaginary surface 30.5 cm above it. The third gauge is the standard type of installation throughout the UK. The fourth gauge consists of a standard copper gauge surrounded by a turf wall which cuts down turbulence around the gauge. This is a standard type of installation at windy sites. To date, in the experiment shown above, the ground-level gauge has caught most rainfall, followed by the turf-wall gauge, the standard gauge and the PVC gauge in that order.

Rainfall distribution

Mean annual precipitation over the globe is difficult to estimate and different figures are quoted. Critchfield, for example, quotes a figure of 86 cm while Penman puts it higher at 100 cm. Rainfall is heavy along the intertropical convergence zone where trade winds meet and also along the polar front. These are the two major zones of low-level air convergence in the atmosphere and unstable vertical motion is common. Rainfall is low at the poles and over the subtropical high pressure belts where atmospheric subsidence occurs and stability is common. Windward coastal zones tend to have larger rainfall totals than continental interiors and leeward coasts in the same latitude because onshore winds bring moist air off the sea. If offshore ocean currents are warm, absolute humidity is relatively high before the air is uplifted at the coast and rainfall tends to be heavy. Cold offshore currents tend to induce fog, low coastal humidities and therefore low rainfall.

Within this very generalized pattern of world-wide rainfall there is immense variation, both in space and time. Rainfall totals are very high in monsoon India, where Cherrapunji has the world's highest annual, six-monthly and monthly rainfall totals. These are respectively 26 461 mm (1042 in), 22 454 mm (884 in), and 9300 mm (366 in). The world's largest daily rainfall, 1870 mm (74 in) was recorded at Reunion Island in the Indian Ocean. For comparison, the highest daily rainfall recorded in Britain was at Dorchester in July 1955 when 280 mm (11 in) fell.

Droughts

Rainfall can be very variable from year to year and even in a very moist country like Britain dry spells are not uncommon. In Britain a drought is officially defined as a period of 15 days, none of which records more than 0.2 mm of rain. The last prolonged drought in Britain occurred in 1975 and 1976. The period from May 1975 to August 1976 was the driest 16-month period since records began in Britain in 1727, and rainfall over England and Wales was only 64% of the long-term average. A 16-month period as dry as this and ending in August can be expected only once in 1000 years. The drought was most intense in the summer of 1976 when only 36% of long-term average rainfall fell between June 1st and August 31st (Figure 9.10). A 3-month period as dry as this can be expected in Britain only once in 300 years

according to the Government's Central Water Planning Unit (see Doornkamp and Gregory).

Cloud seeding

In many parts of the world aridity is the norm and efforts have been made to induce rainfall by *cloud seeding*. The two theories on rainfall formation discussed earlier suggest that clouds can exist without rainfall if ice crystals (in the case of cold clouds) or large supercooled droplets (in the case of warm clouds) are not available to initiate rain drop formation. Silver iodide crystals, injected into clouds from aircraft or released from ground level burners, can cause ice crystals to form at temperatures as high as $-4\,°C$. This seeding technique is therefore popular in cold clouds which reach high altitudes. In the case of shallower thinner, clouds oversized droplets are introduced at the base from an aeroplane, to start coalescence. Cloud seeding was first practised in 1946 when two American scientists, Langmuir and Schaeffer dropped dry ice (solid CO_2) into the top of a supercooled cloud to initiate ice crystal formation. Cloud seeding is now widely practised in the semi-arid areas of south-western USA as part of large-scale irrigation projects. Claims are made that seeding with silver iodide can increase rainfall by up to 15%. These claims are difficult to assess for it can never be proved that rain which falls after seeding would not have fallen naturally anyway.

Urban precipitation

On a local scale cities can affect precipitation. We have already examined the heat-island effect, and this can exist during the day as well as at night. Its effect at daytime is to increase convection over the city. Cities also produce abundant quantities of dust and are often covered by a *dust dome*, a pall of suspended particles from industry and cars which provides innumerable condensation nuclei. In Illinois one study has shown that average annual rainfall between 1949 and 1967 was 12.4% more over a city (Champaign–Urbana) than over the surrounding countryside, while the Metropolitan Meteorological Experiment (METROMEX) in St Louis, USA suggests that summer rainfall totals are 20% in excess of those in surrounding

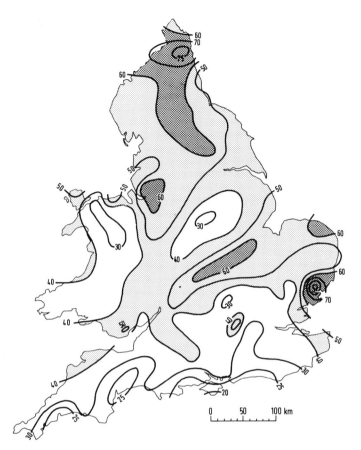

Figure 9.10 Rainfall in England and Wales during the period April 1976 to August 1976 expressed as a percentage of long-term average rainfall in this 5-month period. The drought was most severe in south and south-west England, Nottinghamshire–Lincoln-shire, and central Wales. (Source: *1975–76 Drought: A Hydrological Review*, Central Water Planning Unit, Reading, Technical Note 17, 1976, p. 19.)

areas and condensation nuclei far more abundant (Atkinson, 1978). In central London between 1952 and 1960 rainfall from thunderstorms was 43% more than in neighbouring areas at the same altitude and was attributed by Atkinson (1979) to the heat island, the availability of condensation nuclei, higher urban humidity, and greater rough-ness of the city's ground surface. Considering the lack of vegetation in cities and the rapid run-off from impervious surfaces it may come as a surprise that absolute humidities in cities can be higher than outside. Higher absolute humidities in urban

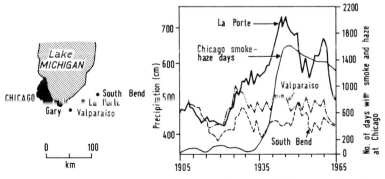

Figure 9.11 Annual rainfall totals over a 60-year period in three towns south-east of Lake Michigan and their relationship to the number of smoke-haze days in the Chicago–Gary area. Valparaiso and South Bend, unlike La Porte, lie outside the path of the pollution plume from Chicago–Gary. Between 1951 and 1965 precipitation at La Porte was 31% greater than in surrounding areas. Thunderstorms and hail storms were respectively 38% and 246% more frequent. (Source: S. A. Changnon, 1968, 'The La Porte weather anomaly—fact or fiction', *Bulletin of the American Meteorological Society*, 49, p. 5.)

areas, however, are now well documented, and result from various forms of human activity such as industrial processing, transport, and domestic washing. Relative humidities, however, are lower than in surrounding areas because temperatures in the city are higher.

With wind speeds at or above 13 km h^{-1} dust is blown downwind and the dust dome becomes a *dust plume*. A study in Indiana, USA, showed that dust plumes from the Chicago–Gary industrial area could extend 50 km downwind to La Porte. Here rainfall has increased dramatically since 1925 even though similar increases have not occurred in neighbouring towns outside the plume (Figure 9.11). Annual rainfall totals at La Porte increased in direct relation to steel output in the Chicago area, strongly suggesting that rainfall here is affected by man's artificial production of condensation nuclei.

10

The Atmosphere in Motion

ACTORS AFFECTING WIND

Pressure

Winds are affected by three factors: atmospheric pressure, earth rotation and friction. The atmosphere behaves very much like a fluid and its weight exerts a pressure on the earth's surface, which in SI units is expressed in Newtons per square metre ($N m^{-2}$). More conventionally, it is measured in units called *millibars*. A millibar is a force of 1000 dynes cm^{-2} and average atmospheric pressure is 1013.2 mb. One millibar is 100 $N m^{-2}$ or 100 pascals. Pressure is not uniform over the earth's surface but it only varies slightly from place to place. High pressures rarely exceed 1040 mb and low pressure is seldom less than 960 mb. This range, only about 8% of average atmospheric pressure, is nevertheless sufficient to initiate large and small-scale horizontal air movements.

In zones of high pressure (anticyclones) the subsidence of the overlying atmosphere forces air to diverge at ground level (Figure 10.1 A) and move outwards towards areas of low pressure. Low pressure areas surrounded by high pressure zones thus become areas of ground level convergence, and there is a net movement of air across isobars at low altitude from high to low pressure at a speed which is dependent on the pressure gradient. The closer together isobars are on a weather map the stronger is the *pressure gradient force*. Winds are strong in such circumstances. Widely spaced isobars, conversely, indicate a low pressure gradient force and gentle winds.

The Coriolis force

Although winds might be expected to move from high to low pressure straight across isobars, they never actually behave in this way. High above the earth's surface, in fact, they move parallel to isobars (Figure 10.1 B I). At ground level they move obliquely across the isobars at varying angles but always towards low pressure (Figure 10.1 B II). The wind which blows parallel to straight isobars is called the *geostrophic wind* and is clearly the product of a pressure gradient force and some other force as well. This other force is the *Coriolis force* which results from the earth's west to east rotation and always acts at *90° to the direction of motion*. The magnitude of the Coriolis force increases with wind speed. A wind which blows parallel to curved isobars is called a *gradient wind*.

Friction

Towards ground level the uneven nature of the earth's surface introduces a third force affecting atmospheric motion. This force is friction and its effect is to progressively reduce the speed of any wind as altitude decreases. Geostrophic wind speeds are therefore higher than wind speeds associated with the same pressure system at ground level. As wind speed towards ground level is reduced so too is the Coriolis deflection, and at ground level the combined reduction of wind velocity and of the Coriolis force has the effect of causing winds to be deflected obliquely across isobars in the direction of the pressure gradient force (Figure 10.1 B II). The angle of deflection across isobars is about 30° over land surfaces.

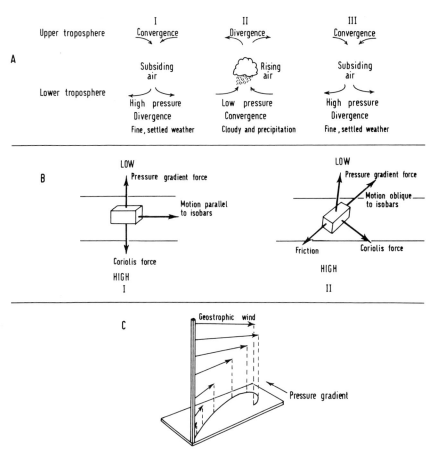

Figure 10.1 A   How convergence and divergence are inter-related in the upper and lower troposphere. (I) and (III) represent anticyclonic conditions. (II) represents cyclonic conditions.

Figure 10.1 B   (I) Air motion parallel to the isobars occurs everywhere in the troposphere except at very low levels and close to the equator. The balance of forces necessary to produce the geostrophic wind is shown here. In the case of the geostrophic wind the Coriolis

force, which always acts at right angles to the direction in which a body is moving, must act in a direction exactly opposite to that of the pressure gradient force. Near the ground friction affects moving air and the three forces in (II) are balanced only when parcels of air move from high to low pressure and cross isobars obliquely.

Figure 10.1 C   The Ekman spiral.
(Modified from R. G. Barry and R. J. Chorley, p. 137.)

Over the sea, where friction is lower, the angle of deflection is about 15°. The relationship between wind direction and isobaric pattern is summarized in *Buys Ballot's law* which states that if you stand with your back to the wind in the northern hemisphere the low pressure is on your left-hand side. In the southern hemisphere it would be on your right.

   The change of wind direction with height as friction effects decrease (Figure 10.1 C) is similar to the change in ocean current direction with depth beneath the ocean surface. W. V. Ekman, a Swedish oceanographer, was the first to establish that ocean currents have spirals of deflection beneath the ocean surface, and deflection spirals

in the atmosphere as well as in the ocean are now called *Ekman spirals*. In the oceans, frictional effects decrease with depth until at a depth of about 100 m ocean currents in the northern hemisphere flow at 90° to the right of winds generating them. We shall refer later to the oceanic Ekman spiral and its significance in oceanic circulation.

   Of the three forces affecting wind speed and direction the Coriolis force is the most difficult to understand. It is usually explained with reference to a rotating turntable as shown in Figure 10.2. This 'explanation' is superficially useful but it ignores the fact that the earth is not a flat disc but a sphere. It also fails to offer any physical reasons

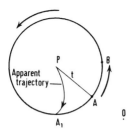

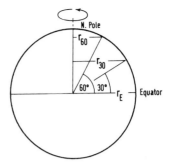

Figure 10.2 Imagine an object thrown by a person from the centre of a turntable P to another person at the edge of the table A. The turntable rotates anticlockwise and in the time taken for the ball to reach the edge of the turntable along the line PAO, A's position moves to B and A₁ moves to A. Although the ball has been thrown in a straight line relative to the earth and to any observer it appears to the people at P and A to have been deflected to the right, i.e. toward A₁. In real life we are on the rotating earth and we therefore receive the equivalent images of people at P and A. Only somebody in space would see things moving in straight lines relative to their points of departure.

Figure 10.3 The distance from the earth's axis of rotation to the bottom of the atmosphere (*r*) decreases with increasing latitude. At the poles of course *r* is zero. Here the Coriolis effect is at a maximum.

for the apparent deflection. A more scientific explanation of the Coriolis effect involves a very important principle of physics: *the law of conservation of angular momentum*. The momentum of a body was originally used by Newton to measure the amount of motion it contained. Momentum is the product of the body's mass and velocity. The conservation of momentum law states that the total momentum of a body stays constant unless it is changed by an external force. A sphere rotating on an axis has angular momentum rather than straight-line momentum such as a moving train would possess, and the earth's angular momentum is the product of its mass, its angular velocity (i.e. the number of degrees it turns through per second) and its radius of curvature. The product of all three remains constant in the absence of any outside force.

Consider now a parcel of air moving north in the northern hemisphere. In order to conserve angular momentum in the rotating atmosphere and in the absence of any change in its mass, the air parcel's angular velocity has to increase as the distance of the earth's atmosphere from the earth's axis of rotation progressively decreases with latitude (Figure 10.3). The parcel is thus progressively deflected to its right by the west-to-east rotation of the earth. In the southern hemisphere a parcel of air moving poleward is deflected to its left. Conversely, a parcel of air moving south in the northern hemisphere progressively invades parts

of the atmosphere which are further away from the earth's axis of rotation. The west-to-east angular velocity of the atmosphere in low latitudes is lower than in higher latitudes and the invading parcel of air is thus slowed down and deflected towards the west, i.e. to its right. Air moving northward in the southern hemisphere is deflected to its left for the same reason. This deflection of all moving bodies to their right in the northern hemisphere and to their left in the southern hemisphere is known as *Ferrel's law*, after Ferrel who first observed the effect.

The conservation of angular momentum provides an incomplete explanation of the Coriolis effect since it can only apply to air moving from one latitude to another. It would not explain, for example, why a parcel of air moving along a line of latitude, and therefore not invading parts of the atmosphere with different angular velocity, is also deflected to its right in the northern hemisphere and to its left in the southern hemisphere. Clearly the real physical explanation of the Coriolis effect is very complex and ultimately involves a very considerable ability in mathematics. Too much non-quantitative description on this particular topic is dangerous. As Hare has noted in his book *The Restless Atmosphere*: 'To try to visualize the physical explanation for this curious force . . . is to run the risk of hopeless confusion.' (Hare, 1961, p. 50.)

We shall therefore not examine the Coriolis force any further. One last point about the three forces affecting winds, however, is worth emphasizing. The student might be forgiven for thinking that wind is initially created by a pressure gradient force, is then deflected by the Coriolis

121

force, and finally slowed down by friction. This is not the case. The three forces do not act in any chronological order but simultaneously, and it is their simultaneous interaction that makes the study of atmospheric motion so complex.

SCALES OF ATMOSPHERIC MOTION

Wind is evidence of the atmosphere in motion, and four scales of motion can be recognized (Table 10.1). In very large, or primary, atmospheric circulation systems vertical motion is slow, less than 3 mm s^{-1}. For this reason it is often said that the primary circulation of the atmosphere is basically horizontal. At local level vertical motion can be intense as in tornadoes. Vertical motion is thus inversely related to the horizontal scale of the circulation system. Before looking at the four scales of motion in more detail it is important to define what wind really is. In calm conditions the atmosphere is usually described as still. This is not strictly true, for in calm conditions the atmosphere revolves at the same speed as the underlying earth. It thus only appears still relative to the motion of the earth. All winds, in fact, are relative. West winds, for example, occur when the atmosphere moves from west to east at a faster rate than that of the underlying earth. East winds occur when the earth moves from west to east faster than the atmosphere. In these conditions the

wind appears to move from east to west. But remember that in all conditions the atmosphere is moving from west to east. It moves in this direction, of course, because it is gravitationally tied to the earth and to the earth's rotation.

PRIMARY CIRCULATION

The basic pattern of global surface pressure and winds is shown in idealized form in Figure 10.4 A. Surface winds blow from the subtropical highs towards the equator, being deflected by earth rotation to right and left of the pressure gradient force in the northern and southern hemispheres respectively. These winds are the north-east and south-east *trade winds* which meet at the *inter tropical convergence zone* (ITCZ), the mean position of which varies throughout the year (Figure 10.4 B). The vertical movement of air near the equator produces a low pressure zone known as the *equatorial trough*. In Figure 10.4 A this low pressure zone is shown on the equator but its position varies as the vertical sun migrates between the Tropics of Cancer and Capricorn. The ITCZ moves with the trough and is always located in it. Being an area of convection, the equatorial trough is an area of vertical rather than horizontal air motion. Winds here are therefore weak and are called the doldrums.

Table 10.1. Scales of atmospheric motion (Modified from Sutton, O. G., 1962, *The Challenge of the Atmosphere* p. 46, Hutchinson)

Rank	Horizontal scale	Systems	Operational significance
Primary	Very large (thousands of km)	General circulation (Trade winds, Continental anticyclones) Long waves	Long-range forecasts (month or more ahead)
Secondary	Large (thousands to hundreds of km)	Weather-producing systems (depressions, small anticyclones)	Short- and extended-range forecasts (day or two ahead)
Tertiary	Medium (tens of km)	Meso-scale disturbances (thunderstorms, tornadoes)	Very short-range forecasts and warnings
Local	Very small (km or m)	Eddies (local winds, frosts)	Advisory services for agriculture

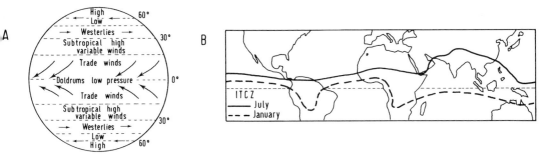

Figure 10.4A Surface winds and pressure as they would exist on a featureless earth. The increasingly strong Coriolis effect towards the poles causes winds in mid- and high-latitudes to blow parallel to lines of latitude, in contrast to the trades.

Figure 10.4B Position of the ITCZ in July and January. (Source: R. A. Muller, p. 112.)

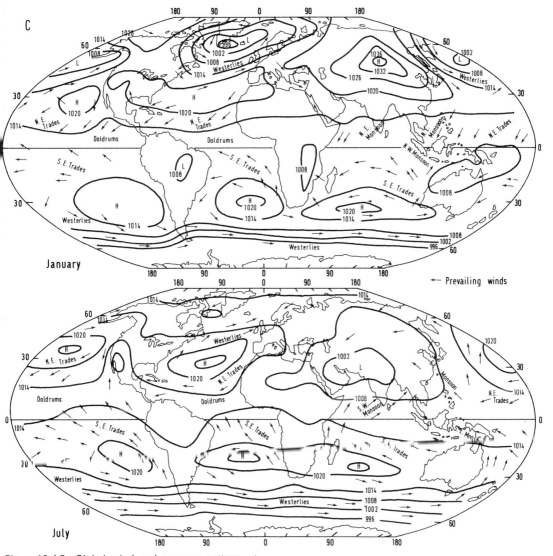

Figure 10.4C Global wind and pressure patterns at ground level in January and July.
(Source: R. A. Muller, p. 112.)

Air subsiding on the poleward margin of the tropical Hadley cell produces the subtropical high pressure belts. Here, subsiding air moves towards the equator as the trade winds and away from, or parallel to, the equator as the *mid-latitude westerlies*. These latter winds, which are far less constant in behaviour than the trades and tend to be more nearly geostrophic, are best defined over the vast expanse of mid-latitudinal ocean in the southern hemisphere (Figure 10.4 C). In the northern hemisphere the distribution of continents disrupts westerly airflows in mid-latitudes. Winds blowing outward from subsiding air over the poles are deflected towards the west, like the trades, and are known as the *polar easterlies*.

The ideal pattern of global surface winds shown in Figure 10.4 A rarely exists in reality partly because of seasonal changes in the sun's vertical position and partly because of the distribution of continents, oceans, and relief. The ideal pattern is, in fact, partly derived from observation and partly from considerations of physics. A very interesting and important physical consideration is the need for the sum total of westerly air movement over the globe's surface to balance the sum total of easterly flow. Too much easterly flow, for example, would slow the earth's rotation by frictional forces between the earth and atmosphere!

Figure 10.4 C shows wind patterns as they really are for January and July. In January the ITCZ moves southward in South America, Africa and Australia, producing low pressure cells in these areas. The south-east trades tend to blow towards these areas at this time of year. With the thermal equator in January over the Tropic of Capricorn the large continental areas of the northern hemisphere become very cold and a particularly large continental anticyclone develops over Eurasia, almost merging the subtropical and polar high pressure areas into one. Around the eastern margins of this anticyclone winds blow southward in those precise latitudes that we might expect eastward-moving air to exist. This is a good example of how continents distort the ideal pattern of atmospheric circulation, and we shall have more to say about the Eurasian winter anticyclone when we discuss the south-east Asia monsoon.

The situation changes in summer as the thermal equator moves over the Tropic of Cancer. Now the ITCZ moves into south-east Asia as the Eurasian continent warms up and a large area of low pressure builds up here. The effects of the northern hemisphere's continents on temperature distribution in July are shown in Figure 10.4 C. Along the 30th parallel occurs an alternating succession of very well-developed high and low pressure areas. The highs occur over the oceans, the lows over the continents. Compare this picture with the ideal pattern shown in Figure 10.4 A.

The upper atmosphere's role in the primary circulation

In Chapter 8 we saw that radiosonde evidence is not easily able to define upper atmospheric circulation outside the Hadley cell. Nevertheless, until quite recently most climatologists still accepted the basic notion of three vertical circulation cells in each hemisphere.

More recent views on the causes of primary circulation in the atmosphere play down the importance of vertical circulation cells of the type proposed by Hadley, Ferrel and others. In particular, the existence of cells in mid- and high-latitudes is now emphasized less than it used to be although the Hadley cell is still regarded as a fundamental part of atmospheric circulation. The mechanisms of energy transfer from low to high latitudes are still not perfectly understood, but the role of horizontal heat energy transfer in the atmosphere is now believed to be more important than the role of vertical cells. It has already been stressed that on a global scale atmospheric motion is basically horizontal and that there are very few areas of pronounced vertical movement. Another characteristic of atmospheric motion in the lower troposphere is that, apart from the trade winds of intertropical areas, flow is basically zonal (i.e. parallel to lines of latitude). There is relatively little meridional flow (i.e. along lines of longitude). Zonal flow, as we have seen, becomes increasingly pronounced with increasing latitude and it is a weakness in the three-cell model of atmospheric circulation that net flow in the mid-latitudes now appears to be westerly, not south-westerly (and therefore poleward) as reported by masters of early sailing ships. Poleward-moving air in mid-latitudes and equatorward-moving air in high latitudes are integral parts of atmospheric circulation in traditional three-cell models, and serve to ransfer equatorial heat energy poleward and to return cold air towards the equator. Westerly zonal winds in mid-latitudes and easterlies in high latitudes are not effective mechanisms for transferring excess heat from low to high latitudes or for returning cold air towards the equator, and meteorologists have therefore begun to search elsewhere for alternative mechanisms by which the necessary energy transfers might be brought about.

A feature of global circulation discovered only in the last 40 years is the presence of wave-like disturbances in the upper troposphere poleward of the tropics. These waves were first studied successfully by Rossby and are called *long waves* or *Rossby waves*. The waves appear to be generated by interaction between air in the middle troposphere and high topographic barriers, principally the Rockies and Andes. To the east of the Rockies, for example, middle tropospheric air moves south-eastward, later to recurve north-eastward. This motion initiates a set of waves

(typically 4 or 5 in number) which encircle the earth poleward of the Tropic of Cancer. These wave patterns appear to have a complete life cycle of about 6 weeks. The cycle is called the *index cycle* and is described in Figure 10.5. The sequence of events in the cycle is still imperfectly understood although Rossby believed that the breakdown of the cells is associated with the poleward movement of moist tropical air into the middle and high latitudes (Crowe, p. 179). Such movements are now thought to be an important mechanism in transferring equatorial heat energy poleward and returning cold air towards the equator. High and low index circulation patterns over Britain and Ireland are shown in Figure 10.6.

Jet streams are very much associated with long waves and were first observed when jet aircraft began to fly at heights of 9 km or more and speeds became unaccountably fast or slow in certain narrow, well-defined, corridors of high-velocity air. There are two well-defined jet streams, one more or less along the line of the polar fronts

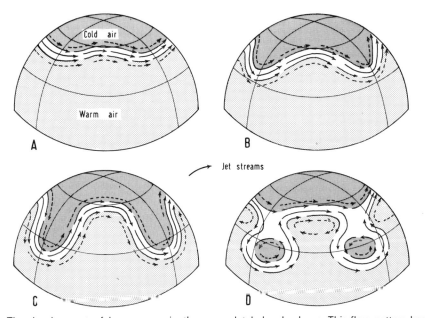

Figure 10.5 The development of long waves in the upper and middle atmosphere of the northern hemisphere. In (A) a cell of cold air lies over the pole and the four or five waves which girdle the globe at about latitude 55 °N are not very pronounced. Atmospheric circulation in these conditions is very much along lines of latitude, and is said to have a high 'zonal index'. In (B) and (C) the zonal index decreases as waves increase in amplitude. Flow now becomes increasingly meridional. Jet stream velocities increase. In (D) cells of rotating warm and cold air are formed. Zonal flow com-

pletely breaks down. This flow pattern has a low zonal index. In (D) the meridional flow transfers cold air southwards and warm air northwards. This is thought to be an important mechanism in the redistribution of incoming solar energy. With the breakdown of the cells in (D) circulation returns to the path shown in (A). Notice how high index flow paths occupy a narrow latitudinal zone and low index patterns stretch down into intertropical latitudes.
(Source: R. A. Muller, p. 122; after Namias.)

A

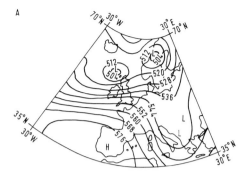

B

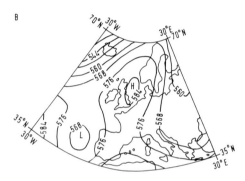

Figure 10.6 (A) High index zonal flow over Britain and Ireland at an altitude of about 5 km (i.e. at 500 mb level), December 1979; and (B) low index meridional flow over Britain and Ireland at 500 mb, August 1976. (Source: N. Betts, 1982, 'Climate' in *Northern Ireland: Environment and Natural Resources*, J. G. Cruikshank and D. N. Wilcock (eds), Queen's University Belfast and New University of Ulster, 1–42.)

wherever they might be at any particular time. The other, the subtropical jet, has a more defined location and lies on the poleward edge of the Hadley cell. Remember that both are features of the upper troposphere only, and both move west to east. A third jet stream, moving east-west, forms in southern Asia during summer. The jet streams, and there are other smaller jets elsewhere in the upper troposphere, are most frequently likened to rivers of fast-flowing air. They may be several kilometres thick and speeds of over 300 km h^{-1} have been recorded in their centres. The origin of the polar jet is linked to the strong temperature contrast associated with the underlying fronts and its principal meteorological importance seems to lie in its relationship with surface depressions. We shall examine these relationships later.

Oceanic circulation

The oceans and atmosphere are so inter-related that it is now appropriate to examine the major features of oceanic circulation. This takes two forms, horizontal and vertical, although as in the atmosphere horizontal motion is dominant. Horizontal circulation is controlled by the winds but because water is denser than air the oceanic circulation is slower. Because oceanic circulation mirrors that of the atmosphere, the ocean, like the atmosphere, can be described as a great heat engine with warm tropical water transferring heat energy poleward while cold polar water is transferred equatorward.

The pattern of ocean currents in a perfectly symmetrical ocean basin would be like that shown in Figure 10.7 A. Each hemisphere would contain three closed loops or *gyres* controlled by the three major surface wind systems. In reality the distribution of continents destroys any idealistic circulation of oceanic water and the three gyres are confined to the Atlantic and Pacific oceans which alone have sufficient north-south extent for their maximum development. Even here, however, the three gyres are not precisely defined (Figure 10.7 B).

A notable feature of oceanic circulation is that west coasts below the 30° line of latitude are characterized by cold currents (e.g. the California current and the Benguela current) while east coasts in these latitudes receive the westward-flowing warm waters of the equatorial currents. Poleward of about latitude 45° the position is reversed. West coasts experience the warm waters of the North Atlantic Drift and the North Pacific current while east coasts suffer the effects of cold currents originating in polar waters (e.g. the Labrador current and the Kamchatka current). The deflection of warm tropical waters eastward across the north Pacific and Atlantic oceans is a product of westerly winds in these latitudes and (to a lesser extent) of continental distribution, while the cold east coast currents of high latitudes are principally a reflection of circumpolar easterlies. Ocean currents, like winds, are subject to the Coriolis effect and are deflected to their right in the northern hemisphere and to their left in the southern hemisphere.

The oceans also have a vertical circulation called the *thermohaline circulation* (see Stewart, p. 36).

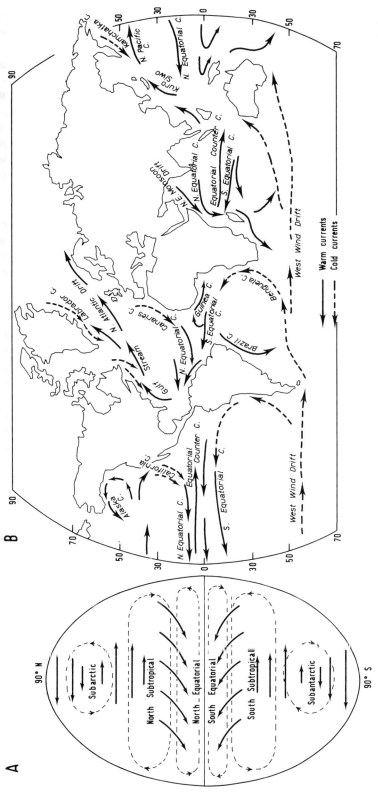

B

Figure 10.7 B Actual oceanic circulation around the globe.
(Modified from H. J. Critchfield, p. 98.)

Warm currents ——→
Cold currents --→

A

Figure 10.7 A Oceanic circulation (broken lines) on a featureless earth. Solid lines are ideal surface winds.
(Source: R. A. Muller, p. 127; after Weyl.)

90° N

Subarctic

North Subtropical

North Equatorial

South Equatorial

South Subtropical

Subantarctic

90° S

This is controlled by density which in turn is controlled by temperature and salinity. Normally, the top few metres of surface water are warmer than the vast body of water beneath because they are warmed by insolation. This vertical distribution of temperature makes the oceans very stable and vertical circulation is slower than in the atmosphere. Because the atmosphere is warmed principally from below this gives it a natural instability the oceans do not possess.

The physical processes governing oceanic circulation are interesting. Like evaporation, freezing increases salinity because although water molecules change state (from liquid to solid) at 0 °C salt does not. Oceanic water in the polar seas therefore has a relatively high density due to its high salinity and so sinks. Because it is so cold and so far removed from solar heat it remains at the ocean bottom for centuries, probably for thousands of years.

To compensate this polar sinking there are other areas where cold water systematically upwells to the surface. Often this is due to the oceanic Ekman spiral discussed earlier, and described at length by Stewart. Off the coasts of California and Chile, for example, surface winds deflected by north-south trending mountains tend to blow parallel with the coast and towards the equator. Within the top 100 m of water the effects of friction decrease and the direction of oceanic flow is affected by wind direction and the Coriolis force. The Coriolis effect always acts at 90° to the direction of motion and oceanic flow within the 'Ekman layer' appears to be principally governed by this effect. Along the California and Chile coasts, therefore, warm surface waters are swept away from the coast and replaced by cold water from below. Off the coasts of both California and Chile, and elsewhere where this effect is observed, the upwelling cold water is rich in nutrients and sustains a great variety of sea life, which in turn often supports a dense seabird population.

Of all the world's ocean currents the Gulf Stream is perhaps the most famous. Like its Pacific equivalent, the Kuro Siwo, the Gulf Stream is a narrow, meandering, fast-moving body of water. According to Muller, it transports 30 times the volume of water in the world's rivers and glaciers. Water in the Gulf Stream continues its journey across the Atlantic as the North Atlantic Drift. This latter current transports warm water originating in the Gulf of Mexico towards north-west Europe, where it ensures relatively high winter temperatures and ice-free coastal waters. The North Atlantic Drift lies at the junction of cold polar waters to the north and warmer tropical waters to the south and as a concentrated line of relatively fast, and mainly zonal, flow in an otherwise slowly circulating body of fluid, it has characteristics not unlike that of the polar jet stream in the atmosphere.

Two particularly interesting and potentially most significant features of the Gulf Stream are the *cold-* and *warm-core rings* that develop from meanders in the Gulf Stream itself. Study of these rings is only in its infancy but their development appears quite well understood. Cold-core rings form when overdeveloped meanders in the Gulf Stream are 'pinched off' at their necks and trap cold water from the North American continental slope in their centres before drifting southward into the Sargasso Sea. Warm rings form by the same process but this time warm water from south of the Gulf Stream is trapped in the centre of a meander developing on the north side of the Gulf Stream itself. The warm ring then drifts northward towards the North American coast. Cold rings have anticlockwise circulation and warm rings have clockwise (anticyclonic) circulation (Figure 10.8). Warm rings are thought to be an important mechanism transferring heat energy poleward, while cold rings are a compensating mechanism transferring cold water equatorward. One estimate states that the heat energy annually carried northward by rings across the Gulf Stream is the approximate equivalent of all the solar radiation reaching the north-western quadrant of the Sargasso Sea. Infrared satellite measurements which are now able to detect global heat flow suggest that these intermediate-scale eddies are probably the most important mechanism of oceanic heat transport between equator and pole.

Oceans are thus important in several respects. Their waters sustain the hydrological cycle (see Chapter 2). They are an important vehicle for the redistribution of heat energy on earth. They heat up and cool down slowly and thus ameliorate climatic extremes on coastal margins. They are also the birthplace of large air masses, which are secondary features of atmospheric circulation and conveniently introduce us to the next section.

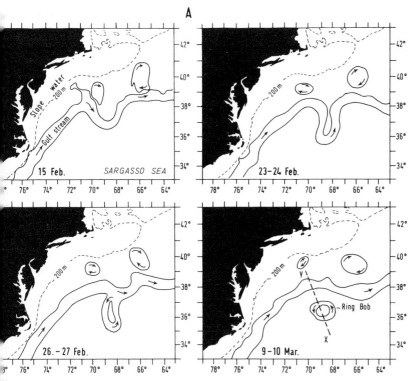

Figure 10.8 A The formation of warm- and cold-core rings in the Gulf Stream. The diagrams were compiled from infrared satellite images and show two warm-core rings north of the Gulf Stream and one cold-core ring (Ring Bob) to the south.

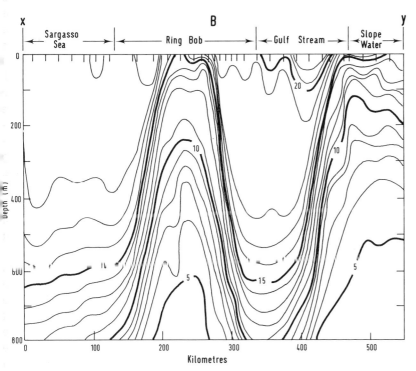

Figure 10.8 B Vertical temperature profiles along section XY. The lines on this diagram join points of equal temperature (°C). Note that Gulf Stream surface water is 6 °C warmer than on the continental slope and in Ring Bob. At a depth of 600 m temperature contrasts are even greater and Gulf Stream water is 10 °C warmer than water on either side.
(Source: (A and B) The Ring Group, 1981, 'Gulf Stream cold-core rings: their physics, chemistry and biology', *Science*, Vol. 212, p. 1093.)

SECONDARY FEATURES OF ATMOSPHERIC CIRCULATION

Air masses

Air masses are large portions of the lower troposphere with more or less uniform temperature and moisture characteristics. They develop over large oceanic or continental areas during anticyclonic conditions. In anticyclones slow atmospheric subsidence occurs and the subsiding air diverges at the earth's surface. Gently diverging air in the lower troposphere gradually assumes the temperature and moisture properties of the surface beneath. When this is uniform, as over large expanses of ocean or continent, air masses develop.

Air masses are classified by their source of origin. The lower case letters 'c' and 'm' indicate continental and maritime sources respectively. Upper case letters indicate source region thus: tropical (T), equatorial (E), polar (P), and Arctic (A). Thus mT air originates in the tropics over an ocean.

Anticyclones are very stable features of the troposphere but air eventually moves out from the source regions and becomes an *air stream*. Air masses are modified as they move out from their source areas. When a warm air mass passes over a cold surface, for example, its environmental lapse rate (ELR) is made less steep near the ground surface, and the lower atmosphere therefore becomes more stable. Weather in such an air stream is generally uneventful. Such surface cooling affects mT air moving north-eastward towards Britain in May and June and often produces fog in south-west England. Instability and a steep ELR result when cold air streams pass over a warm surface. This occurs in the north-east Atlantic when cool mP air moves southward over warmer waters. Instability is triggered off by the western hills of Britain and Ireland, and cumulus clouds with their characteristic showers are produced.

Lying in the mid-latitudes on the western margins of Europe, Britain and Ireland experience air from many different sources and are often said to lie at the battleground of the world's air masses. The approximate frequency of these air masses is shown in Figure 10.9 A. Much of the mT and mP air that affects the British Isles comes as part of

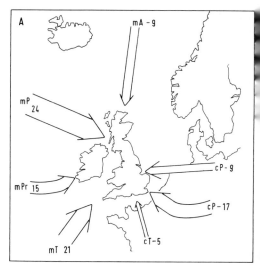

Figure 10.9 A An approximate picture of the percentage frequency of air masses over Britain and Ireland in January. 'mPr' stands for 'polar maritime returning' This is air that originates over polar maritime sources but moves southwards before sweeping north-easterly towards the British Isles.
(Modified from R. G. Barry and R. J. Chorley, p. 234.)

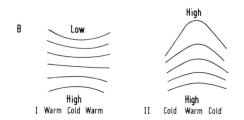

Figure 10.9 B Vertical pressure distribution in cold and warm anticyclones.
(Source: R. G. Barry and R. J. Chorley, p. 148.)

the frontal systems which are such a feature of our climate. Both occur throughout the year. Southwesterly air streams of pure mT air also occur but these are somewhat less frequent than northwesterly air streams of mP air which is our dominant air stream. Northerly air streams bringing cold mA air often occur in winter and become progressively unstable as they move south. They bring snow and sleet to the uplands of Scotland and northern England. Air originating from anticyclones over Europe (cP air) occurs in winter and summer and produces periods of very cold winter weather or very hot summer weather. This air stream, especially the south-easterly branch of it, is particularly well developed under an anticyclonic ridge of high pressure extending outward from Scandinavia over Britain and Ireland. With such a distribution of pressure, eastward-moving depressions are forced north of Scotland. The anticyclone and ridge block their customary passage across Ireland and Britain. For this reason such anticyclones are called *blocking highs*. Another, infrequent, source of very hot weather in Britain is cT air from the Sahara. This occurs on no more than about 12 days per year. The lower layer of this air stream is always very stable and brings very hot, subtropical temperatures in summer and fine, dry, warm weather in winter.

Before leaving the subject of anticyclones a brief note on their vertical structure is relevant. Two types of anticyclone can be recognized. *Cold anticyclones* are best developed over very large landmasses of middle and high latitudes in winter. The subsidence of very cold air, gravitationally sinking under its own weight, produces high pressure at the base of the troposphere, but low surface temperatures cause the air to contract vertically downward thus producing lower pressures aloft. Cold anticyclones formed in this way, such as the Eurasian winter anticyclone of the NE monsoon which we shall discuss later, are therefore shallow features of the atmosphere. *Warm anticyclones*, in contrast, are vertically much thicker. This is the case with the subtropical highs, the subsidence in which is dynamically produced, and maintained, by circulation in the Hadley cell. Such anticyclones are therefore a product of general atmospheric circulation. In such anticyclones the isobaric surfaces (Figure 10.9 B) tend to be convex upward for much greater heights than they are in cold anticyclones.

Cyclones and fronts

When air streams from two different sources converge, conditions become favourable for the formation of fronts. The process of frontal formation is called *frontogenesis*, and the most dynamic front in the earth's atmosphere is the polar front on which develop the 'lows', 'depressions' or 'cyclones' that so regularly affect Britain and Ireland. Altogether, an average of 170 fronts cross the Irish coast each year.

Our modern understanding of depressions (Figure 10.10) began in 1921 with the work of

Bjerknes and Solberg, two Swedish meteorologists. Whenever adjacent liquids or gases of different density and velocity move relative to each other wave disturbances are likely to be generated, as they are for example at the junction between the sea and the atmosphere. Waves forming on the polar front take on a familiar appearance. The lowest pressure is at the apex of the wave. Here, buckling of the polar front is most pronounced because convergence is most severe. Where convergence is most severe, upward moving air is most rapid and here, therefore, pressure is lowest. The wave form grows over a period of days,

The leading edge of a frontal depression is a *warm front*. It is well to remember that fronts are not narrow lines, as they appear on maps, but zones often hundreds of kilometres wide. They also extend upward and have distinctive profiles. A warm front separates cold polar air in front of it (to the east) from warm tropical air in the rear. Warm fronts have a well-defined system of clouds (Figure 10.10 G) and the appearance in the western sky of high-level cirrus cloud gives advance notice of a warm front's impending arrival. There is little dynamic activity on a warm front. Its gradient is gentle (about 1:150) and clouds have little vertical development. Precipitation from frontal cloud reaches the ground only in the area immediately ahead of the front. Any precipitation from high-level cloud on a warm front evaporates before reaching ground level. After the passage of a warm front temperatures rise as warm sector air replaces polar air.

The *cold front* separates warm air in front from cold air behind and is altogether more dynamic than the warm front. Cold air behind the front undercuts warm sector air, forcing it to rise. This is an important trigger action, simultaneously producing adiabatic cooling and releasing any instability in the tropical air. For this reason clouds near a cold front have pronounced vertical development. Cumulus cloud and thunderstorms are characteristic of cold front activity. Another feature of air motion at a cold front is the clockwise veering of the wind direction as the front moves through.

The role of the upper atmosphere is important in the formation of depressions. For a depression to intensify more air has to be removed aloft

131

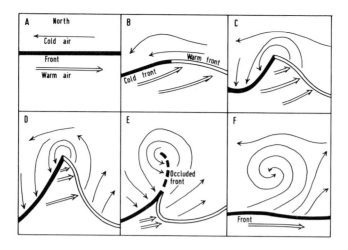

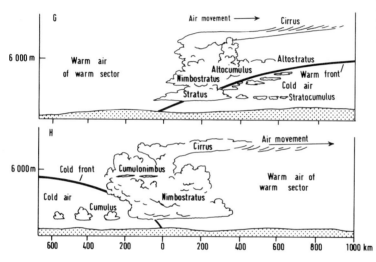

Figure 10.10 Stages in the development and decay of a polar front. (A) Cold air and warm air on either side of the front set up waves much as eddies and whirlpools develop between currents of water moving at different speeds in a river. (B and C) The wave progressively deforms and a well-developed warm sector becomes established between the warm and cold fronts. (D) The cold front, travelling faster than the warm front, begins to catch it up. (E) Cold air behind the cold front undercuts warm sector air and forces it off the ground. This is the process of occlusion. (F) Warm sector air is totally removed above ground level and the wave front eliminated. (G) Cloud forms and a vertical section through a warm front. (H) Vertical section through a cold front.
(Source: H. J. Critchfield, pp. 109, 111 and 112.)

than converges below. The circumpolar jet stream seems to be important in this process. As Figure 10.11 shows, waves on the polar front in the lower troposphere are reflected by sinuosities in the jet stream. Maximum velocity in the jet stream is thought to occur at the apex of a ridge which in Figure 10.11 is shown to be located just to the east of the depression's centre. Another zone of high jet stream velocity is at the point of maximum curvature in the trough but, for reasons we need not explore here, velocities here are not as high as those in the ridge. This means that jet stream air leaving a trough tends to accelerate towards the ridge. The effect of this acceleration is to produce divergence in the upper troposphere between the trough and ridge. This divergence or 'stretching out' of air in the jet stream is similar to the

everyday effects observed when cars accelerate away from traffic lights. As they accelerate the distance between them increases (i.e. they diverge from one another and the column of cars stretches out). Conversely, of course, the distance between cars decreases as they slow down or decelerate at the approach to traffic lights. Now the column length becomes shorter as they converge on one another. High-level divergence, as we have seen earlier, produces low-level convergence. Surface depressions therefore tend to form beneath that limb of a jet stream between trough and ridge, where divergence in the upper troposphere is thought to be at a maximum.

What we have so far said of course relates to the jet stream and surface depressions as seen in plan view. A cross-section through the troposphere

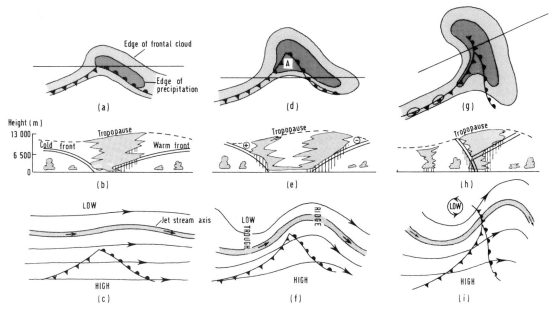

Figure 10.11 Three stages in the life cycle of a depression. Top row: plan view of fronts and cloud and the distribution of precipitation in the lower troposphere. Middle row: cross-section along the section lines shown in the top row. Bottom row: isobar patterns (at about 8 km) and jet stream position in relation to ground level frontal features.
(Source: D. E. Pedgley, p. 154.)

(Figure 10.11) at maximum vertical development of both fronts shows that the jet stream lies at the edge of the warm sector air and moves parallel to the fronts. The '+' sign in Figure 10.11 (e) indicates that the jet stream here is moving away from the reader (i.e. from the south-west). The '−' sign indicates it is moving towards the reader (i.e. from the north-west). This can be verified by watching high-level clouds in the upper troposphere. On the approach of a warm front these move rapidly from the north-west. Above the cold front they move from the south-west (Pedgley, p. 155).

Tropical secondary circulation

Because there are few weather stations in the intertropical region relatively little was known about features of atmospheric circulation here until the advent of earth satellites. The principal front is the ITCZ but because the north-east and south-east trade winds are so similar with respect to temperature and humidity this front is less dynamic than the polar front of the mid-latitudes. When air mass contrasts do appear in the trade wind belt, small troughs of low pressure with a shallow, wave-like plan develop and move westward. These

are the nearest counterpart of the eastward drifting depressions of the polar front but they are rarer and much less active, producing drizzle and steady rain. They are called *easterly waves* and can be hundreds of kilometres long.

Monsoons

The term *monsoon* means seasonal reversal of winds and the most outstanding example of this phenomenon occurs in south-east Asia (Figure 10.12). Smaller monsoons also affect west Africa and south-west USA. The characteristics of the south-east Asia monsoon have been well described by Hare, Miller, and Barry and Chorley. The following account is based on their descriptions of events.

Seasonal temperature contrasts between land and sea lie at the heart of the monsoon mechanism and south-east Asia has such a pronounced monsoon mainly because it lies between permanently very warm seas and the largest land mass in the world. This land mass is very hot in summer and very cold in winter. The monsoon is therefore principally the result of *continentality*, a term referring to the rapid heating and cooling of

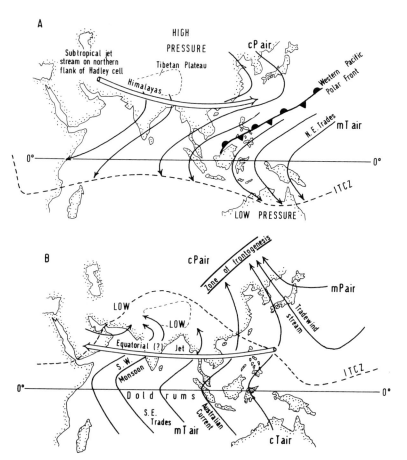

Figure 10.12 Principal characteristics of atmospheric motion during (A) the north-easterly monsoon and (B) the south-westerly monsoon. (Based on F. K. Hare, 1961, pp. 141 and 149.)

large land masses. Other factors, however, play important parts. Earth rotation, the migration of the vertical sun in the intertropical latitudes, frontal formation, topography and the jet streams of the upper troposphere: all contribute.

The winter monsoon is characterized by very cold anticyclonic air over Asia. Polar continental air from this anticyclone moves outwards over China and the west Pacific. The Indian subcontinent, however, is effectively cut off from these winds by the high Tibetan plateau. (Recall that cold anticyclones are very shallow features of the atmosphere.) High pressure over India in winter is a quite separate feature from high pressure over Eurasia and is thought by some climatologists to be principally caused by subsidence resulting from deceleration and convergence in the subtropical jet stream. Subsidence of air above south-east Asia in winter has long been suspected, for as Hare points out, much more air flows southward across the 15th parallel than across the 30th parallel. Clearly the additional air crossing the

15th parallel must be drawn from somewhere and the upper troposphere always seemed the most likely origin.

Monsoon air moving southward over China and the west Pacific ocean is deflected to its right and eventually crosses the numerous peninsulas and archipelagos of south-east Asia as a north-easterly air stream. Heavy rain occurs on east facing slopes but, generally, temperatures are relatively cool for this part of the world when the monsoon is blowing. This is especially the case in India. At the height of the north-east monsoon most of India is subject to cool, dry air originating over the Ganges basin and moving outwards over the Bay of Bengal. It then turns south-westwards and blows as a north-east wind across south India. This airflow path is sometimes regarded as an isolated cell of the northern hemisphere's tropical trade wind circulation.

During the northern hemisphere's winter, the ITCZ lies over north Australia where an intense low pressure cell develops. The north-east trades and the north-east monsoon streams both containing warm, moist, air are attracted towards this cell and change direction to become north-west air streams as they cross the equator. They provide a large area of north Australia with high summer rainfall.

It has to be stressed that the monsoonal flow originating in Siberia and terminating in Australia is not one air stream but consists of air derived from at least three sources. Continental polar air, tropical maritime air and upper troposphere air are all involved. It must also be remembered that the monsoon does not blow all the time. During December and January, depressions originating on the polar front over the Atlantic sometimes cross the Mediterranean and bring light rain to India.

In the south Pacific the temperature and humidity contrasts between two converging air streams, one relatively dry and of polar continental origin blowing out from the Asian continent and the other moist and warm, originating in the tropical maritime air stream of the north-east trade wind belt, produce conditions ripe for frontogenesis. The resulting front is termed the *western Pacific polar front* and it is highly mobile. On it depressions originate, just like those on the polar front of the north Atlantic, and these often move north-east across the Pacific to affect British Columbia, Washington and Oregon.

The summer monsoon

In summer as the ITCZ moves into the northern hemisphere, Asia heats up and cells of low pressure develop. These are particularly pronounced over northern India, but relatively low pressure exists over the whole of Asia and this causes winds to converge here. Three distinct monsoon air streams can be traced, all of them very pronounced reversals of the winter conditions. India receives a south-westerly air stream originating in the south-east trade wind belt of the southern hemisphere. These winds, on crossing the equator, are deflected to their right. Travelling across vast expanses of warm tropical ocean their absolute humidity levels become very high. On being forced to rise over the western Ghats and the Himalayas they release vast quantities of rainfall. These winds do not penetrate beyond the high barrier presented by the Himalayan mountains.

Not all of the Indian subcontinent receives high rainfall. There are some rainshadow areas like parts of the Deccan in the lee of the western Ghats. North-west India and Pakistan also remain relatively dry because they principally experience dry subsiding subtropical air from the continental areas of the Middle East. Any potential convection in moist air from the Indian ocean which may enter these areas is damped down by the subsiding air above.

The Australian current originates as tropical continental air over the Australian desert and moves north-westwards. Being initially dry it produces dry weather in the adjacent islands to the north but as it moves further away from Australia it becomes more moist in its lower layers and potentially unstable. It is responsible for much summer rainfall in Malaya and south China.

A final air stream originates over the Pacific, on the western margin of the subtropical high pressure belt which is more or less stable in summer at latitude 35–40°N and longitude 150°W. Air on the western side of the cell moves towards the low pressure over China and provides Japan with most of its summer rainfall.

There have always been a few anomalies in the weather of the south-east Asian monsoon. One particularly interesting anomaly is that the summer monsoon of India, which of course arrives from the south-west, breaks in India only after it has broken in Burma, to the east (Figure 10.13). This is now explained by some meteorologists as the product of an easterly jet stream, sometimes referred to as the equatorial jet stream, and its ability to evacuate rapidly rising unstable air from the lower atmosphere. One study has correlated the

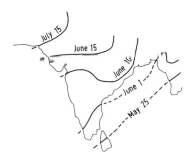

Figure 10.13 Typical starting dates of the south-west monsoon. **Note how they are earliest in the east.** (Source: R. G. Barry and R. J. Chorley, 1969, *Atmosphere, Weather and Climate,* 1st edition, p. 233.)

135

position and strength of this jet, or more precisely
of strong easterly flow in the upper atmosphere,
with the occurrence of rainfall in the south-west
monsoon current. If this relationship is valid it
could possibly explain why the start of the summer
monsoon season advances westward rather than
eastward, as it presumably should if it is principally
the product of surface winds.

Tropical revolving storms

Tropical revolving storms are intense low pressure
areas most frequently called *hurricanes* or *cyclones*
(Figure 10.14 A). According to Critchfield, they
differ from temperate cyclones in several important
respects:

1 They do not have fronts. The trade winds, on
either side of the ITCZ on which the revolving
storms develop, do not have the contrasting
pressure and humidity necessary for frontal formation.
2 They have much steeper pressure gradients than
those which are normally found in depressions.
Pressure gradients of 30 mb per 100 km are
frequent. Atmospheric pressures below 900 mb
have been recorded in the centre of hurricanes
though 940 mb is a more common value.
3 The sequence of weather typical of depressions

is not found in hurricanes. Rainfall, always very
heavy, is more or less evenly distributed across
the storm except in the centre which is always
dry. As for rainfall totals, these are excessive:
a total of 250 mm of rainfall in one day is not
uncommon and 1000 mm in a day has been
recorded.
4 The centre of a temperate cyclone is a region of
ascending air. In a hurricane the eye is characterized by descending air (Figure 10.14 B).
5 In plan, hurricanes are smaller features of the
lower troposphere than temperate cyclones.
Their anticlockwise rotation (in the northern
hemisphere) is also far more marked and much
more compact which is why they are called
tropical revolving storms.

Tropical cyclones have diameters in plan ranging
from 150 km to 1000 km. Surrounding the central
'eyes', usually about 25 km wide, are concentric
bands of towering cumulus cloud. The energy for
the convection in these high clouds comes once
again from condensation and the release of latent
heat. The atmosphere above the tropical oceans is
so humid and the cooling so rapid that latent heat
release is here probably close to a global maximum.
The energy input into a hurricane from condensation is the equivalent of several thousand atomic

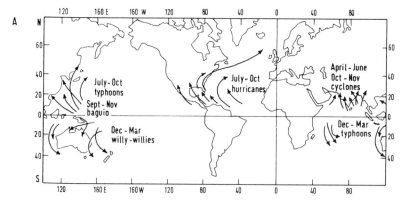

Figure 10.14 A The
distribution and local names
of tropical revolving storms.
(Source: J. J. Hidore, p. 111.)

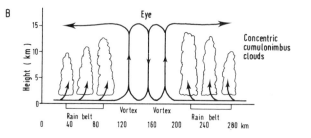

Figure 10.14 B Cross-
section and air currents in a
hurricane.
(Source: H. Flohn, pp. 140
and 141.)

bombs! The moisture content in a hurricane can equal 5 billion tonnes or more.

Excessive wind speeds (over 120 km h^{-1}), high rainfall, and sea surges, typically of 5 m or more and with 10 m waves superimposed, cause much physical damage. On leaving oceanic areas, however, hurricanes are cut off from the evaporation process which fuels their energy supply and they become less intense. Some of the most intense systems, however, do travel a great distance before filling in. Some even reach British seas although in much subdued form.

Hurricane formation is poorly understood. They form most frequently when the ITCZ is some 5° to 10° poleward of the equator, but only over seas with a minimum temperature of 27 °C. At about 10° north and south of the equator the Coriolis force is sufficiently strong to account for the severe revolving nature of the storms. At the equator it is too weak. Note that the ITCZ rarely extends south of the equator in the Atlantic (Figure 10.4) and hurricanes do not form here. Hurricanes are also characteristic of the western and not the eastern oceans, and here the moist layer of air above the oceans is up to 2500 m thick whereas in the east it is only 1250 m thick. These two facts account for some features of their timing and distribution. But the trigger action which initiates the systems remains unknown.

MEDIUM-SCALE MOTION

Tornadoes

Thunderstorms and tornadoes are representative of medium-scale motion in the atmosphere. Tornadoes are localized but extremely violent storms in the lower troposphere, and consist of a very narrow funnel of rotating air which appears to descend from the base of a Cb cloud towards the ground. The base of a tornado does not always stay in contact with the ground but rather moves across it with a skipping motion. Winds in the cloud revolve in a very tight anticlockwise vortex. The diameter of a tornado is often only 100 m. At its centre pressure may be 80 mb less than in the atmosphere outside and winds are therefore extremely violent, sometimes exceeding

500 km h^{-1}. In the Mid-west region of the USA, upwards of 100 tornadoes may be recorded each year. In Britain they are less frequent (about 10 per year) and less intense. Damage to property is caused as buildings in the path of the tornadoes explode due to the rapid drop of pressure outside.

Tornadoes typically form ahead of a cold front in the warm sector of a depression. They result from rapid convection, probably induced by local heating of the ground in summer, and are often associated with thunderstorms in late afternoon. The origin of tornadoes is not fully understood but they appear to form most frequently when the contrasts of temperature and humidity between tropical and polar air on either side of a cold front are at their maximum. Turbulent action along such intense fronts may produce local eddies and some of these may develop into tornadoes. An alternative theory is illustrated in Figure 10.15. Descending downdraughts of Cb air in the right rear of a decaying thunderstorm move in a direction opposite to that of the main air stream. These converging flows shear to the right of each other (in the northern hemisphere) and cyclonic (anticlockwise) motion is set up.

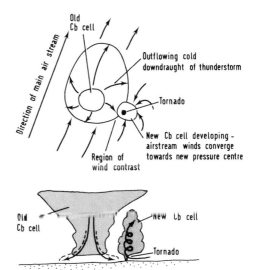

Figure 10.15 A possible method of tornado formation. Notice how downdraughts encourage the dynamic uplift of air along its margins. This may help in releasing the tornado's instability. Alternatively the internal uplift in the tornado may be started by convection. (Source: D. E. Pedgley, p. 115.)

ATMOSPHERIC MOTION ON A LOCAL SCALE

The smallest cells of atmospheric motion occur in the so-called boundary layer which lies at the junction of the earth's surface and atmosphere. Motion in this lowest part of the troposphere is much affected by friction and by sharp contrasts in the nature of the earth's surface itself. The surface contrasts are particularly pronounced at boundaries between land and sea, mountain and lowland, city and countryside.

Land and sea breezes

On a clear afternoon in summer, land surfaces in Britain may be 10 °C warmer than adjacent coastal waters. Sensible heat transfer from the ground to the air increases as the ground warms up and this causes the air column above the land to expand in its lower layers. Expansion of the air column in this way means that above a height of about 300 m there is more air in the atmospheric column over the land than in the atmospheric column over the sea. A pressure gradient from land to sea is thus brought into existence and winds above 300 m in height blow from the land towards the sea. The transfer of air from above the land in this way creates low pressure at ground level and winds therefore blow from the sea on to the land (Figure 10.16 A).

Sea breezes in low latitudes tend to be stronger than in mid-latitudes because insolation here is stronger and temperature differences between land and sea are consequently greater. An interesting feature of sea breezes (see e.g. Pedgley, p. 33) is that they are initially quite gentle and travel across the pressure gradient from sea to land, crossing the coast at right-angles. As the sea breeze wind speed increases so too does the Coriolis force, and the wind becomes more nearly geostrophic with low pressure (over the land) to the left of an observer in the northern hemisphere with his back to the breeze. The winds thus increasingly cross the coast more obliquely. The absence of a marked Coriolis effect near the equator is one reason why sea breezes here extend further inland than in higher latitudes and cross the coast more nearly at right-angles.

At night when the earth cools the sea-breeze effect may be reversed (Figure 10.16 B) as the air

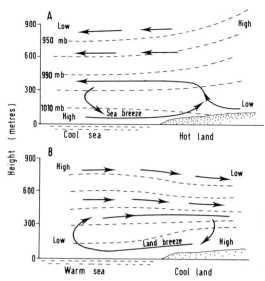

Figure 10.16 Cross-section of a daytime sea-breeze (A) and a night-time land breeze (B) in temperate latitudes. In tropical areas the depth of atmospheric turnover in the sea breeze may be 1000 m. The land breeze is the weaker of the two because temperature differences between land and sea are usually smaller at night than in the day.

column over the land contracts, and a ground level *land breeze*, usually weaker than the sea breeze, may then set in. In summer, *lake breezes* from Lake Michigan reduce lakeside temperatures in eastern Chicago by 16 °C in comparison with areas 10 km inland.

Mountain winds

Anabatic and *katabatic winds* are shown in Figure 10.17. They are gentle winds, rarely exceeding 5 knots. The katabatic wind, which in essence results from the downward sinking of cold heavy air, is a form of *gravity wind* and these can occur on quite a large scale. Cold air in the Alps often sinks and funnels down the Rhône valley to produce the *mistral,* a cold northerly wind which develops in winter and summer, and often adversely affects crop production in the area north of Marseilles. Sometimes the cold air is derived from the rear of a cold front moving southward into the Mediterranean basin during periods of low index, meridional, circulation.

The warm dry wind which sometimes descends the lee side of the Alps is called the *föhn.* Its equivalent in the Rockies and Cascade mountains

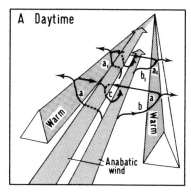

Figure 10.17A   Warm air in contact with the valley sides (a and a₁) rises. Air in contact with the valley bottom moves up the slopes to replace this rising air (b and b₁). Converging air above the centre of the main valley sinks (c) and moves up valley to replace rising air at b₁. An up-valley wind circulation is thus set up.
(Source: R. A. Muller, p. 123.)

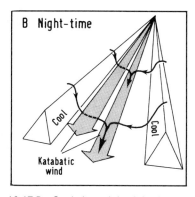

Figure 10.17B   Cool air at night sinks down the valley sides, converges in the valley axis and moves gravitationally down the valley. A down-valley wind is thus set up. If katabatic winds drain into a depression a frost hollow may be established.
(Source: R. A. Muller, p. 123.)

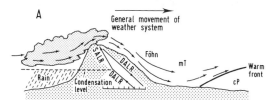

Figure 10.18A   The so-called thermodynamic explanation of the föhn wind. Moist air is forced to rise orographically. Initially, this air rises at the DALR but when condensation levels are reached latent heat is released and the air cools at the SALR. Precipitation falls on the windward slopes. In the lee of the mountains friction drags high level air downward. Exhausted of precipitation this air now contains less moisture than on the windward side and is warmed by compression so that its relative humidity as well as its absolute humidity decreases. It now warms at the DALR. At equivalent altitudes on either side of the mountain range temperatures on the leeward slopes are higher than on the windward slopes.
(Source: H. J. Critchfield, p. 128.)

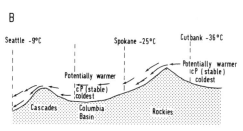

Figure 10.18B   Not all föhn effects involve condensation. The stable-air föhn effect can occur in western USA and Canada during winter when dry high-level anticyclonic air descends from east of the Rockies into the Columbia basin. This air is warmed at the DALR as it descends westwards. This descending air, although warmer at equivalent altitudes than its parent air mass east of the Rockies, is sometimes colder than the Pacific air which it replaces. This is more frequently the case if upper level air in the Columbia basin crosses the Cascades into the Pacific coastlands. Residents of Seattle may feel this föhn effect to be cold and unpleasant even though the descending air itself is being warmed by compression.
(Source: H. J. Critchfield, p. 128.)

of North America is the *chinook*. Descending air in these local winds can reach very high velocities, sometimes exceeding hurricane force east of the Rockies. The traditional explanation, sometimes termed the thermodynamic interpretation, is illustrated in Figure 10.18 A. According to Critchfield, the chinook wind is not always a warm wind in absolute terms even though temperature increases of 22.5 °C in one hour have been attributed to it. Frequently the chinook itelf is below freezing. Always, however, the true föhn or chinook is warmer than the air it replaces and this is its important characteristic. It can cause snow to disappear by ablation (solid → liquid) or by sublimation (solid → gas).

Föhn-like winds can occur in circumstances different from those described in Figure 10.18 A. Sometimes, dry continental air from high altitudes is drawn down the lee side of mountains and is not accompanied by precipitation on the windward slopes. This is called the *stable air föhn effect* (Figure 10.18 B).

Urban winds

We have already seen many instances of how cities develop their own climate. In some cities the heat island seems capable of causing thermally-induced winds to blow in from the surrounding countryside in much the same way as expansion of the air column over land areas can cause sea breezes. Such thermal winds have been documented in Leicester and several cities in North America such as Cincinnati and Toronto. In Toronto they are most marked in winter when temperature contrasts between city and country-side are greatest.

With regard to windspeed the effect of cities is unclear because data are scarce. It appears, however, that windspeeds in central London are about 5% lower than outside, although calm periods are fewer in number (Chandler). These effects are caused by the greater *aerodynamic roughness* of cities and their greater turbulence in comparison with rural areas. The effects of the slightly reduced windspeed are not in themselves dramatic but rather appear to reinforce other climatic effects of the city. Low windspeeds, for example, seem to be a precondition of the heat island effect itself, for it is often destroyed in smaller urban areas when the windspeed exceeds 20 km h^{-1}. In London, however, the heat island effect is more resilient and is maintained in wind speeds up to 40 km h^{-1}. Such a high threshold indicates how well established and resilient are many of man's modifications to his natural environment.

11

Climates of the Present, Past and Future

WORLD CLIMATES TODAY

The pattern of global climates at any one time is determined by a combination of interacting factors such as atmospheric circulation, the distribution of oceans and continents, altitude, air masses and air streams. Many classifications of world climate have been made, principally by Köppen in 1918 and 1923, by Thornthwaite in 1931 and 1948 and by Miller in 1951 Climatic boundaries in Köppen's classification were based largely on plant distributions mapped in the nineteenth century, and he tried to define these boundaries in terms of mean temperature, rainfall and seasonality. The principles of his classification are shown in Table 11.1. His five major climatic divisions are based on temperature. Seasonal rainfall is the basis of his major subgroups and extreme monthly temperature the principal, though not sole, basis of his second subdivision. Using this classification, the

Table 11.1. Köppen's algebraic classification of world climates (after Strahler, pp. 168–169)

Five major temperature groups	Subgroups based on rainfall	Second sub-division
A Tropical (Average monthly temperature >18 °C. No winter. Annual rainfall exceeds evapotranspiration)	m = short dry season of monsoon type f = no dry season w = winter dry season	
B Dry (Annual evapotranspiration >precipitation)	S = steppe (38–76 mm year^{-1}) W = desert (<25 mm year^{-1})	Dry hot (h) = mean annual temperature >18 °C. Dry cold (k) = mean annual temperature <18 °C
C Warm temperate or mesothermal (One month >10 °C. Coldest month <18 °C and >−3 °C)	f = no dry season w = winter dry season s = summer dry season	a = warmest month >22 °C b = warmest month <22 °C c = less than 4 months >10 °C
D Snow or microthermal (Coldest month < −3°C. Average temperature of warmest month >10 °C)	f = no dry season w = winter dry season	a = warmest month >22 °C b = warmest month <22 °C c = less than 4 months >10 °C d = coldest month < −38 °C
E Ice (Average temperature of warmest month <10 °C)	T = tundra F = permanent frost	

141

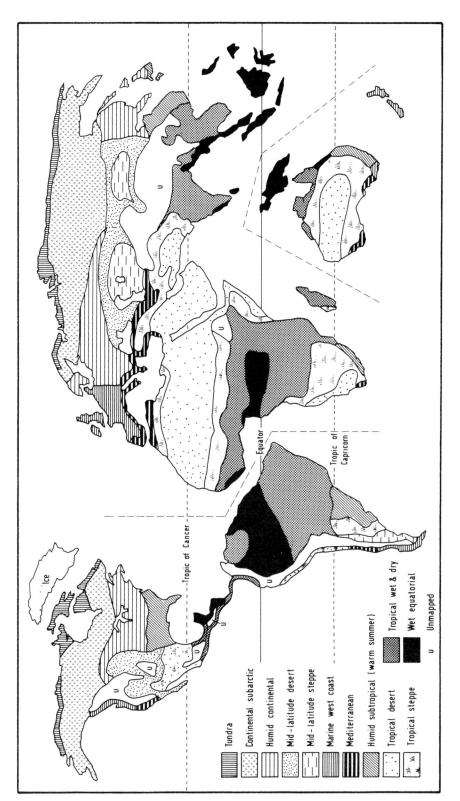

Figure 11.1 World climates classified by dominant air masses. Letters in brackets refer to the nearest equivalent climatic region in Köppen's more complicated scheme.

1 Tundra (ET). This climatic type lies along a frontal zone between polar and arctic air masses. The climate is humid and very cold although oceanic influences modify the climate somewhat. (North of 55°N.)

2 Continental subarctic (Dfc, Dfd, Dwc, Dwd) climates

Figure 11.1 caption contd. on p. 143.

are the source area of cP air. Summers are short, winters long and temperature ranges enormous. (50–70°N.)

3 Humid continental (Dfa, Dfb, Dwa, Dwb). Away from maritime influences in the mid-latitudes, temperatures here are extreme. Continental influences are dominant, although precipitation from the polar front is common. cP air ensures cold winters. (35–60°N.)

Legend:

Tundra
Continental subarctic
Humid continental
Mid-latitude desert
Mid-latitude steppe
Marine west coast
Mediterranean
Humid subtropical (warm summer)
Tropical desert
Tropical steppe
Tropical wet & dry
Wet equatorial
u Unmapped

4(a) Mid-latitude deserts (BWk).

4(b) Mid-latitude steppes (BSk). Here, cP air in winter gives cold temperatures while cT air in summer provides hot weather. Very dry with no maritime influences. (35–50 °N and S.)

5 Marine west coast (Cfb, Cfc). These climates have a maritime location on the axis of the polar front. Weather is cloudy, wet and has a low temperature range. (40–60 °N and S.)

6 Mediterranean (Csa, Csb) climates have classic warm moist winters and hot dry summers with frequent droughts. Winter rain is from the polar front depressions when mP air is frequent. These areas are under the influence of subtropical high pressure zones in summer when mT air masses are dominant. (30–45 °N and S on west coasts.)

7 Humid subtropical (Cfa). Here easterly mT air is dominant all year. Weather is humid with abundant summer rainfall. These regions are subject to revolving subtropical storms. (20–35 °N and S on east coasts.)

8(a) Tropical desert (BWh).

8(b) Tropical steppe (BSh). These climates are situated in regions of subsiding air beneath the poleward limbs of the Hadley cells and are very dry and hot throughout the year. Fog is frequent on the west coasts. (15–35 °N and S.)

9 Tropical wet and dry climates, including the monsoon lands of south-east Asia (Aw, Cwa). Climates here are dominated by movement of the vertical sun which distorts the trade wind circulation to produce incursions of moist mT air into continental areas during summer when rainfall maxima occur. Drier cT air streams dominate in winter. (5–25 °N and S.)

10 Wet equatorial (Af, Am). In these climates uplift along the equatorial trough of low pressure gives heavy convectional storms throughout the year. Temperatures are uniformly high from month to month. (10 °N to 10 °S.)

Areas left unmapped are mountainous. Here climate changes too rapidly to be represented at this map scale. (Source: A. N. Strahler, pp. 170–172.)

code 'Cfa', for example, refers to a warm temperate climate with no dry season and a very hot summer. Florida is an example of such a climatic type.

Thornthwaite's classification was based on precipitation (P) and potential evapotranspiration (PE) and he developed a moisture index from research he carried out in the USA. The moisture index summarizes the availability of soil moisture for plant growth. When P exceeds PE the index is positive. When PE exceeds P the index is negative. A moisture index of zero separates arid from humid areas. Thornthwaite's classification was designed as a contribution towards agriculture and forestry in the USA and therefore, like Köppen's classification, it is closely related to vegetation.

Another basis for classifying world climates is by air mass. This is the basis of the world classification shown in Figure 11.1. Because this classification seeks to explain the causes of world climates it is sometimes described as a _genetic classification_. Other criteria might be temperature, net radiation, or precipitation. These have all been used but provide very elementary categories, within which other aspects of climate important for vegetation, agriculture, geomorphology, and human activity vary considerably.

Classification of world climates is necessary in geography because despite the large range of factors affecting climate it is apparent that certain types are regularly repeated across the globe and define regions in which the physical and biological processes affecting the environment are obviously very similar. An understanding of the distribution of these regions around the world is a first step to understanding how climatic systems work.

It is well to bear in mind several weaknesses of any climatic classification system. These have been described by Miller (p. 82) as follows:

1 All climatic boundaries are in fact transition zones. There are no sharp dividing lines between climatic types. This difficulty is apparent when attempts are made to define where deserts begin. At least six classifications have sought to define this limit and between them they provide 34 possible combinations of mean annual temperature and annual rainfall as definitions of aridity.

2 Most classifications have traditionally used vegetation change as the reflection of a significant climatic boundary. But vegetation also changes gradually rather than suddenly over an area, and may also reflect other controlling factors such as soil and topography which need not be so closely related to climate as vegetation is presumed to be.

3 Most classifications use mean annual values as the basis of regional descriptions of climate, when in effect vegetation is probably as much, if not more, adjusted to the extreme aspects of climate such as the frequency of droughts, frosts and floods. Other controlling factors of vegetation such as windiness are never considered.

The use of mean temperature and mean rainfall in climatic classification is partly responsible for the notion that 'climate is average weather' In some parts of the world such as the equatorial tropics weather varies little from day to day and the average of daily events gives some impression of what the weather is like for most of the time throughout the year. But in countries like the UK the weather is so changeable from day to day that the average daily temperature may actually be experienced on only a small proportion of days in the year. The variability of climate in Britain and Ireland has given rise to the expression that 'here there is no such thing as climate, only weather'.

4 A final factor to bear in mind is that any classification of climate only reflects conditions over the period of time for which records have existed. There is now abundant evidence to suggest that the pattern of world climates has changed considerably since Pleistocene times and may still be evolving. Vegetational changes may lag behind these climatic changes, and it is therefore very possible that today's pattern of world vegetation reflects climatic and other environmental patterns of past years rather than those of today.

THE VARIABILITY OF CLIMATE IN RECENT YEARS

The recent variability of world climate has given new impetus to the study of climatic change. Many scientists from different disciplines (e.g. agriculture, hydrology, meteorological forecasting, etc.) are now investigating whether or not climates are currently changing, and if so, how rapidly and in what direction. Among recent examples of climatic variability in the British Isles were the 1975–6 drought (see Chapter 9) and the 1978–9 winter. In the latter period, both the amount of snowfall and the length of time it remained on the ground exceeded all known records in many upland areas of Britain. Elsewhere in the world extreme climatic events have been common in the recent past (Figure 11.2). Many anomalies have now lasted several years, and one in particular, the Sahel drought, has caused widespread famine.

To appreciate the scale of recent variations in world climate it is helpful to place them in historical perspective. This we can do as a result of techniques developed in the last 50 years which enable us to identify and date the principal changes of climate throughout the late-glacial and post-glacial periods. Most of the material in the rest of this chapter is based on Lamb's work. But see also Gribbin's more recent text.

SOME TECHNIQUES OF HISTORICAL CLIMATOLOGY

Pollen analysis

Pollen grains and spores released by individual plant species are microscopically small but none the less distinctive. Carried into the air by wind, pollen grains eventually fall to the ground and become trapped in sediments. Peat bogs, being devoid of oxygen, preserve pollen grains very well because the grains only decompose slowly and therefore retain their identity for a long time. At any one time the pollen grains trapped in a peat bog are assumed to reflect the composition of vegetation nearby. As the peat bog grows, successive layers of pollen accumulate and a stratigraphic column is formed. Since the composition of vegetation is very largely dependent on humidity, temperature and exposure, the pollen record contained in a vertical section of peat is presumed to be a good indication of how climate has evolved in the area. The study of pollen grains is called *palynology*. In pollen analysis, cores of sediment are extracted from a peat bog or lake. Each core can be several metres long and might represent several thousand years of history. Each distinctive horizon in the core is examined and each type of pollen grain is counted. Variations in the amount of pollen from each plant species which are found in the core are presented in a pollen diagram (Figure 11.3). By matching the various populations of fossil pollen grains in different parts of a core with the pollen produced by vegetation associations in different climatic areas of the world today, the palynologist can infer the sequence of climatic events since the sediment started to accumulate. Suitable sediments for the preservation of pollen have been developing in Britain and Ireland throughout late-glacial and post-glacial times and palynology is the principal source of information about this period.

Figure 11.2   Anomalous features of world climate in 1972 and some of their environmental and social effects:
1   Poor soya-bean crop.
2   Failure of anchovy fisheries.
3   Sahel drought zone.
4   Heavy pack ice.
5   Reduced wheat crop.
6   Failure of the monsoon.
7   Poor rice crop.
Anomalies have continued throughout the 1970s. Extensive flooding occurred in Australia 1973–4. In 1975, Arctic sea-ice reached Iceland's offshore zone in July for the first time this century.
(Source: Anon, 1981.)

Cold
Drought
Benign
Lack of snow
Cool
Wet
Frost
Downwelling
Heavy ice

145

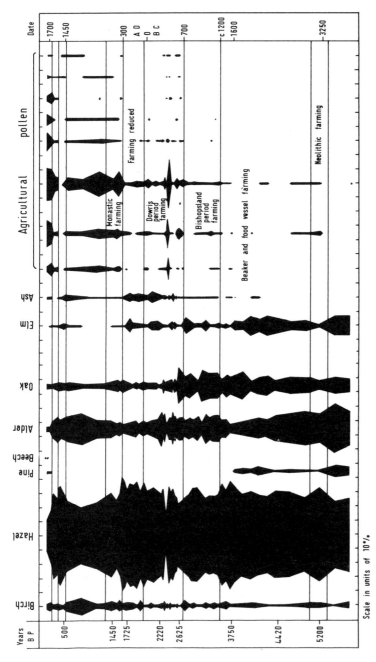

Figure 11.3 A generalized pollen diagram from Red Bog, west of Dundalk, Ireland. The bottom of the diagram represents the end of the post-glacial climatic optimum when elm pollen starts to decline for the first time and agricultural pollen from crops and weeds such as ribwort plantain increase in number. Notice that agricultural pollen increases in relative abundance after about 1200 BC as farming increases. Trees, especially oak and elm, decline after this period and elm is virtually eliminated by 300 AD. About AD 1450 hazel and elm make a resurgence which may be associated with a slight rise in temperature. Right up until 1700 hazel provided most pollen but by this time agricultural pollen had begun to exceed pollen from trees.
(Source: F. Mitchell, 1976, *The Irish Landscape*, Collins, p. 136.)

Oxygen isotopes in oceanic sediments

Another source of information about the environmental history of this period is the ocean bed on which accumulate the remnants of tiny organisms, zooplankton, that live and feed in oceanic surface water. Some of these zooplankton have skeletons containing carbonates derived from seawater and containing two isotopes[1] of oxygen that have proved useful in investigating past events. The two isotopes are oxygen-16 (^{16}O) and the heavier oxygen-18 (^{18}O). During evaporation from the ocean surface, water molecules containing the lighter ^{16}O vaporize more easily than water molecules containing ^{18}O. Since evaporation rates are related to atmospheric and surface water temperatures, it follows that a relatively high ratio of ^{18}O to ^{16}O in the skeletons of what were once surface water zooplankton (see Chapter 12) reflects a period of relative warmth. Conversely, if the $^{16}O/^{18}O$ ratio is relatively high, atmospheric and surface water temperature must have been quite cold when the zooplankton skeletons were deposited. Analysis of $^{16}O/^{18}O$ ratios in the sediment of oceans has been a principal source of evidence about fluctuations in world temperature during the late-glacial period.

Lake levels and inland seas

Closed lake basins (i.e. without tributary or outlet streams) represent another source of evidence about past climates. High lake levels in such basins represent a period when the ratio of precipitation to evaporation was higher than today. Climate was relatively cool and/or moist in such periods. Low lake levels, in contrast, indicate high evaporation rates and/or relatively low precipitation when climate was warm and relatively dry.

Past lake levels are recorded in terraces, some higher than today's lake level, some lower. If the chronological succession of these terraces can be established, then the sequence of climatic types in the area can be established too. Lakes where such terrace evidence is abundant are Lake Bonneville in Utah (USA), Lake Chad and the Caspian Sea. The mean depth of Lake Bonneville at its maximum extent was 300 m and its surface area was 10 times that of its successor, the present Great Salt Lake.

Carbon-14 dating

The methods so far described for examining past climatic events are all relative. They only provide a chronology of what happened but do not tell us when an event occurred. The importance of radiocarbon dating is that it provides absolute dates of certain events in the stratigraphic record from which the dates of all other events can be more accurately determined.

Carbon-14 (^{14}C), a radioactive isotope of carbon, is a constituent of the atmosphere taken in by plants and animals during the carbon cycle (Chapter 12). In any living organism ^{14}C forms a fixed proportion of all carbon ingested. The importance of radioactive isotopes for dating the past is that they spontaneously decay at a known rate. Every radioactive isotope has a known *half-life*. This is the time taken for 50% of the isotope to decay. ^{14}C has a half-life of 5730 years. Thus only half the ^{14}C present in a live specimen will be found in a dead specimen 5730 years old. Only one-quarter of the ^{14}C present in a live specimen will be found in a dead specimen 11 560 years old, and only one-eighth in a specimen 17 290 years old. Comparing the known ratio of ^{14}C to non-decaying carbon (^{12}C) in a live specimen with the ratio found in a dead specimen of that organism, enables scientists to determine the date of death, often to within $\pm 5\%$. The technique is acceptably accurate back to about 50 000 years before the present (see Lamb, 1977, pp. 60–68, for much more precise details of the technique).

Dendrochronology

Dendrochronology is the study of tree rings and is another absolute dating technique often used as a check on radiocarbon methods. Annual growth rings in some trees of high and mid-latitudes

---

1 Different isotopes of a chemical element all have the same number of protons and electrons but different numbers of neutrons. The mass number of an element (the number that appears before it) is the sum of protons and neutrons contained in one atom of that element. The most common isotope of oxygen (^{16}O) contains 8 protons and 8 neutrons. ^{18}O contains 8 protons and 10 neutrons, thus making it slightly heavier. The most common isotope of carbon is ^{12}C which contains 6 protons and 6 neutrons. ^{14}C contains 6 protons and 8 neutrons.

vary in thickness according to climatic severity. Climatic conditions favourable for growth, such as adequate moisture supply and warmth, produce wide rings. Poor conditions produce thin rings. The age of a tree is given by the number of rings it contains and thus its cross-section represents a stratigraphy, or chronological record, of climatic events in its life-time. In California, bristlecone pine trees more than 4000 years old have been used for tree-ring dating.

Archaeological evidence

Sites of past human settlements dating from different post-glacial periods have now been discovered in many parts of the world. Diverse evidence of human occupance (fish bones, charcoal, stone implements, etc.) has been found at many of these sites and can often be accurately dated by radiocarbon techniques. This archaeological evidence can often be used, along with other evidence, to relate man's movements to past climatic events.

Historical evidence

Moving into historical times the evidence of past climatic events becomes clearer. Written records of floods and droughts exist in ancient calendars, in the Bible (e.g. Noah's flood) and in learned manuscripts. In the Middle Ages tithe receipts in Britain provide evidence about harvest yields. By 1800, weather records were being kept at twelve sites in Europe and at five in the eastern USA. By 1850, 168 returns of rainfall were available in Britain and Ireland and by 1900 regular rainfall measurements were being made at 3500 sites.

The 200 years of rainfall and temperature data that now exist, however, often raise more questions than they answer, for they correspond with a period in which man's impact on climate through such activities as building, changing land use, and industry has been most dramatic. Two hundred years, moreover, is a very small fraction (0.01%) of glacial and post-glacial time and, some would say, far too short a record from which to establish future long-term climatic trends with certainty.

CLIMATIC EVENTS IN THE POST-GLACIAL PERIOD

Figure 11.4 outlines the main late- and post-glacial periods now recognized for Britain and Ireland together with their dates, vegetation characteristics, and pollen zones. A pollen zone is a distinctive part of the sedimentary sequence in which particular types of pollen are repeatedly associated together at a large number of sites far removed from each other. Also included in Figure 11.4 is a graph showing probable changes in temperature throughout the period.

The post-glacial period which started about 10 300 years ago (8300 BC) has three main climatic phases. The first, a period of increasing warmth, ended in Boreal times. The second has been called a period of culminating warmth and lasted throughout the Atlantic period. The third, a period of increasing coolness, started at the end of the Atlantic period and lasted until about 1800. There have been oscillations of temperature in each phase and today temperatures are relatively warm.

The chronology of events throughout Britain and Ireland since late-glacial times is worth describing in detail. Pollen studies provide the basis for a recognition of eight climatic periods (marked I to VIII in Figure 11.4) in each of which the assemblage of fossil pollen grains is very distinctive, both here and elsewhere in Europe. The retreat of ice at the end of the Würm glaciation (see Table 7.2) was interrupted by minor advances. These cold phases saw the return of tundra conditions to much of southern Britain. Mosses and lichens flourished. These cold phases are called the Dryas periods after a species of mountain avens (*Dryas octopetala*) which flourished at the time. Periods of marked warming occurred between the Dryas periods but ice retreat was only local. These were the Bølling and the Allerød *interstadial* periods, so-called from sites in Denmark at which these warm phases were first identified.

The post-glacial period begins with the pre-Boreal. Mean annual and winter temperatures began to rise, never again to become as cold as in the Dryas times. Temperatures continued to rise through the Boreal period and may have been higher then than today. Hazel developed north of,

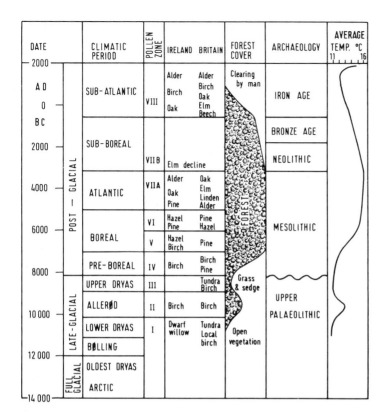

DATE	CLIMATIC PERIOD	POLLEN ZONE	IRELAND	BRITAIN	FOREST COVER	ARCHAEOLOGY	AVERAGE TEMP. °C 11 ... 16
2000 — AD — 0 — BC	SUB-ATLANTIC	VIII	Alder Birch Oak	Alder Birch Oak Elm Beech	Clearing by man	IRON AGE	
2000 —	SUB-BOREAL	VIIB	Elm decline			BRONZE AGE NEOLITHIC	
4000 —	ATLANTIC	VIIA	Alder Oak Pine	Oak Elm Linden Alder			
6000 —	BOREAL	VI	Hazel Pine	Pine Hazel		MESOLITHIC	
		V	Hazel Birch	Pine			
8000 —	PRE-BOREAL	IV	Birch	Birch Pine			
	UPPER DRYAS	III		Tundra Birch	Grass & sedge		
10 000 —	ALLERØD	II	Birch	Birch		UPPER PALAEOLITHIC	
	LOWER DRYAS	I	Dwarf willow	Tundra Local birch	Open vegetation		
12 000 —	BØLLING						
	OLDEST DRYAS						
—14 000 —	ARCTIC						

(left-side bracket labels: POST-GLACIAL, LATE-GLACIAL, FULL GLACIAL)

Figure 11.4 Changes of climate, vegetation and culture in Britain and Ireland since the end of the Pleistocene period. Note the development of forest in post-glacial times and its virtual elimination by man in the last 2500 years for agriculture. Note, also, how average temperature changes mirror the development of forest, except in the last 200 years or so. Temperature data refer to the north-west coast of USA and Canada. (Source: H. H. Lamb, 1977, pp. 79 and 401.)

and higher than, today's boundaries. In Atlantic times post-glacial temperature reached a peak. This is the period known as the *climatic optimum* which lasted in Britain and Ireland from about 5000 BC to 3000 BC. Temperatures were mild all year round, probably 2.5 °C higher than today, and humidity conditions were very suited to the development in England of extensive mixed forests of oak, lime and elm.

The warmth of the climatic optimum was associated elsewhere in the world with the final shrinkage of the world's ice sheets to the position they occupy today. Sea level rose and the end of the Atlantic period saw the flooding of the North Sea (which had been dry in Boreal times) and the Dover Straits.

From about 2000 BC to the present time temperatures declined and most of our blanket peat bogs started to form in this period of climatic deterioration. The general decline of temperature after 2000 BC was interrupted by brief warm periods, one of which from AD 1150 to AD 1300 was as warm as any period in the post-glacial record. During this period vine growing extended into southern Britain (Figure 11.5).

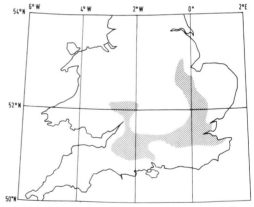

Figure 11.5 Areas of vineyard cultivation in England between 1000 and 1300 AD. Over 60 vineyards ranging in size from 1 to over 10 acres existed in the area. The vast majority were under 2 acres in size. (Modified from H. H. Lamb, 1977, p. 277.)

After AD 1300 the brief interlude of warm weather appears to have ended and colder conditions returned. The period 1300–1400 is known as the 'climatic worsening'. Arctic sea ice and European valley glaciers began to expand, the tree line was lowered, lakes began to freeze

149

more frequently than previously in the historical record, and harvest failures became recurrent as the ground became wetter. Vineyards in Britain were abandoned after 1310 and whole villages were deserted. The deterioration of climate began in 1300 and continued for five centuries. The 14th and 15th centuries in particular saw the abandonment of many farms and villages. Deserted villages in Britain have often been attributed to the Black Death (1348–50) but Lamb points out that the process started before and continued long afterwards. One study of medieval tithe records in the English Midlands showed that the population of rural settlements here declined by a third, and sometimes by a half, between 1290 and 1327.

The sequence—climatic deterioration, bad harvest, famine, village abandonment—seems to have happened frequently in Europe during the 14th, 15th and 16th centuries, and Lamb speculates that a large part of medieval social history might be explained in terms of man's vulnerability to climate.

Between 1540 and 1700 temperatures everywhere became markedly colder and Europe entered the *Little Ice Age*. Glaciers once again expanded and in twelve years between 1540 and 1700 the River Thames at London was completely frozen over. In the last half of the 17th century the Thames was frozen over on six separate occasions, and frost fairs were a frequent occurrence. The last complete freezing of the river was in 1814 (Lamb, 1977, pp. 568–570).

The period since 1800 has been one of steady recovery from the Little Ice Age (Figure 11.4), and during the 1850s and 1860s alpine glaciers once again receded in response to the general warming. Meteorological data are available for much of the northern hemisphere since about 1870 and temperature curves (Figure 11.6) show that between 1880 and 1940 mean temperature in the northern hemisphere rose by 0.6 °C while between 1945 and 1970 it fell by 0.3 °C. This most recent fall has been accompanied by a general increase in snow and ice amounts during the early 1970s.

THE CAUSES OF GLACIATION AND FUTURE CLIMATIC PROSPECTS

Theories on climatic change generally fall into one of three groups. The first group stresses that

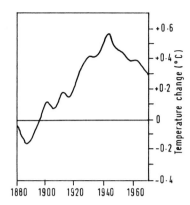

Figure 11.6 Mean temperature changes in mid-latitudes of the northern hemisphere between 1880 and 1970. The zero line represents temperature in 1880 and temperatures in later years are expressed relative to this datum.
(Based on J. M. Mitchell, 1963, 'On the worldwide pattern of secular temperature change', *Changes of Climate*, UNESCO, p. 161.) ·

variations in the amount of solar radiation received by the earth are the fundamental cause of climatic change. These are *astronomical theories*. A second group of theories stresses the importance of changes in *terrestrial* factors such as the earth's albedo or the frequency of vulcanicity. A third group, concerned with climatic changes that may (or may not) have taken place over the past hundred years or so, believes that man's technology can change climate significantly and that such changes may be superimposed on, and even mask, changes taking place due to other factors.

No single theory yet explains climatic change in Pleistocene times although astronomical theories probably enjoy the widest support among climatologists. These theories argue that changes in the receipts of solar radiation were principally responsible for the onset of glaciation. Several factors are important in determining the amount of insolation received by the earth over very long periods but two might be mentioned here. The first is the tilt of the earth's axis. At present this is $23\frac{1}{2}°$ but if it were to increase, by as little as 1°, high latitudes in the northern hemisphere would receive 4% more insolation in summer. A reduction of the earth's tilt would correspondingly decrease the summer insolation in these areas. A second factor is the earth's elliptical orbit around the sun. At *perihelion*, which currently occurs on January 4th, the earth is nearest to the sun and at *aphelion*

(July 5th) it is furthest away. These relationships are not constant and by 1992 the opposite will occur. Perihelion will take place in the northern hemisphere's summer and aphelion in winter. Solar radiation received by the earth at aphelion can be up to 7% less than that received at perihelion.

Neither the earth's tilt nor its elliptical orbit round the sun is constant. Both have certain well-defined cycles lasting 40 000 years and 21 000 years respectively, during which the position of the earth relative to the sun changes in a systematic manner. At certain intervals these cycles combine and bring the earth relatively close to the sun and at other times position it relatively far away. A Yugoslavian astrophysicist, Milankovitch, argued that these latter periods would produce glaciations and predicted six very well-defined cold spells in the last 350 000 years. These cold spells correspond very closely with periods of low oceanic temperature as determined by oxygen isotope analysis of carbonates on the ocean bed (Table 11.2).

Despite the good correlation between Milankovitch's predictions and oceanic stratigraphy, the astronomical explanation of glaciation just described has its weaknesses. Some scientists, for example, argue that glaciation requires not less solar radiation but more, in order to increase the amount of water vapour available in high latitudes for condensation and precipitation as snow. Another criticism is that we have no evidence of regular and intense cold periods in Tertiary times, even though cyclic variations in the earth's ellipse and tilt must have occurred then with the same periodicity as they do now. A final weakness of the astronomical theory in the view of some critics is that the amount of solar energy received by the earth would vary by only a few percent between those times when it was closest to the sun and those times when it was furthest away. This variation, they argue, would probably be too small to initiate glaciation.

It is sometimes suggested that periods of intense volcanic activity might act as trigger actions to initiate periods of glaciation. Dust has a definite scattering effect on solar radiation and large amounts in the atmosphere released during phases of mountain building might severely reduce the insolation received at the earth's surface and start a phase of cooling. The fact that a phase of mountain building in Tertiary times preceded the Pleistocene periods add some apparent support to this theory. But the time period (some 30–40 million years) between the end of Tertiary mountain building and the beginning of the Pleistocene was almost certainly long enough for any atmospheric dust to have settled out.

A second terrestrial theory relates the onset of glaciation to possible changes in the position of long waves in the upper troposphere (see Tullett). Studies have shown that winter conditions in mid-latitude countries of today often differ in severity from year to year, and that these differences can be related to changes in the position of Rossby waves. If a particular pattern of Rossby waves conducive to colder winters and the accumulation of snow were to become more frequent over Britain than they are today it is suggested that glacial conditions in Britain could possibly start again. The key element in this theory is the longitudinal position taken up by Rossby waves in the later stages of the index cycle (Chapter 10) when the amplitude of the waves becomes most pronounced and tropospheric circulation is most markedly north-south (i.e. meridional).

Today the longitudinal position of these waves tends to remain constant. For example, a pronounced trough recurs east of the Rockies in

Table 11.2. Dates of the most intensive periods of glaciation in the last 500 000 years as predicted from analyses of ^{18}O in ocean cores and by Milankovitch's astronomical theory

Oxygen-18 analyses[1] (Years Before Present)	Milankovitch[2] (Years Before Present)
20 000	20 000
65 000	70 000
110 000	115 000
	180 000
245 000	230 000
330 000	330 000
420 000	
505 000	

1 Source: Calder, I. N., 1974, 'Arithmetic of Ice Ages', *Nature*, Vol. 252, pp. 216–18.
2 Source: Fairbridge, R. W., 1960, 'The Changing Sea-Level', *Scientific American*, 202, p. 9.

North America. But if the preferred longitudinal position of these troughs and ridges were to shift, the areas of maximum warmth and cold along any parallel (line of latitude) in mid-latitude would presumably shift too. And the redistribution of temperature could take place without average temperatures along the parallel changing at all.

Imagine, for example, that north-west Europe, with its plentiful supply of precipitation, were to become 5 °C cooler than today and that central Canada were to become correspondingly warmer as a result of a shift in the longitudinal position of long waves. In north-west Europe the number of days with snow lying on the ground could be expected to increase, and if such conditions lasted long enough ice sheets might once again start to accumulate. In Canada melting might be expected. However, modern temperatures in Canada are too far below freezing for such a small temperature increase to cause melting. A more likely effect would be increased snowfall resulting from increased absolute humidity levels as temperatures began to rise. Increased snow and ice amounts in both areas would bring into effect other factors such as increased albedo. This would encourage the further development of ice sheets by the positive feedback mechanisms described in Chapter 1.

The attractiveness of this particular theory is that it provides a mechanism for glaciation in terms of factors which govern our weather today. However, like many other theories of climatic change much of it necessarily remains conjectural and several important questions about climatic change in Pleistocene times remain to be answered. One such question concerns the causes of Pleistocene climatic change in intertropical areas. We shall see in Chapter 14 that the intertropical areas were much drier at glacial maximum than they are now and that in parts of Africa aridity extended to the equator. Were changes in the atmospheric circulation of low latitudes responsible for this climatic change or was it part of a more general worldwide trend towards lower amounts of available moisture which caused forests everywhere to retreat, including the tropical rain forests? These and other questions are currently important topics of research among climatologists and biogeographers.

Another important question concerns the role of the north Atlantic, north Pacific and Arctic oceans in Pleistocene times. If these were covered with ice, where did the moisture come from to supply the snowfall over the ice sheets of the northern hemisphere? These ice sheets would have been dominated by cold anticyclones and subsiding air. They could hardly have generated any precipitation themselves from locally-induced instability. Moist air must have entered the ice cap areas from outside and this suggests that many parts of the northern oceans must have been ice-free at the time of maximum glaciation.

PRESENT TRENDS AND THE FUTURE

As we have seen, temperatures in the northern hemisphere appear to have been falling since 1945. One school of thought (see P. J. Lamb's review of this debate) argues that this trend is principally caused by atmospheric dust from industrialization, and that cooling is concentrated in high latitudes, where the sun's rays pass through the greatest thickness of atmosphere and therefore suffer the greatest scattering. The cold pool of air above polar regions is intensified by the cooling and expands to push upper circumpolar westerlies towards the equator. These in turn push other features of atmospheric circulation towards the equator including the subsiding air in the poleward limb of the Hadley cell which is said to be currently further south by a few degrees latitude than it used to be. Subsidence in this limb, which now lies over the Sahel region in the upper Niger valley, brings drought because it prevents monsoonal air from the Gulf of Guinea penetrating very far into west Africa during summer. The recent Sahel droughts, on this interpretation, have thus been initiated by extratropical cooling, and this in turn is seen as a well-established recent climatic trend. Some supporters of this 'climatic change' theory believe that the monsoons of west Africa may not return until the end of the century.

An alternative theory argues that recent extreme climatic events are just part of the natural variability inherent in any world climatic pattern. Departures from average conditions and the infrequent occurrence of extreme events are to be expected. Theories of the type described in the last paragraph are considered alarmist by this school of thought and it is argued that there is insufficient evidence to suggest that world temperatures are falling significantly. Specific criticisms of the 'climatic change' theory are as follows:

1 The record is not long enough to establish significant trends and to extrapolate these into the future.
2 Dust levels in the atmosphere measured at the Mauna Loa laboratory in the Hawaiian islands already appear to be falling.
3 All other changes in the composition of the atmosphere, particularly the increasing CO_2 levels, are tending to increase world temperature, not reduce it.
4 If the present sub-Saharan droughts are the product of extratropical cooling, why did such droughts also occur in the 1940s when the northern hemisphere was at its warmest since 1800?

A possible local factor encouraging drought in the Sahel is overgrazing. Reduced vegetation increases ground-level reflection and decreases the amount of net radiation absorbed at the earth's surface. This in turn leads to less intense upward atmospheric motion, less cloudiness and ultimately less rainfall. Vegetation growth is thus inhibited and the desert expands. This is the process of *desertification* and it is a widespread phenomenon in the subtropical high pressure belts of north Africa and the Middle East. Pressure on the land in semi-arid areas may thus contribute towards increasing drought even though it need not necessarily be the sole cause.

Many climatologists reject outright the theory that the earth is entering a phase of cooling, and point instead to the more dominant upward trend of world temperatures since 1800, in comparison with which the recent cooling phase has been relatively slight and short-lived. This temperature increase, as we have seen, coincides with man's output of CO_2 from the burning of fossil fuels. If this output continues at its present level (currently we release 5×10^9 tonnes of carbon per year into the atmosphere) world CO_2 levels could double by 2050. According to one estimate, this might cause mean global temperatures to rise by 2 °C. Such a view of likely future changes is widely held and has recently been exhaustively discussed by experts from the World Meteorological Organization, the United Nations Environmental

Programme, and the International Council of Scientific Unions. Some scientists argue that increases in CO_2 levels will be highest in the high latitudes of the northern hemisphere and that temperature increases here will exceed those elsewhere. This will have the effect of decreasing the temperature gradient between equator and poles which is the basic mechanism determining atmospheric circulation. None of these changes is likely in the near future and their specific effects on the worldwide pattern of temperatures and/or precipitation are uncertain. One prediction, quoted by Hargreaves, is that rainfall between latitudes 37°N and 47°N might decrease and that evapotranspiration here may increase by 30%. But these are only estimates, and other predictions are far less dramatic. That is why the World Meteorological Organization helped to establish an International World Climate Programme (WCP) in 1979. Among the subjects it will study is the variability of world climate and some of the likely developments over the next 30–50 years (Anon; Bouille and Doos).

CONCLUSIONS

Major trends in world climate over the past 2000 years are now reasonably well established though extrapolation of these trends into the future is not yet possible with any certainty. The causes of glaciation and of other, less dramatic, types of climatic change are not yet fully understood. One thing, however, is certain. Climatic history tells us that extreme variability is possible and that successive years, decades, and even centuries may depart very considerably from long-term average conditions. In a world of rapidly-increasing population, variations of climate can cause real economic and social problems. Primitive rural societies are most immediately vulnerable, but industrialized societies may have to adjust in the longer term.

Large-scale responses to diminishing water supplies, however, are not without their own implications for climatic change. In 1982, work started in the Soviet Union on a water transfer scheme involving the transport of 20 km³ per year from the Pechora and Sukhona rivers into the Caspian Sea basin. This may yet prove to be the first part of a much grander scheme to divert water southward into the Caspian Sea basin from rivers such as the Ob and Yenisey draining northward into the Arctic Ocean. The Caspian Sea is currently deprived of 37 km³ of water per year because of abstraction in the Volga basin upstream and levels are falling dramatically. According to many scientists, the loss of relatively warm water flowing into the Arctic Ocean from these rivers would significantly change climatic patterns in the northern hemisphere by altering the amount of Arctic ice. It would be ironic if man's response to water shortage, brought about in this case principally by the demands of irrigation in the Volga basin and not by changing climate, were itself to bring about further climatic changes with even more severe consequences! (See Vorupaev and Kosarev.)

Section 4
BIOGEOGRAPHY

12

Flows, Cycles and Systems in the Biosphere

The *biosphere* is that part of the earth containing life, and the basic processes of life are photosynthesis and respiration. These processes involve the cycling of three important chemical elements (hydrogen, oxygen and carbon) between solid, liquid and gaseous forms of matter. Liquid matter, of course, principally exists in the hydrosphere, solid matter in the lithosphere and gaseous matter in the atmosphere. The biosphere therefore exists at the junction of the other three spheres (Figure 12.1) and occupies a relatively narrow vertical zone. Its limits extend from about 7000 m above sea level to about 6000 m below. Man is a natural component of the biosphere and utilizes more parts of it than any other organism. His ultimate dependence on the biosphere and his impact upon it are important contemporary themes of all the sciences, including physical and human geography, and it is therefore appropriate that some time be spent in examining how the biosphere works.

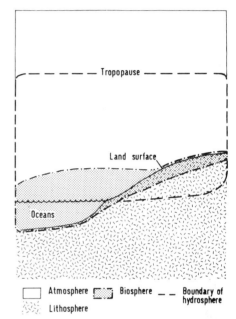

Figure 12.1 An idealized representation of the biosphere in relation to the hydrosphere, atmosphere, and lithosphere.

SOLAR ENERGY—SOURCE OF LIFE

There are seven essential ingredients of life on earth. These are:
1 a supply of either solar energy or chemical energy for food;
2 water;
3 carbon dioxide;
4 oxygen;
5 an appropriate range of temperatures;
6 suitable surfaces on which solids, liquids and gas can interact with each other;
7 an adequate supply of nutrients to encourage growth.

We saw in Chapter 1 that solar radiation is emitted in different wavelengths. Radiation in the visible light part of the spectrum normally agitates molecules in substances on earth and they subsequently release this energy as heat. Green plants behave differently for they contain chlorophyll, a substance that can trap light and convert it into stable chemical compounds edible to other organisms. This is *photosynthesis*, the fundamental mechanism underpinning the production of food on earth. Photosynthesis is a process which *fixes* carbon. Plants take in carbon dioxide (CO_2) through their stomata and water through their roots and, in the presence of light, convert these through their chlorophyll-bearing tissue into carbohydrates (containing fixed carbon) and oxygen (O_2). The carbohydrates, which are sugar-like substances, then become available as food both to the plants themselves and to other animals. The O_2 produced is released into the atmosphere. Photosynthesis is thus the source of the world's oxygen supply, a fact of which some people are more aware than others (Figure 12.2).

Only green plants can photosynthesize, but such plants exist both on land and in water. On land they range in size and complexity from microscopically small algae to trees. In water, *phytoplankton* drifting near the surface perform the same role, absorbing dissolved CO_2 from the top layers of the ocean or lake, where it is readily available, and fixing it as new carbon in their own organic tissue. Green plants are thus the basic creators of food on earth. They are the *producers* or *autotrophs*. The term 'trophic' means 'nourishing' and an autotrophic plant therefore feeds itself: it is self-nourishing.

Although the carbon fixed by autotrophs is the basis of the world's food supply, the autotrophs

Figure 12.2 Photosynthesis is not a process the public is normally aware of. Here, on a North American college campus the public is reminded of its role and importance to human life.

consume a large proportion of it themselves before any becomes available to other organisms. Like other forms of life, autotrophs have to survive when food is scarce. For autotrophs, food is scarce at night when light is unavailable for photosynthesis. Some of the food synthesized as carbohydrate in the day is therefore stored in the green plants for their own food supply at night.

Any organism using carbon as a source of energy has to oxidize it. To do this, the organism takes in atmospheric oxygen. The oxidation of carbon to produce energy is a biochemical process that produces carbon dioxide and water. As a biochemical process, it involves the breaking of molecular bonds in the carbohydrates and the joining of oxygen atoms with all the carbon and hydrogen atoms released in the process. This is *respiration* (see Chapter 1) and the respiration of plants alone consumes about 50% of the fixed carbon they themselves produce in photosynthesis.

The fixed carbon not consumed by autotrophs is available as a source of food to organisms which cannot photosynthesize their own carbon. Such organisms are called *heterotrophs* (i.e. they are nourished by others). Two basic types of heterotroph can be recognized. One type feeds on organic matter to convert it into new forms of living organic tissue. The other type feeds on organic matter in order to break it down into the inorganic constituents from which it was originally built up by photosynthesis. The first type of heterotroph forms part of a *grazing food chain*. The latter forms part of a *decay food chain* (Figure 12.3).

Grazing food chains

The grazing food chain consists of herbivores, carnivores, and omnivores. These three classes of organism exist at different *trophic levels*, i.e. they each derive their food in distinctive ways. At the lowest level of the grazing food chain are herbivores. These obtain their food by grazing directly on the vegetable matter produced by photosynthesis. On land, herbivores have a wide size range: grasshoppers, fieldmice, cattle and deer, for example, all fall into this category. In water the smallest consumers are *zooplankton*, microscopically small animals which feed on such phytoplankton as blue-green algae and diatoms.

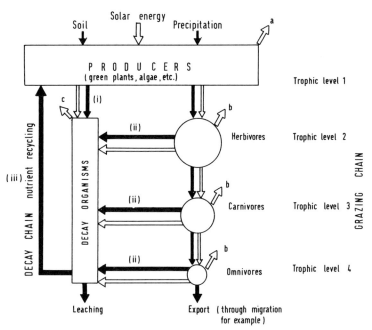

Figure 12.3 Flow diagram showing the relationship between food producers and food chains in a terrestrial part of the biosphere. Flows of energy are shown by open arrows, nutrient flows by solid arrows. Most of the solar energy fixed in the biosphere by photosynthesis is consumed in respiration by plants (a), animals (b), and micro-organisms (c) and all nutrients are recycled passing either directly into the decay chain from the producers (i) or into the decay chain from various parts of the grazing chain (ii). Inorganic nutrients are released by decay and recycled into the soil for re-use by producers (iii). There is some loss of nutrients to plants by leaching of dissolved nutrients to groundwater and subsequently to streams for eventual transfer out of the system. This loss is compensated for by the release of nutrients in rock weathering. Browsing animals also migrate out of the system and these represent a loss of nutrients and of stored chemical energy. (Source: G. M. Woodwell, p. 29.)

Larger aquatic herbivores are insects, snails and fish. Herbivores consume part of the biomass produced by photosynthesis and convert it chemically into a new form of biomass containing proteins and fats. The term 'biomass' refers to the quantity of living material (i.e. stored chemical energy) existing at any particular trophic level.

Above herbivores in the grazing food chain are the carnivores, the meat eaters. These are predatory creatures. Good examples are the wolf, eagle and pike. Carnivores occupy the third trophic level, above producers (1st level) and herbivores (2nd level). Man is an omnivorous animal (i.e. he is both herbivore and carnivore) and he therefore obtains his food from more than one trophic level.

Two features of the grazing food chain need to be stressed. The first feature is its structure. In terms of energy at each trophic level the grazing food chain is shaped like a pyramid, for the simple reason that not all the biomass at each level is passed on as food to the level above. On the first trophic level some of the solar energy fixed as carbon is used to sustain the plants themselves, and is not available for the herbivores as food. In a similar way some of the energy stored in the proteins and fats of herbivores is used to sustain them when they are not eating, and is not available as food to the carnivores. Thus, although chemical energy is transferred up the food chain from one trophic level to another, a large proportion is lost in metabolic respiration at each level. These energy losses are very considerable (Figure 12.4).

A second characteristic feature of the grazing chain is the tendency towards a decreasing number of organisms at each successive trophic level. Because energy (and usually biomass) decrease up the food chain, the amount of available food in any particular area of land decreases up the food chain as well. Carnivores therefore have to roam over longer distances for their food supply than herbivores, and omnivorous man, even in primitive societies, covers larger areas in search of

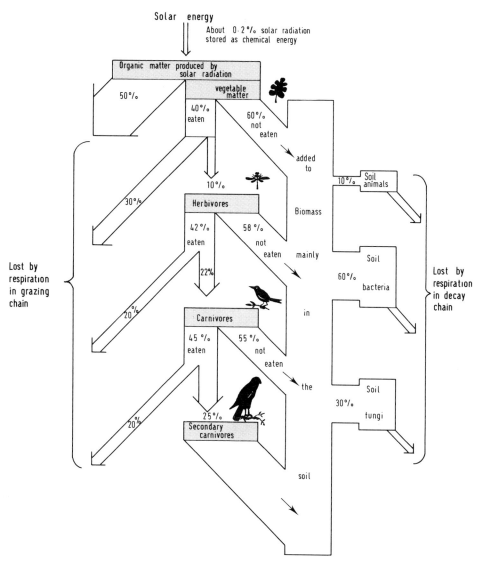

Figure 12.4 Energy flow in a deciduous forest. Note the large losses of energy involved in maintaining normal metabolic functions at each trophic level. Only 0.275% of the total chemical energy fixed by photosynthesis becomes available to the secondary carnivores as food in this particular forest.

food than carnivores. Industrialized man, at the very pinnacle of the food chain, obtains his food from many diverse parts of the world. Eventually, the amount of energy expended in obtaining food equals and then exceeds that obtained from eating it. For all organisms except man, this principle sets the limit for the number of trophic levels in the food chain and the number of organisms on the highest level in a particular part of the biosphere. As we shall see, however, man is prepared to expend more energy in obtaining certain types of food than he derives from eating them.

The decay food chain

The second type of food chain is the decay food chain. This consists of organisms like millipedes and worms that consume leaves and other dead organic matter. Also in this food chain are various forms of bacteria and fungi which break down dead organic matter into its constituent inorganic chemical compounds of carbon, nitrogen, calcium, etc. In this process of biological decomposition, or *biodegradation*, oxygen is consumed by the bacteria in respiration. In the process of biodegradation, water, carbon dioxide and heat are released. Sufficient oxygen may not always be available for bacteria to complete the breakdown of organic compounds into their inorganic constituents. Sometimes oxygen runs out altogether and normal bacterial respiration cannot continue. In these *anaerobic*, or oxygen-starved, conditions the products of biodegradation are not water and carbon dioxide. Instead, partially-decomposed organic matter builds up, often containing the foul-smelling gas hydrogen sulphide (H_2S). Decomposition is only finally complete when the end-products of water, carbon dioxide and other mineral nutrients have finally been released into the soil or atmosphere.

Energy fixed in the biosphere

The rate at which energy flows through the biosphere or through the individual trophic levels of the food chain is very difficult to assess. At the first trophic level the problem can be tackled by measuring the amount of vegetation growth on an ungrazed plant over a certain period of time. Growth in these circumstances represents the difference between the amount of organic carbon fixed as chemical energy by photosynthesis and the amount of fixed carbon consumed in respiration by the plant itself (R_A). Growth is usually called net primary production (NP). The amount of carbon fixed by photosynthesis is gross primary production (GP). Thus

$$GP - R_A = NP.$$

Newbould discusses how these can be determined from field measurements of trunk girths, litter-fall, weights of leaf and root harvests, etc.

For the world as a whole NP has been estimated at 170×10^9 tonnes (see Table 12.2) though it varies markedly from crop to crop. In deciduous trees of the high latitudes, growth is relatively low because photosynthesis principally takes place in summer whereas respiration takes place in summer and winter. Respiration in winter, when photosynthesis is virtually nil, consumes much of the energy fixed in summer. In comparison, agricultural crops such as wheat have relatively high growth rates because they are harvested before any stored energy is used in respiration. The net productivity of autotrophs is the maximum potential food supply for all heterotrophs on the higher trophic levels of the food chain.

RECYCLING OF MATERIALS IN THE BIOSPHERE

There is a distinct contrast between the movement of energy in the biosphere and the movement of materials. Energy moves into, through and out of the biosphere in a complex series of energy transformations. One sequence of energy transformations could be represented as follows. At the first trophic level solar energy becomes chemical energy in the form of fixed carbon. At the second trophic level the chemical energy of fixed carbon is transformed into the chemical energy of fats and proteins. All these forms of chemical energy can be considered as potential energy in that they are a food source and therefore provide a capacity to do work. At the second, third and fourth trophic levels potential energy becomes kinetic energy (motion), and kinetic energy becomes heat energy through frictional effects of that motion and through respiration. Respiration releases heat because oxygen atoms form very strong chemical bonds with other elements in the process, and heat is released as the new bonds are formed. Heat energy is thus the end-product of all energy transformations in the biosphere. As we have seen when we considered the laws of thermodynamics in Chapter 1, heat energy is the most degraded form of energy and cannot be spontaneously transformed into any other form of energy. If the highly structured, well-organized food chains of the biosphere are to be preserved, heat energy cannot be allowed to build up within it. Heat is therefore exported, principally to the atmosphere, and replaced with further inputs of solar energy. It is the continuous input of solar energy and the continuous output of heat which thus maintains the *continuous flow of energy* through the food chains of the biosphere (see e.g. Odum, p. 38).

In contrast to the constant throughput of energy in the biosphere, materials tend naturally to be conserved by *recycling*. Hydrogen, oxygen and carbon are the chemical elements recycled by photosynthesis and respiration. Together with nitrogen, one of the most important nutrients in the biosphere, they account for 99% of all materials circulating in the biosphere.

The carbon cycle

Carbon appears in three principal forms. As a gas, CO_2, it is stored in the atmosphere and in the oceans where it is available for photosynthesis by autotrophs. As carbon it is stored in all forms of vegetation, where it is available as energy for autotrophs and heterotrophs. As carbonate it is stored in accumulating oceanic and lacustrine sediments.

Two virtually separate cycles of carbon exist in the biosphere. In the ocean, carbon is fixed by phytoplankton drifting at the water surface where they are able to absorb light for photosynthesis. The CO_2 they require for photosynthesis is obtained principally from surface oceanic water which is rich in CO_2. Oxygen is an essential product of photosynthesis by phytoplankton, and this oxygen is used by zooplankton which graze the fixed carbon in the phytoplankton as their source of food. Phytoplankton and zooplankton have very short lives and therefore produce a lot of dead organic matter. This sinks to lower levels of the ocean where it is consumed by micro-organisms which, like the zooplankton, rely for their respiration on the oxygen produced by phytoplankton. A by-product of this decomposition is CO_2 which is then dissolved in the water to become available for photosynthesis by phytoplankton. This cycle is thus almost closed (Figure 12.5).

A fraction of fixed carbon contained in the dead plankton sinks to deeper layers of the ocean where it decomposes more slowly. A very small proportion escapes decomposition altogether and accumulates on the bed of the ocean eventually to become fossil carbon in some form of sedimentary rock. The principal reason for this slight rupture of the oceanic carbon cycle lies in the poor vertical mixing of ocean waters which are heated from above and therefore have a very stable temperature distribution (see Chapter 10). Poor mixing means that the oxygen produced by phytoplankton at the surface is not very plentiful in bottom layers and micro-organisms cannot decompose material as efficiently as they can nearer the surface.

The carbon cycle on land is shown in Figure 12.6. It is connected to the oceanic carbon cycle by the exchange of oceanic and atmospheric CO_2. This occurs through turbulent wave action, and normally the atmosphere and oceans exchange the same amount annually with perhaps a slight net annual movement of CO_2 from the atmosphere to the oceans to make up the small amount lost by incomplete biodegradation of dead plankton. Over the last 150 years, however, a second connection between the two cycles has been established in the burning of coal and oil by man (Figure 12.5). Man now oxidizes fossil carbon at a rate sufficient to increase CO_2 levels in the atmosphere by 2 parts per million (2 p.p.m.) every year although, in fact, annual CO_2 concentrations only rise by 0.66 p.p.m. Scientists have put forward two explanations to account for the

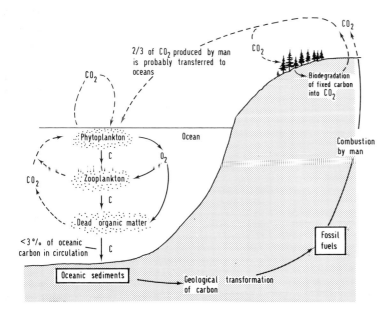

2/3 of CO_2 produced by man is probably transferred to oceans

CO_2

CO_2

CO_2

Biodegradation of fixed carbon into CO_2

Phytoplankton — Ocean

C

O_2

Combustion by man

Zooplankton

C

Dead organic matter

<3% of oceanic carbon in circulation

C

Fossil fuels

Oceanic sediments — Geological transformation of carbon

Figure 12.5 The circulation of carbon in the biosphere. Note that there are two virtually separate cycles, one in the ocean, one on land.

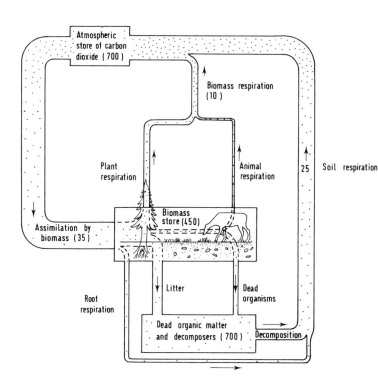

Figure 12.6 The carbon cycle on land. All figures are in tonnes $\times 10^9$. Only 5% of carbon dioxide stored in the atmosphere is fixed as carbon by photosynthesis. About 28% (10×10^9 tonnes) of annually fixed carbon is used by plant and animal respiration and returned immediately to the atmosphere as CO_2. The rest is respired through the soil. Roots of living vegetation account for a fraction of the soil's total respiration of CO_2. The rest comes from micro-organisms in the decay chain.
(Modified from B. Bolin, p. 50 and The Open University, 1975, p. 20.)

missing 1.34 p.p.m. One possibility is that this amount is annually absorbed by increased photosynthesis and fixed as carbon in new vegetation. A second explanation, more probable and more widely-supported, is that CO_2 is currently absorbed by the oceans at a faster rate than has been typical of the recent geological past. Neither of these explanations has yet been confirmed by measured data (see Bolin, p. 55).

Mankind's recent use of fossil fuels releases into the atmosphere, at a very rapid rate, the CO_2 that should have been slowly released into the oceans by respiration. In the late nineteenth century atmospheric CO_2 levels were 290 p.p.m. Now they are 330 p.p.m. According to some climatologists (see Chapter 11) this 12% increase is the source of recent atmospheric warming.

The water cycle

Water has several properties of great importance to life on earth. It expands on freezing as we saw when looking at freeze-thaw as a mechanical weathering process. Because it occupies a larger volume than the same weight of water, ice is also less dense than water and therefore floats. This is

very important to aquatic parts of the biosphere because floating ice insulates living organisms beneath it from the cold atmosphere above. If ice sank to the bottom of lakes because it was denser than water it would rapidly accumulate from the bottom upwards. Fortunately, this does not occur. Ice stays on the surface where it is exposed to solar radiation. It melts rapidly when temperatures rise.

We have seen that water transports heat most effectively in the atmosphere and oceans. It is also a powerful solvent dissolving rock material and transporting plant nutrients through the soil thus making them available for plant growth. Without dissolved nutrients in soil water there would be no photosynthesis, because plants need nutrients for photosynthesis and these nutrients are absorbed through the roots. Add to all these properties its role as a basic ingredient of photosynthesis and it becomes clear why water is essential for life in the biosphere. Because water is so important the hydrological cycle has been studied for many years and we now have a good idea of how water circulates in the hydrosphere (Figure 12.7).

The vast bulk of water is stored in the oceans which hold 97.6% of the world's water, followed

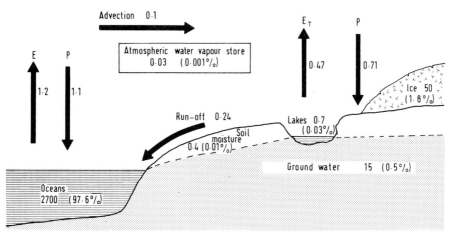

Figure 12.7 The storage and transfer of water in the hydrological cycle. There are six principal stores: the oceans, ice, groundwater, lakes, soil moisture and the atmosphere. Storage figures are expressed in metres per area and were obtained by dividing the volume of water in each store by the earth surface area of 510×10^6 km². The volume of water in the oceans is therefore 2700 m × 510×10^6 km², which equals 1377×10^6 km³. Figures in brackets alongside the storage figures refer to the percentage of the earth's water in each store. Arrows indicate water transfers in the hydrological cycle. P is precipitation, E is evaporation and E_T is evapotrans-piration. Figures for transfer are in metres area^{-1} year^{-1} and are shown for the oceans and land areas separately. Thus 1.20 m are evaporated from the world's oceans and 1.10 m are precipitated back on to them. Because the oceanic surface area of the world is 2.4 times that of the land area, the 0.10 m advected from them represent 0.24 m of precipitation on land. This figure makes good the difference between precipitation and evapotrans-piration over land and is eventually discharged back into the oceans. All figures are approximate.
(Based on H. L. Penman, pp. 41 and 42.)

by ice, groundwater and soil moisture. Water stored in the world's rivers at any one moment is infinitesimal relative to these other stores, and accounts for only 0.0001% of the world's water. Sometimes, continental storage of water lasts for years, decades, centuries or even millenia, and the water discharged into the oceans in any particular year did not necessarily fall in that year as precipitation.

The oxygen cycle

The oxygen we breathe along with other hetero-trophs in the biosphere is diatomic oxygen (O_2) which originates from the photosynthetic splitting of water and CO_2. If we divide the total volume of water on earth (1410×10^6 km³) by the rate at which it is consumed in photosynthesis and re-formed in respiration we can calculate how long it would take every water molecule to be involved in the creation of O_2. The figure we end up with is 2 million years. A similar calculation for CO_2 in-volves dividing the atmosphere's total volume of CO_2 by the rate of its production in respiration and its consumption in photosynthesis. This indi-cates that every molecule of atmospheric CO_2 is recirculated between biosphere and atmosphere

once every three hundred years on average. Atmospheric oxygen is a temporary product of these two cycles and builds up in the atmosphere. Dividing the total volume of atmospheric oxygen by the rates at which it is consumed in respiration and recreated in photosynthesis suggests a re-cycling time of 2000 years (Figure 12.8).

The durations of the cycles shown in Figure 12.8 are average figures for the globe as a whole and are not to be taken literally. All the water molecules on earth do not in fact take turns to be-come involved in photosynthesis. Most probably never become involved at all. Photosynthesis takes place on land (where less than 3% of the world's water occurs) and at the surface of the oceans. Because of the slow circulation of oceanic water most of it never reaches the surface, and so cannot take part in oceanic photosynthesis or be evaporated and advected across continents to take part in photosynthesis there.

Two features of the oxygen cycle are worth emphasizing. One is its great complexity. The oxygen cycle is complex because oxygen reacts readily with most chemical elements in the bio-sphere, and oxygen atoms are therefore bound up in other cycles such as the carbon cycle and water

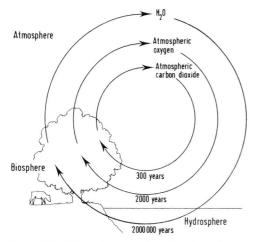

Figure 12.8 Water vapour, carbon dioxide and oxygen (O_2) are circulated in the biosphere, atmosphere, and hydrosphere. Oxygen is circulated as part of each cycle and is exchanged between them, principally in the photosynthesis–respiration cycle.
(Source: P. Cloud and A. Gibor, 'The Oxygen Cycle'. Copyright © 1970 by Scientific American, Inc. All rights reserved.)

cycle. Another feature of the oxygen cycle results from the slight imbalance between the photosynthetic production of O_2 and its consumption by respiration. If all carbon fixed by photosynthesis were broken down by respiration and decomposition then all the O_2 produced by photosynthesis would be consumed. But the fixed carbon is not all broken down. Small amounts of plant material, about 1 part in 10 000 according to Giddings, sink to the bottom of lakes, estuaries, and oceans where they are trapped in sediment and sealed from complete oxidation. The O_2 released by photosynthesis in the original production of the undecomposed organic carbon is therefore able to accumulate in the atmosphere. This process has been continuing for millions of years and explains how the world's oxygen supply has built up over geological time to the point at which it now accounts for 21% of all gases in the atmosphere. This supply could be exhausted only if all carbon in the earth's crustal rocks were brought to the surface by man and burned. If this were ever to happen, atmospheric oxygen supplies would be reduced to a level at which only autotrophs could survive. Fortunately, this prospect is not one which need worry us for it appears that the maximum amount of fossil fuel that man can recover and oxidize would deplete atmospheric reserves by only 1% or 2%.

ECOSYSTEMS—SOME CONCEPTS

The climax ecosystem

An ecosystem is a recognizable unit of the landscape in which plants and animals exchange energy and materials with their environment and each other. The number of interactions are usually so great that they cannot all be described. A study of material cycles and energy flows within an ecosystem, however, reveals a great deal about how it works. In this respect an ecosystem is no different from any of the other functioning systems that we have studied in previous chapters.

It will be recalled that net production at the first trophic level in a food chain is the difference between gross production and autotrophic respiration. An ecosystem consists of animals and micro-organisms as well as plants, and their respiration (R_H) consumes part of the ecosystem's gross production. What remains of initial GP after both these respiration demands have been met is stored in the biomass of both producers and consumers. This increase of biomass in the plant and animal community as a whole represents additional energy stored within the ecosystem and is known as net ecosystem production (NP_E). It should be carefully distinguished from net primary production (NP) and is represented as follows:

$$NP_E = GP - (R_A + R_H).$$

As ecosystems mature, and respiration demands on GP increase, NP_E decreases. When this reaches zero a *climax ecosystem* is said to exist. In such a system all solar energy fixed by photosynthesis is consumed as food within the ecosystem either by plants themselves or by some form of animal life. Every part, or *niche*, of the ecosystem which provides a potential source of food is filled by some organism adapted to the environment of the niche. Thus a mature ecosystem also has diverse forms of animal life within it. With maximum utilization of fixed energy within the system it follows that very little energy is available for export to other systems. Such climax ecosystems take hundreds, maybe thousands of years, to mature and as they mature they become more and more closed in character (see Chapter 2), importing and exporting energy in the form of solar radiation and heat respectively, but recycling more and more efficiently the nutrients needed to sustain them.

Nutrient cycling

All plants require certain chemical elements for growth. Such elements are called nutrients. The principal nutrients required for plant growth are nitrogen, phosphorus, calcium, magnesium, potassium, and sulphur all of which are needed in relatively large amounts. Some nutrients, the so-called trace elements, are only needed in relatively small amounts. Two examples are molybdenum and copper.

Nutrients are normally derived from chemical weathering and some from rainwater. Nitrogen is unique, however, and is derived from the atmospheric reservoir. Only a few micro-organisms and plants can naturally convert atmospheric nitrogen (N_2) into usable nitrate (NO_3^-). This is the process of *nitrogen fixation*. Nitrogen fixation may be either symbiotic, that is in the root nodules of members of the family *leguminosae* (peas, beans, clover etc.) or non-symbiotic, that is, by certain bacteria and blue-green algae. One important crop that fixes nitrogen is lucerne (alfalfa), and this is widely grown in crop rotation cycles for this specific purpose. In the twentieth century, man has learned to fix nitrogen industrially. Nitrogenous fertilizers are now available and their use has led to increased production of many crops including grass.

In a terrestrial ecosystem, nutrients are taken up by plants in dissolved form via roots. They are held by plants (in organic form) until the decomposition of fallen leaves and branches by microbial activity releases them as inorganic nutrients and returns them to the soil. Here they can once again be dissolved and taken up by plants in solution. It follows from this description of nutrient cycling that when growth of biomass is rapid, as in an immature ecosystem, a lot of nutrients are incorporated into the accumulating vegetation. To maintain growth in these conditions, nutrient imports from chemical weathering have to be substantial. The shortage of even one element may be sufficient to limit growth. Such an element would then be a limiting factor. The law of limiting factors was first recognized in 1840 by the biologist Liebig and is known as *Liebig's law of the minimum*.

It states that crop growth is checked by the nutrient in shortest supply. In a mature ecosystem there is less accumulation of nutrients in organic form because there is no net accumulation of vegetation from year to year. Growth of biomass is less, and nutrients are therefore cycled quickly from inorganic to organic and back to inorganic form. Fresh nutrient inputs from weathering are therefore required less and less as the ecosystem matures. Nutrient cycling becomes more and more closed.

Energy flow in plants, crops and ecosystems

The measurement of energy flow through a plant is complex. One technique (described for example by Muller) begins by enclosing individual plants in transparent boxes in order to monitor changes of CO_2 levels. During darkness, when photosynthesis does not take place, the build-up of CO_2 inside the box is a measure of (a) the quantity of stored chemical energy used in autotrophic respiration. During daylight, CO_2 levels are drawn down because the plant uses CO_2 in carbon fixation in addition to the amount it respires. The extent of the drawdown in CO_2 levels inside the box is thus one measure of (b) net production, while the ratio between (b) and (a) establishes the ratio between NP and R_A. Another measure of net production, of course, is the weight of the harvest. If growth in a cabbage over a certain period of time is 10 g and the ratio between NP and R_A is 5:1, then R_A is the equivalent of 2 g. Gross production in these circumstances must be 12 g (i.e. $12 - 2 = 10$).

For a commercial crop the dry matter contained in the harvest is usually used as a measure of above-ground NP. Relationships between NP, R_A and GP can be obtained by experiments on individual plant species contained in various crops and the energy equivalent of crop weights can be determined by measuring the heat energy released by complete combustion of an accurately weighed amount of dry matter from the harvest. Energy units can then be substituted for crop weights (see Chapter 1) and compared with measurements of shortwave and longwave energy received by the crop to determine the amount of energy it fixes.

In natural ecosystems the measurement of energy flows is much more difficult although

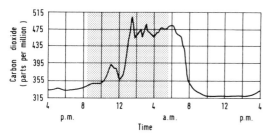

Figure 12.9 Hourly fluctuations of CO_2 at a height of 0.3 m above the ground inside an oak–pine forest during a temperature inversion. These, and similar measurements made at different heights and times, made possible the calculation of respiration rates within the forest.
(Source: G. M. Woodwell, p. 34.)

many ingenious attempts have been made. One experiment has been described by Woodwell for an oak-pine forest ecosystem. In this experiment the night-time build-up of CO_2 was measured during temperature inversions when horizontal movement of air and of CO_2 into or out of the forest was therefore zero (Figure 12.9). Ecosystem respiration, of course, comes from animals and from vegetation. That part of the total ecosystem respiration due to autotrophs was determined by careful field study of respiration rates from individual leaves and branches and from the soil.

From such field measurements a detailed picture of production and respiration in the forest ecosystem has been built up (Figure 12.10). Table

12.1 summarizes the relevant flow statistics. Net ecosystem production is 550 g of dry matter per square metre every year or 21% of gross production. Clearly the system has some way to go before reaching climax status when NP_E will reach zero. Net primary production in the forest is 1200 $g m^{-2} year^{-1}$. This is quite high in comparison with net production in other natural ecosystems (Table 12.2), although it falls below the mean value for temperate forests as a whole. Forests, in fact, are very productive ecosystems along with swamps, marshes and estuaries. Low production occurs in the desert, and oceanic production is lower than that on land (see Woodwell, p. 33). In Table 12.2 agriculture occupies a surprisingly low position. Other estimates put the net production of most agricultural land at about 2000 $g m^{-2} year^{-1}$. Some crops such as sugar cane may have net production values in the region of 7–8000 $g m^{-2} year^{-1}$. Such high values, however, are the result of two factors which do not operate in natural ecosystems. The first is the massive injection into agricultural ecosystems of additional energy in the form of fertilizers. As we shall see later, agricultural ecosystems are not all that productive when considered in relation to all the energy inputs they receive. The second factor is that most crops are harvested before autotrophic respiration in winter depletes the energy fixed by photosynthesis during summer.

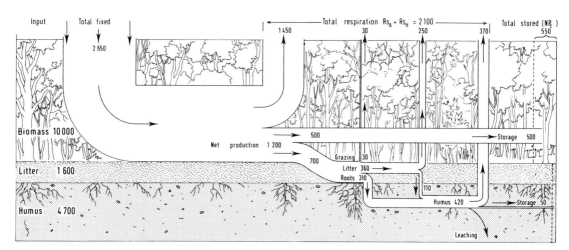

Figure 12.10 Production and respiration in an oak–pine forest ecosystem. Units are grams (of dry organic matter) $m^{-2} year^{-1}$. Production in the forest was determined from measurements of leaf weight, root weight, etc. This forest was found to fix 0.9% of solar energy received.

(Source: G. M. Woodwell, 'The Energy Cycle of the Biosphere'. Copyright © 1970 by Scientific American, Inc. All rights reserved.)

Table 12.1. Production and respiration in an oak-pine forest (Source: G. M. Woodwell, p. 32)

Gross production, GP, (a)	2650	
Autotrophic respiration, R_A, (b)	1450	grams of dry matter
Heterotrophic respiration, R_H, (c)	650	per square metre
Net production, NP, (a−b)	1200	per year
Net ecosystem production, NP_E, (a −(b +c))	550	

Two aquatic ecosystems

Lakes

Lakes, both natural and man-made, are important features of the earth's surface from many points of view. They modify the extremes of climate, especially in continental areas. Their sediments contain important evidence about recent climates and man's impact on his environment, and are therefore valuable sources of information about past landscapes (see Oldfield). Everywhere they are a means of transport and a potential source of water supply and food. In industrialized countries they represent an increasingly important recreational resource, especially close to cities. They are also obvious receptacles for human and industrial waste. Because so many demands, most of them incompatible with each other, are made on lakes their proper management presents many problems. Physical geographers have begun to study lakes for all these reasons and, along with ecologists, have made great contributions to understanding their evolution and how they work as dynamic systems of the landscape. As geographical systems they have already been described in Chapter 2.

Table 12.2. Net primary production in ecosystems

Ecosystem	Area (km² × 10⁶)	Mean net production (g dry matter m⁻² year⁻¹)	World net production (tonnes × 10⁹ year⁻¹)
Lakes and streams	2	250	0.5
Swamps and marshes	2	2000	4.0
Tropical forest	24.5	1900	46.5
Temperate forest	12	1250	15.0
Boreal forest	12	800	9.6
Woodland and shrubland	8.5	700	6.0
Tropical grassland	15	900	13.5
Temperate grassland	9	600	5.4
Tundra	8	140	1.1
Desert	18	90	1.6
Extreme desert, rock and ice	24	3	0.07
Agricultural land	14	650	9.1
Total for land	149	773	115.0
Open ocean	332	125	41.5
Continental shelf	27	360	9.6
Attached algae	0.6	2500	1.6
Total for oceans	361	152	55.0
Total for Earth	510	333	170.0

Modified from R. H. Whittaker, p. 224.

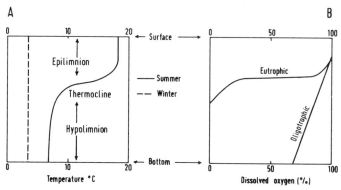

Figure 12.11 A Summer and winter temperature profiles in a temperate lake. Stratification occurs in summer when temperatures in the mixed surface layer (epilimnion) are higher than in the stagnant layer (hypolimnion) and the lake is very stable. Separating these two zones in summer is the thermocline, a narrow zone of rapidly-changing temperature.

Figure 12.11 B Summer profiles of oxygen levels in eutrophic and oligotrophic lakes. In both types of lake during winter the thermocline breaks down and the total profile is saturated with dissolved oxygen (DO).

Lakes in temperate areas function as ecosystems in the following manner. In summer they can be divided into two horizontal zones, an *epilimnion* and a *hypolimnion* separated by a *thermocline* (Figure 12.11). This stratification builds up because of the slow warming of surface layers in summer. In the epilimnion, phytoplankton such as algae and diatoms photosynthesize and release dissolved oxygen. Because warm water overlies cold in summer there is no vertical mixing and dissolved oxygen does not therefore reach the hypolimnion, which cannot produce its own oxygen from photosynthesis because of insufficient light. In autumn and early winter the surface layers cool and begin to sink. Mixing starts to occur and the temperature and dissolved oxygen gradients are eliminated so that there are no temperature or dissolved oxygen gradients in winter.

Four types of vegetation can be recognized around lake margins. At the lake edge is the *emergent zone*. Vegetation here is rooted below water but grows above the lake level. Bulrushes, bur-reed and various sedges belong to this category and sometimes stand a metre or more above the lake surface. Vegetation in the *intermediate* (or floating leaf) *zone* is rooted but grows only to the water surface. Examples are the water lily and pondweed (Figure 12.12). The third zone from the shore is the *submerged zone*. Here are found plants like stoneworts and Canadian pondweed, common in Britain and Ireland, which never reach

Figure 12.12 Lake vegetation, County Mayo. Sedges in the marginal zone and water lilies of the intermediate zone can be distinguished. Note the extensive areas of blanket peat in the background.

the water surface. Beyond these is the *zone of rootless plants* which drift in the water. These plants take in nutrients via roots from the water itself. Duckweed is one example and it may form extensive surface mats. Along with phytoplankton, marginal vegetation is autotrophic. It takes in CO_2, fixes carbon and releases oxygen. When marginal vegetation and phytoplankton die they are decomposed or become food for such herbivores as zooplankton (e.g. water fleas) and water snails. Various species of invertebrate (e.g. beetles, pondskaters) feed on algae and in turn become food for such carnivores as fish and birds. In the deeper zone of the hypolimnion sinking organic matter depletes oxygen levels, especially in summer when lake stratification is marked.

Lakes with steep shorelines and little marginal vegetation produce less organic matter to be decomposed. Oxygen levels in such lakes are therefore higher than in shallow lakes which have more primary production at the lake edges (Figure 12.13). The first type of lake is *oligotrophic* (low in nutrition) and is easily identified by stony shores devoid of vegetation. The second type is *eutrophic* (rich in nutrients). Oligotrophic lakes tend to be deep, narrow-sided and low in phytoplankton. Water is very clear, however, and some phytoplankton is found at great depth because light can penetrate easily. These lakes have high dissolved oxygen levels and low temperatures near the bottom. Many oligotrophic lakes occupy formerly glaciated troughs in north-west Scotland (e.g. Loch Ness), Wales and Ireland. Eutrophic lakes tend to be shallower than oligotrophic lakes

and their dense populations of surface phytoplankton such as diatoms and algae prevent sunlight from penetrating to deeper layers. Most naturally eutrophic lakes in Britain are in lowland areas. They have high rates of productivity and decomposition. Basal oxygen can be depleted to very low levels, especially in summer, by microorganisms in their attempt to decompose all the organic sediment which sinks to the lake bottom from the very productive surface layers. As organic sediment accumulates, the lake becomes progressively shallower and marginal vegetation begins to extend outward from the shore. The lake becomes accordingly more productive, and the organic load to be decomposed increases yet further. Oxygen levels continue to fall and the lake may be eventually de-oxygenated altogether. This is an example of positive feedback in the biosphere. It is the mechanism by which oligotrophic lakes tend naturally to develop into eutrophic lakes as shown in Figure 12.13. We shall see later that the natural sequence of eutrophication, which may take hundreds or thousands of years to complete, can be accelerated by man.

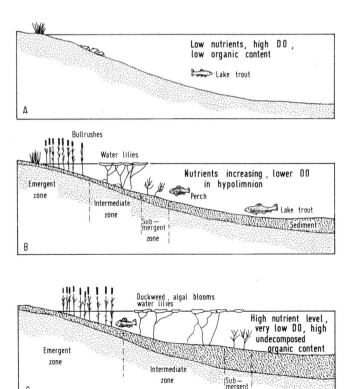

Figure 12.13 The sequence of natural eutrophication in lakes. An oligotrophic lake (A) has little sediment and high DO levels. Sediment enters the lake from tributary streams and enriches the lake with nutrients (B). The lake becomes shallower and more photosynthesis occurs at the lake edges. Although photosynthesis adds O_2 to the water, decomposition tends to remove it. (C) A eutrophic lake in which inorganic sediment and dead organic matter continue to build up on the lake bed. Micro-organisms find it difficult to decompose the organic matter, especially in summer when surface oxygen is unable to mix into lower layers because of stratification. Eventually, the bottom layers become totally de-oxygenated (anaerobic) and higher forms of fish life cannot exist. Such a lake is highly enriched with nutrients. Unfortunately, enrichment goes hand in hand with oxygen depletion. (Source: A. N. Strahler and A. H. Strahler, p. 581.)

Rivers

Rivers as ecosystems have several important features. Being avenues of transport for weathered sediment, there is a constant input and output of nutrients to and from each reach of the river. The dissolved load of rivers can be very large (see Chapter 5). Much of this load provides nutrition for aquatic plants, and net production in rivers can be 10–20 times higher than in lakes. These high production rates are usually the basis of a sophisticated food chain in a healthy river. A healthy river is rich in dissolved oxygen (DO) which it absorbs from the atmosphere by turbulent mixing as it flows over rocks and rapids. Upland rivers and other stretches of river on steep slopes are therefore particularly rich in DO. Such rivers, however, obtain little oxygen from primary production because fast currents inhibit the development of fixed vegetation, and phytoplankton are easily swept away. Downstream, where the gradients are more gentle, aquatic vegetation can become fixed on riffles and other sedimentary deposits. Photosynthesis in such reaches is a principal source of oxygen.

There has been space in this book to describe only three types of ecosystem (woodland, lakes and rivers) although many other types, for example estuaries, may be recognized. (For a longer discussion of Britain and Ireland's major ecosystems, see Angel.) On a world scale, it is possible to identify eight large terrestrial ecosystems called *biomes*. These are desert, tropical grassland, temperate grassland, tropical rain forest, temperate forest, chaparral, coniferous forest, and tundra. The ecosystem concept, on whatever scale it is applied, is important in physical geography (see Stoddart) because it stresses the interactions between vegetation, soil, animals (including man) and mineral cycles. Knowledge of these interactions provides the key to understanding how ecosystems function and how they might best be managed.

A pioneer of ecosystem analysis was E. P. Odum who was among the first to point out that mature and immature ecosystems are both integral parts of the biosphere. Man needs mature ecosystems because they are often the most stable part of the biosphere and serve to protect less stable parts from the impact of extreme events. For example, the closed canopy of a mature forest on the watershed of a drainage basin inhibits soil erosion, and reduces the likelihood of flooding in the lower parts of the drainage basin during heavy storms. But man also needs immature ecosystems with high productivity. Immature agricultural ecosystems provide our food. Immature coniferous forests provide our timber. The proper provision of mature and immature ecosystems is the basis of good land management.

MAN'S IMPACT ON NATURAL ECOSYSTEMS

Agriculture

Agriculture is a means of maintaining ecosystems in a permanent state of early development. Food production is high in such ecosystems, but it is kept high only by early harvesting and by the elimination of pests and other consumers. Both harvesting and pest control involve massive energy inputs to the ecosystem in the form of mechanized transport which consumes fossil fuel. Even the manufacture of pesticides involves fuel consumption at the manufacturing plant.

Another implication of harvesting is that ecosystem nutrient cycles are deliberately ruptured. The harvest is removed from the land before decomposition can release into the soil any organic nutrients bound up in the crop. To maintain soil fertility, man therefore has to add nutrients to the soil either as organic manure or artificial fertilizers, three important constituents of which are nitrogen (N), phosphorus (P), and potassium (K). The production of fertilizers, however, involves fossil-fuel combustion, as does the transport of fertilizers to the farm and of the crop to the market.

By the use of fertilizers and pesticides, man is able to boost primary productivity in agricultural ecosystems to very high levels, and this productivity is increasing all the time. Yields of maize in the USA over the last 40 years, for example, have increased nearly three times, and the most productive agricultural systems can now produce 4–5 times as much dry matter for food as natural ecosystems. But the high outputs of modern agriculture are obtained only at the cost of high energy inputs of the type described earlier. If energy inputs in the form of fuel are compared vith the energy contained in a particular crop, an energy ratio term can be derived which measures the efficiency of an agricultural system in terms of ts use of fossil fuels. Solar energy is excluded from the calculations. In Figure 12.14 the energy atios of various farming techniques as just defined are compared and the inefficiency of modern agriculture becomes apparent. The UK's food supply, for example, contains only 20% of the total fossil fuel energy consumed in its production.

Subsistence agriculture on this basis is therefore 300 times more efficient in its use of energy from fossil fuel than modern agriculture (see papers by Leach and by Simmons).

Man-made eutrophication and oxygen depletion in natural waters

The natural ageing process of eutrophication in lakes has been accelerated by man in several ways.

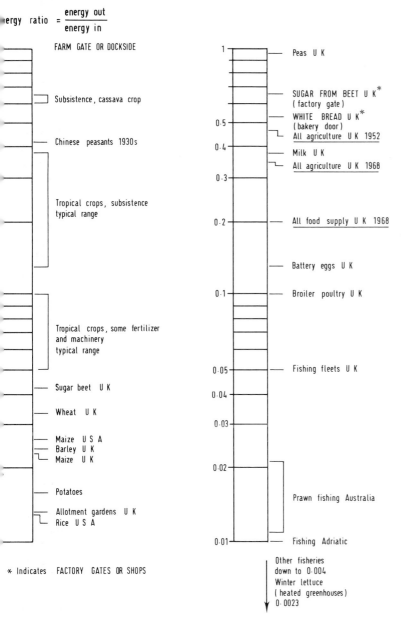

$$\text{energy ratio} = \frac{\text{energy out}}{\text{energy in}}$$

Figure 12.14 Energy ratios for a range of food-producing systems. Energy inputs refer to fossil fuel consumption. A ratio of 1.0 indicates that energy input equals energy output. Foods in the left-hand column therefore contain more energy than was required to produce them. Such agricultural ecosystems might be described as energy-positive. Systems in the right-hand column are energy-negative.
(Source: I. G. Simmons; after G. Leach, p. 8.)

Deforestation in the Middle Ages, for example, produced much sediment which ultimately ended up in the rivers and lakes of Europe. Lakes became shallower as a result and dissolved nutrients, carried into the lakes along with suspended sediment, encouraged primary production of phytoplankton, particularly algae. In natural lakes nutrients are the principal limiting factors. If too many nutrients are added algal blooms develop. These are often visible as mats of floating green vegetation. The decomposition of these blooms by bacteria rapidly exhausts oxygen levels in a lake particularly if the lake is well stratified. Today the principal nutrients involved in eutrophication by man are phosphorus and nitrogen. Phosphorus in lakes comes principally from urban effluent, especially from detergents. The main source of nitrogen is nitrogenous fertilizer, the use of which has been increasing since 1960 throughout Britain and Ireland and many parts of Western Europe. Because of man-induced eutrophication in recent years the dissolved oxygen levels in many of the world's lakes has declined dramatically. By seriously limiting the amount and species of fish that can survive in de-oxygenated water (salmon, for example, require dissolved oxygen concentrations of at least 4 p.p.m.) eutrophication can destroy rivers and lakes as a source of recreation. The most notable example of lakes made highly

eutrophic by industry and agriculture are the Great Lakes of North America. According to one estimate quoted by Giddings, the eutrophication rates induced by man in Lake Erie are 300 times the natural eutrophication rates of the lake.

Rivers, lakes, and estuaries in Britain and Ireland have been receiving sewage from towns and cities for generations. Until quite recently, much of this sewage was totally untreated before it entered the water and its principal constituent was undecomposed organic matter. To break down organic material into its inorganic components vast populations of bacteria develop in the water. Like any non-autotrophic organisms, bacteria in the decay chain need oxygen, and they obtain it from the oxygen dissolved in the water. The bacterial demand for oxygen in aquatic ecosystems is known as the *biological oxygen demand* (BOD). Downstream from a source of organic effluent in a river, oxygen levels fall due to bacterial activity, the effect being known as *the oxygen sag curve* (Figure 12.15).

To reduce the effect of domestic organic effluent on the DO levels of aquatic ecosystems sewage works have been built. These consist of various artificial environments such as filter beds in which organic matter is decomposed by bacteria continuously supplied with oxygen from the atmosphere. Many modern sewage works can reduce

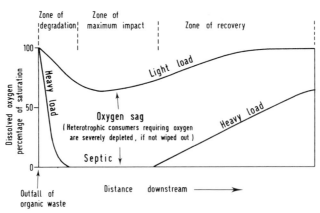

Figure 12.15 An idealized oxygen sag curve in a river downstream of an organic sewage outfall. Immediately downstream of the outfall is the zone of degradation in which BOD rapidly depletes O_2. In the zone of maximum impact the number of bacteria in the stream is at its highest, and if oxygen levels here reach zero septic conditions prevail. In the zone of recovery the amount of

sewage to be decomposed starts to decrease and so too do the number of bacteria in the decay chain. Oxygen levels accordingly start to rise, especially if the river is fast-flowing. Nutrients are converted into inorganic form in this zone and primary producers (algae, etc.) can take up these nutrients and produce O_2 as a by-product of photosynthesis.

BOD levels in organic effluent by 90%. Despite this, vast quantities of sewage, much of it un-treated, are still discharged into marine ecosystems around the coasts of densely-populated areas, and oxygen levels in estuaries and some sheltered seas such as the Baltic and Mediterranean are very low despite current efforts to improve matters.[1] Large stretches of oxygen-depleted water in estuaries can act as effective barriers to the move-ment of fish such as salmon in and out of the river systems. From a salmon fisheries management point of view, it is little use having clean rivers in which fish can breed if they are unable to penetrate a barrier of polluted water in the estuary during the course of their migration to and from the sea.

Water pollution, however, does not derive only from urban sources. Modern intensive farming techniques produce slurries and effluents with larger BOD values than domestic sewage and these are often discharged directly into rural watercourses, sometimes causing severe fish kills. Water quality in Britain's rivers is defined by measuring DO and BOD levels and four grades of quality are recognized. In 1980, 75% of Britain's rivers were considered unpolluted, 18% were of doubtful quality, 5% were poor and 2% were grossly polluted. The situation on estuaries was far worse. Only 50% were unpolluted, 34% were of doubtful quality, 8% were poor and 8% were grossly polluted (National Water Council, 1980, *River Quality—the 1980 survey and future outlook*).

Water use in Britain

The scale of man's impact on the hydrological cycle in Britain is shown in Figure 12.16. Approxi-mately half of Britain's rainfall becomes run-off and 21% of the average daily flow in rivers is used by man for industrial and domestic purposes before being returned to river or coastal waters as effluent. Rivers, of course, do not always flow at their average annual rates. Flows are lower than average in summer and higher in winter. Through-out the year, however, demand remains more or less constant, being if anything higher in summer

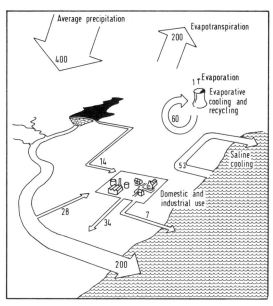

Figure 12.16 Man's impact on the hydrological cycle in England and Wales. Units are $\times 10^6\,m^3\,day^{-1}$. Of the $200 \times 10^6\,m^3$ flowing in Britain's rivers daily, 42×10^6 are used for industrial and domestic purposes. After use, 34×10^6 are returned to rivers and 7×10^6 are dis-charged at sea. Only $1 \times 10^6\,m^3\,day^{-1}$ are added to make up for evaporative losses from industrial cooling processes.
(Source: B. M. Funnell and R. D. Hey, p. 7.)

when natural river flows are at their lowest. To meet summer demand, reservoirs are built to store surplus winter run-off.

Since rivers have traditionally had to act both as sewers and sources of water supply it was natural that reservoirs were traditionally kept upstream and linked to the consumer by gravity-fed pipeline. Many factors now restrict the development of upland water-supply schemes. Reservoirs and pipelines from upland sources are increasingly expensive to build. Suitable sites for reservoirs from a geological point of view are diminishing in number. Opposition from organizations wanting unrestricted access to unspoiled upland areas is increasingly vocal and critical of reservoir con-struction in places as far apart as the Pennines and the Mourne mountains.

For these and other reasons, the current national water strategy is to improve existing storage, to develop underground storage where possible, and to develop new strategic storage sites inland and on estuaries. The Kielder dam (Figure 12.17) is one of the new strategic storage sites. Water

1 The Mediterranean is currently the subject of a clean-up campaign organized by the United Nations Environment Programme and costing £30 000 million between 1980 and 1995.

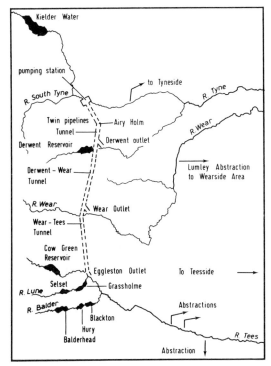

Figure 12.17 The Kielder Water scheme is designed to regulate flow in the Tyne, Tees and Wear rivers. The reservoir, Kielder Water, is the largest man-made lake in Europe and one of ten strategic reservoirs proposed for Britain. It holds $200 \times 10^6 \, m^3$ and was filled in 1982. (Source: C. Kirby, p. 146.)

stored here can be delivered by pipeline and river to a number of outlets as far south as the Tees. The plan is to make this water ultimately available to the Yorkshire Ouse as well. The national strategy is to integrate rivers, pipelines and aqueducts into as flexible a supply system as possible so that water can be transferred quickly from an area of abundant supply to an area of demand. Modifications of the hydrological cycle on this scale will clearly affect natural run-off and aquatic ecosystems and these will have to be carefully

monitored. The major proposed lines of water transfer in England and Wales are shown in Figure 12.18 (see Kirby; Funnell and Hey).

CONCLUSION

Man's impact on the flows of energy and material in the biosphere has three principal effects.

1 Cycles are broken before decay chains can return organic nutrients to the soil, and fertilizers have to be applied to maintain soil fertility.

2 Many of these artificial additions to the biosphere 'leak' from the ecosystems to which they were applied and cause pollution of other ecosystems and food chains.

3 Natural trends in the biosphere towards complex, mature, integrated ecosystems are reversed in man-made agricultural ecosystems. These are designed to increase food production but can do so only if maintained in a permanent state of immaturity by the deliberate eradication of food chains that would reduce net production and harvests.

In the biosphere flows of energy and materials depend on life processes which man can easily destroy. This is why the biosphere is less robust than the atmosphere, hydrosphere and lithosphere. But man's activities in the biosphere also have effects in the atmosphere and hydrosphere. The monitoring of these effects is now undertaken on an international scale and several research programmes have been sponsored by UNESCO and other international scientific organizations. In 1971, for example, the *Man and the Biosphere* programme started and in 1975 the *International Hydrological Programme* (IHP) was set up. It is out of such programmes that we shall hopefully discover how the biosphere might be rationally managed in the future.

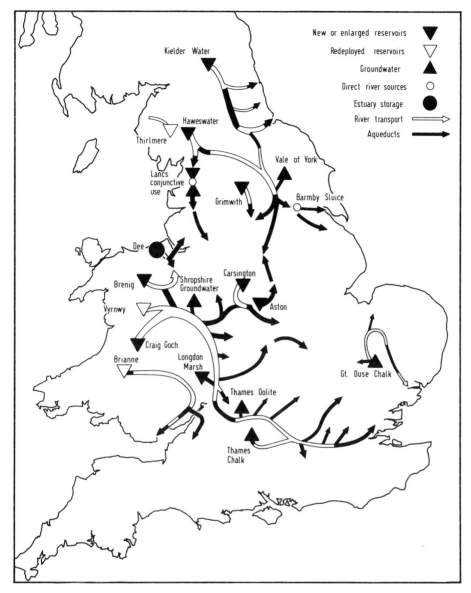

Figure 12.18 The current water storage and distribution strategy for England and Wales. Notice the strategic importance of certain river systems such as the Yorkshire Ouse, the Severn and Thames in transferring water from the wetter north and west to the drier east and south-east. Notice also the new aqueducts designed to transfer water between river systems.
(Source: The Open University, 1975, p. 48.)

13

Soils and Vegetation

Soils and vegetation are the two principal components of natural ecosystems. As such they represent the central subject matter of biogeography which studies the distribution of organisms across the earth and the way in which this distribution has evolved through time. The processes affecting soil and vegetation development are so clearly inter-related by biological activity and nutrient cycling that it is best to study them as inter-dependent parts of the landscape whenever possible.

Soil consists of inorganic rock particles derived from weathering and organic material derived from the decomposition of vegetation. It is vital for vegetation in three ways. It provides a rooting medium in which plants can grow and be supported. It stores water (against the force of gravity) which plants can easily tap, and it stores mineral nutrients in the clay-humus complex and in the soil water.

Soil occupies the uppermost section of the regolith, and its inorganic or mineral fraction is the product of mechanical and chemical weathering. Chemical weathering is important in soil development because it releases important plant nutrients into the soil such as magnesium, phosphorus, potassium, and calcium. Trace elements released by weathering include boron, molybdenum, sulphur and copper, most of which are vital in photosynthesis. The processes of chemical weathering described in Chapter 4 need not be repeated here, but a point worth emphasizing is that fine rock particles in soil are often not completely broken down chemically and may contain a substantial reservoir of weatherable minerals. Chemical weathering, in other words, is a process which goes on in the soil and is not confined to the decomposition of parent rock.

The other source of nutrients in soil is the decomposition of leaves and other dead organic matter. Dead plants, for example, contain nitrogen and magnesium as well as oxygen, hydrogen and carbon and these are all released and returned to the soil as by-products in the decay food chain. Many interesting studies are currently in progress comparing the quantities of nutrients released by decomposition and the quantities filtering through the soil into neighbouring streams.[1] Where the difference between the two amounts is high, the soil is presumed to retain most of the nutrients released by decomposition and to adequately fulfil its role as a nutrient reservoir. Where the difference is low, most of the nutrients produced by decomposition leave the soil, which is unable to retain them, and move into neighbouring streams, to be lost forever to the particular ecosystem which originally produced them. In this situation the weatherable minerals in the soil become an important potential source of plant nutrients, if they are released rapidly enough.

A final point about the decomposition of organic matter is also worth emphasizing. Recall that respiration by the organisms of decay releases CO_2. This is mixed with rainfall, itself already a dilute solution of carbonic acid (H_2CO_3). The decomposition of organic matter thus increases the acidity of water percolating downward through the surface layers of the soil.

---

1 The amount of mineral nutrients in the rainfall is also an integral part of such studies.

ACTORS AFFECTING SOIL AND VEGETATION DEVELOPMENT

Soil development

It is customary to divide factors affecting soil development into two categories: active and passive. The active factors which affect soil development are those which affect weathering and decomposition, i.e. climate and soil organisms. To these can be added three passive factors: parent material, time and topography.

Of the active factors climate is the most significant. Particularly important aspects of climate are annual precipitation and annual evapotranspiration. Where rainfall exceeds evapotranspiration, net water and nutrient movement in the soil is downward. Where potential evapotranspiration exceeds precipitation, net water movement is upward and dissolved nutrients such as calcium are moved towards the surface. Using these criteria soils can be classified as *pedalfers* or *pedocals* (Figure 13.1). Another important climatic factor is annual temperature range. Temperature is clearly related to evapotranspiration but along with soil moisture content it also affects rates of weathering and the activities of soil organisms. Many aspects of the relationship between moisture, temperature and chemical activity in soils are even now not

fully understood. In soils of the hot moist tropics, for example, silica moves down the soil profile in a process known as *desilication*, often leaving iron at or close to the surface. Tropical pedalfers therefore tend to be yellow or reddish in colour reflecting the presence of iron oxides. In temperate pedalfers the iron is mobilized leaving silica near the surface and podsols, the most extreme example of a temperate pedalfer, accordingly have a characteristic surface colour of grey. It is still not perfectly clear how the preferential mobilization of iron in temperate latitudes and of silica in the tropics is related to heat and moisture.

Other active agents in soil formation are soil organisms. In Chapter 12 the role of fungi, bacteria and other micro-organisms in breaking down dead organic matter was described. A particularly important soil organism is the earthworm which ingests both organic and inorganic material. As this material passes through the worm's gut it suffers some mechanical disintegration and chemical breakdown. In this way, decaying surface organic matter and soil grains are dispersed vertically through the soil. Earthworm channels, which are opened up as the worms force and/or eat their way through the soil, allow water and air to move through the soil more easily. Soil in which air moves freely tends to be warm. If air cannot enter, a soil tends to become cold. It

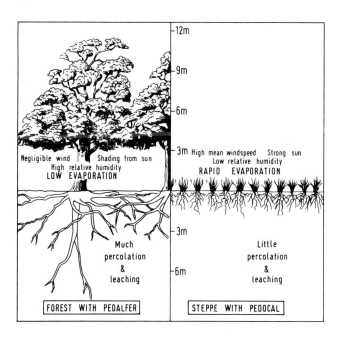

Figure 13.1 Contrasting microclimates, vegetation, and soil processes in pedalfers and pedocals. Pedalfers are so-called because aluminum (Al) and iron (Fe) are prominent constituents. In pedocals calcium (Ca) is present, brought to the upper horizon by evaporation. The term 'microclimate' refers to the climate within 2 m of the ground surface. (Source: S. R. Eyre, p. 119.)

was Charles Darwin in 1881 who made the first scientific study of earthworm activity in soil formation. Since then several studies of earthworm populations have been made. In Russian oak forests, for example, earthworm populations of 2.94 million per hectare have been counted. Populations tend to be lower under ploughed fields (0.88 million ha⁻¹ under wheatfields in Russia) and lower still under very acidic conditions such as the podsol soils of coniferous forests (Bunting, p. 43). Larger burrowing organisms (e.g. the rabbit) also affect soil development, sometimes negatively in that soil structure can be destroyed by extensive colonies.

The three principal passive factors in soil development are parent material, time and topography. The roles of all three are interrelated but this is especially the case with parent material and time. In the early stages of soil development parent material determines the range of chemical elements available. But as the soil–vegetation ecosystem matures, recycling of nutrients between vegetation and soil makes the input from weathering less important. Climate, through its effect on the direction of soil-water movement and decomposition rates, becomes correspondingly more important as time passes and in this way the soils of an area come more to reflect large-scale regional climates rather than local variations of parent material. This has been the conventional view of soil evolution since the work of Dokuchaev in Russia during the 1890s. A mature soil adjusted to climatic and vegetation controls in the way just outlined is termed a *zonal soil*. One which has not had time to become so adjusted is termed *azonal*, while one which reflects local conditions of bad drainage, or the dominance of a distinctive parent material such as limestone, is independent of time and classified as *intrazonal*. The length of time taken for a soil to move from immaturity, when it reflects parent material, to maturity when it reflects climate and vegetation, varies considerably but is seldom specified. Incipient podsolization, however, is sometimes detectable after 200–300 years and becomes quite marked after 1000 years.

Topography is another passive factor. Clearly, soils tend to move down slopes under the influence of gravity and to accumulate at their base. Soils on a steep slope are consequently thin and immature. They are azonal. At the base of a slope

soils may accumulate, often to great depth, in zones of deposition. Such soils are termed *alluvial soils*, along with soils deposited by rivers. Soils a the base of a slope are more prone to bad drainage than soils on the slope itself. Groundwater tends to be close to the surface here and may, in fact reach the surface, excluding air from the soil pores more frequently than on the slopes above. When air is excluded from the soil in this way decomposition slows down, and if flooding is frequent decomposition may be so slow that organic material never breaks down completely. In such circumstances *organic soils* (i.e. peats) may accumulate. *Gleys* are also typical soils of badly drained areas. Like peats they are intrazonal occurring in any climate where precipitation is high in relation to evapotranspiration and where excess water accumulates because of poor drainage. Such soils may be very old and, therefore, are not azonal. Peats, for example, can be very old and are an important source of palynological data (see Chapter 11). The influence of topography on soils (and vegetation) within small areas has led to the concept of a *soil catena* (Figure 13.2).

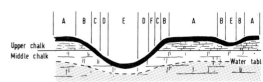

Figure 13.2 The soil catena concept, originally developed by Milne in Africa. In an area of uniform lithology and climate, variations in soil type may reflec topography through its effect on soil and water movement above or close to the ground surface. In this diagram, the depression represents a dry valley in the Chilterns. Sites with the same lettering have similar soil moisture and drainage conditions, and the pattern o mosaic of soils in the area is closely related to topography because of these controls.
(Source: J. G. Cruickshank, p. 49.)

Vegetation development

Factors affecting vegetation development are much the same as those affecting soils. Climate is an obvious active control along with soils and living organisms. Soils are usually referred to as *edaphic controls* and living organisms as *biotic controls*. In regions with pedalfer soils where precipitation is high in relation to evapotranspiration, and where movement of nutrients is predominantly downwards, trees are at a competitive advantage over grasses because of their deeper roots which enable them to extract nutrients from deeper horizons. Grasses with their shorter roots tend to dominate the vegetation when nutrients are brought to the surface by evaporation.

All vegetation requires particular temperature and moisture conditions for each phase of its development, and the constancy of climatic conditions from year to year is important. Many plants are vulnerable to short-term, unseasonal, variations of weather. In a western oceanic climate such as Britain's, for example, where frosts are uncommon, a prolonged spell of subzero temperatures in spring can seriously damage any recent new growth. Seeds and mature plants are less vulnerable.

Another important feature of climate is the distribution of temperature and rainfall throughout the year which determines the length of the growing season. Where temperature and rainfall are both high throughout the year growth is continuous as in the wet tropics. Where only one is acceptably high throughout the year the other factor becomes critical in affecting growth. Thus in Britain and Ireland, where precipitation is generally high in relation to evapotranspiration, moisture availability is seldom a problem, and the growing season is primarily determined by the length of time that temperatures are above the minimum required for growth. In contrast, the growing season in arid and semi-arid areas is determined by the start and finish of any rainfall that happens to occur.

Vegetation adjusts to climate in different ways. In very cold, windy areas vegetation is close to the ground, to make maximum use of whatever terrestrial radiation is available and to minimize exposure to cold winds. In arid areas, another extreme environment, plant leaves are small and waxy, two characteristics that are sometimes said to cut down evapotranspiration losses. Many plants here also have thick spongy stems in which to store water. Such plants are called *succulents*. Many succulents also have a distinctive photosynthetic mechanism called CAM (*crassulalean acid metabolism*) which reduces the need for stomatal opening and conserves CO_2 within the tissues. Reduced stomatal opening cuts down transpiration. In areas of abundant surface moisture some trees, such as willows for example,

appear to be better adapted than others, though why this should be so is usually far from clear. Some trees are sometimes said to transpire more and this might suit them to wet conditions. But do trees transpire at different rates, and if so, why? Is it because of rooting density? Is it to do with colour? Do trees with dark leaves absorb more radiant energy than trees with light-coloured leaves and therefore transpire more? Or is it to do with the fact that trees in wet areas are never short of water and transpire at or close to the potential rate all the time? Clearly there is the real danger of a circular argument in seeking to explain why some plants appear to thrive in wet conditions while others fare less well. Plants which actually grow in standing water or very wet conditions are called *hydrophytes*. *Xerophytes* grow in dry conditions and *mesophytes* in areas of intermediate water availability.

The deciduous habit of seasonally shedding leaves is a protection against cold or freezing temperatures. Plants lose heat through their leaves which have a large surface area in relation to volume (recall that evapotranspiration like evaporation is a cooling process). The shedding of leaves in autumn thus cuts down on heat loss. The photosynthetic process is also inefficient in high latitudes during winter. This is another reason for the deciduous habit.

Topography also affects vegetation. Slopes facing the sun, for example, are relatively warm and dry. Such locations provide especially favourable conditions for vegetation development in cold wet areas. On steep areas soils are shallow and shallow-rooting vegetation is at an advantage. The influence of topography, however, is passive. So too is the influence of time. The idea that vegetation develops through a succession of stages until it is finally adjusted to climatic factors was originally the idea of Clements in the 1930s. On bare ground in moist mid-latitudes a *succession* might begin with a *pioneer community* of lichens and algae (as outlined by Pears, for example, p. 50). These lichens and algae can colonize bare rock surfaces, but as weathering continues to slowly break down rock material, nutrients are released, and mosses may develop on the soil particles accumulating between rock outcrops. These processes continue, parent rock initially determining the primitive soil character.

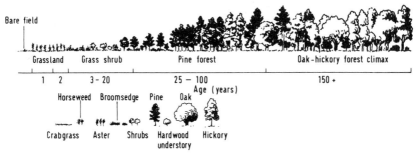

Figure 13.3 Probable sequence of plant succession from grass to climax deciduous forest in a temperate mid-latitude country.

(Source: R. A. Muller, p. 231; after E. P. Odum, 1971, *Fundamentals of Ecology*, Saunders.)

As plant decomposition increases, so too does soil acidity, and weathering and soil formation rates increase. Eventually, grasses replace mosses. With the passage of time and a thickening mantle of soil, shrubs replace grasses and trees replace shrubs. The type of succession that might follow the grass stage is shown in Figure 13.3.

The principal idea underlying the concept of plant succession is that at each stage of development a particular type of plant is dominant, but that it so alters the soil and microclimate as to create conditions more favourable for another species which subsequently invades the area and becomes dominant in the succeeding stage. The stage beyond which no further change naturally occurs is called the *climax vegetation*, and this is dominated by that plant community most closely adjusted to climatic factors. The whole succession is called a *sere. Primary seres* develop on ground previously unvegetated. *Secondary seres* develop on ground from which previous vegetation has been removed or has been arrested for some reason, maybe by fire or clearance by man.

There are several types of sere. *Xeroseres* develop on dry sites. In semi-arid areas a xerosere will stop at the grass stage or even earlier. *Hydroseres* develop in water and *psammoseres* on sand. Local conditions initially dictate the early stages of seral development but site conditions are eventually so modified from the original that all local seres converge towards a regional type dictated by climate. A xerosere in Britain, for example, might start from relatively dry local conditions on very well-drained, weathered, scree material located on the side of a glaciated valley. A neighbouring hydrosere, in contrast, might develop

from a lake from early seral stages dominated by algae. Subsequent development may be as follows (see Pears, for example, p. 51). The accumulation of sediment at the water's edge encourages the development of pondweed which traps more sediment and encourages emergent species such as bulrushes and reeds. Decomposition and sedimentation slowly transform the margins of the lake into dry land, and shrubs succeed the reeds. As each new stage develops with increasing dryness of the lake perimeter, so its predecessor is pushed into the more moist interior. In this way the initial lake becomes smaller and is ultimately completely filled. (The earlier stages of this type of hydrosere are, of course, part of the natural eutrophication process described in the last chapter.) Eventually, trees may come to dominate what was once an aquatic environment and the appearance of the vegetation will more closely resemble the final stages of the xerosere succession than the earlier stages of the hydrosere. Another type of hydrosere succession is shown in Figure 13.4.

The concept of climatic climax vegetation embodies the principle of steady-state equilibrium. We have already referred to two aspects of this equilibrium in Chapter 12. The first of these is the balance between gross primary production and respiration which results in zero net growth of the biomass. Under this condition of balance the amount of solar energy imported equals the amount of heat exported and there is no storage of energy (as chemical energy) in the biomass of the ecosystem. The second aspect of equilibrium is the balance between the uptake of mineral nutrients by plants and the return of these nutrients

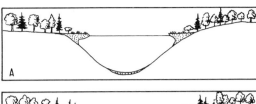

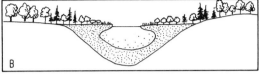

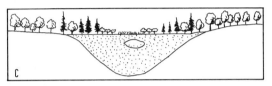

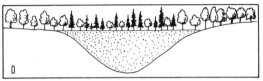

Figure 13.4 A hydrosere succession developing from an initial mat of floating vegetation such as sphagnum moss around the edge of a lake (A). The mat thickens and advances towards the centre of the lake (B). Decomposition of dead organic matter is virtually nil in this environment and the accumulation of poorly decomposed material results in the development of peat in the depression. Shrubs (B and C) and, eventually, trees (D) invade the peat from other forests nearby. (Source: R. H. Whittaker, p. 172.)

to the soil by way of such processes as leaf-fall. Under this condition of balance the amount of nutrients imported into the system equals the amount exported and there is no net storage of these materials within the ecosystem. To these two characteristics of equilibrium can be added a third relating to species composition. In a climax community the reproduction of plants in an individual species is equalled by the death of an equal number of very old plants in the species. Thus the relative frequency within the plant community remains the same and the overall species composition of the community remains stable.

Clements' views on the development of a climax vegetation have been modified by later workers, and two other theories might be described. One argues that a cyclical type of vegetation development is more probable than the indefinite maintenance of a single climax vegetation, once this has been established. In many forests, for example, some dominants produce so much shade that their own offspring saplings are unable to develop to maturity. Such dominants, it is argued, will be replaced by other species less demanding of light. The new dominant species will then allow the light-demanding species to recolonize or regenerate, and these in turn will re-emerge as dominants. In any large area this cyclical evolution is locally at different stages of development and a *vegetation mosaic* comes into existence.

Another view arguing in favour of a mosaic appearance to maturely-developed vegetation stresses that there are few very well-defined boundaries in nature. Climate, soils, topography and vegetation are not uniform over large areas and do not all suddenly and simultaneously change in character along well-defined boundaries. Change from one area to another is more usually gradual. All these factors, it is argued, affect vegetational development to some extent at least, and as each changes at different rates in any one direction so a new combination of vegetational controls comes into existence and a new pattern of vegetation emerges. This is sometimes called the *climax pattern hypothesis* and was developed by Whittaker. It states that a number of different plant communities can all exist at the climax stage, each adjusted to the wide variety of ecological conditions to be found in any area. One type of plant community will, however, be more extensive than all others and this will principally reflect the region's climate. For a longer discussion of this topic see Whittaker (p. 179).

SOME IMPORTANT PROPERTIES OF SOIL AND VEGETATION

Soil properties

Soils are differentiated from one another by texture, structure, degree of profile development, colour, chemistry, and acidity. *Texture* refers to the size distribution of inorganic materials in the soil (Table 13.1; Figure 13.5). To determine texture a soil is first sieved to separate 'fine earths' with diameters less than 2 mm from the coarser fractions of the soil. These fine earths are then allowed

Table 13.1. The international scale of soil particle sizes

Size (μm)	Description	Size (mm)
2000	Gravel and very coarse sand	2.0
200–2000	Coarse sand	0.2–2.0
20–200	Fine sand	0.02–0.2
2–20	Silt	0.002–0.02
2	Clay	0.002

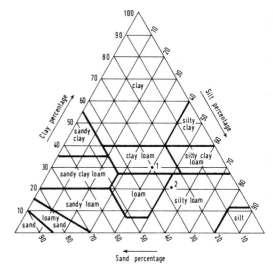

Figure 13.6 Soil classification by texture. A soil containing 30% sand, 40% silt, and 30% clay is a clay loam (1). A soil with 26% sand, 53% silt and 21% clay is a silty loam (2).

to settle gravitationally in a litre flask full of distilled water, and specific gravity measurements of the liquid/sediment mixture, made at specific times, allow the proportion of sand, silt, and clay to be determined (see Pears, p. 34; Cruickshank, p. 231). Reference to an internationally agreed classification scheme, the texture diagram (Figure 13.6), enables the soil to be classified.

A second important soil property is *structure*. Natural aggregates of soil particles are held together by their finest constituents, i.e. by clay and humus colloids. Such an aggregate is called a *ped* and peds can be classified according to their shape. Some are elongated into *columns* or prisms up to 10 cm long with well-defined flat tops, some are platy (i.e. thin and flat), while others are cube-like or *blocky* in appearance (Figure 13.7). Structure affects infiltration of water and the ease with which soil can be ploughed for cultivation. The most favourable type of structure for agriculture is a *crumb structure* in which individual

peds are fine (1–5 mm in diameter). Smaller peds inhibit soil water movement and oxygen penetration. Coarser peds do not easily hold water against the force of gravity. Soil moisture retention is therefore poor and plant nutrients are in limited supply.

Texture and structure both affect the water-holding properties of soil. The strongest force holding water in the soil against the force of gravity is the electrical attraction force between hydrogen atoms in the water molecule which have a slightly positive electrical charge and any oxygen or nitrogen atoms in the soil material which carry negative charges. Clay particles in soil are negatively charged (see later), and these too attract the positive charge on the water molecule. The strength of these attraction forces (called hydrogen bonding) is very powerful when

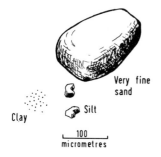

Figure 13.5 The relative size of sand, silt and clay. (Source: R. A. Muller, p. 183.)

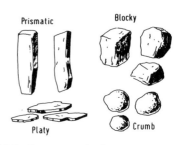

Figure 13.7 Four types of soil structure. (Source: J. G. Cruickshank, p. 58.)

water molecules and soil particles are very close together. As the distance between soil particles and water molecules increases the forces holding water in the soil become less strong and eventually a point is reached when the weight of the water molecule exerts a force exceeding the soil's total retention forces and water is able to drain down to lower horizons[1] (Figure 13.8).

It follows from all this that soils with large proportions of silt and clay, and therefore small pore spaces between individual grains, hold water in the rooting zone of plants more powerfully and for longer periods than soils containing only sand. In sand soil pores are large, retention forces are weak and water drains away freely with gravity. Too much clay in a soil, however, retains water so effectively that large quantities can be removed neither by gravity nor by root action. Such soils tend to remain waterlogged and cold allowing no air to penetrate, and therefore no oxygen. Such soils are *anaerobic*. Some silt or sand is required in a soil to allow drainage and oxygen penetration. The best soils from an agricultural point of view are therefore the loams which contain a mixture of particle sizes.

Early Russian work showed that soils in different climatic zones exhibit contrasting *profiles* below the ground surface. The nature of these profiles represents a third distinguishing feature of soils. Some soils have strongly developed horizontal stratification. Others have none. Organic debris on the surface may be thick, thin or non-existent. In some soils soluble salts lie at the surface. In other soils they are located well down the profile. The recognition by early workers of similar soil profiles across very large geographical areas within which geology varied markedly, suggested that regional climate was the principal factor affecting profile development, or the lack of it.

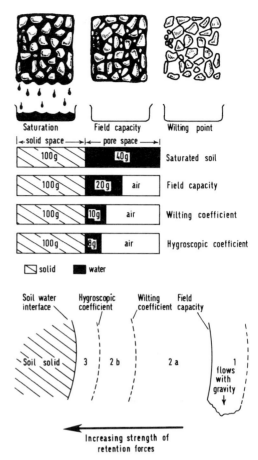

Figure 13.8   Soil-water zones in a loam soil. At saturation, water furthest away from the soil particles is held by weak retention forces and flows out of the soil under the influence of gravity. This is gravitational water (1). The term 'field capacity' defines the maximum amount of water a soil can retain against gravity. A block of soil at field capacity would retain all its water even though suspended over a tray (top diagram). Water held by stronger retention forces than the water which drains out is called capillary water. Some capillary water can be removed by transpiration and is therefore available to plants (2a). As water is removed through the transpiration stream so the distance between soil particles and water molecules decreases and the molecular attraction forces between soil particles and soil water become very strong. Soil moisture retention forces therefore increase, and there eventually comes a point at which the forces involved in transpiration are unable to extract any more water. This is called the wilting point. Water held by retention forces stronger than those at wilting point is usually divided into two categories, namely capillary water unavailable for plants (2b) and hygroscopic water (3). Hygroscopic water exists as a very thin film around each soil particle. Soil moisture retention forces at the hygroscopic coefficient are almost 100 times higher than at field capacity.
(Based on N. Pears, p. 39.)

1 Surface tension is the other principal force involved in holding water against gravity. As we saw in Chapter 1, water molecules in a body of water are joined to each other by hydrogen bonding on all sides. Molecules on the surface, however, are only held from below and this, one-sided bonding 'pulls' surface molecules into the body of the water. This is the phenomenon of surface tension which can work with, or against, the force of gravity. Water droplets adhering to soil particles, or the side of a glass for example, are prevented from moving downwards partly by surface tension forces acting inward towards the centre of mass of the water droplet.

Soil profiles are usually divided into three basic horizontal divisions, an upper A horizon, an intermediate B horizon and a lower C horizon. The A and B horizons are the true soil, sometimes termed *solum*. The C horizon is weathered parent material. In humid climates A horizons are zones from which chemical elements are removed and transferred downward by percolating water in a process called *leaching*. This is the zone of *eluviation*. The B horizons in humid climates are zones of accumulation in which dissolved chemical elements are redeposited. This is the zone of accumulation or *illuviation* (Figure 13.9). In other climatic regions of the world where the balance between downward-moving and upward-moving water is different the characteristics of the A and B horizons differ. Characteristic soil profiles from different

regions of the world are described in the next chapter.

The idea that soil profiles can be used to distinguish between soil types assumes that the dominant movement of soil water is vertical. Even where this is the case the rate of vertical movement will differ locally, and the position of a particular boundary separating two horizons may vary between profiles a few metres apart. To assist in problems of field mapping the concept of a *pedon* was developed. A pedon is an attempt to represent soil bodies in three dimensions. Its maximum area is 10 m² and several pedons in an area are called a polypedon (Figure 13.10). The polypedon is the basic unit of soil survey work (see Cruickshank for a longer discussion).

Colour is a fourth distinguishing characteristic of soils and reflects both mineral and organic content. Dark soils usually contain a high proportion of organic matter, but a grey colour may represent low organic content or reduced iron (ferrous) oxide (see Chapter 4). Soil colours resulting from iron can be particularly confusing. Although ferric oxide is usually red it can also be yellow. Colour can therefore be an unreliable indicator of chemical content. It is also a subjective quality and several observers of a particular soil are quite likely to describe its colour differently. Objective methods of testing soil colour·have been devised which make use of colour charts.

No description of a soil is complete without some description of its chemistry, and the single property which most affects a soil's ability to store chemical elements is its *clay–humus complex*. Clay, as we have seen, is the finest textured inorganic matter in a soil. Humus is soil organic matter which is almost completely decomposed, having lost any traces of plant structure. Both clay and humus are *colloidal*: that is, they expand on wetting and contract on drying. They also 'stick' to other substances in the soil, most notably to any positive ions (see Chapter 4) that might be present.

The process by which the clay–humus complex stores nutrients in the soil can be summarized as follows. The whole clay–humus complex has a negative electrical charge, principally because of the negative charges on the surface of the clay minerals within it. Because of its fine texture the ratio of surface area to volume in the clay–humus

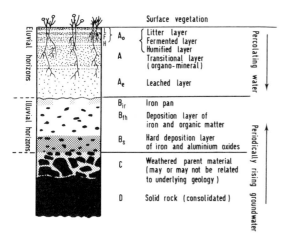

Figure 13.9 A podsol soil profile and its various horizons, not all of which need be present at any one site. The A_o (sometimes 0) horizon contains plant litter and animal remains in various stages of decomposition. Soil organisms gradually make this material semi-soluble and it washes into the A horizon. Well-decomposed organic matter, flaky, black and showing no signs of its original structure is called humus. The surface of the A_o horizon is the recent leaf-fall (L). The fermented layer (F) is partly decomposed and the well-humified layer (H) is humus. The A layer is the layer of mixing between organic and mineral material and the A_e (sometimes E_a) layer is the one from which downward percolating water removes (leaches) both organic and inorganic particles. This layer is often white or grey in colour. The top B horizon (B_{ir}) is a layer of redeposited iron and clay, the so-called ironpan. Its surface is often well defined and separates the zone of eluviation from the zone of illuviation. It can be completely missing. If well developed, the ironpan can impede drainage. Further deposition of clay and of other dissolved material takes place in the B_{fh} layer. The B_s layer is often hard and subject to saturation when ground water tables are high.
(Based on N. Pears, p. 31, and J. G. Cruickshank, p. 105.)

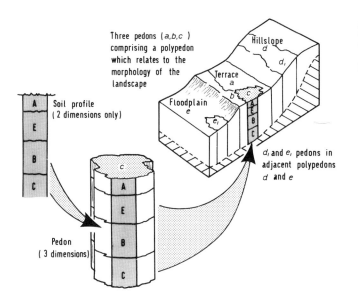

Three pedons (*a,b,c*) comprising a polypedon which relates to the morphology of the landscape

Hillslope
d

d₁

Terrace
a

Floodplain
e

c
b

A
E
B
C

e₁

d₁ and *e₁* pedons in adjacent polypedons *d* and *e*

A
Soil profile
(2 dimensions only)
E
B
C

c

A
E
B
C

Pedon
(3 dimensions)

Figure 13.10 The concepts of soil profile, pedon and polypedon. (Source: E. M. Bridges, p. 357.)

complex is very high, clay minerals, for example, having a surface area 10 000 times that of an equivalent amount of sand. This makes the surface of the clay–humus complex chemically very active.

Rainwater, as we have seen, is a dilute solution of carbonic acid. On percolating through decomposing surface vegetation its acidity increases. Recall from Chapter 4 that acids lose H^+ cations very easily, and that mineral salts in the soil are also separated into positively charged cations and negatively charged anions by hydration. The most common cations in soil released from the weathering of minerals are calcium (Ca^{2+}), magnesium (Mg^{2+}), sodium (Na^+) and potassium (K^+). These cations (also called bases) are the nutrients so important to vegetation growth, and along with hydrogen ions they are all attracted to the negatively charged clay–humus complex. Of the 5 cations just mentioned, hydrogen is attracted and held most strongly to the clay–humus complex followed by calcium, magnesium, potassium, and sodium in that order. As H^+ ions dissociate from the slightly acidic soil water percolating downward from the surface of the ground, they displace less strongly held cations on the clay–humus complex. These then join with the carbonate ion (CO_3^{2-}) from the original solution of carbonic acid, and are transferred down through the soil as carbonate salts in the soil water. This is the process of *leaching*.[1] The exchange of hydrogen ions for bases held in the clay–humus complex is called *base exchange*. When the clay–humus complex is saturated with hydrogen ions it is said to be *hydrogenized* (Eyre).

In wet, cold conditions water moves down through the soil quickly, absorbing CO_2 from decomposing surface organic matter on the way. Evaporation is limited and there is little if any upward movement of water in the soil profile. In this type of situation soils tend rapidly to become acidic, i.e. rich in hydrogen (H^+) ions and deficient in bases. Such soils tend naturally to be infertile. In dry areas by way of contrast even relatively weakly held cations can be stored in the soil for a long time. Annual rainfall is small and vegetation decomposes quickly thus reducing the acidity of percolating water which has less organic matter to penetrate. Such soils tend to be naturally fertile although, clearly, in the extreme case of zero or near-zero rainfall and the accumulation of salts at the soil surface few plants can survive. Even in desert areas, however, irrigation has brought impressive crop yields, and a major agricultural problem in irrigation projects is often one of removing excessive accumulations of base nutrients from the root zone of the crops where they build

1 As pointed out by Muller, the process can be seen in flower pots. Water percolates downward exchanging hydrogen ions in the water for bases in the soil. The bases are later deposited on the outside of the clay flower pots after drainage water has seeped through the pot and evaporated, leaving a white salt deposit behind.

up after being drawn to the surface by evaporation.

Because hydrogen ion concentration in a soil provides such an important indication of how many nutrients may be available for crop growth the pH of a soil is one of its most important properties. Few soils in Britain have pH values higher than 6.5 but organic soils may have pH values of 3.5 or lower. This range might appear low but remember that a soil of pH 6.5 is 1000 times less acidic than one with a pH of 3.5.

A problem for newcomers to soil science is why hydrogen ions held in the soil can be determined from measurements of soil water. The answer is that ions moving to or from the clay–humus complex are temporarily dissociated in the soil water before they bind with the carbonate ions to form carbonic acid or carbonates. If the clay–humus complex is therefore saturated with hydrogen ions it follows that only these will be found in the soil water. If other bases are fixed on the clay–humus complex they too will be temporarily dissociated from it and will lower the concentration of hydrogen ions in the soil water thus raising its pH.

The type of humus present at the soil surface can affect soil pH. Different plants have different nutrient requirements and return to the soil as leaf-litter only those nutrients they have previously stored. Coniferous trees, for example, tend to use little calcium and magnesium unlike grasses which use a great deal. The litter that coniferous trees return to the soil is therefore poor in nutrients and the humus, derived slowly from this litter, is acidic. Acidic litter is called *mor*. Humus rich in nutrients is called *mull* and has a pH of 4.5 or over. Mull and mor are extreme types of humus. In between is a third type, *moder*. The storage and transfer of nutrients between plants and vegetation is very important. A useful diagram to help understanding of nutrient cycling is given in Figure 13.11.

The description of vegetation

Two terms used widely in biogeography are the descriptive concepts of *life-form* and *communities*. Life-form refers to the size, shape and structure of plants in relation to their *habitat*, which in turn can be defined as the sum total of environmental conditions in which a plant is situated. There are six life-forms: trees, shrubs, lianas (climbing vines), herbs (including grass), bryoids (e.g. mosses) and epiphytes (which grow on other plants). Many aspects of plant adjustment to different climatic conditions were described earlier in the chapter. Interesting variations occur, however, even between plants with the same basic life-form, and sometimes these can be interpreted as adjustments to the climatic factor of light. Such a contrast is provided by multilayered and mono-layered trees (Figure 13.12).

Within a forest a variety of life-forms can exist (Figure 13.13), and several questions about the state of *plant succession* can be asked. If the shrub layer is dominated by seedlings and saplings of trees not represented in the canopy layer, the probability is that the young saplings represent an invading species. If tree species in the canopy layer are locally reproducing themselves they should have offspring of all age categories in the lower layers. If a tree species in the canopy layer is *senile* it is unlikely to be represented by any offspring in the lower layers.

A forest with the broad variety of life-forms represented in Figure 13.13 can be described as a *plant community*. In a plant community each different part of the ecosystem provides a combination of light and food sources which can be utilized by different plant and animal species. Bacteria, fungi, and algae belong to the lower forms of plants. They do not have roots, stems or leaves and grow as thin films of vegetation

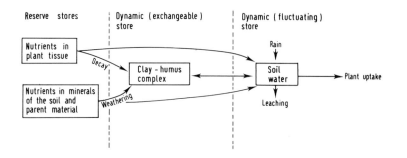

Figure 13.11 There are 4 nutrient stores in a soil vegetation ecosystem. The processes involved in cycling nutrients between these stores are shown as arrows. (Source: S. T. Trudgill, p. 22.)

Multilayered trees   Monolayered trees

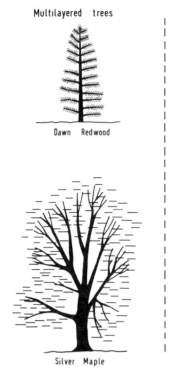

Dawn Redwood   Hemlock

Silver Maple

Sugar Maple

Figure 13.12 Leaf distribution in multilayered and monolayered trees. Multilayered trees have leaves at all points of the branch network. Leaves on monolayered trees are principally located at the ends of branches. It is argued that multilayered trees are at a competitive advantage over monolayered trees in open well-lit spaces, because their leaves do not shade each other as much as those in monolayered trees. Each leaf on a multilayered tree can photosynthesize more efficiently than its counterpart on a monolayered tree and manufacture more chemical energy for growth. In shaded situations, however, the inner leaves of the multilayered tree receive hardly any sunlight. The tree is therefore at a disadvantage over the monolayered tree whose concen- tration of total leaf area at the branch tips is better able to make use of whatever limited strong light is available. Monolayered trees therefore grow relatively well in the shaded layers below the canopy. It is suggested that multilayered trees may dominate the early successional stages of a forest only to be ultimately replaced by monolayered trees. When these finally dominate the canopy multilayered trees probably survive only at the forest edges where light intensities are relatively high, or in gaps within the canopy where monolayered trees have died and allowed light to penetrate to the lower layers of the forest floor.
(Source: H. S. Horn, p. 96.)

attached to rocks, branches and tree trunks. Mosses grow on rocks, while shrubs use whatever light filters down through the canopy layer of the trees above, and extend their roots into the upper layers of the soil from where they derive nutrients. Each plant species in other words occupies a *niche* (see also Chapter 12), a well-defined loca- tion within the vertical and horizontal structure of the ecosystem from which it excludes all other species through competition. This position is also defined with regard to time or stage in the succes- sion of vegetation, according to the climax theory of vegetational development (Figure 13.3).

Canopy layer →

Shrub layer →
Field or herb layer →

Moss layer

Figure 13.13 Vertical strati- fication of life-forms in a forest. Trees are dominant in this ecosystem, and the canopy layer of the trees is virtually closed allowing little light penetration to the shrub layer.
(Based on E. J. Kormondy, p. 134.)

187

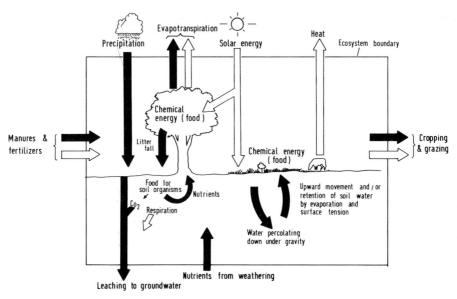

Figure 13.14 The flow of energy and materials into, through, and out of an ecosystem.

FEEDBACK MECHANISMS IN AN ECOSYSTEM

Some of the energy flows and material cycles discussed in this and the previous chapter are represented in Figure 13.14. The main purpose of examining relationships between components within an ecosystem is to identify those links which tend to maintain stability (negative feedback loops) and those which encourage change (positive feedback).

Figure 13.15 shows positive and negative feedback loops between the soil solution nutrient store (status) of an ecosystem and the three processes of weathering, leaching and nutrient cycling. The important negative feedback loop in this diagram is that between nutrient status and weathering and one way in which it works is as follows: increased weathering rates raise nutrient status, which in turn raises the cation content in the clay–humus complex and soil water. This water becomes less acidic, and its capacity for weathering soil minerals therefore decreases. In this way, increased nutrient status tends to reduce weathering in the soil, and reverses the direction of the initial trend in weathering rates.

Consider now the nutrient status/nutrient cycling loop. Here, both links have a positive sign, and the loop illustrates positive feedback. This

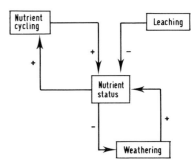

Figure 13.15 A very simplified systems model of the feedback relationships between nutrient status, nutrient cycling and weathering in an ecosystem. Many of the links between nutrient status and weathering on the one hand, and between nutrient status and nutrient cycling on the other, have been omitted. Notice that leaching increases the rate of weathering by lowering nutrient status and thereby increasing soil acidity.
(Source: S. T. Trudgill, p. 82.)

might work as follows. Increased nutrients in the soil solution leads to the development of a larger biomass. The larger the biomass the larger is the quantity of nutrients returned to the soil as organic matter for eventual decomposition. This reinforces the direction of the initial change in that it further raises the nutrient status of the soil. A different illustration of how this positive feedback mechanism might work is the sequence of events that might be expected to take place following natural or man-induced forest clearance. Either way, it leads to a reduced biomass and a lower rate of humus production. Lower humus content in the soil decreases the soil's ability to store nutrients and soil nutrient status therefore falls. Nutrient losses from the soil after forest clearance show up as increased nutrient loads in neighbouring streams and rivers. The loss of soil nutrients in this way restricts the immediate regeneration of a large biomass and thus reinforces the direction of the initial change.

The negative feedback loop between nutrient status and weathering resists both types of positive feedback just described. It slows down any rapid development of biomass because as the nutrient status of the clay–humus complex increases so soil acidity and therefore mineral weathering decrease. Conversely, it accelerates the development of biomass if this is suddenly removed, because the lower base status of the clay–humus complex and of water retained in the soil against the force of gravity both tend to increase mineral weathering. Increased weathering in turn releases nutrients which subsequently makes possible the natural regeneration of vegetation. Weathering of soil minerals, therefore, plays a vital role in the regeneration of any plant community following clearance, and a store of such minerals is necessary if regeneration is to occur. We shall see in the next chapter that many tropical soils do not have such a store and that this is a major problem in their development. For a longer discussion of the feedback mechanisms described here see Trudgill (p. 81).

14

World Soils and Vegetation

SOILS AND VEGETATION OF THE TERRESTRIAL BIOMES

Eight terrestrial biomes were recognized in Chapter 12. Others could be identified for no universal agreement exists among biogeographers as to their precise number. Some authorities claim six, others ten or even eleven. Biomes are areas in which there is a characteristic association of vegetational life-forms and animal life. They are often associated with particular soil types and climates. It should not be assumed, however, that vegetation boundaries necessarily coincide with those of soil and climate. There are three reasons for saying this. The first is that distinct vegetation, soil, and climatic boundaries are rare in nature. The second is that the mapping of vegetation by life-form is not everywhere complete, and the third is that man has markedly modified the distribution of vegetation everywhere in the world, although to varying degrees in different places.

The distribution of the eight biomes to be described is shown in Figure 14.1, and Figure 14.2 shows the distribution of ten major soil types to which reference will be made. The distribution of world climates was shown in Figure 11.1. Alternative ways of representing the association between climate, soils and vegetation are shown in Figure 14.3.

Tundra

Tundra areas are very cold throughout the year with temperatures ranging from −40 °C in winter to only 6 °C in summer. They are regions of permafrost. Although surface soils thaw out in summer they refreeze from the surface downward

in winter, and when water between the zone of permafrost and recently frozen surface ice finally freezes it expands causing surface soils to be heaved upward. These processes occur annually and soil horizons are unable to develop. The permafrost zone in fact acts as an impermeable barrier to the downward movement of percolating water, and waterlogged, anaerobic, gley soils are common.

In such poor soils and low temperatures vegetation is sparse. Trees require a growing season with temperatures above 10 °C and cannot therefore exist in these latitudes. The open landscape is exposed to Arctic winds and only low ground-cover plants such as lichens, grasses, mosses and dwarf shrubs can survive. The tundra biome is therefore the poorest in terms of plant species diversity. It supports such herbivores as voles, lemmings and reindeer, while its carnivore population includes wolves, arctic fox, owls and hawks.

Taiga

The distribution of coniferous forests (taiga) approximately coincides with the continental subarctic climate and its associated podsol soils. These are areas of low precipitation, most of it falling as snow. Evapotranspiration, however, is also low and surplus water moves down the soil profile. The coniferous forest vegetation is evergreen, which enables it to start photosynthesis very early in the year without having to wait for new growth. These trees therefore make maximum use of the limited solar energy input to these high latitudes. They also have shallow rooting systems which allow them to make maximum use of snow-melt. Soils are derived principally from glacial

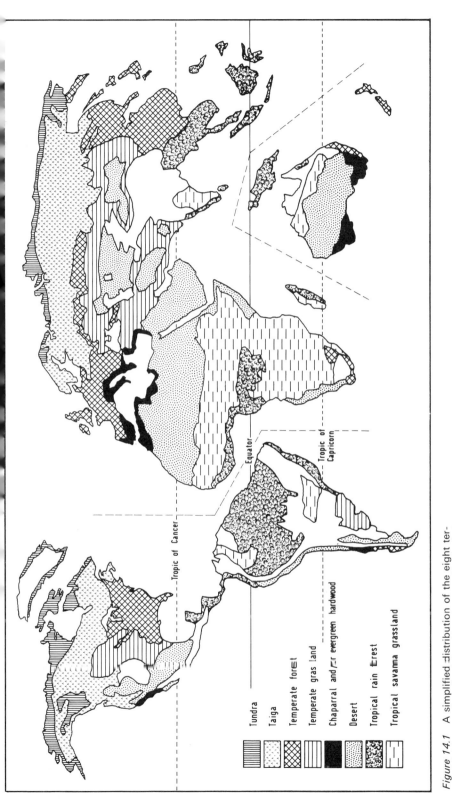

Tundra

Taiga

Temperate forest

Temperate grass land

Chaparral and/or evergreen hardwood

Desert

Tropical rain forest

Tropical savanna grassland

Figure 14.1 A simplified distribution of the eight terrestrial biomes described in this chapter. Unshaded areas represent parts of the world where none of the biomes to be discussed in this chapter has very great areal extent or where several biomes interdigitate in a way too complex to be represented.
(Sources: C. B. Cox *et al.*, pp. 40–41, and A. N. Strahler, plate 4.)

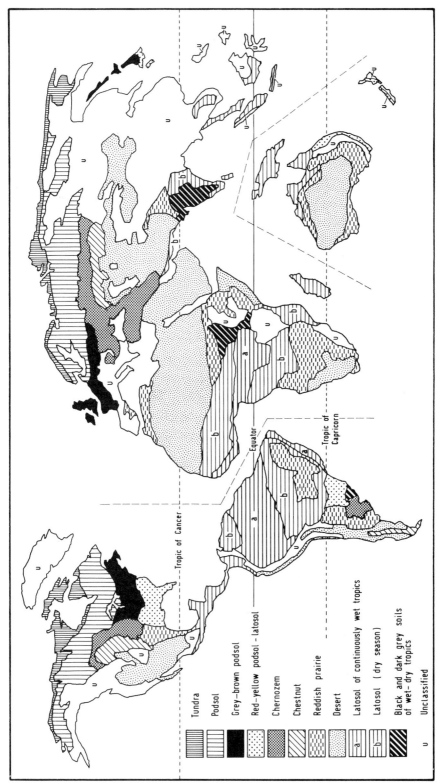

Figure 14.2 A simplified map of some of the world's major zonal soil types. In South America and Africa two types of latosol are distinguished. The letter 'a' refers to soils in areas without a marked dry season while 'b' refers to soils in areas with pronounced wet and dry seasons. This distinction could be made for other parts of the world but is not done so on this map. Mountain and alluvial soils are not represented, and areas where they occur are left unclassified.
(Simplified from A. N. Strahler, plate 3.)

Tundra
Podsol
Grey–brown podsol
Red–yellow podsol - latosol
Chernozem
Chestnut
Reddish prairie
Desert
Latosol of continuously wet tropics
Latosol (dry season)
Black and dark grey soils of wet-dry tropics
Unclassified

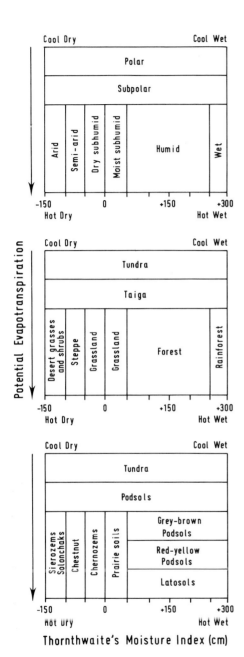

Thornthwaite's Moisture Index (cm)

Figure 14.3 The top diagram shows the eight principal climatic regions identified by Thornthwaite's system of climatic classification (see Chapter 11). The middle diagram shows the types of biome principally associated with each climatic type. The Mediterranean climate lies between the semi-arid and subhumid categories in the top diagram and its associated chaparral biome would lie between the steppe and grassland categories in the middle diagram. Note how moisture availability is uniform throughout the tundra and taiga. Here, temperature is the principal controlling factor on vegetational life-forms. In the other biomes moisture availability determines the distribution of life-forms, each biome experiencing much the same range of PE and temperature. The bottom diagram shows soils in relation to climatic regions.
(Modified from: R. A. Muller, pp. 189 and 233.)

material and are often free-draining and poor in nutrients. The humus is a very acidic mor, the product of slowly-decaying pine needles which are themselves low in nutrient content. Earthworms find this environment extremely unattractive and any mixing of organic and inorganic matter is minimal, the organic matter remaining on the surface for a long time before decomposition.

Classic features of a podsol profile in upland Britain were shown in Figure 13.9. Water percolating through the thick mat of slowly decomposing vegetation becomes acidic and leaches any nutrients present in the eluviated A_e horizon. Often the percolate is so extremely acidic that the clay minerals themselves are dissolved as well as the metallic cations such as iron (Figure 14.4). This leaves the A_e horizon devoid of colloids to retain nutrients and it is left rich in silica. The silica gives the soil its characteristic whitish-grey colour.

Figure 14.4 A grey–brown podsol in Ontario, Canada, showing eluviation of clay from the upper profile and deposition in darker layers below.
(Courtesy, J. G. Cruickshank.)

Inorganic material removed by leaching accumulates in the illuviated B horizons at the top of which an ironpan, sometimes containing clay and humus, may be recognized. This can impede drainage and often has to be broken by deep ploughing when these soils are brought into any form of cultivation. Diversity of flora and fauna is limited because of the extreme conditions. Herbivores in the taiga include deer and various rodents. Carnivores include stoat, lynx, and wolf. Bears are the principal omnivores.

Temperate forest

The principal areas of temperate forest occur in western Europe, eastern USA, eastern China, New Zealand and South America. At least four types of forest are included in this biome which extends across a variety of climatic and soil types. The natural vegetation of lowland Britain and Ireland represents one type. It includes mixed woodlands of oak, beech and other deciduous trees growing in what we usually term a brown forest soil. These soils experience a strong downward movement of soil water, especially in winter when rainfall is high and evapotranspiration low, but in summer when evapotranspiration exceeds precipitation (Figure 14.5) the soils are able to dry out somewhat. Soils here are rich in nutrients because deep-rooted trees are able to extract nutrients from chemically weathered parent rock and return these to the soil as organic matter during leaf-fall in autumn. Humus is of the slightly acidic mull variety (pH 4.5–6.0) and earthworms flourish mixing organic and inorganic material thoroughly. These soils therefore lack the well-developed horizons of *podsols* (Figure 14.6). They are potentially fertile but need lime to correct the slight acidity if grasses are to grow well. Some of the highest wheat yields in the world have been obtained from these soils with the use of fertilizers, manure and nitrogen-fixing crops in a crop rotation system.

In North America, the deciduous forests of the east are similar to those in Britain but a larger number of common species exists, 40–50 in North America compared with 15 or so in Europe. They include hemlock and chestnut as well as oak and beech. As in Europe trees in the canopy layer seldom touch, a lot of light penetrates and a shrub

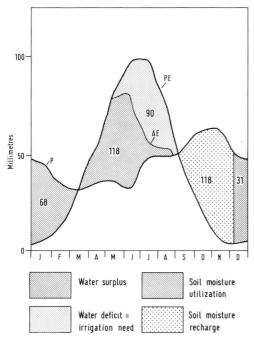

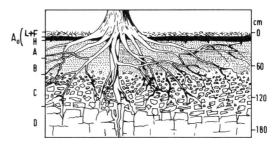

Figure 14.6   A brown forest soil beneath oak forest. These soil profiles are usually thicker than podsols. (Based on S. R. Eyre, p. 67.)

Figure 14.5   A soil moisture budget (in mm) for Margate. From January to March precipitation (P) exceeds potential evapotranspiration (PE), soil moisture levels are above field capacity and surplus gravity water therefore drains away to groundwater. From March to September PE exceeds precipitation. As the soil dries from spring onwards it approaches field capacity. When this stage has been reached transpiration becomes the principal force removing water held in the soil against gravity and this time of year is a period of soil moisture utilization. As the soil moisture reservoir is progressively depleted so the retention forces holding water in the soil increase. Plants find it increasingly difficult to extract water and by May the actual evapotranspiration rate (AE) falls below the potential rate. The difference between PE and AE from May onwards is the amount of water that has to be added to meet the full transpiring capacity of the crops. It is therefore a measure of the irrigation requirement. From September onwards precipitation once again exceeds PE. The first demand on any surplus rainfall is to replace the 118 mm of soil moisture consumed in summer. When this has been done and the soil has returned to field capacity (usually by November) water surplus occurs once again and groundwater recharge takes place.
(Source: K. Smith, p. 78.)

layer flourishes. The areas of grey-brown podsol have provided very good agricultural soil and are very similar to the brown earths of western Europe.

To the north of the mixed deciduous forests, in north-east USA, north-east Europe and north-east China the temperate forest biome includes conifer as well as deciduous trees, while to the south, in south-west Europe for example, conifers and evergreens of the broad-leaf varieties used to be very common including various species of oak. Around the Mediterranean basin most of this mixed coniferous and broad-leafed evergreen forest was destroyed for agriculture by early civilizations and today the dominant vegetation is scrubland, variously called maquis, garrigue or chaparral (see later).

In some mid-latitudinal areas precipitation amounts are very large and temperature ranges are small. In such circumstances *rain forests* have developed as in New Zealand and on the Olympic peninsula of Washington State, USA. In the extreme north-west of the Olympic peninsula annual rainfall can exceed 2500 mm and forest trees including maple, cedar, fir, spruce and hemlock act as hosts for epiphytes some of which have aerial roots that trap leaf-fall and derive both their nutrients and water from this source.

Fauna in the temperate forests is varied. Herbivores include squirrel, mice and rabbits. Carnivores include foxes and bears. Often the different layers in the forest support their own distinctive assemblage of animals.

Temperate grassland

All the world's extensive areas of grassland have been the subject of recurrent debate as to whether they represent a natural climatic climax community or an early stage of sub-seral development, the moister parts of which might eventually develop into some form of woodland if not kept as grassland by grazing and/or fire. Examples of temperate grassland are the prairies of North America, the steppes of central Asia, the pampas of South

America and the veldt of southern Africa. In North America grasslands occur on three types of soil extending in a north-south direction through the centre of the continent. The most easterly of these soils are the prairie soils (not shown in Figure 14.2) where natural grassland is tallest and exceeds 1 m in height. On the chernozems, in the centre of the grasslands, grasses are shorter while on the drier chestnut soils to the west of the chernozems grasses occur in short tufts, often quite far apart.

Of these three soils the *prairie soils* (or brunizems) are pedalfers. Here annual rainfall and evapotranspiration are approximately equal at about 750 mm year^{-1}. Prairie soils have a slightly acidic reaction (pH about 6.0) with few soluble salts in the upper profile and no accumulations of calcium carbonate near the surface. In these respects they are therefore typical of forest soils. The actual surface crumb structure of the soil and its high humus content, however, is the product of dense root networks in the various grasses which grow here. The question which has taxed soil scientists for decades is whether the soils were originally formed under forest which was subsequently replaced by grass, or whether grass is the natural vegetation of this pedalfer-type soil.

Most soil scientists now believe that forest, probably quite open in character, once extended on to the prairie soils. Changes in climate, the advent of man, or both in combination, subsequently resulted in burning of the forest edges deliberately or accidentally, and grassland expanded eastward. Herds of bison, a dominant herbivore of the grasslands and much more numerous in the past than today, would have played a part in maintaining the grassland. Grazing removes the short upper shoots of grasses thereby encouraging new leaf growth at the base of the plants where all new growth is concentrated. The plant is thus encouraged to spread laterally. For a longer discussion on the role of fire in the evolution of grasslands see Pears (p. 112).

Chernozem (or 'black earth') *soils* are less of an enigma. Here grasses are the dominant plants. In areas where chernozems occur, potential evapotranspiration exceeds precipitation and leaching ceases to be a dominant water-moving process in the soil. It still occurs during snowmelt and heavy storms when it removes the weakly-held potassium

and sodium ions from the soil profile, but it never lasts long enough to allow calcium and/or clay minerals to be removed from the A_e horizon. A typical chernozem profile is shown in Figure 14.7. Below recent litter there is no evident development of F and H horizons. Decomposition is rapid, soil organisms abundant, and the humus well mixed. The soil profile may be 1.5 m thick. Humus from decomposed grasses is probably the principal reason for the soil's typical dark surface colour, and is a principal factor in explaining why soils retain bases near the surface. The other factor is the non-solubility of clay in dry, alkaline conditions. Surface pH values may reach 7.5. The retention of calcium carbonate is often marked by the build up of calcium carbonate nodules in the A_e horizon.

To the west of the chernozems and their associated short prairie grasses in North America lie the *chestnut-brown soils* and an even drier climate. Equivalent ecosystems are found in South Africa, southern Spain and central Asia. In these drier areas calcium is retained even more strongly than in the chernozem belt and the C horizon is often completely white. A discontinuous surface cover of grass leads to a lower production of

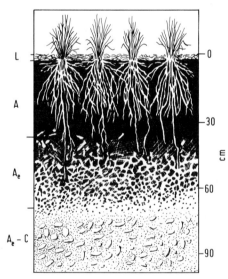

Figure 14.7 A chernozem profile. The dark-coloured A horizon has a crumb structure and a well-developed clay–humus complex. There is no illuviated B horizon and the A_e horizon lies on parent material, sometimes loess. Calcium carbonate is deposited in the A_e horizon by water moving towards the surface as a result of evaporation in dry weather.
(Based on S. R. Eyre, p. 111.)

humus and these factors, together with the very low amounts of soil moisture available throughout the year, make these soils significantly less fertile than the chernozems which have been the world's major wheatlands in both North America and Russia for a century or more. Nevertheless, the superficial similarity of soil types in the chestnut brown and chernozem regions has always tempted farmers to extend the wheat areas on to the former soil types. It was in these regions, and in the more marginal western regions of the chernozem belt, that soil erosion reached a peak in the 1930s when a succession of dry years ended in massive soil erosion throughout Kansas, Colorado, Texas and other states of central USA. Valuable topsoil was removed by wind erosion, the affected area being known as the *Dust Bowl*. A combination of factors was responsible including: drought, the removal by ploughing of the grass roots which bound together the fine clay particles, and the poor management practice of leaving land fallow and unprotected against the wind.

Chaparral

This biome is perhaps best described as dense scrubland with intermittent trees. Trees that can survive are adapted to long dry summers (Figure 14.8) and include eucalyptus and various species of evergreen oak. Trees are seldom close together principally because of their need to tap large

areas for water, and most plant species have very hard, thick, leaves as an adaptation to drought. The growing season occurs in winter when soil moisture is available and evapotranspiration rates are at their lowest. In Mediterranean areas such as Spain, chaparral vegetation is called maquis (Figure 14.9) and in part represents a degenerated form of the area's natural vegetation brought

Figure 14.9 A Dense shrubland and isolated trees in southern Spain. The vegetation shown here is intermediate between chaparral (maquis) and garrigue, the latter consisting of very low-growing shrubs and a well-developed aromatic herb layer. Among the shrubs typical of maquis are broom and gorse.

Figure 14.9 B Cork oak (*Quercus suber*), a tree believed to be formerly more extensive in Mediterranean areas than it is today. It is now principally found in more moist areas. Bark from this tree is used as a source of cork in the bottling of wine.

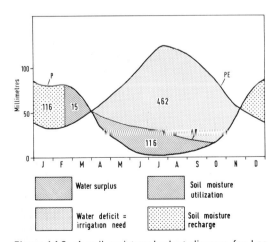

Figure 14.8 A soil moisture budget diagram for Los Angeles in the chaparral biome of California. Units are in mm. Note the very large irrigation requirement, which here equals more than the annual rainfall.

about by burning and overgrazing. Formerly the Mediterranean coastal areas are thought to have been extensively covered by climax evergreen forests in which holm oak and cork oak were common. Maquis then probably existed as climax vegetation only on poorer land. The forest was felled, however, and a pastoral economy was introduced. Soils deteriorated and vegetation too. Today overgrazing, especially by goats, remains a problem in southern Spain and aggravates a long-established problem of soil erosion in the area (Figure 14.10).

Figure 14.10 Two types of soil erosion in southern Spain. Top: gully erosion on unconsolidated sediment from which nearly all vegetation has been removed by goats. Bottom: sheet erosion in an olive grove. Notice the exposed root systems following the removal of topsoil.

Desert

Desert and semi-desert is found in continental interiors of the mid-latitudes. Examples of such areas are the Columbia and Snake basins to the lee of the Cascade mountains in the Pacific north-west of the USA and the Gobi desert in central

Asia north of the Himalayas. These 'cold' deserts often experience subzero temperatures in winter. Closer to the equator are the 'hot' deserts of the world such as the Sahara, Arabian, Atacama, Sonora, Kalahari and Australian deserts. These areas lie beneath the subsiding air of the sub-tropical high pressure belts.

Deserts are usually defined on the basis of annual rainfall. On this definition deserts have under 120 mm of annual precipitation and semi-deserts between 120 mm and 250 mm. This definition ignores both the amount of evapo-transpiration and the distribution of precipitation throughout the year. True deserts are perhaps best defined as areas with a dry season of more than $7\frac{1}{2}$ months with low and infrequent rainfall which often falls in storms. Cactus and other succulents are adjusted to these conditions by virtue of their thick stems for storing water and the very small surface area of their spikes and hairs which function as leaves but cut down on moisture loss (Figure 14.11). Cacti are also shallow-rooting and can use any rainfall that occurs before it is evaporated.

Recall that all plants require water, nutrients and sunlight for growth. In arid areas the requirement in shortest supply is water and this is the limiting factor. Nutrients are not in short supply because there is little gravity water in the soil to remove them. However, the shortage of water makes nutrients generally unavailable for plants which can only absorb them in dissolved form,

Figure 14.11 A Joshua tree (*Yucca brevifolia*) in the Mojave desert, southern California. Leaves on yuccas are thick, which helps to cut down on evapotranspiration losses. Note the tussocky grasses and large areas of unvegetated surface in this semi-arid desert.

and because of the water shortage desert soils contain cations such as sodium and potassium which in more moist areas are easily leached from the soil. For this reason desert soils are potentially fertile and have been brought into very productive use by irrigation schemes such as those in the Columbia basin of Washington State and in the Imperial valley of southern California. The soils do lack humus however, because vegetation is so sparse. Another problem is the build-up of soluble salts in the root zone of plants once irrigation has been introduced. Water applied to desert soils increases the upward transport of salts by evaporation and these are deposited just beneath the surface. Extra water often has to be applied to such soils, not to meet the transpiration requirements of the crop but in order to leach excessive salts from the root zone. The increased salinity of rivers, such as the lower Colorado, as a result of leached cations from irrigated land is one of the inadvertent environmental effects of bringing desert soils into agricultural production. Even so, pressure to expand this production is great for desert soils occupy 20% of the earth's land area.

Zonal soils of the deserts are of two basic types. In the cold deserts, *sierozems* or grey desert soils exist. In the hot deserts soils are of the *red desert soil* variety. Both contain large quantities of calcium carbonate which in the sierozem may occur just beneath the soil surface as a band of hard rock referred to as *caliche*.

Like the autotrophs of this biome the heterotrophs are limited in number and diversity. They include various types of insect, and rodents such as the gerbil. Among the predators are birds of prey and reptiles.

Tropical rain forest

This biome covers large areas of the Amazon and Orinoco basins in South America, much of the Zaire (formerly Congo) basin and Guinea coast of Africa and extensive parts of the south-east Asian archipelago. It is the most diverse ecosystem in the world with over 20 000 species in each of the South American and south-east Asian forests. The African forest with only 7000 species, has a relatively low diversity (Harris, p. 244). Because of their great diversity, tropical rain forests are very heterogeneous, and forty tree species per hectare

have been counted, a figure to be compared with the British norm of about 12 species per hectare. A commercial drawback of diversity is that pure stands of timber are rare and the economic costs of harvesting are consequently high.

The very great diversity of this biome results from environmental and historical factors. Solar energy inputs, for example, are continuous throughout the year and result in high light intensities and continuously high temperatures. Moisture is abundant and precipitation exceeds evapotranspiration in every month. Climatic factors are thus ideal for the growth of vegetation. A second reason frequently advanced to explain the biome's diversity is its age. Most biogeographers would probably agree that its oldest parts represent the oldest ecosystems on earth and some, though not all, would argue that a form of tropical rain forest has been present on earth since Cretaceous times about 100 million years ago. In support of their claim they point to Cretaceous fossils some of which are very similar to plants of today's rain forest. Great age, coupled with hot humid conditions, has thus allowed protracted competition between species to fill every niche the biome has to offer.

The tropical rain forest however is not everywhere of the same age. During the last glaciation it is now believed that the tropical rain forests of South America and Africa contracted into 'core areas' as a result of reduced precipitation all over the earth. During cold glacial spells less water would have circulated in the hydrological cycle and global precipitation would have fallen. Certainly, palynological evidence tells us that forests everywhere in the world retreated at these times, the temperate deciduous and taiga forests occupying only a small part of the areas into which they expanded during interglacial periods. During these advances and retreats of vegetation temperature seems to have been a less important factor than moisture availability.

The core areas into which the tropical rain forests of Africa are thought to have retreated are shown in Figure 14.12, along with the areas into which deserts expanded. These core areas are therefore now thought to be the oldest areas of tropical rain forest in Africa and the richest in terms of species diversity. The maximum retreat occurred about 18 000 BP at the time of the last glacial maxima, since when the tropical rain forests

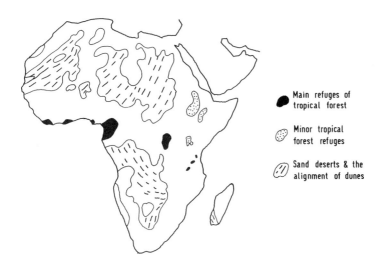

Figure 14.12 The distribution of tropical rain forest and deserts in Africa about 18 000 years BP.
(Source: A. C. Hamilton, 1981, p. 3.)

● Main refuges of tropical forest

⊙ Minor tropical forest refuges

⟨⟩ Sand deserts & the alignment of dunes

have been expanding. As an example of the evidence used in this type of work Hamilton (1981) described two interesting aspects of research undertaken in Uganda. Palynological studies here show that there was no rain forest near Jinja on the northern shores of Lake Victoria between 14 500 BP and 12 000 BP but that it began to expand eastward across Uganda from 12 000 BP onward. Study of the species diversity in the present forests of Uganda show the western forests to be richer than those in the east, suggesting that this was the direction of advance in the postglacial period.

Rain forests have a well-defined structure. Three principal tree layers can often be recognized: an upper layer above 25 m, a middle layer (10–25 m) and a lower layer at about 10 m (Figure 14.13). The largest trees are often very straight, slim and buttressed for support. Most are quite shallow-rooted. It is a common myth that undergrowth is very dense and impenetrable. The concept of tropical jungle with a dense undergrowth of shrubs and bushes is largely untrue principally because there is insufficient light to support vigorous shrub growth beneath the tree canopies. The shrub layer is dense along river banks and in other areas where strong light is able to penetrate from the side to ground level but within the forest proper ground level light intensity can frequently be as low as 1% that of the canopy level. Only a few saplings of trees in the higher layers are able to survive these conditions but enough manage to mature to replace those that die. As in the tem-

perate rain forests epiphytes are abundant and include various types of moss, lichen and fern which use tree foliage and branches as hosts on which to establish their root network.

Within this biome the vast majority of flowering plants are broadleaf evergreen. Some trees do shed their leaves but only a few shed their leaves periodically at one season. There is no need for this type of plant adjustment in a region where autotrophic production is possible throughout the year. Seasonal leaf loss places a species at a competitive disadvantage with other trees. The great diversity of vegetation in this biome supports an equally diverse population of herbivores and carnivores, too well-known to require repetition here. Bird life is particularly varied and enjoys a large variety of foods such as seeds, fruit, insects and nectar.

All soils of freely-drained sites in the humid tropics (and this includes soils in the seasonally wet and dry savanna regions as well as the continually humid rain forests) are called *latosols* (Table 14.1). Latosols of the tropical rain forest are akin to podsols in that leaching is the dominant process in their formation. Humus is deficient, however, not because of slow decomposition as in the taiga, but rather because bacterial decomposition of dead vegetation is so rapid in the warm, moist conditions of the rain forest that it frequently equals the rate of litter supply. Nutrients are quickly released into the soil on decomposition and taken up again by vegetation. Surface soil may therefore be neutral (pH 7.0),

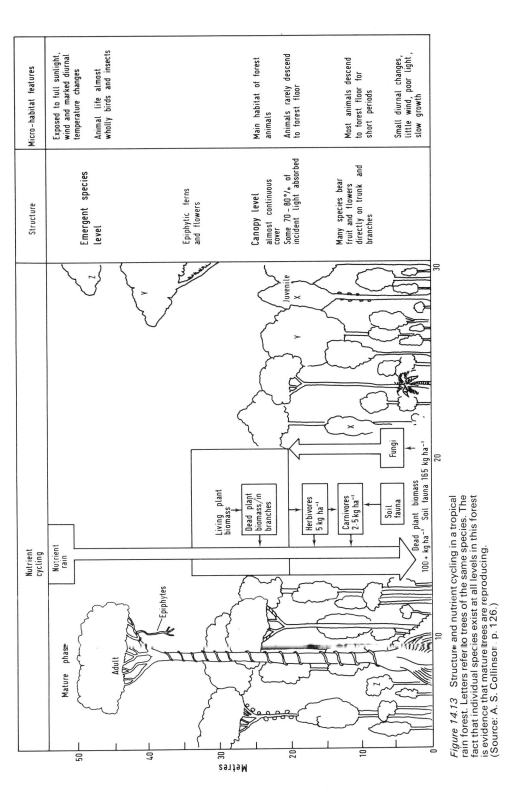

Nutrient cycling	Structure	Micro-habitat features
	Emergent species level	Exposed to full sunlight, wind and marked diurnal temperature changes
		Animal life almost wholly birds and insects
	Epiphytic ferns and flowers	
	Canopy level almost continuous cover	Main habitat of forest animals
	Some 70 – 80% of incident light absorbed	Animals rarely descend to forest floor
	Many species bear fruit and flowers directly on trunk and branches	Most animals descend to forest floor for short periods
		Small diurnal changes, little wind, poor light, slow growth

Figure 14.13 Structure and nutrient cycling in a tropical rain forest. Letters refer to trees of the same species. The fact that individual species exist at all levels in this forest is evidence that mature trees are reproducing. (Source: A. S. Collinson, p. 126.)

Table 14.1. A classification of tropical soils (Source: Young, p. 235)

Climatic zones	Parent materials		
	Acidic (siliceous) or intermediate composition	Basic composition (rich in ferromagnesian minerals)	Acidic composition (highly weathered often on erosion surfaces)
Rain forest (mean annual rainfall >1500 mm)	Leached ferrallitic	Strongly leached ferrisols — 1800 mm — Ferrisols — 900 mm —	
Savanna (600–1500 mm)	Ferruginous	Eutrophic brown soils	Weathered ferrallitic
Tropical high altitude (Height >1500 m)	Humic ferrallitic	Humic ferrisols	
Humic latosols			

(Basisols spans the Basic composition column between Rain forest and Savanna rows.)

though at no great depth it quickly drops to 5.0 and below. Quick uptake by plants is fortunate because the soils have little humus and kaolin, the dominant clay present, has only a limited ability to retain cations. For reasons which are still not understood, silica is dissolved and moved down the profile in the wet humid tropics, while sesquioxides of iron accumulate near the top of the profile giving these soils their characteristic red or yellow colour. The short supply of organic acids because of rapid decomposition may partly explain the insolubility of iron compounds. The removal of silica is called *desilication*. Apart from the contrasting stabilities of iron and silica in podsols and latosols the two soils have another difference. Whereas in podsols mobilized surface cations are redeposited in the B horizons, latosols have no such illuvial layer and leaching may extend down to the water table.

The classification of latosols in Table 14.1 shows that throughout the tropics rock type appears to influence soil type. On siliceous rocks in the rain forest *leached ferrallitic soils* are dominant. These are deep and acidic (pH 5.0–5.5) with very few exchangeable cations to give the soil fertility. *Basisols*, in contrast, occur on basic rocks rich in ferromagnesian minerals. These soils, occupying only 2% of the intertropical areas, have higher humus content and more weatherable minerals.

They therefore retain and produce more nutrients than other latosols and represent some of the most fertile soils in the tropics.

Notice that the term *laterite* does not appear in this classification of tropical soils. Laterite consists mainly of insoluble ferric iron (see Chapter 4) in deposits up to 10 m thick. These have accumulated in the soil as parent material has weathered and as the more soluble cations released by weathering have leached away. Laterite is sometimes known as ferricrete. It is always very hard but may be brick-like or nodular in appearance. It is not a soil and is, in fact, frequently used as a building material.

Another popular myth about rain forests is the supposed fertility of their soil. Nineteenth century explorers of Africa initiated this idea believing that the luxurious vegetation of the rain forests required fertile soils to support them. In fact, apart from the limited area of basisols, soils of the humid tropics are generally infertile, and the forest is maintained only by a closed nutrient cycle between vegetation and soil in which the process of rapid bacterial decomposition and plant uptake is vital to keep the circulation going. Otherwise all the nutrients would be leached. Soils for the most part are acidic and contain no weatherable minerals. Compared with most ecosystems an abnormally large proportion of nutrients is contained in the forest biomass and the closed nature of the nutrient cycle, like the great diversity of the biomass itself, supports the belief that the biome itself is of very considerable age.

Because of the nature of the nutrient cycle removal of tropical rain forest for agriculture is fraught with difficulties. Deforestation has generally been accompanied by a fall in the nutrient status of any ecosystem affected, and the soils, unable to retain nutrients because of their low clay–humus content, do not long retain any applied fertilizers.

In short, the soils of the tropical rain forest provide a poor basis for commercial agriculture and most soil scientists are increasingly of the view that shifting cultivation sometimes called 'slash and burn', 'milpa' or 'bush fallowing' probably represents the best form of agricultural response to this particular biome.

Shifting cultivation is a form of subsistence agriculture which involves the periodic cutting of trees and their subsequent burning. Burning, of course, is a method of decomposition and oxidation which releases nutrients quickly, most to the soil but nitrogen to the atmosphere. Cleared land is sown and harvested for three years and then vacated, the group of shifting cultivators moving on to another area in order to allow the cleared patch to regenerate. This technique prevents complete soil exhaustion and allows the nutrient cycle on the farmed area to be re-established by rapid re-invasion of plant species from neighbouring forest before it is completely and irretrievably disrupted. The soil's limited fertility is thus

conserved and the system can support population densities of 50 km^{-2} of agricultural land (Collinson).

Outside the rain forest the vegetation of intertropical areas is varied (Figure 14.14). Climatic zones in intertropical areas are conveniently distinguished by the length of dry season which tends to increase in duration with distance from the rain forest. The period of rains is very much associated with the movement of the equatorial trough and since this crosses the equator twice in any twelve-month period but reaches each of the tropics only once, it is apparent why the length of dry season tends to increase with distance from the equator. Tropical rain forest cannot exist if the dry season exceeds $2\frac{1}{2}$ months. Between tropical rain forests and deserts, however, several types of vegetation can be recognized. In South America, for example, a threefold division of seasonal forests is apparent (Figure 14.15), deciduous trees becoming relatively more abundant as the dry season lengthens. At the same time the density of trees decreases. An example of semi-evergreen seasonal forest which lies adjacent to the rain forest is the cerradão in Brazil. With more sunlight penetrating the canopy layer this vegetation has a denser shrub layer than the rain forest itself. Trees have no buttresses and seasonal growth rings become apparent. In the deciduous seasonal forest single species become more abundant although even more widely spaced. Thorn woodland is the driest form of seasonal woodland, almost indistinguishable from desert vegetation.

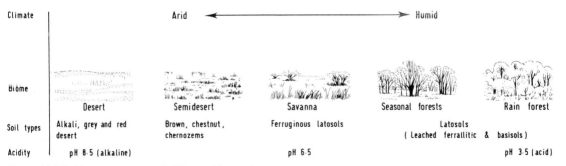

Climate	Arid ←――――――――――→ Humid				
Biome	Desert	Semidesert	Savanna	Seasonal forests	Rain forest
Soil types	Alkali, grey and red desert	Brown, chestnut, chernozems	Ferruginous latosols	Latosols (Leached ferrallitic & basisols)	
Acidity	pH 8.5 (alkaline)		pH 6.5		pH 3.5 (acid)

Figure 14.14 The appearance of different biomes in intertropical areas.
(Modified from M. McNeil, 1964, 'Lateritic soils' in *Scientific American*, Vol. 211, pp. 96–102.)

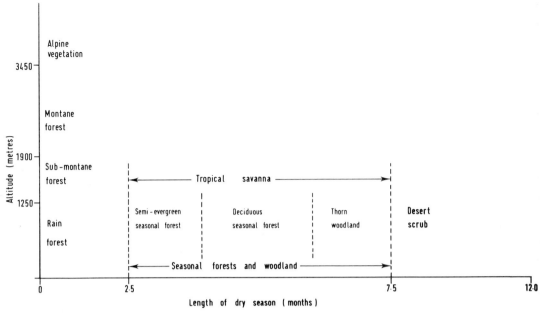

Figure 14.15 Vegetation in intertropical areas and its relationship to the length of the dry season.
(Source: D. R. Harris, p. 241.)

Tropical savanna grassland

In Africa (Figure 14.1) the area between the tropical rain forest and desert is most conveniently described as tropical savanna grassland though parts of it recognizably belong to one of the seasonal forest categories more clearly defined in South America. The principal soils are ferruginous latosols of intermediate agricultural value and suitable for maize and other such annual crops. Tropical savanna grasslands (Figure 14.16) are often described as park-like, a mixture of trees and grass, the latter progressively replacing the former with increasing distance from the rain forest. Grasses can be very tall, sometimes more than 3.5 m high, and characteristic trees are the acacia and the baobab. In Australia the eucalyptus is a widespread tree in the savanna grasslands. In South America, savanna grasslands are best represented by the llanos of Venezuela and the camp sujo of Brazil. A diverse and familiar population of herbivores (antelope, zebra, etc.) graze on the grasslands. Carnivores include lion, leopard, hyena, etc.

The origin of savanna grassland has been debated as thoroughly as the origin of temperate grasslands and similar issues have been raised. The conventional view is that savanna is essentially controlled by fire which destroys tree saplings. Some woody plants with thick barks are fire-tolerant but the grasses with their deep roots

Figure 14.16 Savanna grassland, Kenya.
(Courtesy, D. Ford.)

are more resistant still. Fire-resistant trees and grasses give the savanna its characteristic park-like appearance, the tussock structure of many savanna grasses protecting them from the effects of fire. Only the outer part of the tussock is destroyed by burning and the inner parts are free to regenerate. As in the prairies the effects of grazing, here practised by nomadic and semi-nomadic tribes, is thought to play a part in en-couraging the spread of grasses.

Commercial agriculture on latosols outside the tropical rain forest has met with mixed success but a US government advisory committee, report-ing in 1967, said that 42% of all latosols were potentially arable and accounted for the largest percentage of the world's potential arable land. The vast majority of this potential agricultural latosol lies in the savanna and seasonal forest zones. Many soil scientists, supporting the idea of agricultural development here, argue that shifting cultivation in these ecosystems is wasteful and reflects more the organization of society than poor agricultural potential. The crux of the problem they argue is the retention of organic matter in the soil. If this can be achieved, by manuring for

example, these latosols should develop a capacity for nutrient retention and enhanced fertility. For further discussion of these very important issues see the two papers by Harris and Young from which much of the foregoing account was drawn. See also Table 14.2.

The world's biomes—some general considerations

The brief discussion of world biomes needs to be qualified in three ways.
1 All biomes are evolving and not static. Des-criptions of their present-day structure and appearance tend to suggest that this is how they have always appeared and always will. This is not the case, for ecosystems evolve with time.
2 Biomes have a vertical distribution as well as a horizontal distribution, and high mountain ranges have the same effect on vegetation associations as increasing latitude (Figures 14.15 and 14.17).
3 Of all the world's ecosystems those in the intertropical areas are the least well understood. Detailed measurement of climate, soils, and

Table 14.2. Estimated total land area and potential arable land by broad soil groups (Source: E. M. Bridges, p. 355)

Soil group	Estimated total area (hectares × 10⁶)	Area of potential arable land (hectares ×10⁶)	Potential arable as percentage of total area	Potential arable area as percentage of soil group area
Tundra soils	517	0	0	0
Desert soils	2180	430	3.3	20.7
Chernozems and brunizems	822	450	3.5	54.5
Noncalcic brown soils	291	110	0.8	37.8
Podzols	1920	300	2.4	15.6
Red-yellow podzolic soils	388	130	1.0	31.2
Latosolic soils	2500	1050	8.1	42.0
Grumusols and terra rossas	325	180	1.3	55.4
Brown forest soils and rendzinas	101	30	0.2	3.0
Ando soils	24	10	0.1	41.7
Lithosols	2722	80	0.6	2.9
Regosols	763	70	0.5	9.2
Alluvial soils	595	350	2.4	58.8
Total area	13150	3190	24.2	—

Figure 14.17 Moist montane forest of Mount Elgon on the Uganda/Kenya border. This photograph was taken at about 2500 m. Note the slender, straight, trunks and the lianas. Above montane forest on this mountain is a zone of bamboo forest, followed in turn by a zone of heather and a zone of tundra-like vegetation. Above about 4000 m the mountain is capped with ice. (Courtesy, A. C. Hamilton.)

vegetation in these areas has started to take place only recently and only a small part of the intertropical belt has yet been studied.

INTRAZONAL SOILS

Within any of the zonal soil belts intrazonal soils may occur. These are soils with characteristics dominated by local conditions. In arid areas, for example, gentle depressions in the land surface may periodically fill with water. Fine silt and clay brought into such lakes by floods make their margins impermeable and water, unable to percolate easily into the soil after rainfall, evaporates leaving behind *halomorphic soils*. These soils contain salts of very high solubility such as sodium which in areas with pedalfer-type soils would be one of the first exchangeable cations to be removed by leaching. In these extremely arid environments sodium can be retained. Halomorphic soils are of two types: light-coloured *solonchak soils* and dark-coloured *solonetz soils*.

An intrazonal soil of temperate regions is the *rendzina*, a soil which develops on lime-rich parent material. In Britain rendzinas are found on parts of the scarp slopes in the Chilterns and North Downs. The surface A horizon may contain small angular particles of limestone rubble mixed with organic material. Its dark brown surface colour results from its humus content but the soil lies directly on top of chalk parent material.

Intrazonal soils resulting from excessive surface water can occur in any latitude. When water table levels are so high that dead vegetation is unable to decompose for lack of oxygen a purely organic soil, peat, may develop. Peat therefore develops where accumulation of dead vegetation exceeds decomposition. In Britain and Ireland there are basically two types. *Fen peat* develops when the water table is at the surface and groundwater is rich in basic cations as in the Fenland of East Anglia where water drains towards the lowland from upland areas of chalk and limestone. Base-loving plants such as reeds and sedges develop in fenland.

Where water is poor in bases *peat bogs* develop. They may be of two types. In *raised bogs*, which may initially develop in depressions (Figure 13.4), the centre grows faster than the edge to produce their characteristic dome-shaped appearance. Raised bogs may represent the final stage of the natural eutrophication process described in Chapter 12, an early phase of which is the development of fen peat. *Blanket bog* develops on flat lands or gentle slopes and may have been initiated in some circumstances by the extensive development of an ironpan in podsol soils which eventually so impeded natural drainage as to make the soil waterlogged and decomposition impossible. Raised bogs are especially well-developed in Ireland where they frequently form in former lake basins and inter-drumlin hollows. Blanket bog is common throughout Ireland and the British uplands. In peat bogs, drainage water from surrounding mineral soil does not penetrate on to the bog. Cut off from this nutrient source, growing plants on the bog depend for their

nutrients on rainwater alone. Peat bogs are therefore very acidic environments with pH values as
low as 4.0.

An intrazonal soil much associated with wetlands is the *gley*. Gleys typically develop on river
flood plains and other flat areas under a surface
horizon of organic matter which decomposes only
slowly because of anaerobic and/or cold conditions. Beneath the peaty surface, mineral soil is
frequently or permanently below the water table
and iron compounds are reduced (i.e. broken
down in oxygen-poor conditions) rather than
oxidized. Reduction of the iron to the ferrous state
gives the gley soil a predominantly blue or grey
colour. In dry periods the water table may fall
low enough to allow aeration and oxidation of
iron compounds to take place. Insoluble ferric
oxides are the outcome of complete oxidation
here as elsewhere (see Chapter 4) and produce
the rusty, yellowish-brown mottled appearance of
the characteristic gley (Figure 14.18). Gleying is a
very widespread soil-forming process in Britain
and Ireland (see, for example, Cruickshank, p.
144).

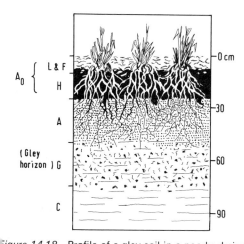

Figure 14.18 Profile of a gley soil in a poorly-drained
area. L—undecomposed grasses, sedges and mosses.
F+H—peat in various stages of decomposition, black
and structureless. A—mixed peat and inorganic material,
greyish-brown in colour. G—gley horizon containing
bluish-grey clay due to reduced iron content with red/
yellow mottling around organic material where some
oxidation has been possible.
Modified from S. R. Eyre, p. 169.)

SOIL AND VEGETATION OF BRITAIN AND IRELAND

In a small area like Britain and Ireland only two of
the world's major zonal soils are represented:
podsols and brown earths (grey-brown podsols).
The purest podsols occur in north-east Scotland
(Moray, Aberdeen, Banff) and in the Southern
Uplands. Brown earths are found throughout
England. The lower parts of the Welsh uplands are
intermediate in character between podsols and
brown earths. Cruickshank describes them as acid
brown earths. Many of our soils are intrazonal
rendzinas, gleys and peats. Gleys are widespread
in lowland valleys of England, and peats, along
with peaty gleys, are widespread in the uplands
of Wales, the Pennines and Scotland. The very
highest parts of Scotland and Wales have localized
azonal soils in the form of *lithosols* formed on
scree slopes. A possible classification of Britain
into regions of relatively uniform climatic processes from the point of view of soil formation is
shown in Figure 14.19.

In terms of vegetation Britain and Ireland both
bear the impact of man's uninterrupted activities
over several thousand years and there is little or
no 'natural' vegetation left. Most of Britain and
Ireland is suitable climatically for mixed deciduous
woodlands with oaks probably the dominant individual species. Two types of oak are found. In
the wetter parts where soils are generally lower in
nutrients and thinner the shallow-rooted sessile
oak is more common, while in the drier east where
soils are less acidic and nutrients more freely
available the deeper rooted pedunculate oak
occurs. To the north and west of the mixed
deciduous oakwoods, in many parts of the Scottish
Highlands for example, birch and pine tend
to dominate whatever remnants of semi-natural
woodland still exist. Altogether, some 8.5% of
Britain is wooded today and the figure is lower for
Ireland. The limited amount of woodland that
exists is liberally scattered across a wide range of
conditions. Only the very highest upland areas or
the undrained wetlands of the lowlands are totally
devoid of some form of woodland.

Other forms of vegetation include *moorlands*
of heather, mosses, bracken, and grasses. These
occur above the limit of agriculture today on land
that may have been forested during the climatic

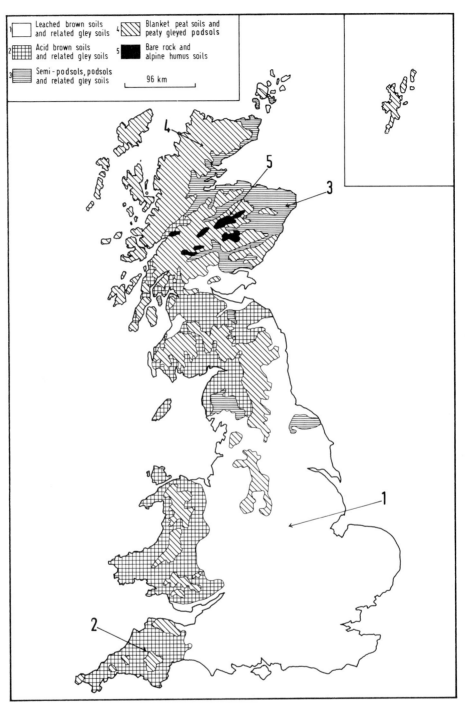

Figure 14.19 The approximate distribution of soil regions and associated climates in Great Britain. Average annual temperatures are 10 °C lower in mountainous parts of Scotland than in south-east England, evapotranspiration is therefore lower and leaching higher with consequently lower surface retention of nutrients. Soil region 1 experiences a warm, dry climate with mean annual temperatures above 8.3 °C and rainfall under 1000 mm year^{-1}. In region 2 the climate is warm and wet (mean annual temperatures above 8.3 °C and annual precipitation above 1000 mm). Region 3 is cold and dry (mean annual temperatures in the range 4.0–8.3 °C and precipitation under 1000 mm year^{-1}). Region 4 is cold and wet (4.0–8.3 °C, precipitation over 1000 mm) and region 5 is very cold and wet (under 4 °C and over 1000 mm).

(Source: C. P. Burnham, p. 27.)

Legend:
1 — Leached brown soils and related gley soils
2 — Acid brown soils and related gley soils
3 — Semi-podsols, podsols and related gley soils
4 — Blanket peat soils and peaty gleyed podsols
5 — Bare rock and alpine humus soils

96 km

optimum (Chapter 11) and contain many plant species typical of *heathlands*, but this term is usually reserved to describe open, dwarf shrub communities which exist on poorer soils within the altitudinal limits of agriculture.

Man's impact on soils and vegetation in Britain

The post-glacial history of man's impact on the ecosystems of Britain and Ireland began with the fishing, hunting and gathering economies of Mesolithic man (Figure 11.4) about 9000 years ago. In general, however, these primitive people lacked the technology to cut down the mixed woodlands that probably covered 80% or more of Britain and Ireland at the time. The first significant clearances were probably made by Neolithic man for cultivation, settlement and the feeding of animals. There is some fossil pollen evidence to suggest that the decline of elm in upland areas is associated with the development of Neolithic farming about 5000 BP. At about this time cereal pollen occurs for the first time often accompanied by pollen from weeds. It is sometimes speculated that Neolithic man may have used elm twigs and bark as an animal fodder in winter. This is still apparently the practice in parts of Sweden today. Alternatively the elm may have been progressively killed by grazing animals eating the tree bark. Peat started to form as a blanket on the hills about a thousand years after the elm decline and most probably represents a climatic deterioration towards wetter conditions.

The next major phase of forest clearance came with the Romans who removed woodland for cultivation and defence and for the development of cities and road networks. But the most important phase of clearance was started by the Saxons in the sixth century and was continued by them for several centuries more. Most of Britain's villages were established by Anglo-Saxon settlers. During the medieval period timber was used as a fuel, for domestic building and for ship construction, and woodland was cleared at an accelerated rate. The

process continued as the area under agriculture expanded and it was not until the establishment of the Forestry Commission in 1919 that the position started to be reversed.

One of the major changes to Britain's vegetation currently taking place is the afforestation of upland areas. These new forests now cover 20% of the upland area, and represent a deliberate effort to reduce the cost of timber imports into Britain. Quite recently, the Forestry Commission discussed the possibility of planting a further 1.8 million ha by the year 2025. Planting on such a scale would raise the forestry cover to 50% of the upland area in Britain (Calder and Newson).

Afforestation has marked effects on evaporation and streamflow. Recent studies by the Institute of Hydrology at Plynlimon in Wales showed that run-off from a small forested catchment in the upper Severn drainage basin was 19% less than from an adjacent grass-covered catchment in the upper Wye, the difference being accounted for principally by the evaporation of precipitation intercepted by the forest canopy in the Severn catchment. The reduced streamflow brought about by afforestation has implications for other land use in upland areas, notably water supply undertakings. Many upland catchments used for reservoirs are also extensively planted with conifers, and run-off into them most probably declines as planted forests mature and canopies close. Indeed it was a civil engineer with the Fylde Water Board in Lancashire who first observed a loss of inflow into water supply reservoirs on the upper Hodder river and thought that afforestation was responsible. The Plynlimon study has confirmed these earlier views and shown that afforestation and reservoirs are not exactly compatible types of land use in upland areas. More generally, the study also illustrates that processes in the biosphere, atmosphere and hydrosphere are strongly interconnected and that changes in one demonstrably affect the others. This is perhaps the most important theme in physical geography and environmental management.

References,
Other Sources of Information*
and Suggested Reading†

GENERAL

Giddings, J. C., 1973, *Chemistry, Man and Environmental Change*, Canfield Press, 472 pp.

Leopold, L. B. and Davis, K. S., 1972, *Water*, Time-Life International, 200 pp.

Muller, R. A., 1974, *Physical Geography Today—A Portrait of a Planet*, CRM Books, 518 pp.

Strahler, A. N., 1973, *Introduction to Physical Geography* (3rd ed.), Wiley, 468 pp.

Strahler, A. N. and Strahler, A. H., 1974, *Introduction to Environmental Science*, Hamilton, 633 pp.

CHAPTERS 1 AND 2

Chorley, R. J. and Kennedy, B. A., 1971, *Physical Geography—A Systems Approach*, Prentice-Hall, 370 pp.

*Chorley, R. J., 1962, 'Geomorphology and general systems theory', *United States Geological Survey Professional Paper*, 500-B, 10 pp.

Gates, D. M., 1971, 'The flow of energy in the biosphere', *Energy and Power*, (a Scientific American publication), 43–54.

*Rothman, M. A., 1963, *The Laws of Physics*, Pelican, 246 pp.

*Schumm, S. A. and Lichty, R. W., 1965, 'Time, space and causality', *American Journal of Science*, Vol. 263, 110–119.

Spanner, D. C., 1964, *Introduction to Thermodynamics*, Academic Press, 278 pp.

CHAPTER 3

Burke, K. C. and Wilson, J. T., 1976, 'Hot spots of the earth's surface', *Scientific American*, Vol. 235, Aug., 46–57.

†Clapperton, C. M., 1977, 'Volcanoes in space and time', *Progress in Physical Geography*, Vol. 1, 375–411.

†Clapperton, C. M., 1978, 'The Edinburgh Volcano', *Geographical Magazine*, Vol. 50, June, 608–612.

*Jordan, T. H., 1979, 'The deep structure of the continents', *Scientific American*, Vol. 240, Jan., 92–107.

Kittleman, L. R., 1979, 'Tephra', *Scientific American*, Vol. 241, Dec., 132–142.

*Leet, L. D. and Judson, S., 1971, *Physical Geology* (4th ed.), Prentice-Hall, 687 pp.

Moorbath, S., 1977, 'The oldest rocks and the growth of continents', *Scientific American*, Vol. 236, Mar., 92–104.

*Pollack, H. N., and Chapman, D. S., 1977, 'The flow of heat from the earth's interior', *Scientific American*, Vol. 237, Aug., 60–76.

†Rittman, A. and L., 1976, *Volcanoes*, Orbis, 128 pp.

Siever, R., 1974, 'The steady state of the earth's crust, atmosphere, and oceans', *Scientific American*, Vol. 230, June, 72–79.

The Open University, 1971(a), *The Earth, its Shape, Internal Structure and Composition* and *The Earth's Magnetic Field*, Science Foundation Course, Units 22 and 23, Open University Press.

The Open University, 1971(b), *Major Features of the Earth's Surface: Continental Movement, Sea-floor Spreading and Plate Tectonics*, Science Foundation Course, Units 24 and 25, Open University Press.

Thornbury, W. D., 1961, *Principles of Geomorphology*, Wiley, 618 pp.

Toksoz, M. N., 1975, 'The subduction of the lithosphere', *Scientific American*, Vol. 233, Nov., 88–98.

*Wilson, J. T., 1963, 'Continental drift', *Scientific American*, Apr., 16 pp.

'Wylie, P. J., 1975, 'The earth's mantle', *Scientific American*, Vol. 232, Mar., 50–63.

CHAPTERS 4, 5, 6 AND 7

Allen, J. R. L., 1970, *Physical Processes of Sedimentation*, Allen and Unwin, 248 pp.

Andrews, J. T., 1975, *Glacial Systems*, Duxbury, 191 pp.

Bagnold, R. A., 1954, *The Physics of Blown Sand and Desert Dunes*, Methuen, 265 pp.

*Bird, E. C. F., 1970, *Coasts*, M.I.T. Press, 246 pp.

Bowen, D. Q., 1978, *Quaternary Geology*, Pergamon, 221 pp.

†Butzer, K. W., 1978, 'Climate patterns in an unglaciated continent', *Geographical Magazine*, Vol. 51, Dec., 201–208.

'Carr, A. P., 1978, 'The long Chesil shingle', *Geographical Magazine*, Vol. 50, July, 677–680.

Carter, R. W. G., 1975, 'The effects of human pressures on the coastlines of County Londonderry', *Irish Geography*, Vol. 8, 72–85.

Carter, R. W. G., 1979, 'Recent progradation of the Magilligan foreland, County Londonderry', *Publication du CNEXO: Actes de Colloques No. 9*, pp. 18 and 20.

†Clark, M. J., 1978, 'Geomorphology in coastal zone management', *Geography*, Vol. 63, 273–282.

Cooke, R. U. and Warren, A., 1973, *Geomorphology in Deserts*, Batsford, 374 pp.

Davies, J. L., 1972(a), *Geographical Variation in Coastal Development*, Oliver & Boyd, 204 pp.

Davies, J. L., 1972(b), *Landforms of Cold Climates*, M.I.T. Press, 200 pp.

Derbyshire, E., Gregory, K. J. and Hails, J. R., 1979, *Geomorphological Processes*, Dawson Westview, 312 pp.

Douglas, I., 1969, 'The efficiency of humid tropical denudation systems', *Transactions of the Institute of British Geographers*, 46, 1–16.

Dunne, T., 1979, 'Sediment yield and land use in tropical catchments', *Journal of Hydrology*, Vol. 42, 281–300.

Dury, G. H., 1963, 'Rivers in geographical teaching', *Geography*, Vol. 10, 10–00.

Dury, G. H., 1970, 'General theory of meandering valleys and misfit streams' (in) G. H. Dury (ed.), *Rivers and River Terraces*, Macmillan, 264–275.

Dury, G. H., 1977(a), 'Underfit streams: retrospect, perspect and prospect' (in) K. J. Gregory (ed.), *River Channel Changes*, Wiley, 281–296.

*Dury, G. H., 1977(b), 'Peak flows, low flows, and aspects of geomorphic dominance' (in) K. J. Gregory (ed.), *River Channel Changes*, Wiley, 61–74.

Embleton, C. and King, C. A. M., 1968, *Glacial and Periglacial Geomorphology*, Edward Arnold, 608 pp.

Fairbridge, R. W., 1960, 'The changing level of the sea', *Scientific American*, Vol. 202, May, 70–79.

Fairbridge, R. W. (ed.), 1968, *The Encyclopedia of Geomorphology*, Van Nostrand Rheinhold, 1295 pp.

†Fairbridge, R. W., 1979, 'Ice-covered wasteland that became America', *Geographical Magazine*, Vol. 51, Jan., 294–300.

†*Flint, R. F., 1964, *Glacial and Pleistocene Geology*, Wiley, 553 pp.

French, H. M., 1976, *The Periglacial Environment*, Longman, 309 pp.

Graf, W. L., 1979, 'The development of montane arroyos and gullies', *Earth Surface Processes*, Vol. 4, 1–14.

†Gregory, K. J., 1978, 'Valley carved in the Yorkshire Moors', *Geographical Magazine*, Vol. 50, Jan., 276–279.

*Gregory, K. J. and Walling, D. E. (eds), 1979, *Man and Environmental Processes*, Dawson Westfield, 276 pp.

Gregory, K. J. and Park, C. C., 1976, 'The development of a Devon gully and man', *Geography*, Vol. 61, 77–82.

Gross, M. G., 1972, *Oceanography: a view of the earth*, Prentice-Hall, 581 pp.

Holeman, J. N., 1968, 'The sediment yield of the major rivers of the world', *Water Resources Research*, Vol. 4, 737–747.

Holmes, A. D., 1965, *Principles of Physical Geology*, Nelson, 1288 pp.

Hutchinson, J. N., Prior, D. B. and Stephens, N., 1974, 'Potentially dangerous surges in an Antrim mudslide', *Quarterly Journal of Engineering Geology*, Vol. 7, 363–376.

Komar, P. D., 1976, *Beach Processes and Sedimentation*, Prentice-Hall, 429 pp.

Leopold, L. B. and Maddock, J., 1953, 'The hydraulic geometry of stream channels and some physiographic implications', *United States Geological Survey Professional Paper*, 252.

Leopold, L. B., Wolman, M. G. and Miller, J. P., 1964, *Fluvial Processes in Geomorphology*, Freeman, 504 pp.

Matthes, G. H., 1951, 'Paradoxes of the Mississippi', *Scientific American*, Apr., 7 pp.

Morisawa, M. P., 1968, *Streams, Their Dynamics and Morphology*, McGraw-Hill, 175 pp.

*Newson, M. D., 1980, 'The geomorphological effectiveness of floods—a contribution stimulated by two recent events in mid-Wales', *Earth Surface Processes*, Vol. 5, 1–16.

Ovenden, J. C. and Gregory, K. J., 1980, 'The permanence of stream networks in Britain', *Earth Surface Processes*, Vol. 5, 47–60.

†Park, C. C., 1977, 'Some approaches to the study of stream channels', *Classroom Geographer*, Jan.

Paterson, W. S. B., 1969, *The Physics of Glaciers*, Pergamon, 250 pp.

Robinson, A. H. W., 1953, 'The storm surge of January 31st—February 1st, 1953', *Geography*, Vol. 38, 134–141.

Sawyer, K. E., 1975, *Landscape Studies—an Introduction to Geomorphology*, Edward Arnold, 148 pp.

Stephens, N. and Synge, F. M., 1967, 'Pleistocene shorelines' (in) G. H. Dury (ed.), *Essays in Geomorphology*, Heinemann, 404 pp.

†Sugden, D., 1978, 'Extremes of a glacial planet', *Geographical Magazine*, Vol. 51, Nov., 119–128.

†Velitchko, A. A., 1979, 'Soviet glaciers were late developers', *Geographical Magazine*, Vol. 51, April, 472–478.

Washburn, A. L., 1973, *Periglacial Processes and Environments*, Edward Arnold, 320 pp.

West, R. G., 1968, *Pleistocene Geology and Biology*, Longman, 377 pp.

*Wolman, M. G. and Miller, J. P., 1960, 'Magnitude and frequency in geomorphic processes', *Journal of Geology*, Vol. 68, 54–74.

†Wright, L. D. and Thom, B. G., 1977, 'Coastal depositional landforms: a morphological approach', *Progress in Physical Geography*, Vol. 1, 412–459.

Young, A., 1972, *Slopes*, Oliver and Boyd, 288 pp.

†Young, J. A. T., 1977, 'Glacial geomorphology of the Aviemore-Loch Garten area', *Geography*, Vol. 62, 25–34.

CHAPTERS 8, 9, 10 AND 11

Anon, 1981, 'CO_2 and the effects of human activity on climate: a global view', *Nature and Resources*, Vol. 17, No. 3, 2–5.

Atkinson, B., 1978, 'The Atmosphere: recent observational and conceptual advances', *Geography*, Vol. 63, 283–300.

Atkinson, B., 1979, 'Urban influences on precipitation' (in) G. E. Hollis (ed.), *Man's Impact on the Hydrological Cycle in the United Kingdom*, Geo. Abstracts, 123–133.

Barry, R. G. and Chorley, R. J., 1976, *Atmosphere, Weather and Climate*, Methuen, 432 pp.

Bouille, B. W., and Doos, B. R., 1981, 'Why a world climate programme?', *Nature and Resources*, Vol. 17, No. 1, 2–7.

†Butzer, K. W., 1978, 'Climate patterns in an unglaciated continent', *Geographical Magazine*, Vol. 51, Dec., 201–208.

Chandler, T. J., 1965, *The Climate of London*, Hutchinson, 292 pp.

Critchfield, H. J., 1974, *General Climatology*, Prentice-Hall, 446 pp.

Crowe, P. R., 1971, *Concepts in Climatology*, Longman, 589 pp.

†Doornkamp, J. C. and Gregory, K. J., 1976, 'The great drought recorded', *Geographical Magazine*, Vol. 49, 297–301.

Flohn, H., 1969, *Climate and Weather*, McGraw-Hill.

Gribbin, J., 1978, *Climatic Change*, Cambridge University Press, 280 pp.

Hargreaves, G. H., 1981, 'Water requirements and man-induced climatic change', *Journal of the Irrigation Division, Proceedings of the American Society of Civil Engineers*, Vol. 107, 247–255.

Hare, F. K., 1961, *The Restless Atmosphere*, Hutchinson, 192 pp.

*Hare, F. K., 1973, 'Energy-based climatology' (in) R. J. Chorley (ed.), *Directions in Geography*, Methuen.

Hidore, J. J., 1974, *Physical Geography: Earth Systems*, Scott, Foresman and Co., 418 pp.

*Lamb, H. H., 1970, 'Climatic variation and our environment today and in the coming years', *Weather*, Vol. 25, 447–455.

Lamb, H. H., 1977, *Climate, Past, Present and Future*, Vol. II, Methuen, 835 pp.

Lamb, P. J., 1979, 'Some perspectives on climate and climate dynamics', *Progress in Physical Geography*, Vol. 3, 215–235.

Miller, A. A., 1959, *Climatology*, Methuen, 317 pp.

Oort, A. H., 1970, 'The energy cycle of the earth', *The Biosphere* (a Scientific American publication), Freeman 14–23.

Pedgley, D. E., 1962, *A Course in Elementary Meteorology*, HMSO, 189 pp.

Penman, H. L., 1970, 'The water cycle', *The Biosphere* (a Scientific American publication), Freeman, 37–46.

†Rozanov, B. G., 1977, 'Soviet deserts are reclaimed', *Geographical Magazine*, Vol. 50, Dec., 162–165.

Sellers, W. D., 1967, *Physical Climatology*, University of Chicago Press, 272 pp.

Smith, K., 1975, *Principles of Applied Climatology*, McGraw-Hill, 233 pp.

Stewart, R. W., 1969, 'The atmosphere and the oceans', *The Ocean* (a Scientific American publication), Freeman, 28–38.

Sutton, O. G., 1962, *The Challenge of the Atmosphere*, Hutchinson, 227 pp.

Tullett, M. T., 1970, 'The nature of climatic change', *Weather*, Vol. 25, 465–470.

Vorupaev, S. and Kosarev, H., 1982, 'The fall and rise of the Caspian Sea', *New Scientist*, April, 78–80.

Ward, R. C., 1963, 'Measuring potential evapotranspiration', *Geography*, Vol. 48, 49–55.

CHAPTERS 12, 13 AND 14

†Armstrong, P. H., 1973, 'Changes in the land use of the Suffolk sandlings, a study in the disintegration of an ecosystem', *Geography*, Vol. 58, 1–8.

Angel, H., 1981, *The Natural History of Britain and Ireland*, Book Club Associates, 256 pp.

Bolin, B., 1970, 'The carbon cycle', *The Biosphere* (a Scientific American publication), Freeman, 49–56.

*Bormann, F. H. and Likens, G. E., 1979, *Pattern and Process in a Forested Ecosystem*, Springer Verlag, 253 pp.

Bridges, E. M., 1978, 'Soil, the vital skin of the earth', *Geography*, Vol. 63, 354–361.

Bunting, B. T., 1967, *The Geography of Soil*, Hutchinson, 213 pp.

Burnham, C. P., 1970, 'The regional pattern of soil formation in Great Britain', *Scottish Geographical Magazine*, Vol. 86, 25–34.

Calder, I. R. and Newson, M. G., 1979, 'Land use and upland water resources in Britain—a strategic look', *Water Resources Bulletin*, Vol. 15, 12 pp.

Cloud, P. and Gibor, A., 1970, 'The oxygen cycle', *The Biosphere* (a Scientific American publication), Freeman, 59–68.

Collinson, A. S., 1977, *Introduction to World Vegetation*, Allen and Unwin, 201 pp.

Cox, C. B., Healey, I. N. and Moore, P. D., 1976, *Biogeography—an Ecological and Evolutionary Approach*, Blackwell, 194 pp.

Cruickshank, J. G., 1977, *Soil Geography*, David and Charles, 256 pp.

Eyre, S. R., 1963, *Vegetation and Soils*, Edward Arnold, 324 pp.

Funnell, B. M. and Hey, R. D., 1974, *The Management of Water Resources in England and Wales*, Saxon House, 162 pp.

†Frenzel, B., 1979, 'Europe without forests', *Geographical Magazine*, Vol. 51, Aug. 756–761.

†Graham, M., 1973, *A Natural Ecology*, Manchester University Press, 251 pp.

Hamilton, A. C., 1981, 'The quaternary history of African forests: its relevance to conservation', *African Journal of Ecology*, 19, 1–6.

Hamilton, A. C., 1982, *Environmental history of East Africa—a study of the Quaternary*, Academic Press, 328 pp.

Harris, D. R., 1974, 'Tropical vegetation: an outline and some misconceptions', *Geography*, Vol. 59, 240–250.

Horn, H. S., 1975, 'Factors affecting forest succession', *Scientific American*, May, Vol. 232, 90–98.

Kirby, C., 1979, *Water in Great Britain*, Pelican, 162 pp.

Kormondy, E. J., 1969, *Concepts in Ecology*, Prentice-Hall, 209 pp.

Leach, G., 1975, *Energy and Food Production*, International Institute for Environment and Development, 151 pp.

Newbould, P. J., 1967, *Primary Production of Forests*, International Biological Programme Handbook, No. 2, Blackwell, 62 pp.

Odum, E. P., 1966, *Ecology*, Holt, Rinehart and Winston, 152 pp.

Oldfield, F., 1977, 'Lakes and their drainage basins as units of sediment-based ecological study', *Progress in Physical Geography*, Vol. 1, 460–504.

Pears, N., 1977, *Basic Biogeography*, Longman, 272 pp.

*Pennington, W., 1970, *The History of British Vegetation*, Unibooks, 152 pp.

Penman, H. L., 1970, 'The Water cycle', *The Biosphere* (a Scientific American publication), Freeman, 39–45.

*Russell, Sir J. E., 1970, *The World of the Soil*, Fontana, 285 pp.

Smith, K., 1972, *Water in Britain*, Macmillan, 272 pp.

Simmons, I. G., 1980, 'Ecological functional approaches to agriculture in geographical contexts', *Geography*, Vol. 65, 305–316.

*Spurr, S. H., 1970, 'Silviculture', *Scientific American*, Vol. 240, Feb., 62–75.

Stoddart, D. R., 1965, 'Geography and the ecological approach—the ecosystem as a geographic principle and method', *Geography*, Vol. 50, 242–251.

The Open University, 1975, *Introduction and Unifying Themes Environmental Health*, Units 1–2 of the course in Environmental Control and Public Health, Open University Press, 149 pp.

Trudgill, S. T., 1977, *Soil and Vegetation Systems*, Clarendon, 180 pp.

*Watts, D., 1978, 'The new biogeography and its niche in physical geography', *Geography*, Vol. 63, 324–337.

Whittaker, R. H., 1975, *Communities and Eco-systems*, Macmillan, 386 pp.

Woodwell, G. M., 1970, 'The energy cycle of the biosphere', *The Biosphere* (a Scientific American publication), Freeman, 23–36.

Young, A., 1974, 'Some aspects of tropical soils', *Geography*, Vol. 59, 233–239.

Index

ablation   76, 77, 78, 83, 84, 139
abrasion   43, 72, 79
accretion (wind)   64–5
accumulation zone   77–8, 79
acid rain   31–3
adiabatic cooling   110, 111–13, 131
    see also lapse rate
advection   108
afforestation   209
aggradation   38, 58, 90
agricultural ecosystems   166–7, 170–1
air masses   130
    and climate   142–3
albedo   99, 104, 150
alluvial fan   57, 85
alluvial plain   57
alluvial soils   178
anaerobic conditions   160, 169, 183
anions   31
anticyclones   119, 124, 130–1, 134
arête   79
arroyo   56
asthenosphere   18, 19, 24
atmosphere
    circulation   101–3, 122–6, 152
    composition   96
    pressure   111, 119, 123, 130
    stability   97, 111–13, 130, 131, 135
    structure   97
    vapour pressure   107, 110
attrition   42
autotrophs   157–8, 166

backshore zone   66
bankfull stage   46, 52
basal slip   78, 80
basalt   19, 24, 72
base exchange   185
base level   51, 90
batholith   25, 26
beach   66–71
    as open system   11
bedload trap   41–2, 43, 44
berm   66, 71, 72
biodegradation   159–60
biological oxygen demand (BOD)   172
biomass   158, 164, 165, 180
biome   170, 190
    types of   190–206

biosphere   156, 174
blanket bog   206
blocking highs   131
boulder clay   79, 82
braiding   50, 85
Buys Ballot's law   120

caldera   25
Caledonian period   23
caliche   199
carbon dioxide   3, 4, 31, 96, 161–2
    and atmospheric warming   100, 104–5, 153, 162
    and measuring energy flows   165–6
carbonation   31
carbonic acid   31, 185
carbon-14 dating   147
catena   178
cations   31, 32, 185
chaparral   191, 197–8
chernozem   192, 193, 196
Chesil beach   67
chestnut-brown soil   192, 193, 196
clay   182–3
clay-humus complex   184–6
climate
    post-glacial   144–50
    regional classification   141–4
    in relation to world soils and vegetation   193
    trends in   152–4
    variability in   144–5, 152–3
climatic climax vegetation   180–1, 195
climatic optimum   149
climatic terraces   90, 93
climax ecosystem   164
clouds   111, 113–15
    cumulus   5, 130, 131, 136
    and fronts   131–2
    seeding   116
    thundercloud   112
coalescence model of raindrop formation   110–11
coast
    bars   66, 67
    classification   73–4
    cliffs   72
    landforms   66
    sediment traps   68
colloidal swelling   30
condensation   4, 101, 102, 103, 109–11, 113, 136
    nuclei   110–11, 116–18

conduction   100
continental accretion   23
continental drift   23–4
continental shelf   26, 67
continental slope   67
convection (atmosphere)   5, 99, 108, 116, 122, 136, 137
core rings   128–9
corestones   33
Coriolis force   119–21, 126, 138
crag and tail   82
Crater Lake, Oregon   25
craton   20, 23, 24
current meter   39–40
cuspate foreland   69–70
cusps   71
cycles
    carbon   160–2
    hydrological (water)   5, 128, 162–3, 173–4; as closed system   8, 9
    nutrient   165, 170, 186, 188, 201
    oxygen   163–4
    photosynthesis-respiration   4, 164
    vegetation   181
cyclones   *see* depressions *and* hurricanes

Dalmation coast   74
dams
    and hydroelectric power   6
    and river sediment   38–9, 53–4
dating techniques
    archaeological and historical   148
    carbon-14   147
    oxygen-isotope   147, 151
    pollen analysis   144, 146, 200
    radioactive   23, 147
    tree rings   147–8
dead ice   76, 79
decay food chain   159–60, 176
deflation hollow   58
deforestation   104, 172, 189, 203
deglaciation   76, 82, 83, 85–6
degradation   38, 58
deltas   53–4
denudation   29
deposition
    on coasts   66–74
    in deserts   57–8
    by ice   82–5
    in oceans   26
    by rivers   38, 39, 44, 50, 52, 53, 54, 57–8, 84, 85, 90

deposition (*contd.*)
  on slopes 35–6
  by wind 64–5
depressions 65, 131–3
desert
  climate 143
  landforms 56–8
  soil 192
  vegetation 179, 191, 198–9
desertification 153
desilication 177, 202
dew point 110
diorite 24
doldrums 122
drainage basin 11, 29
drainage network 54–5
droughts 116–17, 144, 152–3
drumlins 83–4
dust (atmospheric) 97, 105, 110, 116, 151
dust dome 116
dust plume 118
dyke 25, 26, 27
dynamic equilibrium *see* equilibrium

earth, density 18, 28
earthquake 9, 18–22, 37, 65
ecosystem 164–70, 187–9
  production (productivity) 164, 166–7
efficiency, in energy transformations 4, 10, 50–1, 159, 171
Ekman spirals 120, 128
eluviation 184
endogenic forces 18
energy 2–7, 8, 9
  budgets 77, 99–103
  chemical 2, 160
  conservation of 6
  electrical 6
  flows 8–10, 13, 14, 159–60, 165–6, 188
  geothermal 9
  gravitational 2–3
  heat 3–7, 9, 50, 98–105, 125, 128, 136, 160, 165
  kinetic 3–6, 35, 59, 61, 65, 98, 107, 111, 160
  latent heat 4–5, 96, 100–3, 108, 111–13, 136
  nuclear 2
  potential 2–7, 9, 14, 50, 51, 59, 61, 65, 160
  solar 2–5, 9, 12, 60, 76, 96–101, 105, 108, 150, 156, 160, 180
  tectonic 9
  transformations 3–7, 9, 51, 60, 100–1, 103, 160
ephemeral streams 56
epicentre 18, 19
equatorial climate 143
equifinality 15
equilibrium 7
  dynamic 13, 14–15, 39, 107
  steady state 13–14, 22, 37, 39, 48, 68, 77, 83, 180
equilibrium line altitude 77
erosion
  on coasts 65–7, 73, 74
  in deserts 56
  by ice 78–82
  in rivers 13, 38–9, 47–8
  on slopes 35–7
  of soil 197, 198

threshold 56
erratics 84
eskers 84
eustacy 87, 88, 90
  see also sea level changes
eutrophication 169, 171–2
evaporation 4–5, 14, 15, 64, 100–1, 102, 106–9, 147
evapotranspiration 107–9, 163, 177, 179, 195, 197, 198, 199
exfoliation 30, 31

faults 27–8, 83
feedback loops 12–13, 188–9
  see also positive feedback *and* negative feedback
Ferrel's cell 102
Ferrel's law 121
fetch 60
firn 75
fjord 74
flood 39, 44, 46
  bankfull 46, 52
  coastal 65
  defined 44
  flash flood 56
  hydrograph 39, 40, 41
fluvioglacial deposits 67, 83, 84–5, 86
fog 113, 115, 130
fold mountains 22–3
folding 27
food chains 157–60
foreshore 66
forest
  ecosystem 11, 166
  rain forest 195
  soils 177, 195
  structure 187, 200–1
  temperate forests 191, 193, 194–5
  tropical rain forest 191, 193, 199–203
fossil fuels 104, 161–2, 171
free face 37
freeze–thaw mechanism 29, 33, 78–80, 82, 89–90
friction 7, 160
  in crustal plates 21
  in river channels 50
  by wind 64, 119–20
  see also energy, heat
fronts 131–3

gauging station 40–1
geological succession 87
glacial diffluence 82
glacial drift *see* till
glacial meltwater 52, 76, 78, 79, 81, 84, 85
glacial overflow channels 85–6
glacial transfluence 82
glacial trough 80–1
glaciation, causes of 150–2
glacierization 75–6
glaciers 77–84
  depositional landforms 82–4
  erosional landforms 79–82
  flow path 77, 79, 81
  mass budgets 77–8
  shear planes 78, 83
  velocity 78
  see also ice sheets, moraine, proglacial landforms
gley soil 178, 190, 207

graben 28
graded river 39
grassland
  temperate 191, 193, 195–7
  tropical (savanna) 191, 193, 204–5
greenhouse effect 100, 105
groundwater 9, 34
groynes 68
Gulf Stream 128–9

habitat 186
Hadley cell 102, 124, 152
hail 112, 117
hanging valley 80
headwall gap 79, 80
heat transfers (global) 101–3
heterotrophs 157
hoar frost 110
horst 28
hot-spot volcanoes 20, 21, 23, 24
humidity
  absolute 107–8, 117
  relative 107–8, 111, 118
hurricanes 136–7
hydration 31, 185
hydraulic geometry 48–9
hydrogen bonding 4, 182
hydrograph 40–1
hydrological cycle *see* cycles
hydrolysis 31
hydrophytes 179
hydrosere 180–1
hydrosphere 156, 163

ice, density of 75
ice contact features 83, 84
ice crystal model of raindrop formation 111, 116
ice-dammed lake 85–6
ice sheets 12, 75–6
  decay 76
  thickness 87
  see also glaciers *and* moraine
ice wedges 90, 93
igneous rocks 24–6
illuviation 184
index cycle 125
infiltration capacity 34
inshore zone 66
interglacial periods 88
interstadial periods 148
intertropical convergence zone (ITCZ) 116, 122–4, 133, 134, 135
inverted relief 27
involutions 89
ionic compounds 31, 32, 185
ironpan 184, 206
irrigation 199
isostacy 28, 65, 87
  see also sea level changes

jet streams 125–6, 132–3, 134, 135
joints 33, 71, 81, 82

kames 84
kame terraces 84
kettle hole 84
kimberlites 19
knob and basin topography 84

laccolith 25, 26

lake
  hydrosere 180–1
  strandlines (terraces) 85, 147
  systems 11, 167–9
lake breezes 138
laminar flow 35, 56
land breezes 138
landslide 9, 36–7
lapse rate
  environmental (ELR) 97, 111, 130
  dry adiabatic (DALR) 111, 139
  saturated adiabatic (SALR) 112–13, 139
latent heat *see under* energy
laterite 202
latosols 192–3, 200, 202–3, 205
lava 22, 23, 24–6
leaching 184, 185, 200
leaf-fall 179, 200
Liebig's law of the minimum 165
lithosphere 18, 19, 21
Little Ice Age 150
littoral drift 59, 62, 68
loam 182
loess 90, 93
longshore bar 69, 71
lysimeter 109

magma 19–22, 24–6
man's influence on the environment 53–4, 68, 73, 104–5, 116–18, 140, 150, 153–4, 171–4, 199, 209
mantle 18, 19, 21, 23
mass movement 35–7, 89
Mediterranean
  climate 143
  vegetation 197–8
mesophytes 179
mesosphere 98
metamorphic rocks 25–6
meteorological station 99, 108–9, 115
mid-Atlantic ridge 19–21
models
  atmospheric circulation 102
  earth's crust 22
  ecosystem 188
  raindrop formation 110–11, 116
  slope evolution 37
monsoons 133–6, 143
mor 186, 194
moraine
  cross valley 85–6
  recessional 83
  terminal (or end) 70, 78, 82–3
  valley glacier 80, 84
mountain building 21–3, 26
mudflows 35–6
mull 186, 194

nearshore zone 66, 67
negative feedback 12–13, 14, 37, 49, 50, 71, 188–9
niche 164, 187
nickpoint 51, 81
nitrogen dioxide 96, 115
nitrogen fixation 165
nutrient cycle *see under* cycles

ocean
  basins 25–6
  ice sheets 152
  trenches 20, 22

oceanic circulation 126–9
offshore zone 66
oligotrophic 169
orogenesis 22
osmosis 106
overgrazing 56, 153, 198
overland flow 34, 56
oxidation 30, 157
oxygen 3, 4, 30, 96, 163–4
  dissolved oxygen (DO) 159, 170, 172
  sag curve 172
ozone 97, 98, 115

pampas 195
Pangaea 23, 24
parallel retreat 57
paternoster lakes 81
peat
  bogs 206–7
  soil 178
  stratigraphy 144, 146
pebbleometer 40, 42
pedalfer 177, 196
pediment 57
pedocal 177
pedon 184–5
periglaciation 80, 89–91, 93
permafrost 89–90, 190
permeability (soil) 34
pH 32, 186
phase change 28
photosynthesis 3, 4, 156–7, 161–4, 165
piedmont plain 57
pingo 90–1, 93
plant community 186–7
plant life-forms 186–7
plant production (productivity) 160, 165, 170, 180
plate tectonics 19–24
playa 58
Pleistocene 88, 89, 91–2, 199–200
plucking 79, 81
plumes 21, 23
podsol 184, 190, 192
pollen analysis *see under* dating techniques
pollution
  air 96, 98, 115
  water 172–3
positive feedback 12, 152, 188
post-glacial chronology 144–50
prairie 195–6
precipitation 115–18
  see also hail, rainfall, snow
pressure melting 18–22, 78, 79, 80
pressure release mechanisms 28, 29, 30, 72, 81
proglacial landforms 85–6
psammosere 180

radiosonde balloon 97, 102
radiation
  balance (global) 98–101; (local) 103
  counter 100, 103
  solar *see* energy, solar
  terrestrial 9, 98–101, 103, 115
rain gauge 115
rain shadow 113, 135
raindrop formation 110–11
rainfall 35, 108
  and climate 141–3
  distribution (global) 115–16

and erosion rates 48
and fronts 133
in hurricanes 136
impact of 35
and run-off 56
urban areas 116–18
raised beaches 88
raised bog 206
randkluft 79
rating curve 40, 41
reduction 29
  chemical 30
refraction 61
regelation 78, 81
regolith 29, 32, 33, 176
regression analysis 12
rejuvenation 51
rendzina 206
respiration 4, 157, 161–4, 165–6
ria 74
rift valley 21, 23, 28
rip-current 71
rivers
  base level 51, 90
  channel morphology 15, 38, 48–51; in deserts 56
  competence 43
  deposition 38, 39, 44, 50, 52, 53, 54, 57–8, 84, 85, 90
  discharge 39–40, 43–50
  ecosystems 170
  erosion 13, 38–9, 44, 47–8
  flood plain 52–3
  long profile 51
  and man's interference 6, 38–9, 53–4, 55, 56, 154, 172–3
  meanders 51–3
  networks 54–5
  as open systems 38–9
  sediment transport 38–48, 50, 53, 54, 56
  velocity 38–40, 48–50
roche moutonée 81
Rossby waves 125, 151

saltation 40, 42, 64
sand dunes 70, 72
saturated overland flow 34
saturation zone 34
savanna *see under* grassland
scree 32–3, 37
sea breezes 138
sea-floor spreading 19
sea level changes 67, 72, 73, 87–8
  and river base level 51
sea wave 60, 69
sediment traps (coastal) 68
sedimentary rocks 25–6
seismic waves 18, 19
self-regulation 13
seres 180
Severn bore 60
shadow zone 18, 19
sheetfloods 56
shifting cultivation 203
sial 18, 19, 21
sierozem soil 199
sill 25
silt 182–3
sima 18, 19, 21
slopes 14, 34–7, 57
smog 115
snow 75, 76, 111
soil
  acidity 176, 186

soil (*contd.*)
  and agricultural potential   205
  azonal   178
  in British Isles   207–9
  and climate   177–8, 193
  creep   35, 48
  development   176–8
  erosion   197, 198
  halomorphic   206
  intrazonal   178, 206–7
  moisture budget   195, 197
  organisms   177–8
  profile   183–4
  regional classification   192
  structure   182
  texture   181–2
  water   183
  zonal   178
solar constant   2
solar radiation   *see* energy, solar
solarimeter   99
solifluction   89, 93
solonchak soil   58, 206
solonetz soil   58, 206
spit   68–9
steady-state   *see* equilibrium
steppe   143, 193, 195
stilling well   40, 41
stomata   106
stone polygons   90, 93
storm surge   65
stratigraphic record   58
stratosphere   97–8
stream frequency   54
stream order   54–5
subduction   21, 22, 26
sublimation   76, 111, 139
submarine canyon   66, 68
sunshine recorder   99
surface creep   64–5
surface wash   35
suspended sediment   40, 42, 44–6,
  64
systems
  boundaries   10–11, 59
  closed   8, 22, 59, 67, 164
  defined   8
  diversity in   15, 16
  elements   12
  isolated   8
  links   15
  open   8, 9, 11, 38–9, 59, 77,
  164
  stability   *see* negative feedback
    and equilibrium

storage in   9, 11, 13, 14, 72–3,
  160–4, 180, 186
  see also energy flows *and* cycles
swash   61, 62, 66, 68
swell wave   60, 68

taiga   190–4
talus   57
tectonic forces   18
temperature
  atmospheric   97–8   *see also*
    lapse rate
  and climatic classifications   141
  in continental and maritime areas
    104
  inversions   97, 115
  oceanic   126–9
tephra   24–5
terraces
  climatic   90, 93
  lake   147
  rejuvenation   51
  thalassostatic   90
thermodynamics, laws of   6, 7, 51
thermosphere   98
threshold value   56–7
threshold velocity (of wind)   64
throughflow   34, 56
thunderstorms   112, 117, 131,
  137
tides   62–4
tidal wave   *see* tsunami
till   79, 83
trade winds   122–3
transpiration   106–7, 179
trophic levels   157–60
tropical climates   143
tropical rain forest   191, 193,
  199–203
tropical revolving storms   136–7
tropical soils   200–5
troposphere   97
truncated spur   80
tsunami   65
tundra   142, 190–3
turbidity current   66
turbulence   35, 62, 97

U-shaped glacial trough   80
underfit stream   51–2, 93
urban climates   104, 116–18, 140
urstromtäler   85

valley steps   81
varves   85–6

vegetation
  of British Isles   207–9
  and climatic types   143, 193
  climax   180–1
  factors affecting development
    178–81
  of lake margins   168–9
  mosaic   181
  post-glacial changes   149
  regional classification   190–3
  in relation to soil type   193
  its role in erosion prevention   48,
    56, 73
  succession   179–81, 186
  veldt   196
  volcanoes   19, 22, 23, 24–6
water
  in photosynthesis   3
  in plants   106
  pollution   172–3
  properties of   31
  in respiration   4
  supply domestic   8–10, 173
  transfer schemes   153–4, 174–5
  vapour   4, 96, 100, 102, 107–8
  see also cycles, hydrological
water table   34
waterfall   51, 81
watershed   11
wave-cut platform   72, 88
waves   59–62, 66, 71
weathering   29–33, 72, 89, 176,
  189
  chemical   30–2, 72, 165
  physical   29–30, 37, 64, 79, 80,
    90
  products   32–3, 176
winds   119–27, 138–40
  anabatic   138–9
  chinook   139
  on coasts   60, 64
  in deserts   58
  föhn   138
  geostrophic   120, 124
  gradient   119
  katabatic   138–9
  mistral   138
  in periglacial areas   90
  urban   140
World Climate Programme   153

xerophytes   179
xerosere   180

zooplankton   147, 157